Thinking Critically: What Does It Mean?

Thinking Critically: What Does It Mean?

Edited by
Dariusz Kubok

DE GRUYTER

This publication was made possible due to funding from the Deutsch-Polnische Wissenschaftsstiftung for the project „Tradition und Formen der Kritik in der europäischen Philosophie" (2016–2017).

ISBN 978-3-11-065393-9
e-ISBN (PDF) 978-3-11-056747-2
e-ISBN (EPUB) 978-3-11-056722-9

Library of Congress Cataloging-in-Publication Data
A CIP catalog record for this book has been applied for at the Library of Congress.

Bibliographic information published by the Deutsche Nationalbibliothek
The Deutsche Nationalbibliothek lists this publication in the Deutsche Nationalbibliografie; detailed bibliographic data are available on the Internet at http://dnb.dnb.de.

© 2019 Walter de Gruyter GmbH, Berlin/Boston
This volume is text- and page-identical with the hardback published in 2018.
Cover image: Kim Jonas Meier / EyeEm / getty images
Printing and binding: CPI books GmbH, Leck

♾ Printed on acid-free paper
Printed in Germany

www.degruyter.com

Table of Contents

Dariusz Kubok
Critical Thinking and Philosophical Criticism – an Outline of the Problem —— 1

Sebastian Śpiewak
Criticism as Paradoxatism. The Heraclitean Critique of the Notion of Opinion —— 11

Janina Gajda-Krynicka
Criticism as the Basis for the Procedures of Hypothetical Dialectic in Plato's Philosophy —— 25

Dariusz Olesiński
Aspects of Criticism in Plato's Philosophy —— 47

Zbigniew Nerczuk
References to Plato's *Theaetetus* in book Γ (IV) of Aristotle's *Metaphysics* —— 65

Dariusz Kubok
Conversation and Conservation. Two Kinds of Anti-Dogmatic Criticism in the Philosophy of Politics and their Antecedents in Ancient Greek Forms of Skepticism and Fallibilism —— 73

Adam Grzeliński
The Critical Dimension of Locke's Epistemology —— 93

Tomasz Kubalica
The Old and New Critique of Pure Reason based on Immanuel Kant and Jakob Friedrich Fries —— 111

Andrzej J. Noras
Criticism as It Was Understood by Hermann Cohen —— 127

Beata Trochimska-Kubacka
Hermann Cohen's Critical Exposition of Kant's Critique of Taste —— 139

Ryszard Kleszcz
Criticism and Rationality in the Lvov-Warsaw School —— 161

Adam Jonkisz
Rationality and Criticism in the Views of the Philosophers of the Lvov-Warsaw School and K.R. Popper —— 173

Christoph Demmerling
More than Words: from Language to Society. Wittgenstein, Marx, and Critical Theory —— 191

Peggy H. Breitenstein
Reflexive Social Critique. On the Dialectical Criticism of Ideology According to Marx and Adorno —— 213

Renata Zieminska
Skepticism and Atheism. Three Types of Relationships —— 237

Piotr Świercz
Criticism in Political Philosophy. On the Advantages of Pragmatism over Ideologized Politics in Light of the Works of Witold Gombrowicz —— 251

Agnieszka Woszczyk
Consolatio **or Critical Methods? Reflections on Philosophical Counseling** —— 265

Dariusz Rymar
Plato's Dialectics as a Method of Critical Reflection on Art —— 281

Register —— 299

Dariusz Kubok
Critical Thinking and Philosophical Criticism – an Outline of the Problem

Abstract: The following article constitutes an introduction to the problem of critical thinking and philosophical criticism. Above all, the main problem areas and ways of grasping these problems will be outlined. The possible relations between criticism and philosophy will be subject to analysis, enabling a better grasp of the specificity of philosophical criticism. Three basic models of these relations will be distinguished: (1) the identity of criticism and philosophy, (2) the subordinance of criticism to philosophy, and (3) the superordinance of criticism to philosophy. In addition, the main forms of criticism will be discussed, namely: separative criticism, antidogmatic criticism, and epistemological criticism. The goal of these reflections is to clarify the essence of both critical thinking and philosophical criticism.

Keywords: critical thinking, criticism, antidogmatism, critical philosophy

In a general sense, there seems to be universal agreement that people should think critically, and criticism is a desired trait in our relation to the world. This agreement is based on the silent premise that our understanding of the critical attitude is something clear and obvious. It is commonly believed that both the understanding and applicative validity of the critical attitude do not raise major doubts. However, problems appear when it becomes necessary to specify what exactly critical thinking is, i.e. to conduct a critical analysis of the critical attitude. In that situation, the initial universal agreement must undergo a fundamental deepening, ridding itself of its ostensible self-satisfaction. The situation is even clearer in reference to philosophy. It is not very controversial to claim that philosophy is/should be critical; the real problems appear when the justified question, "What does that mean?" is posed. There is no doubt that reflections on the essence of criticism belong to the sphere of broadly-understood philosophical investigations, and in the history of philosophical thought the problem of criticism was thematized both as a separate subject and within the context of other problems. At the same time, we must remember not to limit our understanding of the critical approach to any one of the particular forms it took within the history of philosophy. It is too often the case that criticism is associated solely with a chosen philosophical conception (e.g. Kant's philosophy, the Frankfurt School, etc.), which markedly narrows and directs the sphere of investigation.

Therefore, it seems worthwhile to undertake reflection on this issue, conducting analyses on the presence and significance of criticism in the European philosophical tradition. Its weight is attested to by the fact that it constitutes not only a theoretical challenge, but also contributes to an understanding and formation of many aspects of societal life. Currently, we can observe many forms that a deficit of the critical approach takes, leading to dangerous phenomena in modern culture. For this reason, in-depth reflection on criticism can lead to a better understanding and dissemination of the values connected with a critical approach in various parts of the public sphere, as well as to a deepening of both social and intercultural dialogue, and the idea of deliberative democracy that is so crucial in today's world.

Generally speaking, critique is a particular cognitive action that accompanies scientific, practical (e.g. ethical or aesthetic), or creative cognition. Critique is both the act of critiquing itself, and the product of this act in the form of opinions, statements, or critical texts. In terms of critique as a product, we must remember that not every judgment is a critical judgment. Existential and subsumptive judgments are certainly not critical, while value judgments are. Thus, we can say that critiquing boils down to evaluation. Evaluations differ, however, and for this reason it is not emotional evaluations that will be taken into account, but utilitarian evaluations which claim that something is in some way good (useful, beneficial, justified) for something (someone).[1] Various types of critique can be distinguished based on different criteria. In terms of the "addressee," critique can be directed at a person, an attitude, a behavior, an object, a conception, a theory, etc.; critique can be verbalized or nonverbalized, personal or impersonal, local (specific) or global, explicit or implicit, while in terms of critique as the product of an action, it can be the result of a prior process of critical reflection or spontaneous. In attempting to define the specificity of philosophical criticism, we must say that it is critique directed at ideas (conceptions, theories), impersonal, verbalized, typically global in scope and usually explicit, being above all the result of critical thinking. Philosophical criticism can take the form of a feature of thought, cognitive attitude, investigative approach, methodological procedure, or even a given philosophical stance. The hidden complexity of critical thinking and philosophical criticism can only be revealed through in-depth systematic-problem-oriented and historic-philosophical reflections such as those contained in this volume.

In general, philosophical reflections on critical thinking should take into account the problem of the relationship between criticism and philosophy, philo-

---

[1] See: Pelc 1998, pp. 7–25.

sophical criticism can be something wholly different from critical philosophy. The first is a type of criticism and should be analyzed from the position of the extensional precedence of criticism; critical philosophy, on the other hand, is understood as a particular type of philosophy for which criticism constitutes a fundamental feature. This is not to say that in certain cases philosophical criticism does not coincide with critical philosophy. Various views concerning the relationship between criticism and philosophy appeared in the European history of ideas. They can be grouped into specific and general models, keeping in mind the understandable arbitrariness usually present when historical positions are cleansed into "pure" models, which necessarily blurs the specific and concrete differences between these views.

The first model assumes an identification of criticism and philosophy. According to this view, every philosophy (science) is by nature critical, and criticism is philosophical, because all forms of value judgments characteristic of criticism must take into account philosophical reflection on values. In this case, even spontaneous acts of criticism are based on a more or less conscious understanding of values. Values so-understood, even those accepted spontaneously or in connection with tradition, have their own philosophical provenance. On the other hand, every philosophy, besides constructive elements, also possesses critical, polemic, revisionary elements, even when it declaratively presents itself as positivistic (e. g. Comte's philosophy). This model's perception of philosophy as critical by nature occurs within the sphere of metaphilosophical reflection, which may lead to the thought that every philosophy is critical in light of its metaphilosophy. If we were to accept this idea, however, the problem of philosophy's criticalness would in fact only be relocated to its metalevel. The second model, on the other hand, assumes that criticism is extensionally subordinate vis-à-vis philosophy. In this case, criticism is emancipated from particular philosophical systems, and historically emerges from the process of their evolution. The development (progress) of philosophy is therefore connected with a tendency towards the intensification of criticism. On the other hand, if criticism is understood as a component of a specific philosophy, it often morphs into a polemic, making it vulnerable to the accusation of partiality, which Hegel suggestively condemned.[2] The third model can be understood as strategy for fighting the polemic nature of criticism. This model assumes the superordinacy of criticism over philosophy. Examples include Kant's views, and, in a more radicalized form, Habermas' remarks treating critique as the only valid method of

---

2 See: Hegel 1970, pp. 171–188.

practicing philosophy.³ This precedence of criticism over philosophy is most often understood as the emancipated "superpolemicness" of criticism, which transcends specific philosophical positions.⁴

Philosophical criticism can also be viewed from the perspective of critical rationalism's precedence in culture and science, as it is viewed in Popper's thought. According to Popper, one can accept two types of attitudes toward tradition: a critical attitude, or an attitude of uncritical acceptance. "But we can free ourselves from the *taboos* of the tradition; and we can do that not only by rejecting it, but also by *critically* accepting it."⁵ Popper's overt admiration for the philosophical tradition begun in Ionia is not surprising, though it is worth noting that the basis for this admiration was the "Greek tradition of philosophical criticism" (Popper 1998, p. 23). Popper adds: "It was momentous innovation. It meant a break with the dogmatic tradition which permits only *one* school doctrine, and the introduction in its place of a tradition that admits a *plurality* of doctrines which all try to approach the truth by means of critical discussion" (Popper 1998, p. 23). On the one hand, the then-new tradition of philosophical criticism, which grew out of the superordinate critical attitude, opposed the dogmatic tradition (though, as the history of philosophy demonstrates, it did not replace it altogether), and on the other, referring back to Marquard's dictionary,⁶ it preached polymythical thinking in place of dogmatism's monomythical approach.

In my opinion, it is possible to view the relationship between criticism and philosophy in yet another way. It allows us to examine philosophical criticism from the perspective of criticism's essence as a general attitude, which in its primary dimension – as separative criticism – precedes and makes rationalism, including critical rationalism, possible. For this purpose, it is necessary to specify our understanding of the essence of philosophical criticism (as an expression of critical thinking), distinguishing it from criticism as such; this will involve the

---

3 See: Habermas 1987, ch. 3.
4 The types of relationships between criticism and philosophy mentioned above are discussed in detail in: Symotiuk 1987, pp. 12–22.
5 Popper 1968, p. 122. Popper adds: "My thesis is that what we call 'science' is differentiated from the older myths not by being something distinct from a myth, but by being accompanied by a second-order tradition–that of critically discussing the myth. Before, there was only the first-order tradition. [...] This second-order tradition was the critical or argumentative attitude. It was, I believe, a new thing, and it is still the fundamentally important thing about scientific tradition" (Popper 1968, p. 127).
6 See: Marquard 2000, pp. 97–111.

proposal of a typology of criticism. Before I discuss this issue, however, I will make a few general remarks on the critical attitude and on criticism as such.

Above all, it is necessary to distinguish the critical attitude from all forms of captiousness and defiant attitudes. The critical attitude assumes intellectual distance, while captiousness, like defiance, is somewhat mechanical. However, the main difference boils down to the fact that the critical approach should be both allocritical and autocritical, while captiousness and defiance are solely allocritical. In autocriticism, the objects being critiqued are the cognitive acts and products (statements) of the critique's author, while in allocriticism, these same objects are critique in reference to everyone but the critique's author.[7] Thus, we can say that autocriticism is a characteristic feature of the critical attitude, or at least sufficiently distinguishes this attitude from other types of evaluation. In his remarks entitled *Some Principles for a New Professional Ethics*, Popper writes: "A self-critical attitude, frankness, and openness towards oneself become, therefore, part of everyone's duty" (Popper 1998, p. 64). In the context of distinguishing criticism from a defiant attitude, Polish scholar Z. Cackowski made interesting remarks concerning the positive, though rather crude, nature of the latter. Defiance can be understood as a distinctive and simple preventative measure against the "stickiness of thinking," i.e. the phenomenon of thoughts "sticking" to what is known, grounded, and sanctified by tradition or authority.[8] We can treat the critical attitude in an analogous way; it also possesses a "therapeutic" dimension, as it contradicts the "stickiness of thought" characteristic of dogmatic attitudes on a higher, theoretical level. Thus, the critical attitude can be perceived as the ability to free oneself from the embrace of ostensible or insufficiently justified tradition. Philosophical criticism, as a specific form of criticism, would play an "ungluing" – though not necessarily subversive – role in reference to philosophical views. We can say that the critical attitude is not of a purely "abolishing" (negative) nature, but that its nature is also, even above all, creative and positive, enabling us to rethink the premises and theses of the convictions we hold.

From this it follows that a fully-developed critical attitude must recognize and maintain a proper distance from its extremes, which I call subcriticism and supercriticism. The first is characterized by an insufficient critical capacity (critical actions), such that does not perceive and/or permits certain dogmatic solutions. The second is an exaggerated way of not recognizing theses that are sufficiently justified (at least for the time being); it may be expressed through

---

7 See: Kubok 2015a, pp. 261–281.
8 See: Cackowski 1983, p. 9.

a total and destructive questioning of obvious judgments. It is worth noting that certain thinkers understand criticism solely or above all as supercriticism, which allows them to perceive only destructive elements in it and treat it as a threat, or even a disease, present in culture.[9] On the other hand, subcriticism is well-described in the history of philosophy, e. g. in the works of Kant and his successors. We can say that subcriticism enables or leaves an open field for positive dogmatism, while supercriticism is frequently linked with negative dogmatism,[10] agnosticism, and in extreme cases – nihilism.

It is a commonly-held belief that the critical attitude is an antidogmatic attitude, though it is necessary to specify what is meant by the term "dogmatism." While this term has predominantly negative connotations today, the same cannot be said about the original Greek meaning of the noun "δόγμα" (belief, statement, opinion, tenet) and the adjective "δογματικός" (tending towards and/or teaching a certain doctrine).[11] The antidogmatic critical attitude consists in not recognizing statements that lack sufficient justification, having been the object of prior investigation. Today, the label "dogmatist" is given to someone who accepts certain judgments in a stronger way than is warranted, while simultaneously not paying sufficient attention to potential doubts and alternative solutions. A key topic of debate among scholars is the problem of the scope, or level of sufficiency of "proper justifications" and "potential doubts." A. Plantinga defines dogmatism as follows:

---

[9] For example, we can indicate the views of Merleau-Ponty or Scheler, who understood criticism as resentment that does not take obviousness into account. See: Scheler 1994, pp. 8–9. It is worth noting that certain phenomenologists' negative opinions about criticism go hand in hand with the principle of obviousness and presuppositionlessness that they presume. Next to the moderate criticism he himself accepts, Tadeusz Kotarbiński, a representative of the Lvov-Warsaw School, distinguishes a totally destructive, decadent, and purely subversive form of criticism that he calls critical hyenism. See: Kotarbiński 1958, pp. 255–283.

[10] In Kant's view, criticism stands in opposition to both dogmatism and skepticism. Kant lists the following necessary stadiums of philosophy: dogmatism, skepticism, and criticism. See: Kant 1993, p. 595. For Kant, criticism was meant to go beyond dogmatism and skepticism. Due to a different understanding of the term "skepticism," I believe the latter can be called negative dogmatism, because it proclaims the impossibility of finding truth. In reference to the original division of philosophy made by Sextus Empiricus (*Pyr.*, I, 1–2), Barnes uses the phrase "negative metadogmatism" (Barnes 1992, p. 4254). Therefore, Kant's criticism stands in opposition to both positive and negative dogmatism (metadogmatism).

[11] "The word 'dogmatist' in contemporary English has a pejorative tone – it hints at an irrational rigidity of opinion, a refusal to look impartially at the evidence. In its ancient sense the word lacked that tone: a dogmatist was simply someone who subscribed to dogmas or doctrines" (Annas/Barnes 1985, pp. 1–2).

> Like 'fanaticism,' dogmatism is ordinarily a term of abuse, and a term one doesn't apply to oneself. (How often do you hear someone describe himself as a dogmatist?) The term has a variety of analogically related uses. In one use, to say of someone that she is a dogmatist is to say that she holds her views more strongly than is appropriate, more strongly than the evidence warrants, for example; alternatively, it is to say that she holds her views uncritically, without paying sufficient heed to objections and alternatives, or to the limitations of human reason (see Kant). 'Dogmatism' is therefore an indexical term; whether you properly apply it to a given doctrine or belief depends upon where you yourself stand (Plantinga 1992, pp. 108–109).

The critical attitude understood as an antidogmatic attitude should assume the potential revision of both currently-held convictions and the degree to which they are justified.

In modern literature, criticism is also understood as a metaphilosophical position declaring that all philosophical reflections must be based on and preceded by epistemological investigations. Such a view can take on many forms. For example, T. Kotarbiński, in his commentary on Riehl's views,[12] describes criticism as understanding the task of philosophy as a critique of knowledge, meaning the investigation of the truth conditions and objectivity of cognition. Simultaneously, he accepts the understanding of criticism as a stance according to which philosophy cannot be metaphysics.[13] Such an understanding of criticism, i.e. one that emphasizes the fundamental role played by epistemological reflection, is commonplace in philosophical literature. It is important to note that Kant's philosophy, or more broadly, Kantianism in its various forms, can be considered a particular form of this type of criticism.

> Many such forms of Kantian criticism may exist, though there is an unchanging set of ideas characteristic for this type of critical approach. Kant understands criticism at its source as a kind of trial: criticism does not end with the conviction of reason; it must also indicate its origins, scope, and boundaries. We may say, then, that pure reason stands before its own tribunal, it pronounces its own verdict, and, at the same time, its power, is its self-limitation. From this perspective, dogmatism is understood as the action of pure reason without the prior critique of its own authority (Kubok 2015b, pp. 16–17).

---

12 It is worth mentioning A. Riehl's monumental work: *Der philosophische Kritizismus und seine Bedeutung für die positive Wissenschaft. Geschichte und System.* 3 Bände, Leipzig 1876–1887. Especially noteworthy in view of the understanding of philosophical criticism is Band 1: *Geschichte und Methode des philosophischen Kritizismus* (1876).
13 Philosophical seminar under the direction of Prof. Tadeusz Kotarbiński. Academic year 1934/35. (Protocols of the meetings). See: Kotarbińska 1977, p. 140.

Critical thinking and philosophical criticism can be analyzed from various perspectives. According to my earlier suggestion, we can discuss philosophical criticism (as a form of critical thinking) as distinct from broadly-understood criticism.[14] In my research, I distinguish the most important types of criticism from the point of view of philosophical criticism. Thus, separative criticism is the most general and fundamental type, as it genetically precedes all rational reflection, including philosophical reflection, since it is already present in prereflective action,[15] and appears in full force in rational discourse. In the most general sense, separative criticism refers to the ability to distinguish, divide, or separate; the critical capacity understood thus consists in delineating the proper boundaries and divisions, thus enabling further reflection or action. Separative uncriticism manifests itself in the lack of ability to make fundamental distinctions, thus resulting in a confusion of spheres of reflection or action, in categorical shifts, or in a certain broadly-understood lack of measure. Antidogmatic criticism, on the other hand, being based on separative criticism, boils down to opposition to all dogmatic claims, whether they take the form of positive dogmatism or negative dogmatism (negative metadogmatism). This type of criticism, which opposes the behavior of dogmatists accepting certain statements in a stronger way than these deserve to be accepted, permits the potential revision of currently-held convictions. Epistemological criticism, which is of a metaobjective nature, is based on the presumption that epistemological (or epistemologico-methodological) reflections precede all other types of philosophical investigations, including cosmological, theological, and ontological investigations, among others.[16] One particular form of epistemological criticism so understood, supplemented by antidogmatic criticism, is broadly-understood Kantianism. In

---

[14] The verb κρίνω means above all: 1) "separate," "divide," "part," "distinguish," 2) "order," "arrange," 3) "pick out," "select," "choose," "prefer," "decide," 4) "judge," "pronounce," 5) "expound," "interpret," 6) "inquire," "investigate," 7) "contend," quarrel," 8) "bring to trial," "accuse," "condemn," "criticize." On the other hand, the verb κριτικός can be translated as: "able to distinguish," "able to discern," "critical," "separated," "picked out," "chosen." See: Liddell, Scott 1940.

[15] Aristotle held that already in animals the inborn critical faculty (faculty of discrimination) in the form of sense is more primary genetically than any rational faculty. "ἀνάγκη ἄρα ἔχειν μέν τινα δύναμιν, μὴ τοιαύτην δ' ἔχειν ἢ ἔσται τούτων τιμιωτέρα κατ' ἀκρίβειαν. φαίνεται δὲ τοῦτό γε πᾶσιν ὑπάρχον τοῖς ζῴοις. ἔχει γὰρ δύναμιν σύμφυτον κριτικήν, ἣν καλοῦσιν αἴσθησιν" Arist., *Analytica posteriora*, 99b32–35. When it comes to animal souls, Aristotle recognizes two faculties (δύο δυνάμεις): the faculty of discrimination (τῷ τε κριτικῷ) and the faculty of motion (τῷ κινεῖν). The first faculty is "the work of thought and sense" (ὃ διανοίας ἔργον ἐστὶ καὶ αἰσθήσεως) Arist.: *De anima*, 432a15-17.

[16] Kubok 2015b, pp. 14–17.

general, we can say that philosophical criticism may be connected with each type of criticism mentioned above, as well as with any configuration thereof. However, due to the rudimentary nature of separative criticism, it seems that this type cannot be omitted. The particular forms of critical philosophy that appeared throughout the history of philosophy can be analyzed within the context of the types of criticism mentioned above. Of course, it goes without saying that this is only possible way of reflection on the complex problem of critical thinking, philosophical criticism, and critical philosophy.

The value of critical thinking, thinking that maintains a proper distance from both subcriticism and supercriticism, is universally accepted and preached. However, this acceptance must be accompanied by in-depth reflection on critical thinking's essence, forms, and centuries-long tradition. The European philosophical tradition undertook reflection on the problem of criticism from the outset. This monograph contains studies in the history and forms of philosophical criticism. In accordance with the critical attitude, the studies presented in this publication do not lean toward any particular solutions; rather, they should be treated as an incentive to continually reiterate one of the most important questions concerning critical thinking: What does it mean?

Bibliography

Annas, Julia/Barnes, Jonathan (1985): *The Modes of Scepticism. Ancient Texts and Modern Interpretations*. Cambridge, England: Cambridge University Press.

Barnes, Jonathan (1992): "Diogenes Laertius IX 61–116: The Philosophy of Pyrrhonism". In: Wolfgang Haase (Ed.): *Aufstieg und Niedergang der römischen Welt. II: Principat*, Band 36.6. Berlin/New York: de Gruyter.

Cackowski, Zdzisław (1983): "Wartość myślenia krytycznego". In: *Człowiek i Światopogląd* 12.

Hegel, Georg Wilhelm Friedrich (1970): *Werke in zwanzig Bänden, Jenaer Schriften 1801–1807*. Frankfurt am Main: Suhrkamp.

Habermas, Jürgen (1987): "The Idea of the Theory of Knowledge as Social Theory". In: Jürgen Habermas: *Knowledge and Human Interest*. Cambridge: Polity Press.

Kant, Immanuel (1993): "Welches sind die wirklichen Fortschritte, die die Metaphysik seit Leibnizens und Wolffs Zeiten in Deutschland gemacht hat?". In: Immanuel Kant: *Werkausgabe*. 6. Bd, Hrsg. von W. Weischedel. Frankfurt: Suhrkamp.

Kotarbińska, Janina (1934/35): "Seminarium filozoficzne pod kierunkiem Prof. Tadeusza Kotarbińskiego. Rok akademicki 1934/35. (Protokoły posiedzeń)". In: *Studia Filozoficzne* 6, pp. 122–141.

Kotarbiński, Tadeusz (1958): "Dążności rozkładowe postępu wiedzy (The Destructive Tendencies of the Progress of Knowledge)". In: Tadeusz Kotarbiński: *Wybór pism*. Tom II. Warszawa: PWN, pp. 255–283.

Kubok, Dariusz (2015a): "Allocriticism and Autocriticism in the Views of Xenophanes of Colophon". *Littera Antiqua* 10–11, pp. 261–281.

Kubok, Dariusz (2015b): "Comments on the Sources of Greek Philosophical Criticism". In: *Folia Philosophica*, vol. 34. Special Issue: *Forms of Criticism in Philosophy and Science*. Ed. by Dariusz Kubok. Katowice, pp. 9–31.

Liddell, Henry George/Scott, Robert (1940): *A Greek-English Lexicon. Revised and augmented throughout by Sir Henry Stuart Jones with the assistance of Roderick McKenzie*. Oxford. Clarendon Press.

Marquard, Odo (2000): *Abschied vom Prinzipiellen. Philosophische Studien*. Stuttgart: Reclam.

Pelc, Jerzy (1998): "Krytyka i krytycyzm w nauce". In: H. Żytkowicz (Ed.): *Krytyka i krytycyzm w nauce*. Warszawa, pp. 7–25.

Plantinga, Alvin (1992): "Dogmatism". In: Jonathan Dancy/Ernest Sosa (Eds.): *A Companion to Epistemology*. Oxford UK: Blackwell Publishers.

Popper, Karl R. (1998): "Back to the Presocratics". In: Karl R. Popper: *The World of Parmenides: Essays on the Presocratic Enlightenment*. Ed. by Arne F. Petersen, with the assistance of Jorgen Mejer. London and New York: Routledge.

Popper, Karl R. (1968): *Conjectures and Refutations: The Growth of Scientific Knowledge*. New York: Harper & Row.

Riehl, Alois (1876–1887): *Der philosophische Kritizismus und seine Bedeutung für die positive Wissenschaft. Geschichte und System*. 3 Bände. Leipzig.

Scheler, Max (1994): *Ressentiment*. Transl. By L.A. Coser, W.W. Holdheim. New York: Marquette University Press.

Symotiuk, Stefan (1987): *Pojmowanie krytycyzmu i modele krytyki w polskich sporach filozoficznych XX wieku*. Lublin.

Sebastian Śpiewak
Criticism as Paradoxatism.
The Heraclitean Critique of the Notion of Opinion

Abstract: This paper is focused on the critical approach of Heraclitus of Ephesus. His theory of logos can be viewed in the light of broadly-understood criticism, which was one of the distinctive features of the nascent philosophy at that time. It has been deemed important to analyze the Heraclitean critical project mainly as a form of critique of existing opinions (especially scientific and philosophical opinions), to which the name of "paradoxatism" shall be suggested as the most appropriate. Heraclitus' criticism as "paradoxatism" turns out to be the main consequence of his view on the logos as the relevant object of cognition and knowledge in spite of its paradoxical nature in the case of the ordinary human cognitive attitude.

Keywords: criticism, critique, polymathy, Heraclitus, opinion

> παίδων ἀθύρματα [...] τὰ ἀνθρώπινα δοξάσματα
> "Human opinions are toys for children"
> (Diels, Kranz[1] 1966, 22 B 70, transl. Kahn 1979, p. 55.)

When discussing the origins of Western European philosophical reflection, one cannot omit the problem of the broadly-understood critical attitude, which should be considered one of the most vital or even constitutive features of philosophical thinking in general. More categorically speaking: philosophy must be critical, and there is no philosophy where criticism is lacking. In this context, it is worth noting that the famous thesis on the sources of philosophy which first appears in Plato's dialogues (Plato 1900, 155d 2–4) and then in Aristotle's *Metaphysics* should be supplemented as follows: the astonishment referred to by these thinkers is perhaps first, and no one can deny this crucial step in the development and flowering of philosophy; nevertheless, being a necessary factor does not make it a sufficient one.[2] For it is the reaction to this first impulse of

---

[1] Further cited as D-K.
[2] After all, it seems clear enough from the words of the Stagirite (Aristotle 1924, 982b 12–19) that astonishment alone cannot be recognized as a sufficient condition enabling one to distinguish philosophizing from other forms of loosely defined human rationalities (in this particular case –

astonishment that really matters for philosophizing, and the response of the astonished man cannot be arbitrary; it must constitute a critical form of explanation.

1 The Earliest Forms of Criticism in Greek Philosophy

It is symptomatic that the critical attitude found at the Greek root of philosophy in Asia Minor was so comprehensive that it had as its object was not only the traditions in large part founded on epic mythology (i.e. Homeric and Hesiod's poems), but also all other competing attempts to explain the world and its riddles, even those attempts that no longer appealed to supernatural factors like the gods or divine powers. Indeed, the first philosophers were critical of the customs of their time, but what is perhaps of greater importance – they were above all critical of each other.³

It is also true that very often the scarcity of original texts of the so-called pre-Socratics makes it impossible to point out strong and direct evidence of the critical relationship between philosophers of the oldest period – something which holds true especially in regards to the great representatives of the Milesian school: Thales, Anaximander, and Anaximenes. Excluding the doxographical tradition, one cannot find any explicit critical comments of these thinkers on their predecessors. Scientific or philosophical dependence can by only assumed from the recognizable development of ideas and concepts proposed for the same problem and question, namely that of the ultimate source and principle of world order (ἀρχή). In this case, it is not until the competing theories and possible arguments are compared that the earliest philosophical critical attitude can be discerned, and only insofar as the reconstruction of a line of thought is possible to carry out. For only then is critical thinking seen at work. But the situation is utterly different when one considers extant fragments of Heraclitus' work, where critical remarks are surprisingly frequent and, as can be supposed for now, constitute the very core of Heraclitus' philosophical message. Thus, we can say that

---

φιλομυθία). The alternative proposal would consist in accepting the view that every human activity in which some sort of astonishment can be found is in some way a form of philosophy, but then the central problem remains of how one can establish the very beginning of philosophy, if its essential function were to be different from the explanation typical for myth.
3 Therefore, it would be fitting to agree with the accurate general view of G.E.R. Lloyd, who deemed the practice of critical discussion one of the three most important elements of the Ionian study of nature (Lloyd 1970, p. 15).

Criticism as Paradoxatism. The Heraclitean Critique of the Notion of Opinion — 13

Heraclitus was the first philosopher who used criticism with full awareness as a well-thought out tactic of his philosophy.

Now, the question arises who or what was the precise addressee of his attacks and why. What was the motive behind such a robust attack against the contemporary intellectual life of Hellas? Possible answers to this question presented below specify the characteristics of this first known (at least from the extant fragments) complex project of Greek criticism and indicate that the main grounds for Heraclitus' famous critique were his understanding of the notion of knowledge and especially its status. In this sense, as will be shown, Heraclitus' criticism turns out to be nothing but paradoxatism – that is to say: reflection oriented against widespread human opinions (παρὰ τῆς δόξης).

2 Heraclitean Criticism

Strictly speaking, it is not the author of the theory of logos, but another Ionian, namely Xenophanes of Colophon, who should be mentioned as the first thinker to refer critically to well-known figures of his time.[4] In his scoffing verses, Xenophanes attacks Pythagoras and his belief in the transmigration of the soul (D-K. 1966, 21 B 7, 3–4). However, this observable scorn for the religious views of the founder of the Pythagorean brotherhood is nothing compared to the concentrated assault carried out by Heraclitus, who was a contemporary of Xenophanes. The addressees of Heraclitus' often ruthless critique who are known by name are: Homer (D-K. 1966, 22 B 56; B 42); Hesiod (D-K. 1966, B 57; B 40), already ridiculed in Xenophanes' poem but only by allusion; Pythagoras (D-K. 1966, B 129; B 81); Xenophanes (D-K. 1966, B 40) himself; Hecataeus of Miletus (D-K. 1966, B 40); and Archilochus of Paros (D-K. 1966, B 42).

Technically speaking, one could ask whether the choice of these personages was a matter of coincidence and perhaps a consequence of Heraclitus' alleged iconic misanthropy. This would mean that there is no theoretical background behind his malignant comments, no philosophy to discover in his critique, and no hidden agenda in his discourse. However, all these assumptions, even though possible, would be quite unbelievable[5] in the case of the legendary ὁ

---

[4] Thus, one is inclined to ascribe to Xenophanes' philosophical activity the label of "allo-criticism," but this is not to say that it exhausts the issue of his idea of criticism, as D. Kubok has clearly shown (Kubok 2015, p. 262).

[5] See Kahn's discussion on the character of Heraclitus' book and his dark style (Kahn 1979, pp. 3–9). It would be of great importance to examine in detail the role of Heraclitus' critique

Σκοτεινός – "the dark," whose prominent postulate remained constant and can be expressed in the following words: φύσις [...] κρύπτεσθαι φιλεῖ (D-K. 1966, 22 B 123).[6] If so, then one feels obliged to seek a place for the critical part of the extant fragments in the whole conception of the Ephesian, the very core of which is focused around the term λόγος.

As a consequence, the most obvious answer to the dilemma of what the rationale for Heraclitus' condemnation of chosen representatives of the Greek παιδεία was would be that they had simply failed to achieve wisdom, which in turn had been achieved by Heraclitus himself, who had been able to recognize that the superior object of the propounded knowledge could be nothing but the logos.[7] In this sense, the figures mentioned by name in Heraclitus' fragments are all guilty of being unaware of what is common to all (ξυνός or κοινός) – a charge which for Heraclitus must have been sufficient evidence of their hopeless idiosyncrasy,[8] since he described it as a kind of deafness to the meaning of λόγος (D-K. 1966, 22 B 34) and still more often as a state of dreaming (D-K. 1966, B 73; B 1; B 89), where reality (that which is true independently of anyone's, even Heraclitus' own teaching, as the message of fragment B 50 indicates: οὐκ ἐμοῦ, ἀλλὰ τοῦ λόγου ἀκούσαντας [...]) is obscured by people's subjective views and concepts. For this very reason Sextus Empiricus reports: "Therefore it is necessary to follow the common (ξυνῶι) [that is, the universal (κοινῶι): for 'common' means 'universal']: but although the Logos is common (ξυνοῦ) the many live as though they had a private understanding (ἰδίαν φρόνησιν)" (D-K. 1966, 22 B 2, Transl. Kirk 1975, p. 57), which remains in perfect agreement with the words of a fragment provided by Plutarch: "The world of the waking is one and shared (ἰδίαν ἔχοντες φρόνησιν), but the sleeping turn aside each into his private (ἴδιον) world" (D-K. 1966, 22 B 89, transl. Kahn 1979, p. 31).

---

of prominent men of his time in the general scheme of his theory of logos – a task to which the present article lays claim only as a form of contribution.

6 On the problematic notion of φύσις in Heraclitean philosophy, see e.g. the works of G.S. Kirk, (Kirk 1975, pp. 227–231); Ch.H. Kahn (Kahn 1979, p. 105); K. Mrówka (Mrówka 2004, p. 330). It seems fully justified to say that the discourse of Heraclitus was supposed to reflect the very structure of the world, being its objective. In this sense, the words of the Ephesian are like those of the god Apollo: ὁ ἄναξ, οὗ τὸ μαντεῖόν ἐστι τὸ ἐν Δελφοῖς, οὔτε λέγει οὔτε κρύπτει ἀλλὰ σημαίνει (D-K. 1966, 22 B 93; see also: B 54).

7 It should not be surprising, then, that the best possible description of this wisdom in Heraclitus' work is the notion of the accordance (ὁμο-λογία) explicitly presented in the following words: οὐκ ἐμοῦ, ἀλλὰ τοῦ λόγου ἀκούσαντας ὁμολογεῖν σοφόν ἐστιν ἓν πάντα εἶναι (D-K. 1966, 22 B 50).

8 "Idiosyncrasy" is used here in the sense of personal and privately valid views.

Both cited fragments should be considered of paramount importance for understanding the specificity of Heraclitean criticism due to two vital pairs of opposites that appear: 1) common or universal (ξυνός or κοινός) – private (ἴδιον); and 2) one (ἕν) as opposed to many (πολλοί). These pairs of opposites build tension between the sphere of human cognitive habits[9] and the precisely established "profile" of the pursued ultimate truth of λόγος. It is because of this tension that the hypothesis of the paradoxical nature of truth and subsequent hypothesis of paradoxatism in Heraclitus' philosophy can be formulated.

3 An Outline of the Problem of πολυμαθίη

It is vital to emphasize that what is opposed in fr. B 2 to the one, common and/or universal *logos* is not so much many people as their differentiated ways of grasping the world in its apparent, superficial (and therefore obvious) and manifold aspects. For Heraclitus, these ways of grasping the world cannot be classified as knowledge, but only as so-called πολυμαθίη, which he attributed to the chosen four most outstanding figures (δοκιμώτατοι of fr. B 28, as one can suspect) of the contemporary culture. As can be read in a well-known attack on this type of comprehension: "πολυμαθίη does not teach understanding (νόον). For it would have taught Hesiod and Pythagoras, as well as Xenophanes and Hecataeus" (D-K. 1966, 22 B 40, transl. S.Ś.). There is an on-going debate in the literature about how this accusation should be interpreted, especially in view of the fact that the Ephesian is the probable author of the neologism πολυμαθίη. Two different read-

---

[9] On a different note, it might be worth considering that the role of accustomed activity, or simply: "habit," has a much broader meaning in Heraclitus' philosophy than is usually connected with the sentence: ἦθος ἀνθρώπωι δαίμων – "Man's character is his fate" (D-K. 1966, 22 B 119, transl. Kahn, p. 81), where it functions in the sphere of moral reflection. It seems that ἦθος understood as "custom," "usage," "disposition" (Liddell, Scott, Jones, McKenzie 1996, p. 766 [further cited as LSJM]) also has its place in the context of the Ephesian's criticism of the inappropriate attitude towards the problem of knowledge and its object. Therefore, Heraclitus can say that "He who does not expect will not find out the unexpected, for it is trackless and unexplored" (D-K. 1966, 22 B 18, transl. Kahn 1979, p. 31; see also: B 47 and B 97), as well as that "Incredibility escapes recognition" (D-K. 1966, 22 B 86, transl. Kahn 1979, p. 69). The evident hint for the gnoseological reading of ἦθος can be found in fragment B 78, where human ἦθος is contrasted with divine ἦθος from the perspective of the ability to achieve insight or understanding. Now, following e.g. M. Marcovich (Marcovich 2001, p. 478), one can say that the term ἦθος here means nothing more than "innate nature," but this hardly solves the problem of what the "innate nature" of human beings consists in when it comes to human cognitive capabilities.

ing are possible depending on which part of the word is emphasized – the first part (πολυ-), or the second (-μαθίη).

Firstly, there is a natural tendency to understand πολυμαθίη as "much knowledge," that is to say: knowledge on many things, or "encyclopaedic" knowledge associated with a great amount of factual material that does not have to be thematically linked.[10] There can be no doubt that this notion of knowledge can be applied to all four figures from fragment B 40 and there is no problem in finding meaningful justification for doing so in each case. Each of them was, in his own way, indeed an erudite.

Hesiod had to be considered a polymath since he was the author of works pertaining to a wide array of what men should know about the gods; the world, its genesis and laws; morality; agriculture; and even hygiene. Arguably, thanks to both his poems (*Theogony*, as well as *Works and Days*) he earned the nickname διδάσκαλος πλείστων πλεῖστα – "the teacher of many things for most men" (D-K. 1966, 22 B 57, transl. S.Ś.). It also cannot be denied that the Pythagorean μαθήματα, if only this notion is applicable to Pythagoras himself, consist in a variety of diverse studies, as has been pointed out (Jaeger 1946, p. 162; Fritz von 1974, p. 37), including not only the sort of knowledge that nowadays would be called "scientific," but also religious elements which, as was seen above, were the objects of mockery in Xenophanes' fragment B 7.[11] Assuming that πολυμαθίη is nothing more than a disposition, founded on "amassed knowledge," to express opinions about different subjects, one also has to agree that this type of activity was characteristic for Xenophanes, who had always displayed a willingness to discuss any given problem (Heidel 1943, p. 267), as evidenced by extant fragments of his poems. The same can be said for the fourth figure – Hecataeus, a geographer and *logographoi* credited with the creation of the second (after Anaximander's project) map of the known world. He was already known as ἀνὴρ πολυπλανής "the man who travels a lot" (D-K. 1966, 12 A 6, 3) in ancient times, a fact that links him with the research activity of Xen-

---

10 Regarding this reading of πολυμαθίη, the following translations can be listed: 1) "erudition" (Cherniss 1951, p. 335); 2) "amassed knowledge" (Guthrie 1985, p. 415); 3) "mere collection of material" (Curd Kenig 1991, p. 531); 4) "much learning" understood either as: "great deal of knowledge," "mere accumulation of information" (Kahn 1979, p. 107–108.), or simply as: "knowledge of many things" (Burnet 1924, p. 58); 5) "factual knowledge in various specific fields" (Fritz von 1974, p. 37). The German equivalent would be "Vielwisserei" (Diels, Kranz 1964, p. 160; see also: Gigon 1968, p. 241; Zeller 1876, p. 654, n. 1).
11 See p. 13 above.

ophanes (D-K. 1966, 21 A 11; A 15; B 21; A 49; B 21a; A1).[12] The main consequence of πολυπλανίη would not only be broad, extensive geographical knowledge, but also ethnographical knowledge, traces of which can be found in the work of Xenophanes (D-K. 1966, 21 B 16).

As has been shown above, the first interpretation of πολυμαθίη is flexible and can be applied to all four cases. For this reason, the threat of unfalsifiability is quite real. But what is even worse, this first interpretation is so broad that it enables us to apply the notion of πολυμαθίη to Heraclitus himself. For one cannot deny that the Ephesian was a typical example of an erudite of his time. The fact that he undertook a critique of distinctive standpoints in itself indicates that he had a great deal of knowledge on different subjects and different opinions. Moreover, one can easily find clear confirmation of the need for extensive study in his aphorisms: "Men who love wisdom must be good inquirers into many things indeed" (D-K. 1966, 22 B 35, transl. Kahn 1979, p. 33), and more vividly: "Seekers of gold dig up much earth and find little" (D-K. 1966, 22 B 22, transl. Kahn 1979, p. 31). If this is the case, what does it mean that amassed knowledge does not teach understanding, given that such knowledge appears to be something recommendable in eyes of the Ionian? For now, let it suffice to say that the hypothesis emphasizing the first part of the word πολυμαθίη is simply too broad and hence needs some refining.

Secondly, the problem of πολυμαθίη can be viewed in light of the extended critique of Pythagoras which is presented in fr. B 129 and B 81, where the object of Heraclitus' discontent seems to be not so much the results of searching (the "mass of information") as the way these results are attained. Consequently, the second, and not the first, part of the word πολυ-μαθίη is considered key for understanding the attack on the figures mentioned in B 40. According to this interpretation, it is not the breadth of knowledge that is criticised, but rather the lack of sufficient activeness on the part of the researcher as a cognitive agent. This automatically solves the problem of the possibility of taking Heraclitus as an erudite, which indeed he was.

Scholars who are in favour of this second interpretation frequently evoke the alleged specificity of the Greek verb μανθάνω, which is the root of the second part of the analyzed term (e.g. Barnes 1982, p. 115). The meaning selected from the wide semantic range of μανθάνω – "learn," especially "by study," would explain what the main motive behind belittling the role of the mentioned figures was. It is none other than the receptiveness characteristic of the process

---

[12] On the Colophonian's intensive travelling and the possible destinations of his journeys, see e.g the comments of W.A. Heidel (Heidel 1943, p. 270) and O. Gigon (Gigon 1968, p. 156).

of learning, which is also confirmed in the semantic field of the verb μανθάνω (μ. τί τινος – "learn from" (LSJM 1996, p. 1079)). In this sense, the fault of the polymaths criticised by Heraclitus would lie not in their acquaintance with a great deal of various facts, but rather in their passive, thoughtless attitude toward adopting existing opinions and beliefs, as such an attitude renders the attainment of certain and reliable knowledge of the world impossible. For this reason, an adequate translation of πολυμαθίη could be "much learning from others."[13]

No doubt Heraclitus considered himself a genuine and self-contained philosopher[14] who despised the vacuity of a society (D-K. 1966, 22 B 121) that could not recognize what and who was the most valuable and the best – ἄριστος (D-K. 1966, B 49). It is also doubtless that he blamed this state of affairs on those who had been deemed teachers, as the example of the meaningful critique of Hesiod in fr. B 57 clearly demonstrates and which in general terms is again expressed in the following complaint: "What wit (νόος) or understanding do they have? They believe the poets of the people and take the mob as their teacher, not knowing that 'the many are worthless' (πολλοὶ κακοί), good men are few (ὀλίγοι δὲ ἀγαθοί)" (D-K. 1966, B 104, transl. Kahn 1979, p. 57).

Thus far, the cited evidence seems to confirm the second reading of πολυμαθίη. Problems arise when one tries to apply it to all the figures in B 40, that is to say, to people who in the strongest possible terms expressed their originality and

---

[13] It is also worth noting other descriptive proposals of scholars. So C.A. Huffman, who in his translation of this term actually tries to summarize the whole interpretation: "Typical translation for *polymathia* in fragment B 129 ('much learning' Kahn, 'learning of many things' KRS) fail to give it the negative connotation it clearly has. My suggested translation '*a bunch of things learnt from others* [italic – S.Ś]' tries to bring out the sarcastic reference to the lack of unity in the learning by the use of 'bunch' and at the same time to emphasize that the learning derives from others rather than from one's own insight" (Huffman 2008, p. 44, n. 61). Similarly J. Barnes, who describes polymaths as those, who: "[...] have acquired a large stock of opinions from other men" (Barnes 1982, p.115), and also Verdenius, who emphasizes the contrast between independent researching and "[...] borrowing other's people wisdom [...]" (Verdenius 1947, p. 281). H. Granger, whose interpretation refers to the specific understanding of ἱστορίαι, expresses the characteristics of polymaths even more plainly. In his opinion, πολυμαθίη is: "the 'knowledge' based on book-learning alone"(Granger 2004, p. 249).

[14] Diogenes Laertius reports that Heraclitus: "[...] ἤκουσέ τ' οὐδενός, ἀλλ' αὐτὸν ἔφη διζήσασθαι καὶ μαθεῖν πάντα παρ' ἑαυτοῦ [...]" (Diogenes Laertius 1964, IX 5, 2–4.), which should be recognized as the prerequisite and perhaps even the benchmark of the cognitive attitude toward the truth proclaimed by the Ephesian, who after all is also the author of the famous sentence: ἐδιζησάμην ἐμεωυτόν (D-K. 1966, 22 B 101).

uniqueness[15] and none of whom, therefore, except Pythagoras, deserve to be accused of thoughtlessly borrowing pieces of information from others.

It should be considered symptomatic that scholars who prefer the second reading are all busy with the problem of Pythagoras' κακοτεχνίη ("artful knavery," as Ch. Kahn translates it). Looking at the content of fragment B 129, where there is talk of "choosing from these compositions" (ἐκλεξάμενος ταύτας τὰς συγγραφάς) and "making one's own wisdom" (ἐποιήσατο ἑαυτοῦ σοφίην), it is easy to show that Heraclitus could have ascribed the despised receptiveness or any other form of philosophical dependence on others to Pythagoras, but this is still not enough to prove that there is any strong connection between Pythagoras' κακοτεχνίη and the notion of πολυμαθίη, that is to say: that πολυμαθίη consisted exclusively in borrowing from others or, simply speaking, "plagiarism." One explanation of the attempt to link πολυμαθίη with the receptiveness found in Pythagoras' doctrine is perhaps the fact that in fr. B 129 the charge of πολυμαθίη is repeated and reapplied only to the son of Mnesesarchus. The latter's activities are closely elaborated and supplemented by an unambiguous invective in fr. B 81: κοπίδων ἐστὶν ἀρχηγός [i.e. Πυθαγόρης – S.Ś] – "Pythagoras was the prince of imposters" (D-K. 1966, 22 B 81, transl. Kahn 1979, p. 41), but there is no trace of evidence that the same argument is applicable under the same conditions to Hesiod, Hecataeus, or Xenophanes. This leads to the conclusion that the second interpretation of the notion of πολυμαθίη is too narrow to include all of criticised thinkers.

4 The Hypothesis of "Paradoxatism"

A possible solution to the dilemma of how one can understand the charge of πολυμαθίη that meets the requirements of including: 1) all of the addressees of Heraclitus' critique, 2) the principle according to which erudition is a prerequisite of knowledge (B 35 and B 22), and 3) the precept of active research instead of passively conducted learning (B 129, B 104), can be found in all those passages where the problem of human opinions is set in opposition to the established features of the pursued logos.

---

[15] So did Hesiod in the famous passage of his *Theogony* (Hesiod 1966, 22–34). As for Hecataeus, the famous opening of his work leaves no doubts as to his originality and self-assertion (Demetrius of Phalerum 1901, 12, 8–10). Similarly, Xenophanes, whose thought is akin to Heraclitus' when the emphasis is put on the problem of the critique of the thoughtless receptiveness of learning from others (D-K. 1966, 21 B 10; B 3).

One can doubt if it is a mere coincidence that the notion of νόος[16] is used both in B 40, where πολυμαθίη is the form of "knowledge" ascribed to the attacked thinkers, and in B 104, where Heraclitus proves the inadequacy of learning. This can mean that in the first place Heraclitus tried to indicate the distinctness of the desired knowledge in regards to both the forms of cognitive products known to him (πολυμαθίη as "a great deal of information" or simply: "erudition") and to the ways of attaining it (πολυμαθίη as "much learning," especially: "from others" [Pythagoras' κακοτεχνίη]). In both cases, the lack of νόος makes it impossible to guarantee the grasping of what is common, universal, constant (ἀεὶ ἐών (D-K. 1966, 22 B 1)), and first and foremost – one, thereby leaving room for the private worlds of dreamers, as Heraclitus would have said, namely for the multitude of idiosyncratic opinions. In this sense, what Heraclitus tried to say was that philosophical knowledge should be determined by its proper object and must therefore d i f f e r from a mere acquaintance with superficial facts that themselves can never break through to what is real, but unseen. Moreover, the very assumption that reality could be divided into two spheres among which one remains hidden from men proves the well-known fact that in Heraclitus' philosophy the ultimate truth exhibits its paradoxical nature.[17] But this occurs chiefly as a result of human beings' wrong cognitive attitude toward the world. Indeed, the Heraclitean φύσις loves to hide, but only from those who choose to stay asleep and blind to what really matters in the understanding or grasping (νοεῖν) of reality. For this reason, the object of knowledge (λόγος) is described mostly negatively in the Ephesian's thought when it is referred to in the critical context; it is un-expected (ἀνέλπιστον), in-credible (ἄπιστον), in-conclusive (ἄπορον), and un-explored (ἀνεξερεύνητον) (D-K. 1966, 22 B 18; B 86).

The paradox of the pursued truth is to be found not so much in its nature (in its ontological status), but rather in the way human beings typically relate to it.

---

16 On the function of νόος see the classical study by K. von Fritz (Fritz von 1974, pp. 23–85). For the sake of argumentation, it is worth citing a basic trait of the activity of this "organ" already present in Greek epic poetry: "[...] *noos* which penetrates beyond the surface appearance discovers the real truth about matter. There can, then, be no different *nooi* in this situation, but the *noos* in this case is obviously but one. What is of still greater importance, with this connotation of the term *noos*, the later distinction, so important in Pre-Socratic philosophy, between a phenomenal world which we perceive with our senses but which may be deceptive and a real world which may be discovered behind the phenomena seems in some way naïvely anticipated" (Fritz von 1974, p. 25).

17 As M.M. Mackenzie has persuasively shown, the whole of Heraclitus' doctrine can be read from the perspective of the art of paradox led by the complementarity of two principles: "unity of opposites" and "opposition of unity." (Mackenzie 1988, p. 1–37; see also: Hölscher 1974, p. 231; Curd Kenig 1991, p. 541).

Not until the last man recognizes the logos will its nature cease hiding and being paradoxical. For the paradox (παρὰ τῆς δόξης) can only last while there is some *doxa* to challenge and eventually deny it: "The majority of men do not notice [or apprehend] the thing they meet with, nor do they know [or comprehend] them when they have learned (μαθόντες) about them [or when they are taught], but they seem to themselves [or imagine] to do so (ἑωυτοῖσι δὲ δοκέουσι" (D-K. 1966, 22 B 17, transl. Marcovich 2001, p. 15). Therefore, it is nothing other than a strong conviction as to the special status of logos that requires of the Ephesian a comprehensive critique of the most prominent figures of his time. This means that his idea of paradoxical truth has the effect of "paradoxatism," which should be defined in terms of a total war against the action of δοκέω and its product: δοκέοντα or δοξάσματα – opinions.

The attack on polymathy conducted in fr. B 40 and complemented by the critique of learning, which goes far beyond Pythagoras' κακοτεχνίη and even beyond the context of the issue of πολυμαθίη (as fr. B 17, cited above, has proved), is only an exemplification of Heraclitus' critical approach, not its core. Opinions have an unambiguously negative connotation in his philosophy, that is to say, they cannot be understood as something positive as they are in the criticised proposals of Hecataeus and Xenophanes, where δοκέω and its products can be used as effective tools of cognition in place of ultimate truth or what is certain (τὸ σαφὲς as Xenophanes would have said (D-K. 1966, 21 B 34, 1)). At the same time, this would explain why in B 40 both Ionian thinkers are separated from the mythological and/or religious (one could say: "dogmatic") views of Hesiod and Pythagoras by means of the phrase: αὖτίς τε ("and also"). For Heraclitus they are guilty not only of preaching doctrines that when opposed to the logos must be considered mere δοκέοντα – a charge that could certainly have been applied to Hesiod and Pythagoras, who were certain of the veracity and accuracy of their knowledge. However, it is too weak for the specificity of the Ionian enlightenment embodied by Hecataeus and Xenophanes, since both Ionians claimed that opinions understood as cautious conjectures should suffice to carry out a rational interpretation of world.[18] Moreover, it is Xenophanes' thesis that these opinions (and not the exhaustive or ultimate knowledge proposed by Heraclitus) are all that human beings can aspire to: δόκος δ' ἐπὶ πᾶσι τέτυκται –"opinion is allotted to all" (D-K. 1966, 21 B 34, 4, transl. S.Ś.).

---

[18] See especially the already cited intro of Hecataeus, where ridiculed beliefs of the Greeks are to be replaced by the (rational) opinions of the Ionian: Ἑκαταῖος Μιλήσιος ὧδε μυθεῖται· τάδε γράφω, ὥς μοι δοκεῖ ἀληθέα εἶναι· οἱ γὰρ Ἑλλήνων λόγοι πολλοί τε καὶ γελοῖοι, ὡς ἐμοὶ φαίνονται, εἰσίν (Demetrius of Phalerum 1901, 12, 8–10).

Bearing in mind Heraclitus' scorn for those who were supposed to be the most trustworthy in his time, it should come as no surprise that these thinkers were deemed δοκιμώτατοι, which linguistically corresponds with the object they recognized and defended, namely opinions: "What the most esteemed (δοκιμώτατος) man (among the Greeks) knows (γινώσκει) and maintains (φυλάσσει) are but fancies (or false opinions – δοκέοντα)" (D-K. 1966, 22 B 28, transl. Marcovich 2001, p. 78).

In the eyes of the author of the theory of logos, δοκιμώτατοι were highly esteemed or famous only for their subjective viewpoints, which manifested themselves as mere polymathy. Such polymathy should not be confused with wisdom, since the shortest path to notability (εὐ-δοξίαν) should lead only through the recognition of what is good (D-K. 1966, 22 B 135). In this sense, Heraclitus was fully aware of the mentioned thinkers' opinion-forming capability for the rest of the Greeks and this was the main rationale for his critical attitude towards them.

Bibliography

Aristotle (1924): "Metaphysica". In: *Aristotle' Metaphysics: a revised text with introduction and commentary*. Vol. 1–2. William David Ross (ed.). Oxford: Clarendon Press.

Barnes, Jonathan (1982): *The Presocratic Philosophers*. London, Boston: Routledge and Kegan Paul.

Burnet, John (1924): *Greek philosophy. Part I: Thales to Plato*. London: Macmillan.

Cherniss, Harold (1951): "The Characteristics and Effects of Presocratic Philosophy". In: *Journal of the History of Ideas* 12. No. 3, pp. 319–345.

Curd Kenig, Patricia (1991): "Knowledge and Unity in Heraclitus". In: *The Monist* 74. No. 4, pp. 531–549.

Demetrius of Phalerum (1901): "De elocutione". In: *Demetrii Phalerei qui dicitur de elocutione libellus*. Ludwig Radermacher (ed.). Leipzig: Teubner.

Diels, Hermann/Kranz Walther (eds.) (1966): *Die Fragmente der Vorsokratiker. Griechisch und deutsch*. Bd. 1–3. Dublin, Zürich: Weidmann.

Diogenes Laertius (1964): *Vitae Philosophorum*. Vol. 1–2. H.S. Long. Oxford: E. typographeo Clarendoniano.

Fritz von, Kurt (1974): "Nous, Noein, and Their Derivatives in Pre-Socratic Philosophy (Excluding Anagxagoras)". In: Alexander P.D. Mourelatos (ed.): *The Pre-Socratics*. Garden City, NY: Anchor, pp. 23–85.

Gigon, Olof (1968): *Der Ursprung der griechischen Philosophie von Hesiod bis Parmenides*. Basel, Stuttgart: Schwabe.

Granger, Herbert (2004): "Heraclitus' Quarrel with Polymathy and 'Historiê'". In: *Transactions of the American Philological Association* 134. No. 2, pp. 235–261.

Guthrie, William Keith Chambers (1985): *History of Greek Philosophy*. Bd. 1: *The Earlier Presocratics and the Pythagoreans*. Cambridge: Cambridge University Press.

Heidel, William Arthur (1943): "Hecataeus and Xenophanes". In: *The Amercian Journal of Philology* 64. No. 3, pp. 257–277.
Hesiod (1966): *Theogony*. Martin Litchfield West (ed.). Oxford: Clarendon Press.
Hölscher, Uvo (1974): "Paradox, Simile, and Gnomic Utterance in Heraclitus". In: Alexander P.D. Mourelatos (ed.): *The Pre-Socratics*. Garden City, NY: Anchor, pp. 229–238.
Huffman, Carl A. (2008): "Heraclitus' Critique of Pythagoras' Enquiry in Fragment 129". In: *Oxford Studies in Ancient Philosophy* 35, pp. 19–47.
Jaeger, Werner (1946): *Paideia: the Ideals of Greek Culture*. Vol. I: *Archaic Greece, The Mind of Athens*. Oxford: Basil Blackwell.
Kahn, Charles (1979): *The Art and Thought of Heraclitus. An edition of the Fragments with Translation and Commentary*. Cambridge: Cambridge University Press.
Kirk, Geoffrey Stephen (1975): *Heraclitus. The Cosmic Fragments: a Critical Study with Introduction, Text and translation*. Cambridge: Cambridge University Press.
Kubok, Dariusz (2015): "Allocriticism and Autocriticism in the Views of Xenophanes of Colophon". In: *Littera Antiqua*. No. 10/11, pp. 261–281.
Liddell, Henry George/Scott, Robert/ Jones, Henry Stuart/McKenzie, Rodercik (1996): *A Greek-English Lexicon: With a Revised Supplement*. Oxford: Clarendon Press.
Lloyd, Geoffrey Ernest Richard (1970): *Early Greek Science: Thales to Aristotle*. London: Chatto and Windus.
Mackenzie, Mary Margaret (1988): "Heraclitus and The Art of Paradox". In: *Oxford Studies in Ancient Philosophy* 6, pp. 1–37.
Marcovich, Miroslav (2001): *Heraclitus: Greek text with a short commentary. Second Edition Including fresh Addenda, Corrigenda and a Select Bibliography (1967–2000)*. Sankt Augustin: Academia Verlag.
Mrówka, Kazimierz (2004): *Heraklit. Fragmenty: nowy przekład i komentarz*. Warszawa: Scholar.
Plato (1900): "Theaetetus". In: *Platonis Opera*. Vol. 1. John Burnet (ed.). Oxford: ethypographeo Clarendoniano.
Verdenius, Willem Jacob (1947): "Notes on the Presocratics". In: *Mnemosyne, Third Series* 13, pp. 271–289.
Zeller, Eduard (1876): *Die Philosophie der Griechen in ihrer Geschichtlichen Entwicklung*. Teil 1: *Allgemeine Einleitung: Vorsokratische Philosophie*. Leipzig: Leipzig Fues.

Janina Gajda-Krynicka
Criticism as the Basis for the Procedures of Hypothetical Dialectic in Plato's Philosophy

Abstract: The aim of this article is to demonstrate that the critical attitude, expressed in the need for a constant verification of conclusions and findings, is the basic condition for the realization of dialectical procedures in Platonic philosophy. This necessity appears at each stage of the realization of dialectical procedure: in synoptic, *hypothetical*, and diairetic dialectic, and results in an evolution of Platonic thought from the doctrine of Forms, presented in the so-called Middle Platonic texts (*Phaedrus, Phaedo, Republic, Symposium*), through the stage of the critique of the doctrine of Forms (*Parmenides*), to the conception of principles – *archai* (*Philebus, Timaeus*, the so-called 'unwritten doctrines' – *agrapha dogmata*). The Author accepts and justifies the idea that dialectical procedures are realized in the intellect of the philosopher, contrary to the conceptions of the so-called Tübingen-Milanese School, which asserts that this can only occur in acts of live speech and cannot be objectified in a written text. She also accepts that the dialectical procedure leading to knowledge of the first forms of being as an argument ultimately justifying the existence of things – phenomena in the overt sphere of reality, is made up of three stages: 1) the synoptic, sensory view of phenomena, ordering them into sets, existing *on account of* transcendent general concepts; 2) the formulation of constantly verified hypotheses, establishing the ontic status and place of being of general concepts; and as the culmination of the prior stages, 3) the ability of defining phenomena in the overt sphere through work conducted on pure concepts, without reference to the sensory view. This article places special emphasis on the hypothetical procedures, due to the fact (among other things) that *hypothetical* dialectic is omitted in the secondary literature, or identified with either the simple acceptance of assumptions, premises of inference, or with hypotheses in the field of mathematics. Due to the leading role of hypothetical dialectic, philosophical hypotheses require special verification. Hence the conclusion that criticism, the critical attitude, is a basic predisposition for philosophizing in Platonic philosophy.

Keywords: Plato, dialectic, synopsis, hypothesis, diairesis, criticism, method, definition, critical attitude, verification.

The definition, role, and function of dialectic in Platonic philosophy have been objects of debate and controversy[1] since the time of Aristotle.[2] There can be no doubt that διαλεκτική τέχνη – the "art of dialectic" – was known and practiced in the Greek *oikoumene* long before Plato, though the state of pre-Platonic philosophers' legacies does not permit a precise reconstruction of this art's procedure. In the work of the late bio- and doxographer Diogenes Laertius, we can find the assertion – cited from Aristotle – that dialectic was invented by Zeno of Elea.[3] However, the same Diogenes Laertius attributes the "invention of 'investigative procedure'[4] in the form of questions and answers" (Οὕτως πρῶτος ἐν ἐρωτήσει λόγον παρήνεγκεν), as well as the introduction of the concept of "dialectic"[5] into philosophy, to Plato. What did this "'investigative procedure' in the form of questions and answers" consist in, and what was its goal?[6] In pre-Platonic philosophy, its goal was surely the justification and confirmation, critique, or even refutation of an investigative thesis, an opinion commonly accepted on the

---

[1] In historical overviews (such as e.g. Dürr 1947), or works of the representative of the so-called Tübingen (Krämer 1959, Krämer 1994, Gaiser 1963, Szlezak 1993) or Milanese Schools (Reale 1991), dialectic is understood as inquiry into truth/knowledge by way of a method of questions and answers in acts of live speech; the works of Ch. Kahn (Ch. H. Kahn 1966, 1973, 1996) concentrate above all on the linguistic aspects of the procedure and the concept itself; F. Cornford (Cornford 1932 and Conford 1935), accepting Zeno of Elea's definition, concentrates on the necessity of verifying the findings of dialectic; D. Scott's interesting piece (Scott 1999) emphasizes dialectical procedures' being conditioned upon the conception of anamnesis; it is worth noting that a majority of the literature concerns diairetic dialectic (Sayre 2006 and Sayre 2007; Lloyd 1965; Philip 1966.

[2] Arist., *Analitica priora* 46a ff., *Analitica posteriora* 96a-97b et passim.

[3] Diogenes Laertius (Diogenes Laertius, VIII 57, 2, see also IX 25, 12), where the doxographer, citing Aristotle (ed. Rose, frgm. 65, derived from the lost work *Sophist*) attributes the invention of *dialektike techne* to Zeno of Elea, and referring to Plato (*Phaedrus*, 261d), calls him the 'Eleatic Palamedes,' which suggests that the Greek tradition accepted that dialectic was already being used during the time of the Trojan War.

[4] This is how I translate the term "logos" in the cited passage from Diogenes Laertius; with the ambiguity of this term even in Plato's writings, such a translation is validated by the fact that the term λογισμός is used interchangeably with λόγος by Plato in *Phaedrus*, see: 249c, 265d – 266b; see also *Phaedo*, 65c, where he describes the sphere in which being is revealed with the verb form λογίζεσθαι; cf. *Phaedo*, 66a, where he uses the term λόγος. In *Phaedo*, the term *logos* is synonymous with the term λογισμός, which I translate as: reasoning, argument, inference.

[5] Diogenes Laertius, III 24, 10.

[6] See: Ch.H. Kahn's piece (Kahn 1996) dedicated to the search for the etymology of the term (concept) "dialectic"; I accept that of the many etymologies Kahn examined, the most justified one is that, which derives the term from the phrase: δία τὸν λόγον [to investigate, to seek], in which the term λόγος (used interchangeably with λογισμός) signifies reasoning, inference; see fn. 4.

grounds of tradition or authority, or of a statement in the form of a proposition that lays an absolute claim to truth.[7] Thus, the function dialectic served was one of critique and verification.

In the scant (extant) legacy left behind by pre-Platonic philosophers, such a procedure can be found in the extant fragments of Parmenides of Elea's poem. In it, Parmenides – in contrast to the philosophers of nature, later called "physicists" by Aristotle – determines the predicates of being and proves their truth, starting from the irrefutable axiomatic[8] statement that being (τ' ἐόν) is (ἔστιν), while non-being (μὴ ἐόν) – its opposite – is not (οὐκ ἔστιν),[9] rejecting both the illusory testimony of the senses and linguistic messages in favor of strictly intellectual inquiry. In his conception of being, which initiated the philosophical ontology of the West and diametrically changed the hitherto conception of philosophy and its object, Parmenides refutes both wide-spread, every day opinions (beliefs – δόξαι) and the theories of the philosophers of nature, which accept motion, change, generation and destruction, multiplicity and divisibility, as well as the possibility of making statements about what exists in many times and modes. We can venture the thesis that on the basis of the extant fragments of the poem *On Nature*, it will be possible to reconstruct the model of pre-Platonic dialectical procedures in both of their aspects: proving the truth of a thesis, and refuting the opposing thesis. The thesis-conception of Parmenides stands in opposition to the conception of the *physicists* in several areas of inquiry, of which the most important should be considered the object of philosophy: for the *physicists* accept that this object is (and should be) the nature of reality (φύσις), while Parmenides considers this object to be being (τ' ἐόν, τὸ εἶναι) and situates the *physicists*' theories within the sphere of the "opinions of mortals" (βροτῶν δόξαι).[10] The philosopher walks the "way of truth," whereas the *physicists* –

---

[7] Perhaps this is why Aristotle considered Zeno of Elea the creator of the "dialectical skill"; called "Parmenides' shield" (Plato, *Parmenides*, 12c-e), Zeno defended the ideas of his mentor Parmenides in the treatise *On Nature*. However, historians of philosophy are still puzzled by the question of whether Aristotle – a doxographer – relayed the views of his predecessors faithfully, on the basis of the source texts, or whether he cited them e.g. from memory or on the basis of other accounts. The faithfulness of Aristotle's account was questioned, if not definitively undermined, in the works of H. Cherniss (Cherniss 1935 and Cherniss 1944).

[8] Presumably, the point of departure for Parmenides' conception of being and its predicates is, in fact, an analytical *a priori* proposition, in which a predicate irrefutably follows from an act of linguistic reference.

[9] Diels Hermann, Kranz Walther (1960), *Die Fragmente der Vorsokratiker. Griechisch und Deutsch*, Zürich: Weidmann, hereinafter cited as DK 28 B 2, B 6, B 8.

[10] DK 28 B 1, 18; B 1, 53; B 8, 61.

the way of opinions, from which it is best to keep one's distance.[11] The critique of the *physicists'* theories is accomplished in Parmenides' poem by way of a method, which may have given rise to the elenctic method attributed to Socrates, presented in Plato's early dialogues and often called "Socratic." The philosopher from Elea, in his argumentation rejecting generation and destruction, motion and change, seemingly accepts the *physicists'* conception, only to reduce it to absurdity: thus, for example, if – tracking Parmenides' line of argument – we accept that being is generated, or comes into being, we have to accept that it was generated from something that is different from it, i.e. from non-being, but non-being is not; if we accept that it is destructible, then it must turn into something that differs from it, i.e. into non-being, but non-being is not (it is necessary to emphasize that ancient philosophy did not have the concept of nothingness); the situation is similar with proving the immutability, immovability, and uniformity of being.[12] Parmenides' argument thus boils down to unmasking absurdity of both the *physicists'* conceptions and all results of a sensory view based on sense perception. It is worth noting that the sophist Gorgias of Leontini uses the same method in his treatise *On Nature or the Non-Existent* in order to reduce the conception of Parmenides and his student, Melissus of Samos,[13] to absurdity, showing the consequences and aporias to which its acceptance would lead. Parmenides' conception of being and cognition, as well Melissus' invalid attempt at translating it into *physics*, thus contain, according to the sophist, irresolvable aporias, which necessarily lead to the negation of any possibility at all of being, cognition, or predication.[14] Moreover, Plato himself subsequently makes use of this same method several times: in the dialogue *Parmenides*, in whose first part, under the guise of the Parmenides, Plato subjects his own doctrine of Forms to critique, revealing its aporias (see: Plato, *Parmenides*, 131a ff., 132a ff., 133, 133b ff., 136a – c); or in the dialogue *Sophist*, when behind the mask of the Eleatic Stranger he commits "patricide" on Parmenides,

---

[11] DK 28 B 8, 18; the polemical aspect is also reflected in the subtitles (possibly assigned later) of sections of the poem: "The Way of Truth," in which Parmenides presents his conception, and "The Way of Opinion(s)," against which he argues, or even refutes. It should be emphasized that attempts present in the secondary literature (Reale 1993, pp. 139 ff.) at finding a so-called "third way," which combine the sensory view with the intellect's investigations and allow for being to be identified with the nature of reality, stand in contradiction to both Parmenides' text and doxographical testimony (e.g. Plato's *Sophist*, or Aristotle's *De coelo* 298b, *Physica* 207a); for further reading, see J. Gajda-Krynicka 2007, pp. 283 ff.
[12] DK 28 B 8, 5 – 21.
[13] Its content was passed down to us in the Pseudo-Aristotelian treatise *On Melissus, Xenophanes, and Gorgias* (980b nn), as well as in Sextus Empiricus' *Adv. Math.*, VII 65 (DK 82 B 3).
[14] For more on this issue, see: J. Gajda-Krynicka 2009.

undermining the latter's conception of the one immovable being (Plato, *Sophist*, 239e, 249c).

The texts indicated above only show us one of the procedures comprising the "dialectical skill": its critical aspect is realized through the method of the *reductio ad absurdum* of a thesis or conception which the philosopher, or sophist, wants to negate. Therefore, we do not know whether pre-Platonic philosophers used these procedures solely as a polemical and critical tool; due to the fact that the extant texts at our disposal are few and fragmentary, we cannot establish precisely which route led them to determine e.g. what the first form of being was *in ordine essendi* in the form specified as *arche* or *archai* – Thales' water, Anaximander's *apeiron*, Heraclitus' *Logos*. We are left only with attempts at reconstructing the line of thought of these philosophers on the basis of extant fragments, doxographical testimony, as well as a few irrefutable axioms, described by Aristotle in book II of the *Metaphysics*.[15]

In these attempts at reconstructing the thought process of pre-Platonic philosophers, as well as the development of pre-Platonic philosophy, an important role is played by questions (ἐρωτήσεις) as indispensable components of dialectical procedures. It is therefore possible to put forward the thesis that every piece of text preserved, or even every philosophical text at all, is an answer to some question. It is therefore necessary to try to recreate the questions which, in the process of philosophy's development and the route leading to certain conceptions, are more important than the answers. However, it must be emphasized here that the role of questions does not determine the understanding of philosophy as in fact realized only in acts of live speech, or interpersonal communication,[16] and therefore unable to be fixed in writing – textual form. The concept of "question" includes, on the one hand, the critical assessment of existing conceptions, and on the other hand, the discovery and articulation of problems that those conceptions have not solved – the very term "question" is, in a sense, a sort of mental shortcut. As an example, we can refer to the evolution of the con-

---

[15] Above all, the belief – originating in the pre-philosophic period – that the chain of cause and effect cannot be infinite, or the principle of noncontradiction, as well as the conviction – clearly present in the oldest literary texts – that the whole of reality (τὰ πάντα) is comprised of two spheres: the overt sphere, accessible to the senses, and the covert sphere, which, beginning with Platonic philosophy, is identified with transcendence.

[16] Since the 1960's, an increasing number of scholars (Krämer 1959, Krämer 1994, pp. 1–20, Gaiser 1968, Reale 1991, Szlezak 1993) accepts the idea that the "true" Platonic philosophy cannot be reconstructed on the basis of the texts, because the "true" philosophy was taught at the Academy for a small group of "initiated" listeners. This stance is based on two passages from Plato's writings: *Phaedrus*, 275c ff, *Letter VII*, 341c ff.

ception of the *arché/principle* in the thought of the first Ionian philosophers: each successive philosopher gains an additional reference point in his investigations in the form of the conception of his predecessor. Each subsequent conception of *arché* is therefore born, on the one hand, in the process of constructive criticism of the previous conception, and on the other, during the search for answers to further questions that appear throughout the course of observation and thinking. Thus, for example, in the evolution of the Ionian philosophy of nature's conception of *arché*, Anaximander rejects Thales' water in favor of his own conception of *apeiron*[17] after a critical (unsuccessful) verification of his predecessor's theory, consisting in the formulation of a series of questions about the conditions that proto-substance – *arché* in its world-generating function – would have to fulfill, and which water failed to fulfill. In turn, as a result of questions about how life identical to motion is possible, a modification of the ontic status of *arché* is made in Anaximenes' conception – the *arché* is air, because what is alive must breathe. The next philosopher, Heraclitus of Ephesus, asks a question unarticulated by his predecessors – the question of the source and genesis of thinking; for this reason, his conception of the proto-substance (*Logos*) attributes both rationality and a normative function (beyond its world-generating function) to this substance.[18]

However, to whom and in what form does the philosopher ask these questions? How would the investigative procedure "in the form of questions and answers" look like "in practice"? Was it – as scholars from the Tübingen and Milanese School would have it – realized in acts of live speech in a shared process of investigating truth with someone else, regardless of whether it be a philosopher, an adept, or a layman?[19] This idea is unacceptable for several reasons. Above all, this is due to the fact that there were no actual (and probably are none to this day within the sphere of philosophical inquiry) possibilities of such interpersonal acts of communication, which would fulfill all the conditions of solving problems and "inquiring into truth," or attaining knowledge.[20] Heraclitus could not,

---

[17] I translate the term *apeiron* (ἄπειρον) as "indefinable proto-substance," i.e. one that cannot be defined through reference to elements subject to sense-perception (like Thales' water).
[18] For more, see: Gajda-Krynicka 2007, pp. 65–73 *et passim*.
[19] Such an understanding of dialectic could justify the "critique" of writing (see fn. 18), because text fixed in a written account cannot defend itself – the notation breaks the continuity of the communicative situation, it distances the written statement of the message sender from its recipient and breaks the linguistic contact – essential in communication – between the sender and recipient of the message.
[20] Here, it is necessary to refer to what is known as "Jakobson's law" (Jakobson 1989, vol. II, pp. 77–125), according to which philosophizing is a discourse, whose point of departure lies in the triple relationship between the three factors comprising an act of speech: the message

for obvious reasons, have held discussions with the Pythagoras he mocked[21] or asked questions of the philosophers from Miletus. Moreover, in order for the conditions of model effective discourse to be fulfilled, the philosopher would have to have worthy partners of inquiry, akin to alter egos. With whom could a philosopher hold a dispute (διαλέγεσθαι), even if he did manage to cross the boundaries of time and space? Let us consider three possibilities: another philosopher, who seeks the same and by means of the same methods, who, as Plato writes in *Phaedrus*, "is able to divide things by classes and to comprehend particulars under a general idea"[22] (*Phaedrus*, 273e); another philosopher, who seeks something different and by different means, who has faith in sense perception – a sophist, or "son of the earth," who "runs away into the darkness of not-being" (*Sophist*, 254a), or a "late learning old man," as Plato described his adversary, Antisthenes – someone, who seeks e.g. not the good as such, on account of which all individual good exists, but good in action, at home, or at the agora, not justice as such, but concrete assessments of deeds or laws, who "sees a horse, but not 'horseness'"; and finally, an adept or layman, who – for the time being, or forever – remains at the stage of a sensory view of things; (the latter can be divided into two groups: those who are, as Socrates states in *Theaetetus*, "pregnant with thought" (*Theaetetus*, 150d ff.) – and it is to them that Plato directs his doctrines and writings, and those, whom Plato scornfully calls the "multitude" (*polloi*) and sends away to learn from the sophists).

Let us consider the second possibility mentioned above: in a dialectical discourse, we seek the truth of being with a philosopher holding views opposed to our own – when it comes to Plato's writings, let him be one of the sophists, who so often appear on the pages of the dialogues, or one of the pre-Platonic physicists cited explicitly or hidden beneath the descriptions: "ancient wise men" (*Philebus*, 16c), or "Sicilian Muses" (*Sophist*, 242d), or even Antisthenes, who held a diametrically different stance than Plato on the issue of the ontic status of general concepts.[23] Such discourse would necessarily be polemical (and Anti-

---

sender, its recipient, and the message itself. This relationship would determine the necessity for additional elements in the communicative act. For an act of communication to exist, three things are indispensable: context (the message must be verbalized and must mean something), contact (there must be a physical – temporal-spatial – and psychological relationship between the sender and recipient of the message), and a code either common to the sender and recipient, or unambiguously translatable.

21 DK 22 B 40, 3; B 81, 6.
22 All quotes from Platonic writings, with the exception of *Letter VII*, are taken from the English translation by R. G. Bury (1966).
23 See: Kalaš/Suvák (2014).

sthenes and Plato's discourses were polemical, as portrayed in the writings of the founder of the Cynic School), but substantive polemical arguments are not born *ad hoc*, during the discourse itself. Did Plato succeed in persuading Antisthenes, for that matter? Did the Platonic Socrates persuade Callicles in the dialogue *Gorgias*? Does Callicles help Socrates to define the Socratic conception of happiness or philosophy? A polemic with the sophists or "sons of the earth" is possible only if it has been preceded by lengthy preparation, leaving aside the fact that Plato often polemicizes with those who are long deceased and thus unable to respond (this is why, in the dialogues, Plato often uses a literary device later legitimated by Lucian of Samosata in his *Dialogues of the Dead*, e. g. when he evokes the sophist Protagoras from the grave in the *Theaetetus*). Such polemic is important and formative for the dialectical process and for the philosopher's search, but it is only one part of the dialectical method. In Plato's writings, such polemics are, in a sense, symbols or metaphors for *elenchos*. However, *elenchos* is only an introduction to proper dialectic. In discourse with a physicist or sophist we will not come to the same conclusions; the physicist or the sophist will not be of service to us, because he will not go the same way we do. Let us consider the third option: the discourse participant is a layman or an adept. Such situations do indeed appear in Plato's writings. The layman, however, not being "pregnant with thought," will not help in the joint investigation into the truth of being. It can only serve as a model for practicing the elenctic part of the dialectical procedure; he is always just a sparring partner. The adept, on the other hand, listens willingly; one can write in his soul, but only what one has previously worked out, in the intellect and in solitude, through *logismoi*.

Therefore, there is no appropriate discourse partner for the philosopher-dialectician. The dialectical process is realized not in live discourse, but in the philosopher's intellect. Live discourse can only be found on the pages of the Platonic dialogues as a record of dialectical procedure written for the voices of actors. Even with such a record, however, in none of the writings will we find a situation defined by the common-place understanding of dialectic, in which the term *logos* is understood as live discourse.[24] Plato frequently emphasizes that dialectical

---

24 The form of the Socratic dialogue itself could suggest a discursive form of investigation, because – seemingly – the Platonic Socrates, Parmenides, Eleatic Stranger either engage in a "duel of words," or – like Theaetetus – "help" Socrates solve a problem. Nevertheless, especially in the so-called dialectical dialogues (*Parmenides, Sophist, Statesman, Theaetetus*), the partner of the dialogue's protagonist is merely a figurehead, a stage character, who allows the dialectical procedures realized in the philosopher's intellect to become objective, show how they are implemented, and which rules within them should be followed. In the *Sophist*, for example, when the Eleatic Stranger is asked in what form he would like to present his position, he rejects

procedures are realized within the soul or intellect of the philosopher (*Theaetetus*, 189c – 190a), and these declarations are particularly valuable to us, because in the development of Greek philosophical thought this is the first time we are dealing with the complete and extant set of a philosopher's writings – the entire *Corpus Platonicum*.

Their analysis leads to a few conclusions in regards to dialectic and dialectical procedures. It must be emphasized yet again that in none of the Platonic writings do we find the explicit statement that dialectical procedures are realized in discourse, in acts of interpersonal communication. Dialectic as a method is, on the one hand, a tool serving the attainment of truth (ἀλήθεια), regardless of whether we seek the "truth of realities" (*Phaedo*, 99e) or that, which is accessible to us through the sensory view: why they are how they are, i.e. ordered in some way and able to be gathered into collections, and why, *on account of what they are how they are, they are best* (*Phaedo*, 97d), or truth identical with the first beings *in ordine essendi, on account of* which there are things, and thus the "truth of realities." Dialectical procedures are supposed to provide us with certain knowledge of that sphere of reality that appears in the sensory view, to enable cognition of the covert sphere, that is, that realm of being, *on account of* which there are things – the first principles and causes, regardless of whether they are Forms or principles – *archai*, as well as, after the philosopher has cognized them, the secondary cognition of the overt sphere, already more accurate and better, because it is not based only on the illusory senses, but realized on the basis of pure concepts. On the other hand, dialectic identifies with philosophy, without losing the status of a method. What enables a reliable dialectician to be a philosopher – as opposed to the twisted procedures of the sophists, for example – is the constant verification of the results of procedures, a critical attitude not only in regards to the accomplishments and conceptions of others, but above all to his own, which is beautifully described through metaphor in *Letter VII* as "rubbing and sparking" (*Letter VII*, 344b ff.).

What, then, does Platonic dialectic consist in?[25]

---

the form of an exposition (*logos*) in favor of an apparent dialogue with the young Theaetetus. It is apparent, because – as he himself notes – he asks to receive an unlearned youth as a partner in the apparent dispute (*Sophist*, 217d).

25 It is worth noting that in many remarks on Plato's dialectic, its individual stages are not distinguished (*Republic*, 537c, *Phaedrus*, 249b *et passim*). This is undoubtedly due to the assumption that the term "dialectician" can only be used in reference to one, who has mastered all of the procedures. In the secondary literature, scholars frequently identify dialectic with only one procedure, concentrating either on the elenctic procedures in the early dialogues, or on diairesis, see: fn. 1.

In Plato's writings we do not find an exposition explicitly dedicated to dialectic, but we can reconstruct it in all its complexity on the basis of almost every dialogue, or at least find it functioning in every dialogue. It is therefore necessary to make a selection of texts; the dialogues I will be referring to are: *Phaedrus, Symposium, Phaedo, Parmenides, Sophist*, as well as, irrespective of the dispute over the authenticity of the letters historically attributed to Plato, *Letter VII*.[26] It should be emphasized here that, although Plato speaks in many places about dialectical procedures as a whole, dialectic is a skill comprised of three stages, which must be implemented consistently in a specific order. The first stage of dialectical procedure is so-called *synoptic dialectic* or *collection*; the second stage is what I refer to as *hypothetical dialectic*; and the third and final stage is *diairetic dialectic* or the *method of division*. Dialectic can thus be referred to as a path; however, while it has a beginning, it does not, in fact, have an end, because it requires constant critical verification – returning to the beginning and continually traversing it anew.

Let us take a look at what the beginning of this path of dialectic looks like, a path accessible only to those, who are "pregnant with thought." It begins with the sensory view, which must nonetheless be achieved not on the basis of individual, detached perceptions, ascertaining that something is and is somehow, but such a special form of insight that Plato calls *synopsis* (σύνοψις), and the one who can implement it, *synoptikos aner* (συνοπτικὸς ἀνήρ).[27] The objects of such insight are *things*,[28] which are somehow: beautiful or ugly, large or small, individual or multiple, similar or dissimilar, simple or complex. They are "ordered" in such a way that sets, species, and genera can be distinguished; among *things* a certain hierarchy of values can be established, their generation and destruction are perceptible and subject to certain laws. The world of *things* is a cosmos – an ordered structure, though its order, built according to some algorithm, hides its efficient cause before the eyes of the viewer, for it would be in vain to it seek in the *things* themselves, though *things*, skillfully viewed by the

---

[26] I omit research positions and secondary literature on this issue out of necessity, on the premise that even if we recognize *Letter VII* as inauthentic, it had to have originated within the Platonic Academy; for this reason, it can be considered an exposition of dialectical procedures that was faithful to the teachings of Plato.

[27] The synoptic view (*Republic* 537c 7) is the opposite of the form of perception Heraclitus (DK 22 B 40, 3) called "much and varied learning" (πολυμαθίη), i.e. perceiving each object separately, in isolation from others. The synoptic, on the other hand, who begins to practice the art of dialectic, can "perceiv[e] and bring[–] together in one idea the scattered particulars" (*Phaedrus*, 265d).

[28] In his earlier dialogues, Plato still refers to them as τὰ ὄντα.

synoptic, reveal to the philosopher that such a cause must exist *somewhere*. The first stage of the dialectical method thus teaches a *synoptic* view of reality: reducing many sensory perceptions to a *single* form, the first form of the dialectic of *things*, which results in the conviction that there must be some form of being, on account of which things, states, or phenomena have a certain quality, and can be classified and assigned to specific collections. Thus, on the path of synoptic dialectic, the formulation of a general concept occurs, first in the form of a name, like redness or beauty, which covers a given set of things: red things or beautiful things, or even the actions of the righteous. The name, in turn, determines the question of its ontic status – whether it is an *empty name*, or whether it corresponds to a form of being that cannot be recognized by the eyes, because searching for it in *things* threatens the seeker with blindness (*Phaedo*, 99d – 99e). The first stage of synoptic dialectic can no longer provide answers to these questions, because its capabilities end with the formulation of a general concept, which we can identify with a definition. The stage of synoptic dialectic that leads to knowledge of the ontic status of names/general concepts is one, which Plato described in *Phaedrus* as the path leading out from the ranks of individual perceptions and gathering them into one, into such a form as Plato (in his mid-Academic period) saw in the Forms. This new form is above and beyond individual things,[29] it is eternal and always the same, though things change and pass away, or lose their qualities. Not everyone can attain knowledge of the ideas – not everyone has dialectical predispositions, since not everyone is "pregnant with thought." Only the "synoptic" can enter onto the dialectic path, who does not stop at perceiving and registering perceptions in the belief (*pistis*) that a thing is as it appears, but rather asks: why is it, and on account of what? The synoptic, who treats the synoptic sensory view as *hupolepsis* – an initial assumption, preparation for the noetic view of such a form of redness or beauty or of a geometric figure, which is not a red or beautiful thing or a concrete figure, but is a form of redness or beauty in general that is no longer subject to a sensual view. It is not an easy procedure. It is seemingly easy to order visible things, like horses, into collections, to distinguish horses from trees, to conclude that, in view of the fact that phenomenal horses are born, grow, and perish only to continually appear anew in a perpetual cycle of birth and death, there must be some "horse-

---

29 "In considering the nature of anything, must we not consider first, whether that in respect to which we wish to be learned ourselves and to make others learned is simple or multiform, and then, if it is simple, enquire what power of acting it possesses, or of being acted upon, and by what, and if it has many forms, number them, and then see in the case of each form, as we did in the case of the simple nature, what its action is and how it is acted upon and by what?" (*Phaedrus*, 270d).

ness" that determines the existence of particular horses. But it is much more difficult, for example, to organize into collections and bring to one form what appears to cognitive agents as beautiful: for some, this may be jewels or costumes, for others – youths (*Symposium*, 210 ff.),[30] and thus, what is mutable and transient, while for others, beautiful deeds or even knowledge. Objects of admiration and desire should therefore be ordered differently than phenomena or artifacts, though they are phenomena or artifacts by definition, remaining in the *overt* sphere of reality. In regards to these objects, it is necessary to seek a different criterion of gathering into collections and ordering, than one merely based on external traits, a criterion no longer situated only in the sphere of the sensory view, but in the sphere of emotions and sensations, which in the Platonic conception of the soul shown in *Phaedrus* (249b nn) is proper to the appetitive soul – in the sphere of Eros. One traversing the path of synoptic dialectic will thus draw a distinction between perceived objects that arouse his desire or admiration, and those that are indifferent to him. One who does not stop at the above arrangement will ask the questions: why is this the object of emotion, why does that man or artifact arouse this feeling, why are these objects – various and seemingly dissimilar phenomena – in this particular collection? The next stage of the procedure, which is still within the sphere of synoptic dialectic, is the discovery that within the collection of desirable objects are those that are beautiful, but in spite of their mutability, transience or destruction, emotions remain, although their object is no longer a phenomenon, but that, *on account of which* the phenomenon exists – namely, beauty itself.

How, then, does the being *on account of which* there are collections of phenomena – beauty itself, differ from beautiful things, how is "horseness" different from a horse? First and foremost, it was, is, and always will be the same, as opposed to phenomena, which are born, change, and pass away. Moreover, unlike individual things, it is that, which is general. In addition, it is inaccessible in the sensory view, though it undoubtedly must be in some kind of relation to things. Thus, in the procedures of synoptic dialectic, it may be identified with a general concept, but this is where the possibilities of *synopsis* and the sensory view end. Is the noetic view still within the scope of synoptic dialectic? Is the synoptic able to break away from earth and move within the sphere of pure concepts using the power of his intellect? There is no doubt that the limit of synoptic dialectic's po-

---

30 The most beautiful and complete description of synoptic dialectic can be found in Plato's *Symposium* (201d-212b), where Plato's Socrates, quoting the words of the priestess Diotima, discusses the degrees and stages of moving from the love and admiration of beautiful bodies to grasping the necessity of existence of the essence of incorruptible beauty, which is manifested in the objects and bodies in which beauty fades.

tential is the determination/discovery of general concepts and their relation to individual things. However, knowledge of where they are – what their ontic status is, how they are, and what the particular relation between general concepts and individual objects is, is beyond the capabilities of synoptic dialectic. Synoptic dialectic organizes things of the phenomenal world into collections and establishes the necessary relation of ontic or metaphysical reference, but the sphere to which it refers remains beyond its cognitive capabilities.

Thus, another question arises: where and how are these general concepts? What is their ontic status? What cognitive faculties can reach them and allow for their cognition? In Platonic dialectic, this question initiates a great dispute about the ontic status of general concepts, which was later referred to as the "problem of universals" in medieval philosophy. The adept of dialectic who is trained in the synoptic view has three choices: 1. general concepts have an ontic status, they are beings in the way the being of Parmenides is, and since they are not subject to the sensory view, they must be in the covert sphere of reality, which we may call transcendent; 2. general concepts do not have an ontic status – they are merely names (this was this position of Plato's adversary, Antisthenes); and 3. general concepts exist in things (this was Aristotle's). In order to solve this problem, the dialectician must embark on the path identified with philosophy: the path leading to the discovery of the form of the first being/beings *in ordine essendi*.

The next stage of the dialectical path is which I call hypothetical dialectic,[31] described most fully by Plato in *Phaedo*.[32] The dialectician must therefore embark on a second journey, to use the metaphor from the *Phaedo*, to reach his destination – to discover that the principles and causes of what is, the form of being that determines the form of *things*, must be sought beyond the sphere of *things*, beyond the phenomenal world. In this search, one must break away from investigating things and move on to a search within the sphere, and at the level, of what Plato calls *logoi* or *logismoi*; this begins with the formulation of a *hypothesis*, which in the process of pure thought is to indicate the first forms of being.

---

[31] From the term: ὑπόθεσις. It should be emphasized that Plato uses this term in many senses, including as a way of describing the premises in deductive reasoning, the initial assumptions of a thesis to be proven, or the premises in a mathematical proof (*Meno*, 86e ff.), see: Kahn 1996, pp. 305 ff.; I accept that this term does not gain the meaning of the second stage of dialectical procedure until the dialogue *Phaedo*. It should be noted that in the works dedicated to Platonic dialectic with which I am familiar (see: fn. 2), hypothetic dialectic is not distinguished as a separate form of dialectical procedure, nor does the term hypothetical dialectic itself appear.

[32] Plato's Socrates calls this stage the "second voyage" (δεύτερος πλοῦς, *Phaedo* 99d); following Reale (1991) I will use the beautiful phrase: "second sailing."

In the *Phaedo*, Plato's Socrates states that when he got tired of investigating *beings* in *things*, he began a search with the acceptance of a "statement [proposition – JGK], which I consider strongest" (λόγος ἐρρωμενέστατος – *Phaedo*, 100a), emphasizing that he does so in every case of dialectical investigation, i.e. undertaking an attempt to find the non-empirical cause of things or phenomena, as well as an attempt to justify why something is how it is. Socrates goes on to give an example of such a hypothesis: "I am going to try to explain to you the nature of that cause which I have been studying, and I will revert to those familiar subjects of ours as my point of departure and assume that there are such things as absolute beauty and good and greatness and the like. If you grant this and agree that these exist" (*Phaedo*, 100b).

It may be concluded from Socrates' previous arguments that such a form of hypothesis was already formulated as a result of synoptic dialectic, as a result of the synoptic view of things. Moreover, it could not be formulated as a statement of sufficient power only within the realm of pure thought, which consciously rejected all contact with things. This would be admitted by Socrates' students, who – though unfamiliar with the hypothetical method – could follow the Teacher as he walked the path of synoptic dialectic. Hypothetical dialectic is the stage of the path in which the philosopher undertakes reflection on the ontic status and place of beauty, good, or greatness as such, firmly certain that they cannot not exist, but which certainty – it must be emphasized – was attained in the process of synoptic dialectic, the basis of which is the sensory view. The result of the ἐν λόγοις investigation, however, is to determine – in the form of a strong assertion – that beauty, the good, or greatness as such are differently and elsewhere than things, and that they determine the characteristics of the collections of beautiful, good or great things subject to them through relations of participation, presence, and imitation. This assertion allows us to establish the kinds of relationships that exist between beauty, the good, or the great, and beautiful, good, or great things by way of deduction: "...if anything is beautiful besides absolute beauty it is beautiful for no other reason than because it partakes of absolute beauty; and this applies to everything" (*Phaedo*, 100c). The first Socratic *hypothesis* is not a dogmatic and authoritative assertion. As mentioned above, this is an initial premise, formulated on the basis of the results of the synoptic view, which is to serve as the foundation for purely *logical* arguments realized in the realm of pure thought, *en logois*.

This *hypothesis* must, however, be subject to two forms of verification. First and foremost, it is necessary to check whether the conclusions flowing from it are compatible with each other (*Phaedo*, 101d), as well as – in specific cases – to explore other possibilities, i.e. to check if the specific trait determining whether a thing belongs to a given collection could not be different and of different origin than that one cause that gives the thing its name and qualities, though it differs from the thing itself: "If anyone tells me that what makes a thing beautiful is its lovely color, or its shape or anything else of the sort, I let all that go, for all those things confuse me, and I hold simply and plainly and perhaps foolishly to this, that nothing else makes it beautiful but the presence or communion (call it which you please) of absolute beauty, however it may have been gained; about the way in which it happens, I make no positive statement as yet, but I do insist that beautiful things are made beautiful by beauty. For I think this is the safest answer I can give to myself or to others, and if I cleave fast to this, I think I shall never be overthrown [...]" (*Phaedo*, 100c–100e).

This form of verification of the hypothesis concerns the investigation of particular forms of the Form – thing (or phenomenon) relation mentioned above, such as: beauty as such and beautiful things, or the good and good things.[33] The hypothesis itself, however, requires justification in the realm of pure thought, that is, the discovery of a proposition of a greater degree of generality from which the initial hypothesis would necessarily follow by way of deduction. This justification may require the formulation of a series of increasingly general hypotheses, until one finally comes to a hypothesis that justifies everything, while not requiring justification itself. This hypothesis would then constitute an argument of ultimate justification, both methodologically and ontologically, as well as validating philosophy, understood as the path to the first forms of being. For Plato in the *Phaedo*, this argument of ultimate justification is the existence of a form of being *other* than the phenomenal form accessible by way of sense-perception – the existence of Forms, the *true* being, different from things, *primary* in relation to them, while in the axiological order, or rather in Plato's ontology of values, superior on account of qualities that things do not possess: eternity, permanence, unity, and perfection.[34] It is a form of being, on account of which things exist, while it itself does not exist on account of nothing, since the reason for its being is within itself. It may be assumed that, at this stage of the development of Platonic thought, the philosopher, by way of hypothetical dialectic, has already come up with the argument of the final justification in the form of answers to all the questions that synoptic dialectic did not solve, including the answer to the question of the cause of all generation and destruction. The

---

33 In his story about the "second sailing," Plato's Socrates does not use the term "idea" (Form; εἶδος) yet. This term does not appear until the short summary Phaedo presents to Echecrates: "As I remember it, after all this had been admitted, and they had agreed that each of the abstract qualities [τῶν εἰδῶν] exists and that other things which participate in these get their names from them" (*Phaedo*, 102b).
34 See: Gajda 1993, pp. 84 ff.

conception of two worlds, one of which gives the other names, figures, qualities, and traits, seems in Plato's *Phaedo* an assertion of such generality and certainty that it could solve all problems in the field of physics, epistemology, ethics, and axiology; moreover, it allows the philosopher to answer questions of an existential or eschatological nature. It allows for the formulation of coherent arguments for the immortality of the soul – arguments, which at this stage of the development of Platonic thought appeared to the philosopher as unshakable and strong, as they were entailed by that most general and irrefutable claim. Hypothetical dialectic – that "second sailing" – thus led Plato's Socrates of the *Phaedo* period to the seemingly safe harbor of the doctrine of Forms, though not for long, because the dialectician, Socrates/Plato of the mid-Academic period, made a mistake in his art, to which he himself later admits.

It will be pointed out to him in *Parmenides*, by the elder Plato himself – who developed and improved his *dialektike techne* throughout the course of his life – hidden behind the mask of the Parmenides.[35] The Platonic doctrine of Forms of the mid-Academic period can be reduced to a proposition formed in the long dialectical process; its roots lie in the synoptic view of things, but at some point, breaking with its synoptic roots, it gained in Platonic thought the status of an axiom that no longer required proof or verification. In the Platonic doctrine of Forms of the mid-Academic period, Forms – the figures themselves, beauty as such or the good as such – the model-efficient causes of things – are defined like Parmenides' being as unborn and indestructible, simple, eternal, immutable, immobile, and identical only with themselves, somewhat axiomatically, because their status in the most general strong *hypothesis* is determined by the fact that they are by definition different from generated and perishing, mutable and complex things. The younger Plato, in establishing the form of the Form – things relationship, simply failed to test all possibilities; he did not subject the doctrine of Forms to proper verification, nor did he subject Parmenides' conception of being to critical analysis, which in consequence led to insurmountable aporias in the doctrine of Forms.

---

[35] I take Plato's *Parmenides* to be a work that reflects the breakthrough that occurs in Platonic philosophy during the period that I call the mid-Academic stage, the period, in which Plato shaped and presented a relatively coherent and consistent philosophical system in such writings, as: *Republic, Phaedo, Phaedrus,* or *Symposium.* This system elucidated and explained the nature of reality at this stage of development of Plato's philosophical thought by referring to the first principles, which Plato – for the first time in the history of Greek thought – situated above and beyond the phenomenal world, granting them the status of transcendent beings, and called forms.

The severe judge of the Platonic doctrine of Forms – the elder Plato, hidden behind the mask of Parmenides – demands verification from the younger Plato for that form of hypothetical dialectic that the Philosopher introduced in *Phaedo*, when Socrates, formulating his strong assertion of the highest degree of generality, in a sense stopped there, without taking into account the consequences that the opposite *hypothesis* would entail. Parmenides-Plato – older and richer in experience and knowledge, and trained in dialectical sophistry by the Megarian dialecticians – demands from the younger Plato that to every *hypothesis*, regardless of its generality and power, he assign the opposite *hypothesis* and examine their consequences by comparing and juxtaposing conclusions: "I mean, for example, that in the case of this very hypothesis of Zeno's about the many, you should inquire not only what will be the consequences to the many in relation to themselves and to the one, and to the one in relation to itself and the many, on the hypothesis of the being of the many, but also what will be the consequences to the one and the many in their relation to themselves and to each other, on the opposite hypothesis. Or, again, if likeness is or is not, what will be the consequences in either of these cases to the subjects of the hypothesis, and to other things, in relation both to themselves and to one another, and so of unlikeness; and the same holds good of motion and rest, of generation and destruction, and even of being and not-being. In a word, when you suppose anything to be or not to be, or to be in any way affected, you must look at the consequences in relation to the thing itself, and to any other things which you choose,—to each of them singly, to more than one, and to all; and so of other things, you must look at them in relation to themselves and to anything else which you suppose either to be or not to be, if you would train yourself perfectly and see the real truth. Socrates asks him to give an example of this process. That, Parmenides, is a tremendous business of which you speak [...] (*Parmenides*, 136a–c). This is an enormous effort – "That, Parmenides, is a tremendous business of which you speak [...]."

It is indeed laborious and arduous work – Plato himself reminds us of the hardships of hypothetical dialectic when he describes it in *Letter VII*, in which, towards the end of his life, he demonstrates the universality of his model of philosophizing: "There is a certain true argument..." (*Letter VII*, 342 ff.).[36] Plato points out that although he has discussed this many times before, he sees the need to present it again. This *logos alethes* is the process, subjected by Plato to strict rules, of achieving cognition of the "being that truly is," which

---

[36] Literally: ἔστι γάρ τις λόγος ἀληθής, which would be better translated as: there is a true judgment, whose object is a set of dialectical rules.

may appear in the soul of the cognizer, as long as he follows the dialectical rules, in the "fifth appearance of the being." However, this "fifth appearance" will not come to those who have not come to know the first four: names, definitions, things in their bodily form (arising and perishing), and knowledge ("knowledge and intelligence and true opinion" – ἐπιστήμη καὶ νοῦς ἀληθής τε δόξα – 342c). This brief Platonic exposition, regardless of who it was actually authored by, fulfills three functions in *Letter VII* that justify the need for a critical attitude in dialectical procedures – on that philosophical path leading to the cognition of the first being. First, it shows the pride and foolishness of one claiming to be a philosopher after reading one of Dionysius II's books; second, it emphasizes the necessity of a continual verification of conclusions and findings, not only in hypothetical procedures; and third, it reveals wherein the essence of philosophizing lies (340c). It is indeed hard work, continuous and essentially endless – an effort, to which one must devote himself entirely and completely.

In this brief exposition, the author shows us that dialectic is a process that has a beginning: it is that, on account of which each thing appears[37]: thus, first a name (ὄνομα),[38] next, a definition (λόγος) – as if in answer to the question: what is a circle?, then – as "something" third, an "image" (εἴδωλον) appears, e. g. a circle made of wood, or drawn in the sand. These three "appearances" constitute the basis for the procedures of synoptic dialectic, which determine the necessity for gaining knowledge (ἐπιστήμη) through hypothetical dialectic, which is referred to as the fourth "something." One who has analyzed these four "appearances" may receive a fifth, in which he will see the pure form of the first being through the eyes of his soul/intellect – γνωστὸν τε καὶ ἀληθῶς ἐστιν ὄν (*Letter VII*, 342b).

What does grasping the first four appearances consist in? Plato writes: "But it is the methodical study of all these stages, passing in turn from one to another, up and down, which with difficulty implants knowledge..." and further: "For in learning these objects it is necessary to learn at the same time both what is false and what is true of the whole of Existence, and that through the most diligent and prolonged investigation, as I said at the commencement; and it is by means of the examination of each of these objects, comparing one with another—names and definitions, visions and sense-perceptions,—proving them by

---

[37] In the Greek text, the term "appearance" or "presentation" does not appear.
[38] It may seem surprising that the author of *Letter VII* lists name as the first thing that appears, despite the fact that in Platonic philosophy, all cognition begins with a sensory view; however, already in Plato's time, insight into phenomenal reality was frequently mediated by names (it is hard to imagine that the average Athenian then had seen an elephant or a hippopotamus, for example, but he knew these names).

kindly proofs and employing questionings and answerings that are void of envy — it is by such means, and hardly so, that there bursts out the light of intelligence and reason regarding each object in the mind of him who uses every effort of which mankind is capable" (*Letter VII*, 344b ff.)[39].

Plato's description leaves no doubt that in the quest for true knowledge and in anticipation of the "fifth appearance," the hypotheses put forth must constantly be verified by examining their strength and legitimacy in confrontation with things, subjecting them to all sorts of *experimentum crucis*. We can thus venture the thesis that the philosophical predispositions Socrates attributed to the "pregnant with thought" consist equally in striving for cognition, the ability of a synoptic view, and, perhaps most importantly, a critical attitude.

Many scholars of Platonic dialectic identify the proper dialectical procedure with *diairesis* – that stage of the path in which the dialectician/philosopher is working with pure concepts, treating the first two stages as preparation for proper philosophical work.[40] In fact, we can find such statements in Plato's writings themselves (*Phaedrus*, 266c, 277c, *Republic*, 537c, *Sophist*, 218b *et passim*), though, as noted above, with the exception of *Letter VII* we do not find a strict exposition or doctrine of dialectical procedures in the Platonic dialogues due to the nature of these dialogues. (As was also noted, the secondary literature does not treat *hypothetical* dialectic as a part or stage of dialectic at all). In the *Republic* and the *Sophist*, Plato writes that the next form of dialectic – diairetic dialectic – constitutes a somewhat higher degree of initiation, which can only be achieved after the philosopher has grasped the *truth of being*. It can therefore only be achieved within a group of philosophers, because only a philosopher can make the proper divisions necessary to obtain certain knowledge in the form of definitions, though the objects of this knowledge are things-phenomena in the overt sphere of reality. Thus, the philosopher returns to earth in a sense, which does not mean that he cannot err.

How would the definition of an object from the (phenomenal) world of things, formulated by a diairetician, differ from a "common sense" definition formulated *ad hoc* by Theaetetus or Young Socrates? Diairetic procedure, which, as indicated above, only philosophers can realize after having mastered the synop-

---

[39] Transl. Benjamin Jowett (1892).
[40] Such as Sayre (2006, pp. 15 ff, 19 ff), who accepts that late Plato resigns completely from synoptic procedure in favor of the so-called theory of paradigms, or Cornford (1932), who, in analyzing books VI and VII of the *Republic*, requires of dialectic only mathematical knowledge; see also Kerferd (1981, pp. 62–76), who identifies dialectic with the sophistic skills of argumentation and eristics, from which it differs only in that it is not based on a play on words and meanings.

tic and hypothetical procedures, is realized in the sphere of pure concepts and requires skill in their ordering and classification. The examples from the Platonic *Sophist* and *Statesman* demonstrate that in this procedure, the philosopher always takes the most general concept to which the object under investigation can be assigned as his starting point. In the case of the so-called *nomina agentis* Plato analyzes, like sophist, angler, and politician, the most general concept will, of course, be activity. An adept diairetician must be able, within the sphere of that concept, to identify types of activity and divide them into groups by referring to synoptic and hypothetical procedures, in order to reach such an activity in which a sophist or angler participates using the method of successive divisions. It is to such a skill that Aristotle was referring when he stated that the theorist, or philosopher, would know more about shipbuilding than the most skilled practitioner in the field. But such a skill would not be possessed by one who had not previously mastered the art of the synoptic view and did not find the argument of ultimate justification for the existence of those phenomena that can be sorted into collections in the arduous and continually verified procedures of *hypothetical* dialectic.

Bibliography

Source Texts:

Diels Hermann/ Kranz Walther (1960): *Die Fragmente der Vorsokratiker.* Griechisch und deutsch von H. Diels, hrsg. von W.Kranz. Bd. 1, Berlin 1960.
Ross, William David (1924): *Aristotle's Metaphysics.* A Revised Text with Introduction and Commentary by W. D. Ross. Vol. 2. Oxford.
Ross, William David (1964): Aristoteles: *Analytica priora et posteriora.* William David Ross (ed.). Oxford: Clarendon Press.
Long, Herbert Strainge (1964): *Diogenis Laertii Vitae Philosophorum.* 2 vols. Oxford: Clarendon Press.
Burnet, John (1900): *Platonis opera.* Oxford: Clarendon Press.

Translations:

Jowett, Benjamin (1892): *The Dialogues of Plato translated into English with Analyses and Introductions by B. Jowett,* M.A. in Five Volumes. 3rd edition revised and corrected. Oxford University Press.
Bury, Robert Gregg (1966): *Plato in Twelve Volumes.* Transl. by R. G. Bury. Cambridge, Mass.: Harvard University Press, London.

Kalaš, Andrej/Suvák, Vladislav (2014): *Antisthenis Fragmenta. Antisthenove Zlomky.* Andrej Kalaš, Vladislav Suvák (eds.). Bratislava: Vydavateľstvo Univerzity Komenskeho.

Secondary Literature:

Cherniss, Harold (1935): *Artistotle's Criticism of Presocratic Philosophy.* Baltimore: Johns Hopkins Press.
Cherniss, Harold (1944): *Aristotle's Criticism of Plato and the Academy.* Baltimore: Johns Hopkins Press.
Cornford, Francis Macdonald (1932): "Mathematics and Dialectics in the Republic VI-VII". In: *Mind* 41, pp. 37–52.
Cornford, Francis Macdonald (1935): *Plato's theory of knowledge: the Theaetetus and Sophist of Plato.* London: Routledge & Kegan Paul.
Dürr, Karl (1947): "Die Entwicklung der Dialektik von Plato bis Hegel". In: *Dialectica* 1, pp. 45–61.
Gaiser, Konrad (1968): *Platons ungeschriebene Lehre: Studien zur systematischen und geschichtlichen Begrundung der Wissenschaften in der platonischen Schule.* Stuttgart: Klett.
Gajda-Krynicka, Janina (2003): "Pismo/tekst a dialektyka w filozofii platońskiej". In: *Roczniki Humanistyczne KUL* LI, z. 3.
Gajda, Janina (1993): *Platońska droga do idei. Aksjologiczny rodowód platońskiej ontologii.* Wrocław: Wydawnictwo Uniwersytetu Wrocławskiego.
Gajda-Krynicka, Janina (2007): *Filozofia przedplatońska.* Warszawa: Wyd. Naukowe PWN.
Gajda-Krynicka, Janina (2008): "Dialektyka jako metoda postaci dialektyki platońskiej". In: U. Wollner (ed.): Problem epistemé v antike. Banská Bystrica.
Gajda-Krynicka, Janina (2009): "Gorgiasz sofista czy filozof? Gorgiasz z Leontinoi w świetle platońskiej doksografii sofistyki". In: A. Pacewicz (red.): *Kolokwia Platońskie Gorgiasz*, Wrocław: Wyd. Uniwersytetu Wrocławskiego.
Jakobson, Roman (1989): "Poetyka w świetle językoznawstwa". In: R. Jakobson: *W poszukiwaniu istoty języka.* T. II. Wybór, red. nauk. i wstęp Maria Renata Mayenowa. Warszawa: PIW.
Kerferd, George B (1981): *The Sophistic Movement.* Cambridge – London – New York: Cambridge University Press.
Krämer, Hans J. (1959): *Arete bei Platon und Aristoteles. Zum Wesen und zur Geschichte der platonischen Ontologie.* Heidelberg: Winter.
Krämer, Hans J. (1994): "Das neue Platonbild". In: *Zeitschrift fuer philosophische Forschung* 48, pp. 1–20.
Kahn, Charles H. (1996): *Plato and the Socratic Dialogue. The philosophical use of a literary form. Cambridge:* Cambridge University Press.
Kahn, Charles H. (1966): "The Greek Verb 'To Be' and the Concept of Being". In: *Foundations of Language* 2 (3), pp. 245–265.
Kahn Charles H. (1973): *The Verb 'Be' in Ancient Greek.* Dordrecht: Reidel.
Lloyd, A. C. (1965): "Plato's description of Division". In: R. E. Allen (ed.): *Studies in Plato's Metaphysics.* London: Routledge & Kegan Paul.

Philip, James. A (1966): "Platonic Diairesis". In: *Transactions and Proceedings of the American Philological Association* 97, pp. 335–358.
Reale, Giovanni (1991): *Per nuova interpretazione di Platone*. Milano: Vita e pensiero.
Reale, Giovanni (1993): *Historia filozofii starożytnej. I. Od początków do Sokratesa*. Transl. E. I. Zieliński. Lublin: Wydawnictwo Katolickiego Uniwersytetu Lubelskiego.
Runciman, W. G. (1962): *Plato's later epistemology*. New York: Cambridge University Press.
Robinson, Richard (1953): *Plato's Earlier Dialectic*. Second Edition. Oxford: Clarendon Press.
Sayre, Kenneth M. (2007): "Dialectic by Negation in Three Late Dialogues". In: S. Stern-Gillet, K. Corrigan (eds.): *Reading Ancient Texts. Volume I: Presocratics and Plato. Essays in Honour of Denis O'Brien*. Leiden – Boston: Brill.
Sayre, Kenneth M. (2006): *Metaphysics and Method in Plato's Statesman*, Cambridge: Cambridge University Press.
Scott, Dominic (1999): "Platonic Recollection". In: Gail Fine (ed.): *Plato 1: Metaphysics and Epistemology*. New York: Oxford University Press.
Szlezak, Thomas Alexander (1993): *Platon lesen*. Stuttgart – Bad Cannstadt

Dariusz Olesiński
Aspects of Criticism in Plato's Philosophy

Abstract: This article constitutes an attempt at outlining the essence of the Platonic type of philosophical criticism (*resp. zeteticism*). This is achieved through the indication of its most important aspects, which in turn allows us to situate Plato's views between positive and negative dogmatism. The key in characterizing these aspects is the acceptance of Plato's metaphilosophical perspective, which itself testifies to the presence of critical reflection in Plato's thought. The perspective of asking about the nature of philosophy leads to the designation of two basic aspects, within whose framework signs of philosophical criticism are indicated. The first of these aspects is the anthropological-psychological aspect, which is connected with Plato's conception of *eros*; the second, the methodological aspect, concerns Platonic dialectic. Both of these aspects are ultimately combined in the profile of the aim of dialectical knowledge, which turns out to be understanding, constituting a critical form of philosophical knowledge.

Keywords: Plato's philosophy, criticism, metaphilosophy, dialectics, heuristic procedure, noesis

Plato's Metaphilosophical Perspective

There are many keys serving a comprehensive reading of the *Corpus Platonicum* – one of these is undoubtedly the search for an understanding of what philosophy is. An important issue that shaped the path of Platonic philosophy was the question of philosophy's essence, of the proper understanding of philosophical activity, which historically was just being shaped. Plato therefore tried to characterize the nature of philosophical thinking primarily by distinguishing it from other contemporary forms of intellectual activity (sophistry, poetry, rhetoric, eristics, or mathematics).

Accepting this metaphilosophical perspective is a testimony to the critical attitude and self-reflectivity present in Plato's philosophy. An attempt to answer the question of the nature of philosophy on the basis of Plato's dialogues leads to the designation of two basic aspects of reflection within which signs of philosophical criticism can be sought. The first aspect concerns the anthropological and psychological dimension, as well as the related Platonic concept of *eros*, while the second concerns the methodological dimension – namely, Platonic dialectic. Both of these dimensions are ultimately intertwined in the attempt to characterize the goal of philosophical (*resp.* dialectical) inquiry – which turns out to be understanding – as its nature has both a psychological and methodological aspect.

As is widely known, various multifaceted disputes and controversies are connected with Plato's thought and concern the interpretation of virtually every aspect of his philosophy. Generally speaking, however, the main tradition of interpreting Plato (extending from antiquity to modern times) can be reduced to a constant oscillation between "the Scylla of Scepticism and the Charybdis of Dogmatism" (Tigerstedt 1977, p. 103).

Most contemporary approaches that view Platonism as a specific doctrine or system consider Plato a dogmatist, explicitly or implicitly referring to the tradition of Neo-Platonism. On the other hand, the aporetic nature of many Platonic dialogues, as well as the frequent lack of conclusivity on key issues, has prompted many researchers to attribute to Plato a skeptical stance – just as he was interpreted by the long tradition of "Academic skepticism" (Annas, Barnes 1985, pp. 13–14; Tigerstedt 1977, p. 104; Woodruff 1986, pp. 23–25; Press 1996, p. 508).

The one-sidedness of these interpretative positions provokes a search for an intermediate interpretation, breaking with the doctrinal extremes of each of them and at the same time inserting Plato into the tradition of ancient Greek criticism. L. Stefanini sought to identify such an intermediate interpretation, deeming it "constructive skepticism" ("la scepsi costruttrice"), and thus a specific type of skepticism that should be distinguished from the traditional meaning:

> The term by which I characterize Platonic thought has acquired its meaning from the use far different from the original one, because by skeptic it is intended commonly to be understood the one who employs unlimited faith in his own reasoning to demonstrate the inconsistency of every reasoning, dogmatic demolisher of every dogma. The degenerate skepticism are self-destructive, because the only consistent attitudes for a radical negation would be the suspension of any judgment: the silence (Stefanini 1949, XXXIII- XXXIV).

It must be borne in mind that ancient Greek sources of criticism are most often associated with the attitude and views of Socrates, who – independently of the positions taken by scholars in regards to the so-called "Socratic problem" – is considered to be the *spiritus movens* of Plato's dialogues. He is not only considered a critical thinker, but also a symbol of criticism that is important for philosophy as such. What is significant in this context, L. Strauss (in his famous debate with A. Kojève) defined the Socratic way of philosophizing as *zetetic*.

This term derives from the Greek *zetein*, meaning to search, to seek, and philosophy for Socrates is a searching, a seeking, an eros for wisdom. This term best reflects the nature of criticism on the grounds of Greek philosophy, and especially that of Plato. In L. Strauss' opinion, philosophy in the original meaning of the term is nothing but knowledge of one's ignorance; therefore, it is inherently skeptical or, more precisely, *"zetetic"*:

> What Pascal said with antiphilosophic intent about the impotence of both dogmatism and skepticism, is the only possible justification of philosophy which as such is neither dogmatic nor skeptic, and still less "decisionis" but zetetic (or skeptic in the original sense of the term) (Strauss 2000, p. 196).

Socratic Erotetic Zeteticism

In the *Symposium*, Plato, in presenting Diotima's story, contained in it a description of the nature of philosophical activity in light of which it appears as divine ignorance (similar to the ignorance repeatedly declared by Socrates). According to this message, man entangled in phenomenal earthly existence can only come closer to the eternal, immutable, and true (which is identified with the Form of Beauty in the dialogue) through divine Eros' power, but cannot achieve this goal fully. For Eros, as the mythological child of poverty (Πενία) and wealth (Πόρος), is a constant, insatiable desire for fulfillment, and thus for attaining a state of fullness and completeness (*Symposium*, 203b–203e). In Plato's dialogues, Socrates is the personification of this erotic power (etymologically representing philosophy as the "love of wisdom"); it is he who possess the specific skill that allows him to be a marvelously skilled hunter for wisdom – described as erotic art (τὰ ἐρωτικά) (*Symposium*, 198d) – which is "daimonic" in its nature, because like its possessor, the *daimôn Erôs* in the *Symposium*, is always in a state between wisdom and ignorance (Belfiore 2012, pp. 17–18).

With the help of this skill, Socrates tries to shape the *eros* of his interlocutors – awaken it and direct it towards sublime goals connected with the attainment of knowledge. The awakened *eros* is to lead Socrates' interlocutor (as well as readers of the dialogues) to the awareness of an essential lack, which is simultaneously an awareness of true being and knowledge, and of the fact that the interlocutor does not possess them. G. A. Press points out that the resulting tension is unavoidable because it is determined by the complex, hybrid nature of Eros itself:

> This is due to the hybrid nature of Eros. Diotima suggests that the lover, always intermediate between Need and Resource, somehow moves from a state in which Need is greater than Resource to one in which Resource predominates over Need. And yet both Resource and Need are always there, as inseparable ingredients in the nature of Eros (Press 2000, p. 157).

One who really begins to associate with Socrates, and more precisely with his particular dialectical method, is persuaded to follow his line of argument (περιαγόμενον τῷ λόγῳ), and consequently:

> [...] he submits to answering questions about himself (διδόναι περὶ αὑτοῦ λόγον) concerning both his present manner of life and the life he has lived hitherto (*Laches*, 187e).[1]

This is in line with the Platonic message stating that the ultimate goal and message of the Socratic elenchus should be *giving an account of somebody's life* (ἔλεγχος τοῦ βίου, *Apology*, 39c8).

Within the framework of this method, by means of a dialogic argumentative scheme determined by a series of questions and answers, Socrates rejects the subsequent theses of his interlocutor if they are inconsistent with the initial views and attitudes declared by the latter.

In this context, one can understand the aporetic and ambivalent character of many Platonic dialogues, due to the fact that their goal is to provide their recipients with the tension connected with experiencing being in the in-between position, and, what follows, with critical self-consciousness. On the one hand, they try to suggest the existence of an eternal, perfect, and desired world; on the other hand, they point out that for the *dramatis personae* involved in the dialogue, as well as for their author, and consequently also for their readers, there is no access to this world – in any case, not easily and directly.

The love of wisdom (philosophical knowledge) motivated by the power of Eros turns out to be the most fundamental and universalizing cognition, because only the philosopher desires to gain knowledge on the whole of reality (*Republic*, 475c – d). For this reason, his soul deserves to be called "magnificence" (μεγαλοπρέπεια), because only it truly wants to come to know everything (θεωρία παντός) and

> [...] is always reaching out to grasp everything both divine and human as a whole (*Republic*, 486a).

In light of the allegory of the cave outlined in *The Republic*, the philosopher, as a man who loves wisdom, must make an attempt at exiting the cave of ignorance as part of the process of "conversion of the soul" (ψυχῆς περιαγωγή), which is a synonym for liberation (*Republic*, 521c); he must liberate his soul not only from sense cognition, but also from itself – in the process of self-transcendence and of

---

[1] All translated passages of the Platonic dialogues contained in this article are taken from: Cooper, John M. (eds.) (1997): *Plato: Complete Works*. Indianapolis: Hackett.

turning toward the ultimate goal of self-knowledge, i.e. toward the world of forms and, ultimately, the Good. From a psychological perspective, this can only be accomplished through the power of *eros*, which expresses the intentional reference of reason to the Good – reason, which must go beyond itself in search of what justifies it and constitutes its meaning (Schindler 2007, p. 206). Rejecting the mundane in favor of the heavenly promise, the philosophical *eros* reveals itself to be a peculiar "perversion" expressing the Platonic form of criticism (Roochnik 1987, p. 127).

The desire of *eros* does not presuppose the existence of the object of that desire; rather, it is an intention of communing with it, full of longing. Thus, the forms "exist" and can be recognized, but only within a specific discourse that seeks to grasp them. In this context, they appear as philosophical postulates, or simply as conditions for the intelligibility of philosophical discourse. The activity of reason taken analogously to the activity of *eros* turns out to be a continuously undertaken, insatiable effort, since the return movement of the soul (ψυχῆς περιαγωγή) is not a one-time act, but a cyclically returning path of *anabasis – katabasis*, the way of the philosopher which not only exits the cave, but also leads back into it (Huard 2006, pp. 126–127). And precisely as a way, philosophy in the Platonic sense does not consist in possessing knowledge, but rather in the loving pursuit of it, which confirms its essentially critical, not dogmatic character (Simpson 2001, pp. 70–71).

Moreover, Socrates' *zeteticism*, which is realized through the *elenchus* method, typically leads to an *aporia* – a situation in which the thesis initially accepted by the opponent is shown to be discordant with his other beliefs. This means that the set of statements that the interlocutor has accepted is contradictory, and hence he must admit that he does not know what he claimed to know. From a psychological point of view, as a specific state of awareness of one's own "lostness," the *aporia* that Socrates' interlocutors lapse into is meant to lead to an awakening discovery (ἐξευρεῖν) connected with the recognition of one's own ignorance, or at least to the identification of one's own cognitive limitations (*Meno*, 84b–c). Therefore, it is not destructive, but turns out to be a necessary condition for possible attempts at overcoming these limitations, and, what follows, for taking up a path of development and self-transcendence, thus expanding the individual's sphere of self-knowledge.

It is significant that Socrates' attitude could not serve as a clue to leaving the state of aporia for his interlocutors – at least not directly; this was mainly due to his conscious and purposive use of irony. This irony is variously understood by scholars (Schlosser 2014, pp. 11–18); in many cases, it is seen as a procedure more fitting the eristic ploys of the sophists than the Platonic Socrates' process of seeking truth, suggesting an inconsistency in his attitude, i.e. the incompatibility of his words and actions, because he ironically hid his knowledge, knowing the answers to the questions he asked his interlocutors (Robinson 1953, pp. 8–10). Indicating the deeper meaning of Socratic irony, it can be understood as the concealment of one's own stance and attitude, as their removal (*Republic*, 336c–337a; Nehamas 1998, pp. 11–13). Consequently, on the court of elenctic confrontation, room is left only for the interlocutor, his knowledge, and his attitude, as they are to be the object of dialectical investigation.

Irony identified as a strategy of avoiding one's own stance corresponds perfectly with the oft-emphasized paradoxicality inherent in the nature of Socrates' philosophy, as well as with his own difficult-to-classify attitude, succinctly expressed in the Platonic dialogues with the term ἄτοπος (*Symposium*, 221d; *Theaetetus*, 149a), which accurately conveys the meaning of the Socratic critical attitude. The only answer Socrates seems to give to his interlocutors is another question that constitutes the further course of philosophical discourse, with the awareness that it never reaches its desired aim, because it is only love, and not the possession of wisdom.

Therefore Socratic philosophical discourse is fundamentally interrogative, and thus critical. As D. Roochnik indicates:

> [...] the question assumes that an answer is desirable and, in some sense, possible. The question thus puts the questioner in a position in-between total knowledge and total ignorance.[...] The questioner is not totally ignorant, for he knows enough (about himself and the object of his question) to pose the question; he is not totally knowledgeable, for he lacks an answer (Roochnik 1987, p. 127).

In *Meno*, in a conversation with the title character, Socrates significantly notes that this is the essence of all reliable cognition:

> Do you realize what a debater's argument you are bringing up, that a man cannot search either for what he knows or for what he does not know? He cannot search for what he knows – since he knows it, there is no need to search – nor for what he does not know, for he does not know what to look for *(Meno*, 80d–e).

That we already have some access to what we do not yet know is a rather puzzling matter (and in the dialog Plato employs in this context – rather as a heuristic device – his famous conception of *anamnesis*), but more important is, Socrates warns us, that without some kind of philosophical piety, we would fall prey to a sophist's trick, and "*it would make us idle, and fainthearted men like to hear it, whereas my argument makes them energetic and keen on the search* (ἐργατικούς τε καὶ ζητητικοὺς)" (*Meno*, 81d–e). Thus, in the light of previously mentioned comments, Socrates is a interrogative philosopher or *erotetikos*, zetetic *skeptic*, and this kind of skepticism differs from nihilistic skepticism, for example Pyrrhonist skepticism, because its very search presumes a meaning, or an aim; nihilistic skepticism attacks both dogmatism and tireless searching that assumes the possibility of truth.

Dialectic as an Heuristic Procedure

The fact that Socrates is the critical (*resp. zetetic*) philosopher *par excellence*, or more generally the personification of philosophical criticism seems fairly obvious. What is less obvious, even controversial, is deciphering the views and intentions of Plato himself, who leads to the confrontation of the form of philosophy and philosophical attitude of Socrates with such a completely contrary ideal of knowledge in his works that it could have been authored by a skilled dialectician. The Platonic dialogues contain two separate and incompatible conceptions, which clash most distinctly in the *Republic:* the vision of the philosopher guided by the power of Eros and exemplified by Socratic ignorance, and the vision of the forms and the Good, knowledge of which is the aim of the philosopher-king and a necessary condition of the proper functioning of *Kallipolis*. Thus the interpretation of Socrates as a *"zetetic"* philosopher is antithetic to the philosopher-kings, who according to G. Fried are

> "echonic" philosophers (from the Greek 'echein', to have, to hold), for they alone "possess" the truth [...] Plato does not represent [Socrates] as the type of philosopher that the internal argument of the Republic establishes as paradigmatic (Fried 2006, p. 163).

An expression of the tension between these two visions is the prevailing controversy between the doctrinal (systematic and dogmatic) and nondoctrinal (skeptic) lines of interpreting Platonism. An attempt at resolving this fundamental tension is a particular form of *developmentialism* advocated by G. Vlastos. According to this stance, the recipients of Plato's dialogues are confronted with the difficult task of reconciling the skepticism of Socrates, who flaunts his own ignorance, with the metaphysical doctrine called the "theory of forms." G. Vlastos attempts to solve this problem by distinguishing the views of the historic Socrates (present mainly in the early, aporetic dialogues) from those of mature Plato (Vlastos 1991, p. 46). Thus, in light of *developmentialism*, we can perceive in the dialogues Plato's transition from an early fidelity to the historical Socrates to his own, mature and independent views.

However, some scholars representing the "third way" of interpretation oppose the above conception. These scholars believe that the tension present between "the Socratic" and "the Platonic" in the dialogues constitutes one of their essential features. This tension is thought to boil down to Plato's intended contrast between the form and the content of his work, and is caused not so much by respect for the historical Socrates, as it is by the dialogical way of thinking characteristic of Platonic philosophy.

I use the term "third way" to refer to a new tendency in interpreting Platonic thought, alluding to the title of a monograph edited by F. Gonzalez that is representative in this regard (Gonzalez 1995). This new interpretative trend encompasses the views of various scholars, who – despite their declared differences – share a characteristic preference for philological-literary readings of Plato's dialogues over analytical readings. For this reason, they view the dialogue form and style as philosophically significant for Plato's thought. They therefore deny the claim that his philosophy was dogmatic and aimed at expressing itself in the form of a doctrinal system, and question the developmental theory and its chronology.[2]

The interpretative stance represented by scholars sympathetic to the "third way" is highly significant due to the topic of reflection chosen, as it fits into the trend of seeking an intermediary stance between dogmatism and skepticism and thus suggests situating Platonic thought on the side of philosophical criticism. As F. Gonzalez indicates, the main alternative (competing) traditions of interpreting Platonic thought lead to a paradox:

> The skeptical interpretation can account for the form of Plato's writings only by minimizing their positive philosophical content, while the 'doctrinal' interpretation can uncover their content only at the cost of considering their form little more than a curiosity and even an embarrassment (Gonzalez 1995, p. 13).

The critical character of Plato's philosophy is evident not only at the level of content (the indication of the cognitive possibilities of man) but also that of method. In this regard, Plato's metaphilosophical reflection that seeks to understand the nature of philosophical activity points in the most general way at dialectic; for on the grounds of Platonic philosophy, dialectic can be identified with philosophy, at least with philosophy viewed from a methodological perspective.

The conceptual tension (between "zetetic" and "echonic" philosophy) present in Platonic thought and outlined earlier also manifests itself in the method of philosophizing, because the dialectic explained in the *Republic*, as it is to be in-

---

[2] Examples of philosophers who argue in this manner include: H. G. Gadamer (1978), Ch. L. Griswold (1988), F. Gonzalez (1998, 2000), G. A. Press (1996, 2000), D. A. Hyland (1995, 2004), G. Fried (2006) and D. C. Schindler (2008).

corporated into the education of the philosopher-kings, seems to no longer represent the "negative" function attributed to the practice of the *elenchus*, rather it has a "positive" function incorporating arguments in order to achieve a sure and true understanding of reality. Generally speaking, the process of dialectical cognition in the form we know mainly from the early, so-called "Socratic," dialogues presents itself as the ability to pose the appropriate questions and give appropriate responses. Thus, it is – at least to certain degree – a non-discursive practical skill, a particular type of *know-how*.

In Plato's later works, an additional and specifically Platonic conception of dialectic appears, in which dialectic is understood, on the one hand, as a dialectical method of hypothesis,[3] and on the other, as a dialectical method of diaresis and synagogy.[4]

In his description of the dialectical method of hypothesis, Plato introduces

> [...] an argumentative structure within which a statement, namely the hypothesis, is postulated as a starting point, i.e., a principle prior to the other statements in the structure. The other statements in the structure are judged to be true if they can be explained by the hypothesis; they are judged false if inconsistent with the hypothesis (Tuominen 2008, p. 28).

D.T.J. Bailey thinks that as is the case with musical harmony, the relationship of agreement between individual hypotheses formulation within the framework of hypothetical procedure can be understood analogously to the symphony of sounds present within the structure of a musical composition (Bailey 2005, pp. 104–106). Thus, a given hypothesis and its consequences, as well as the consequences themselves, are in a relationship (in *Phaedo* Plato describes it as *symphōnein*) that is generally described in modern methodology as explanation. We are thus speaking of a procedure in which a hypothetical thesis gains credibility due to its reference to something that constitutes its explanation, and *vice versa* – the explanation itself gains credibility if it explains something that we have already established is true. In the explanatory process so understood, a mutual strengthening of the explanandum and explanans occurs; consequently, a given conception gains greater explanatory power, deepening our ability to understand the reality described by this conception. As Ch.H. Kahn puts it:

> The method functions not simply by drawing a linear chain of deductions but by building up a complex theory or constructing a model. Whatever is incompatible with some basic

---

[3] Presented in *Meno* (86e–87b), *Phaedo* (99c–d); (99e–100); (101d–e), and *Republic* (510b–511d).
[4] Presented in *Sophist* (219a–237a), *Statesman* (258b–267c), and *Phaedrus* (265a–266b).

feature of the model, as specified in the hypothesis, will be "out of tune" (diaphōnein) or fail to accord. But the positive relationship of "being in accord" (symphōnein, synāidein) is not mere consistency. It means fitting into the structure, bearing some positive relationship to the model by enriching or expanding it in some way (Kahn 1998, p. 316).

Within the framework of the explanatory process of discovering (ἀνευρήσειν) how a given hypothesis could be true (*Phaedo*, 100b), its consequences are investigated – i.e. individual cases of its occurrence within the phenomenal sphere (particularizing explanation). In turn, the generalizing explanation that proceeds in the opposite direction begins with a concrete phenomenon and aims at demonstrating why this phenomenon occurs. Within the framework of the dialectical method, a given hypothesis is therefore verified in a circular process determined by the cyclical coupling of the two complementary directions of argumentation – *anabasis* (generalizing explanation, "ascent") and *katabasis (*particularizing explanation, "descent").

Thus, this method is not so much about deductive reasoning, as it is about explanation understood as an heuristic procedure, which – in contrast to algorhythmic procedure – does not guarantee reliable assurance of the obtained result. However, because of its creative nature, it is especially useful in attempts at dealing with complex and problematic issues, among which we can certainly count philosophical issues.

The Platonic method of hypothesis thus introduces an important change in the understanding of the task that stands before philosophical argumentation. It turns out that it is not meant to conduct proofs on the basis of the first principles (dogmatically assumed axioms); rather, it should begin its investigation with the opinions and uncertain convictions initially assumed, attempting to find the principles that would justify these convictions (Scolnicov 2003, p. 11). Hence, contrary to the dogmatic interpretation, proper dialectical argumentation is not so much deductive-apodictic, as it is critical-investigative. In consequence, dialectic does not aim at achieving the apodictic certainty to which deductive entailment aspires. Certainty would eliminate the investigative curiosity lovers of wisdom need in their quest for knowledge, and could even destroy the meaning of this quest altogether.

In addition, in dialogues such as *Phaedrus, Sophist,* and *Statesman*, Plato presents a methodological procedure composed of two aspects, namely collection (συναγωγή) and division (διαίρεσις). Its direct aim is to find a definition that would express the nature of a given thing as adequately as possible. Significantly, as in the case of dialectic the makes use of hypotheses, the process of collection and division is a two-way method. First, when collecting, we ascend towards what is more general, and then come down by dividing the general into its specific elements (Tuominen 2008, pp. 32–33).

In order to produce an accurate collection combined with division, one has to distinguish the classes and subclasses according to natural similarities and differences between things. Socrates compares this with the work of a skillful butcher who knows how to cut according to natural joints (*Phaedrus*, 265e). This attests to the fact that – as was the case with the method of hypothesis discussed above – this method likewise cannot be reduced to analytical-deductive procedure based on apriorical, conceptual considerations – it is much more heuristic and circular in nature. Because this method fails to add new quality into our description of Platonic criticism, I will not discuss it further in this article.

Understanding as the Aim of Philosophical Knowledge

It is often considered that the dialectic presented in the *Republic* is concerned with knowledge in terms of *"a conception of knowledge which has received the most philosophical attention in modern times: 'propositional knowledge', or knowing that such and such is the case"* (Brickhouse/Smith 1994, p. 43). Especially in Platonic scholarship focused on systematic and doctrinal readings of Plato's Socrates, it is common to identify the type of knowledge that Socrates seeks as "propositional" in nature, as an effect of the Socratic search for "definitions" or another words – as the "apodictic discourse." Such a stance is taken by (among others) advocates of the esoteric reading of Plato's philosophy, which is represented today by so-called the *Tübingen-Milanese School*. It is characteristic of this interpretation to identify the Good with the One and to emphasize its absolute transcendence vis-à-vis being (Krämer 1966, pp. 36–37, Krämer 1969, pp. 1–30; Reale 1984, pp. 341–366). According to representatives of this School, the Good so understood allows for an adequate explanation of the dialectical transition from the level of hypotheses to the level of what is not hypothetical (Olesiński 2012, pp. 50–52).

In consequence, this interpretation treats hypotheses as definitional propositions, presupposing the Good, which is in a certain sense "contained" within them; this leads to the way of *anabasis* being understood as a process consisting in abstracting the Good from those hypotheses, and the way of *katabasis* – as the deductive derivation of particular propositions from the axiomatic truth about the Good. This interpretation ascribes a deductive and propositional nature to knowledge of the final principle, as it is to be knowledge of its definition.

Against this view, philosophical knowledge, as a unique form of insight into the true nature of Being emerging from the dialectic, can be described simply as "understanding." In response to doctrinal interpreters who want to equate philosophical knowledge with the type of sure and certain knowledge we find described by Descartes, F. Gonzalez states:

> The word episteme as used in Plato's dialogues should be translated not as 'knowledge' but as 'understanding.' In other words, Platonic episteme is not 'justified true belief'; instead, its meaning is closer to that of our word 'understanding' (Gonzalez 1998, p. 177).

In famous *Letter VII* Plato describes such knowledge as being of a different nature than the knowledge associated with propositions. The argument that Plato initially offers is directed at all those who attempt to express the greatest and first objects of philosophy in words and begins by distinguishing between five components of philosophical knowledge: the name (ὄνομα) of a thing, the account (λόγος), the image (εἴδωλον), the knowledge itself (ἐπιστήμη), and finally object of this knowledge – the thing itself or the form (*Letter VII*, 342a–b). Names, accounts, and images are a necessary but not sufficient means for attaining knowledge of the true being or essence of a thing, because they are radically defective:

> These things, moreover, because of the weakness of language (διὰ τὸ τῶν λόγων ἀσθενές), are just as much concerned with making clear the particular property (τὸ ποῖόν τι) of each object as the being of it (τὸ ὂν ἑκάστου) (*Letter VII*, 342e–343a).

Here we find a critical reflection on the fallibility and radical limitations of both human knowledge and language. What truly separates the fourth from the fifth stage is that the fourth still lives at the level of propositional discourse, and thus reveals the "quality" of the thing, but is not able to provide understanding of the Being of the thing. As Plato notes in a further passage:

> [...] the being of an object and its quality are two different things and that what the soul seeks (ζητούσης) to know is not the quality, but the being (οὐ τὸ ποιόν τι, τὸ δὲ τί), each of the four offers the soul what it does not seek, so that what is said or shown by each is easily refuted by the senses (*Letter VII*, 343b–c).

This statement suggests that the four stage do not offer the soul the being it seeks, but instead the quality it does not seek. The being which the soul seeks to know is the essence of a thing or its form and by "quality" here appears to be meant any property that might be predicated of a thing. Accordingly, to say that *logoi* can express only how something is qualified (ποιόν τι) is to say that they can only predicate something of something else. Thus, the particular weakness of language (regardless of whether it appears in unwritten or written form) lies in the fact that it cannot adequately express what either the subject or the predicate is in itself, because it can only assert one of the other. For this reason, language cannot adequately express the forms, or the proper objects of dialectical knowledge.

R. Ferber's polemic with H. Krämer is significant in this context, as it fits into the contemporary form of the dispute between dogmatism and skepticism in the interpretation of Plato's thought. Like other "esotericians" who consider the theory of the "unwritten doctrines" crucial for a proper understanding of Plato's philosophy, H. Krämer assumes that all the evidence supporting the functioning of the *agrapha dogmata* is at the same time evidence of the systematic and apodictic nature of his philosophy.

Such a view must be rejected, R. Ferber argues, due to the fact that Plato left *agrapha dogmata* unwritten because they were only opinions and not knowledge (Ferber 1984, pp. 154–59). Moreover, in analyzing *Letter VII*, he shows that since four means of knowing something cannot provide the philosopher with knowledge of a thing's true being, such knowledge can never be attained and consequently, it makes a "theory of forms" strictly speaking an impossibility (Ferber 1991, pp. 43–50). H. Krämer, who considers the forms objectively grounded and certain knowledge about them possible, holds a position of positive dogmatism in the debate cited above, whereas R. Ferber – one of negative dogmatism.

It is possible, however, to hold a non-dogmatic stance on this issue, as do representative of the "third way." For example, D. Hyland indicates the criteria that constitute any given theory – comprehensiveness, consistency, provability, confirming instances – and argues that the reflections concerning the problem of the forms in the dialogues do not fulfill any one of them. In his opinion, Plato's intention in his dialogues was never to present a coherent view on the conception of forms; they are always understood in a way that is context-dependent, appearing as the most adequate replies to various questions and problems discussed by Socrates' interlocutors on various occasions (Hyland 2003, pp. 257–272).

In turn, F. Gonzalez, rejecting the existence of the Platonic "theory of forms," emphasizes that the forms are normative. This is not to deny the essential role the forms play in Platonic philosophy; rather, it concerns the type of knowledge we can possess about forms and the Good, because it is a form of insight or understanding that, although emerging from the discursive process of dialogue, is itself non-discursive. The forms are normative, and thus manifest themselves through the dialectic process, which unceasingly points to language's inability to express them directly, but also enables the forms to manifest themselves indirectly (Gonzalez 2003, pp. 31–83). Therefore, understanding is possible when we immerse ourselves deeply in the dialogue itself; this consists in the interaction of many of its aspects – including multiple perspectives, a specific situation, character play, irony, arguments organized in a specific way, and decisions made by the characters in the dialogue. All of this is to grant insight that would be unachievable in other ways.

The knowledge Plato has in mind is propositional, but never only propositional. The propositional aspect is a necessary but insufficient condition of philosophy: according to Plato, we need the ability to express what we have cognized, even if our words will never directly contain what we are trying to express (Schindler 2008, p. 34). But in the structure of the dialectical process, it is not ultimately about words or even definitions (in light of *Letter VII*, a definition is merely an intermediate stage, not the ultimate goal of philosophical knowledge), but about understanding, which has a discursive and non-discursive aspect, and is the fruit of not only theoretical knowledge, but also of practical experience.

In the dialectical melting pot, not only successive components of philosophical knowledge clash, but also the results of the cognitive activity of particular dialectic methods – elenctic investigation, the hypothetical justification of basic propositions, the search for and refinement of definitions by way of the collection and division method – in such a way that a spark of understanding is ignited in the soul of the philosopher from time to time (*Letter VII*, 341c – d). In this context, it is worth citing the three moments of the *zetetic* model of philosophy outlined by G. Fried:

> [...] we have three moments in the zetetic journey: the liberation from the bonds (deconstruction), the ascent upward (preconstruction), and the return to the cave (reconstruction) (Fried 2006, p. 167).

On the basis of this model, we can now more precisely outline the elements comprising the critical nature of broadly understood dialectical knowledge. It begins with the stage of philosophical *deconstruction* (expressing the negative function of dialectic), thanks to which we can recognize our ignorance and confront it, identifying the existing cognitive barriers and limitations. Thus, the prejudices, beliefs, and the habits we are subject to are revealed through dialectical investigation. Next, in the *preconstruction* stage, we must be open to reinterpretations, revisions, and the possibility of rejecting what dialectic has revealed to us as inadequate. The final stage is that of *reconstruction*, in which there is a moment of enlightenment of the mind and acquisition of new forms of understanding that were hidden in the human world to which we belong. Ultimately, this stage leads back to the deconstruction stage, thus initiating another hermeneutic cycle.

In this context, a noteworthy view on the nature of nonpropositional knowledge was presented by D. Hyland (Hyland 1995, pp. 179 – 195). Hyland distinguished between two types of *noesis: archaic* and *telic*. These types are essentially poles of one and same noetic view, between which – in its "ascent" and "descent" (in *anabasis* and *katabasis*) – the propositional dialectic process plays out. Neither of them is absolute, guaranteeing an apodictic certainty of insight. For this reason, understanding as the ultimate aim of dialectical (*resp.* philosophical) knowledge is of a critical-hermeneutic nature, and may be subject to gradation or a continual deepening: in reference to the object it is more or less insightful, whereas in reference to the subject – more or less conscious (self-reflective). Philosophical knowledge thus turns out to be ultimately possible, but only in the form of critical knowledge, as in the conception of understanding outlined above, of which both the propositional process and nonpropositional act are key, integral components. At the same time, this knowledge should be understood not in terms of the attainment of certainty, but as a process of continuous improvement of eidetic insight, achieved within the cyclically renewed dialectic process.

Bibliography

Annas, Julia/Barnes, Jonathan (1985): *The Modes of Scepticism: Ancient Texts and Modern Interpretations*. Cambridge: Cambridge University Press.
Bailey, D. T. J. (2005): "Logic and Music in Plato's Phaedo". In: *Phronesis* 50 (2), pp. 95–115.
Belfiore, Elizabeth S. (2012): *Socrates' Daimonic Art: Love for Wisdom in Four Platonic Dialogues*. Cambridge: Cambridge University Press.
Brickhouse, Thomas C./Smith, Nicholas D. (1994): *Plato's Socrates*. Oxford: Oxford University Press.
Cooper, John M. (eds.) (1997): *Plato: Complete Works*. Indianapolis: Hackett.
Davey, Nicholas (2006): *Unquiet Understanding: Gadamer's Philosophical Hermeneutics*. New York: State University of New York Press.
Ferber, Rafael (1984): *Platos Idee des Guten*. Sankt Augustin: Verlag Hans Richarz.
Ferber, Rafael (1991): *Die Unwissenheit des Philosophen oder Warum hat Plato die "ungeschriebene Lehre" nicht geschrieben?* Sankt Augustin: Academia Verlag.
Fried, Gregory (2006): "Back to the Cave: A Platonic Rejoinder to Heideggerian Postmodernism". In: Drew A. Hyland/John Panteleimon Manoussakis (eds.): *Heidegger and the Greeks: Interpretive Essays (Studies in Continental Thought)*. Indiana: Indiana University Press.
Gadamer, Hans-Georg (1978): *Truth and Method*. New York: Crossroad Publishing.
Gonzalez, Francisco J. (eds.) (1995): *The Third Way: New Directions in Platonic Studies*. Lanham, Maryland: Rowman & Littlefield.
Gonzalez, Francisco J. (1998): *Dialogue and Dialectic: Plato's Practice of Philosophical Inquiry*. Evanston, Illinois: Northwestern University Press.

Gonzalez, Francisco J.(2003): : "Plato's Dialectic of Forms". In: William A. Welton, (eds.): *Plato's Forms: Varieties of Interpretation.* Lanham, Maryland: Lexington Books, pp. 31–83.
Griswold, Charles L. (1988): "Plato's Metaphilosophy: Why Plato Wrote Dialogues". In: Charles L. Griswold (eds.): *Platonic Writings/Platonic Readings.* Pennsylvania State University Press.
Huard, Roger L. (2006): *Plato's Political Philosophy: The Cave.* Washington: Algora Publishing.
Hyland, Drew A. (1995): *Finitude and Transcendence in the Platonic Dialogues.* Albany: State University of New York Press.
Hyland, Drew A. (2003): "Against Platonic Theory of Forms". In: William A. Welton (eds.): *Plato's Forms: Varieties of Interpretation.* Lanham, Maryland: Lexington Books, pp. 257–272.
Hyland, Drew A. (2004): *Questioning Platonism: Continental Interpretations of Plato.* Albany: State Universty of New York Press.
Kahn, Charles H. (1998): *Plato and the Socratic Dialogue: The Philosophical Use of a Literary Form.* Cambridge: Cambridge University Press.
Krämer, Hans J. (1966): "Über den Zusammenhang von Prinzipienlehre und Dialektik bei Platon". In: *Philologus* 110, pp. 35–70.
Krämer, Hans J. (1969): "*Epekeina tes ousias.* Zu Platon, *Politeia* 509b". In: *Archiv für Geschichte der Philosophie* 51, pp. 1–30.
Krämer, Hans (1990): *Plato and the Foundations of Metaphysics.* Albany: State University of New York Press.
Nehamas, Alexander (1998): *The Art of Living: Socratic Reflections from Plato to Foucault.* Berkeley, Los Angeles, London: University of California Press.
Olesiński, Dariusz (2012): "Plato's Conception of the Good in *The Republic*". In: Agnieszka Woszczyk, Dariusz Olesiński (eds.): *Being and Logos. Categorical and Generic Analyses of Being in Classical Philosophy.* Kraków: Oficyna Wydawnicza "Impuls", pp. 39–54.
Press, Gerald A. (2000): *Who Speaks for Plato?: Studies in Platonic Anonymity.* Lanham, Maryland: Rowman & Littlefield.
Press, Gerald A. (1996): "The State of the Question in the Study of Plato". In: *The Southern Journal of Philosophy* 34 (4), pp. 507–532.
Robinson, Richard (1953): *Plato's Earlier Dialectic.* Oxford: Clarendon Press.
Roochnik, David (1987): "Erotics of Philosophical Discourse". In: *History of Philosophy Quarterly* 4, pp. 117–29.
Schindler, D. C. (2007): "Plato and the Problem of Love: On the Nature of Eros in the Symposium". In: *Apeiron* 40 (3), pp. 199–220.
Schindler, D. C. (2008): *Plato's Critique of Impure Reason: On Goodness and Truth in the Republic.* Washington: Catholic University Press.
Schlosser, Joel A. (2014): *What Would Socrates Do?: Self-Examination, Civic Engagement, and the the Politics of Philosophy.* Cambridge: Cambridge University Press.
Simpson, Tim (2001): "The Limits of Knowledge and the Desire for Wisdom". In: Anthony Anderson (ed.): *Philosophical Studies in Education.* Dayton: Ohio Valley Philosophy of Education Society, pp. 65–74.
Stefanini, Luigi (1949): *Platone.* Seconda Edizione Aggiornata. 2 Vols. Padua: Cedam.
Strauss, Leo (2000): *On Tyranny.* Chicago: The University of Chicago Press.

Tigerstedt, Eugène N. (1977): *Interpreting Plato*. Stockholm: Almqvist & Wiksell.
Tuominen, Miira (2008): *Apprehension and Argument: Ancient Theories of Starting Points for Knowledge*. Finland: University of Helsinki.
Vlastos, Gregory (1991): *Socrates: Ironist and Moral Philosopher*. New York: Cornell University Press.
Woodruff, Paul (1986): "The Skeptical Side of Plato's Method". In: *Revue International de Philosophie* 40, pp. 22–37.

Zbigniew Nerczuk
References to Plato's *Theaetetus* in book Γ (IV) of Aristotle's *Metaphysics*

Abstract: The so called "Secret Doctrine", presented by Plato in *Theaetetus* and attributed to Protagoras and disciples of Heraclitus, is one of the main sources of the critical and skeptical ideas in ancient philosophy. Its main contentions (phenomenalism, subjectivism, the view of relativity and indeterminacy of things, method of antilogic etc.) were acknowledged by Pyrrho and, revived by Aenesidemus, can be found incorporated into the skeptical tradition in the works of Sextus Empiricus. This is the reason why the reconstruction of the reception of Plato's *Theaetetus* is of an outmost importance for our understanding of the development of ancient skepticism. The paper points out the references to the "Secret Doctrine" (Plato's *Theaetetus*) in book Γ (IV) of Aristotle's *Metaphysics*. Based on the references contained in this book, it can be concluded that the Stagirite, opposing those who accept the possibility of contradictory judgments, abundantly presents the position of the "upholders of flux" contained in the dialogue and repeatedly recalls the arguments from the discussion conducted in *Theaetetus*. The interpretation of these references to *Theaetetus* gives an opportunity not only to better understand Aristotle's criticism in book Γ (IV) of Aristotle's *Metaphysics*, but also to give an insight into the sources of later skepticism.

Keywords: Ancient philosophy, sophists, Protagoras, Plato, Aristotle, critical philosophy, skepticism, transmission and reception.

Aristotle's *Metaphysics*[1] is not only a philosophical masterpiece, but also a collection of texts, which are of foremost doxographical importance. It contains numerous quotations and references to other philosophical works and as such constitutes a rich source of information about pre-Aristotelian philosophy.

The analysis of doxographical elements in Aristotle's writings (not only included in *Metaphysics* itself) represents significant value for researchers for at least two reasons. First, the recognition and interpretation of other works, which Aristotle refers to in *Metaphysics*, may be helpful not only in reconstructing the context of discussions included in it, but also in better understanding of Aristotle's objectives pursued in *Metaphysics*. Secondly, the analysis of passages

---

[1] The project was financed by the National Science Centre and was approved by a decision no. DEC-2013/09/B/HS1/01996.

may also contribute to better interpretation of those writings, which Aristotle refers to, by providing an opportunity for deeper reconstruction of literature lost over the years and by deepening our understanding of preserved writings.

A discussion on the "Law of contradiction" in the book Γ (IV) of *Metaphysics* provides a suitable opportunity for our analysis. The aim of our presentation is to demonstrate that a large part of arguments, which are developed by the Stagirite, were actually inspired by the content of the so-called "Secret Doctrine" depicted in Plato's dialogue *Theaetetus*. The main thesis here is that not only the direct mentions of Protagoras' "man-measure" principle contained in books Γ and K, but also a large number of other passages refer to the debate directly from *Theaetetus*.

A significant part of Plato's *Theaetetus* is focused on the discussion of the so-called "Secret Doctrine" (*Tht.*, 151e–187a). This extended and thoroughly elaborated philosophical construct finds its beginning when a definition of knowledge is presented as "perception" (*Tht.*, 151e1–2). This, in turn, initiates further consideration of Protagoras' *man-measure* dictum, which is substantiated with the theory of the nature of perception (the so-called theory of *metaxy*) and the doctrine of universal flux.[2]

The "Secret Doctrine" rests on some fundamental philosophical principles, which result from the "theory of the mechanism of perception" ("metaxy") and the "doctrine of flux". According to the "Secret Doctrine":

1. perception (αἴσθησις) is knowledge (*Tht.*, 151e2–3),
2. perception is the same as appearance (φαντασία) (*Tht.*, 152c1–2),
3. each perception (appearance) is true (e. g. *Tht.*, 152c5–6),
4. each individual determined by his particular affections (πάθη) is a measure (κριτήριον) of all things (Protagoras' "man-measure" principle is repeated five times in *Tht.*: 152a2–4; 160d9; 161c4; 170d2; 183b8),
5. people (or even the same person at different times) have conflicting appearances (*Tht.*, 152b2–3),
6. the notions of truth and falsity are abandoned[3] and replaced by the categories of "better and worse" (*Tht.*, 167b3–4),
7. there is neither "one" (*Tht.*, 152d2–3) nor "being" (*Tht.*, 152e1) – there is just "becoming" (motion is a principle) (*Tht.*, 152d7–e2),

---

[2] "Although ostensibly introduced as an account of sensation, the theory which Theaetetus is now initiated, will actually propose far reaching ontology, which has repercussions not only for perception, but also for language, knowledge, and the very conception of rationality itself" (Desjardin 1990, p. 33)

[3] Dupréel 1948, p. 54; Guthrie 1987, p. 187.

8. "things" (χρήματα) are constituted in the process of constant interconnection between the passive and active element (*Tht.*, 157a; 160c); χρήματα are not substances (*Tht.*, 160bc), they have neither essence nor identity (*Tht.*, 152d; 156e; 159a; 160ab; 166b); they are undefined (*Tht.*, 183ab) and relative (*Tht.*, 156e; 157ab; 160b5–9),
9. the language which is in use does not comply with the reality in flux. All forms, which suggest "rest", "stillness" or "immutability" (verb "to be" [*Tht.*, 152d–e], the determinative and possessive pronouns such as "something", "somebody" "mine", "this", "that" and "any other word that implies making things stand still", [*Tht.*, 157b]) should be abolished; the most fitting words and forms of speech are: "becoming" instead of "being", the participle forms (*Tht.*, 157b) and phrases such as "not more than" (*Tht.*, 182e3–183a1), "so and not so" (*Tht.*, 183a9–b5).
10. since there is no "being" and everything is in motion, there is no contradiction (οὐκ ἔστιν ἀντιλέγειν) and contraries can be predicated alike in relation to each subject ("method of antilogic", *Tht.*, 152d; 166b).

William David Ross in his commentary to *Metaphysics* has already pointed to references to *Theaetetus*, found in the books G and K.[4] Ross remarked that Aristotle refers to the "Secret Doctrine" when he:
1. directly invokes Plato's argument from *Theaetetus* against Protagoras' position: (*Met.*,1010b12: ὥσπερ καὶ Πλάτων λέγει – *Tht.*, 171e; 178b9–179b5),[5]
2. rejects the identity of impression and perception,[6] which was the starting point of the discussion in *Theaetetus*[7] (*Met.*, 1010b3: ἡ φαντασία οὐ ταὐτὸν τῇ αἰσθήσει – *Tht.*, 152c1: φαντασία ἄρα καὶ αἴσθησις ταὐτόν),
3. discusses the issue of dependence of perception on affections[8] (*Met.*, 1010b8–9: καὶ ἀληθῆ πότερον ἃ τοῖς καθεύδουσιν ἢ ἃ τοῖς ἐγρηγορόσιν – *Tht.*, 157e1 sqq.),

---

4 Aristotle 1948.
5 "And again, with regard to the future (as Plato says), surely the opinion of the physician and that of the ignorant man are not equally weighty, for instance, on the question whether a man will get well or not" (Aristotle 1948, p. 277).
6 "Appearance is not the same as sensation" (Aristotle 1948, p. 277).
7 "Then, seeming and perception are the same thing in matters of warmth and everything of that sort" (Plato 1921, p. 43).
8 "And whether truth is as it appears to the waking or to the sleeping" (Aristotle 1948, p. 277).

4. shows the discrepancy between the antilogical position and the real-life practice which has at its basis the discrimination of what is better or worse[9] (*Met.*, 1008b27: ἀλλὰ περὶ τὸ ἄμεινον καὶ χεῖρον – *Tht.*, 171e–172b),
5. makes use of the expression "so and not so" in order to describe the indefiniteness of things resulting from the acceptance of the antilogical position[10] (*Met.*, 1008a31–32: οὔτε γὰρ οὕτως οὔτ' οὐχ οὕτως λέγει – *Tht.*, 183a).

However, the passages reported by W. D. Ross constitute only a part of references to the "Secret Doctrine". Aristotle evokes the discussion from *Theaetetus* when he:
1. quotes Protagoras' *man-measure* principle[11] (*Met.*, 1062b13–14: καὶ γὰρ ἐκεῖνος ἔφη πάντων εἶναι χρημάτων μέτρον ἄνθρωπον – *Tht.*, 152a2–4: φησὶ γάρ που πάντων χρημάτων μέτρον ἄνθρωπον εἶναι, τῶν μὲν ὄντων ὡς ἔστι, τῶν δὲ μὴ ὄντων ὡς οὐκ ἔστιν) and discusses this dictum interpreting it in the context that is known from the dialogue (*Met.*, 1007b20–29; *Met.*, 1009a6–15; *Met.*, 1062b12–19),
2. quotes the fundamental thesis of the "Secret Doctrine"[12] (*Met.*, 1062b14–15: οὐδὲν ἕτερον λέγων ἢ τὸ δοκοῦν ἑκάστῳ τοῦτο καὶ εἶναι παγίως – *Tht.*, 161c2–3: ὡς τὸ δοκοῦν ἑκάστῳ τοῦτο καὶ ἔστιν),
3. searches for the sources of contradictory judgments in the observation of the world of senses (*Met.*, 1009b1–2 – *Tht.*, 151e–187a) and in the confinement of the reality to sensible things (*Met.*, 1010a1–3 – *Tht.*, 151e–187a),
4. outlines the arguments of the opponents of the Law of contradiction, which correspond to the arguments from *Theaetetus:* from "the number or fewness" (*Met.*, 1009b2–3 – *Tht.*, 158d); from the number of upholders (*Met.*, 1009b3–6 – *Tht.*, 159b); from the fact that animal impressions are contrary to human (*Met.*, 1009b7–8 – *Tht.*, 154a); from different perceptions of an individual at different times (*Met.*, 1009b8–9 – *Tht.*, 154a),
5. points out the consequences of the "antilogical position" (parallel to Plato's opinions in *Theaetetus*) resulting in denial of the substance and the essence of things (*Met.*, 1007a20–1; 1010b26–30 – *Tht.*, 152d; 156e; 159a; 166b) and denial of language and communication (e.g. *Met.*, 1010a12–13 – *Tht.*, 157b; 179e; 180b) and the acceptance of the view of the indefiniteness of the reality (*Met.*, 1008a27–30 – *Tht.* 183b),

---

[9] "Hence, as it seems, all men make unqualified judgments, if not about all things, still about what is better and worse" (Aristotle 1948, p. 272).
[10] "Again, however much things may be so and not so" (Aristotle 1948, p. 271).
[11] "For he said that man is the measure of all things" (Aristotle 1928, no pagination).
[12] "That which seems to each man also assuredly is" (Aristotle 1928, no pagination).

6. revokes the thesis of the identity of thought and sense perception (*Met.*, 1009b12–13 – *Tht.*, 158b; 161d; 166e; 167a; 167b; 167c)[13],
7. points out the absurd consequence of the Secret Doctrine that if there were no "animate things" with their senses there would be no reality (*Met.*, 1010b30–1011a3; 1011b5–7 – *Tht.*, 152c5–6; 160ab),[14]
8. rejects the demand of finding the judge of everything (*Met.*, 1011a2 – *Tht.*, 158c sqq.),
9. uses "turnabout" (περιτροπή) argument (*Met.*, 1011a16 – *Tht.*, 168c2–171c7).

A logical question, therefore, is about the reason for Aristotle's interest in the "Secret Doctrine" included in *Theaetetus*. The discussion in book Γ of *Metaphysics* is concerned with the definition of "the most certain principle", i.e. the Law of contradiction, and the refutation of arguments of its opponents. From Aristotle's own words (*Met.*, 1011b13–15), it may be pre-supposed that this part of the book Γ could originally have been formed as a separate and coherent investigation (*Met.*, 1005b5–1011b22).

The Stagirite recognizes a wide spectrum of views, which are contradictory to his "most certain" principle. According to him, one of such views is Protagoras' "man-measure" principle (1007b22), which involves the acceptance of the premise that "it is possible to affirm or to deny anything of everything" (or in a different wording: "contradictory statements are both true").

The reference to the "man-measure" principle, which (as it is explained in *Theaetetus*) justifies the sophistic method of setting up contradictory statements on one subject (called "antilogic", "dissoi logoi", "enantiologia"), introduces the discussion about the philosophical implications of this standpoint. In his consideration of Protagoras' principle, Aristotle evokes various arguments offered in the "Secret Doctrine" for the sake of the "antilogical position", clarifies its theses, and, ultimately, refutes them. The Stagirite's view is that the "Secret Doctrine", which involves and justifies "antilogic", ultimately results in the denial of definiteness of things and of knowledge. This is done in acceptance of their total relativity and the impossibility of language and communication.

References to *Theaetetus* in *Metaphysics* book Γ provide an opportunity to investigate the manner in which Aristotle uses other sources, to examine the relation between Plato's and Aristotle's criticism of the "Secret Doctrine" and, fi-

---

13 "It is no doubt more than accidental that Plato places *phantasiai* and *doxai* side by side (*Theaet.* 161e8; cf. Sextus Empiricus *Adu. mathematicos* 7.60), also *aistheseis* and *doxai* (αἱ κατὰ ταύτας sc. [αἰσθήσεις] δόξαι, 179c3 f.), and Aristotle *phainomena* and δοκοῦντα (*Metaph.* 1009a8), though they are not of the same kind or class" (Classen 1989, p. 20).
14 See: Dupréel 1948, p. 24.

nally, to discuss if Aristotle's account contributes to the solution of the problem of attribution of this theory and to our knowledge about Protagoras.

On the basis of references to *Theaetetus*, it may be observed how intertextual Aristotle's work really is. Although in the case of references to the dialogue, Aristotle provides no direct information on a specific source he is drawing from, in books Γ and Κ there are at least three short quotations from *Theaetetus*, which are tightly woven with Aristotle's argumentation (these are: (1) homo-mensura [1062b14–15], (2) "that which seems to each man also assuredly is"[15] (τὸ δοκοῦν ἑκάστῳ τοῦτο καὶ εἶναι παγίως [1062b14–15]), (3) the negation of the identity of appearance and perception [1010b3]). There are also numerous references to various theses of the "Secret Doctrine" and arguments for and against this theory.

It is worth noting that direct references to *Theaetetus* (though present already in chapters 3. – 4.) are accumulated in a large passage in chapters 5. and 6., in which Aristotle outlines, scrutinizes (1009a6–1010a15), and refutes (1010a15–1011b22) the main views of those who uphold the "Secret Doctrine". The accuracy of Aristotle' account testifies that the Stagirite either had the text of *Theaetetus* itself or (what is more likely) held the notes from the dialogue before his eyes. Apart from one direct mention of Plato's argument, which can be identified as an argument from *Theaetetus* (*Met.*, 1010b12), he does not make any other suggestions, which could help determine Plato's dialogue as his source.

Examining the above detailed references, we may extensively learn about the way Aristotle makes use of his sources. The Stagirite draws excerpts from the dialogue freely and adapts them to his needs. The structure of the report is convoluted. Views and arguments from *Theaetetus* are widely scattered and modified. The Stagirite is not concerned with providing any literal and faithful report, but is focused more on the matter at issue. Because of his focus on the problem, Aristotle seldom names a particular "upholder" of reported views, but rather tends to use plural, descriptive or impersonal forms: "our opponent" (1006a12–13; 1008a29), "many writers about nature" (1006a2), "those who say this" (1007a20), "those who share the view of Protagoras" (1007b22–23), "some people" (1008b1), "the professed followers of Heraclitus" (1010a11) etc.

So, what is the relation between Plato's and Aristotle's refutation of the "Secret Doctrine"? Aristotle certainly shares Plato's criticism drawing similar conclusions from Protagoras' "man-measure" principle and revoking some arguments from Plato's refutation of this theory such as: "from future advantages" (*Met.*, 1010b12 – *Tht.*, 178b9–179b5), from different appearance of a thing to the sight of each of the eyes (*Met.*, 1011a27–28 – *Tht.*,165b2–c10), and "turnabout"

---

[15] Aristotle 1928, no pagination.

argument (περιτροπή) (*Met.*, 1008a27 – *Tht.*, 168c2–171c7). But the main implication of the "man-measure" principle (that "all things would be one") and the majority of the counterarguments are either Aristotle's own or are derived from unknown sources.

Another interesting question is what we can learn about the "Secret Doctrine" from Aristotle's account. Unfortunately, Aristotle's report does not solve the perplexed issue of the attribution of this theory. The Stagirite associates the "Secret Doctrine" with certain interpreters of Heraclitus and "those who share the view of Protagoras" (*Met.*, 1007b22), thereby repeating what we may learn from the dialogue itself.

The answer to our final question concerning the issue whether Aristotle's account on Protagoras' "man-measure" dictum contributes to our knowledge on the sophist, must also be negative. There is nothing in Aristotle's report that would go beyond *Theaetetus* and could suggest that the Stagirite refers directly to the original writing of Protagoras. However, it is certain that all three comments on the "man-measure" principle (in books Γ and K) are interpreted within the context, which perfectly matches the presentation of this principle in *Theaetetus*. This observation may at least support the view that Aristotle trusted Plato's account on Protagoras' statement illustrated in *Theaetetus*.

Based on the references enumerated above, it can be concluded that the Stagirite, opposing those who accept the contradictory judgments, derives views and arguments of the "partisans of flux" contained in the dialogue. A closer examination of these references to *Theaetetus* may give an opportunity to better understand both Aristotle's arguments targeted against those who deny the principle of contradiction and the manner in which Aristotle uses Plato's dialogue.

Bibliography

Aristotle (1928): *The Works of Aristotle*. Vol. VIII: *Metaphysica*. 2nd edition. Oxford: Oxford University Press.

Aristotle (1948): *Metaphysics*. A Revised Text with Introduction and Commentary by W.D. Ross. Oxford: Oxford University Press.

Classen, Carl Joachim (1989): "Protagoras' Aletheia". In: P. Huby and G. Neal (eds.): *The Criterion of Truth. Essays Written in Honour of George Kerferd*. Liverpool: Liverpool University Press, pp. 13–38.

Desjardins, Rosemary (1990): *The Rational Enterprise: Logos in Plato's* Theaetetus. Albany, NY: State University of New York Press.

Dupréel, Eugène (1948): *Les Sophistes. Protagoras, Gorgias, Prodicus, Hippias*. Neuchâtel: Éditions du Griffon.

Guthrie, William Keith Chambers (1987): *A History of Greek Philosophy. The Later Plato and the Academy.* Vol. 5. Cambridge: Cambridge University Press.
Plato (1921): Theaetetus. Sophist. Cambridge, Massachusets: Harvard University Press.

Dariusz Kubok
Conversation and Conservation.
Two Kinds of Anti-Dogmatic Criticism in the Philosophy of Politics and their Antecedents in Ancient Greek Forms of Skepticism and Fallibilism

Abstract: The aim of my paper is to indicate the Greek antecedents of select conceptions in the field of modern political philosophy and to reveal the durability of certain interpretations of Greek skepticism and fallibilism in fields other than traditionally-understood ancient epistemology. My reflections concentrate on the views of M. Oakeshott and K.R. Popper and are based above all on their correspondence from 1948. I attempt to show the similarities and differences in these views from the perspective of anti-dogmatic criticism, whose roots are located in Greek thought. In this sense, the philosophy of politics will be treated as a sort of adaptational test of the life-span of ancient ideas, in this case – to particular versions of skepticism and fallibilism. In this context, special attention should be paid to problems connected with man's cognitive limitations; the way rationalism is understood; the critique of Utopianism; and the role of tradition and humility in human life.

Keywords: skepticism, fallibilism, anti-dogmatic criticism, political philosophy, conversation, conservation, M. Oakeshott, K.R. Popper.

When examining the tradition and forms of criticism in European philosophy it is necessary first to specify how criticism is to be understood in these reflections. "Criticism" has a broad range of meanings and is diversely interpreted depending on one's conception, the historical and theoretical context, and on the normatively understood tasks of philosophy and science. Whether criticism and the critical approach are understood colloquially or spontaneously is also significant. I must note that I limit myself in these reflections to philosophical criticism broadly understood as anti-dogmatic criticism,[1] thus not connected with any particular philosophical school or philosophical conception (e.g. Kantian philosophy, the Frankfurt School, etc.). It is almost a truism to say that philosophy is/

---

[1] In regards to the essence and types of philosophical criticism, see: Kubok 2015a, pp. 9–31.

should be critical; however, a very non-trivial problem is what this means, i.e. how such criticism should be defined.

The aim of my paper is neither to conduct a detailed analysis of anti-dogmatic criticism in the field of the philosophy of politics, nor an attempt at analyzing various forms of skepticism and fallibilism (as symptoms of anti-dogmatic criticism) in Greek philosophy. Each of these subjects deserves a separate in-depth study. The aim of this paper is, on the one hand, to indicate the ancient Greek antecedents of select conceptions in modern political philosophy, and on the other, to reveal the durability of certain notions of Greek skepticism and fallibilism in fields other than traditionally-understood ancient epistemology. The field I have in mind in the second case is modern political reflection that takes into account or implicitly assumes fundamental philosophical premises, especially those connected with anti-dogmatic criticism. In this sense, the philosophy of politics will be treated as an adaptational test of the life-span of ancient ideas, in this case skepticism and fallibilism. Among the many modern conceptions in the philosophy of politics, I will limit myself to two thinkers: Michael Oakeshott and Sir Karl Raimund Popper. There are at least four reasons for this choice. First, both can be considered important and influential representatives of broadly-understood anti-dogmatic criticism in the field of political philosophy. Second, we have direct access to their polemic on rationalism, conversation, tradition, and above all on man's cognitive limitations. For this reason my main point of reference (aside from their own writings) will be two letters from 1948: Oakeshott's letter to Popper from January 28, 1948, and Popper's reply from January 31, 1948.[2] Third, the Greek (in the sense of the Greek anti-dogmatic approach) antecedents of their conceptions in political philosophy have not been sufficiently demonstrated.[3] Fourth, their versions of anti-dogmatic criticism dif-

---

[2] As noted by the Michael Oakeshott Association, "The following two letters have been made courtesy of the Hoover Institution Archives and Melitta Mew, the copyright holder. The text has been transcribed (as is) with footnotes by Efraim Podoksik, Hughes Hall, Cambridge. The third letter has been made available courtesy of the Oakeshott Archives, LSE." http://www.michael-oakeshott-association.com/pdfs/mo_letters_popper.pdf, accessed: 16.02.2017. I will be referring to this edition in my article.

[3] The literature on Popper's ties with the Greeks is prolific, not to mention Popper's own texts on ancient thought in the context of epistemological and methodological problems. Much less is written on attempts at demonstrating the Greek sources of Popper's political philosophy in appropriately-interpreted Greek anti-dogmatism. When it comes to the historical sources of Oakeshott's thought, they have been examined much more thoroughly. For example, W.J. Coats, Jr. lists the following thinkers as the most significant sources (in his language: "his contemporaries") of Oakeshott's thought: Montaigne, St. Augustine, Hegel, Hobbes, Benjamin Constant, Rousseau, and Hume (W.J. Coats, Jr, 2000). See also: Wood 1959, pp. 647–662; Rayner 1985,

fer from one another (though certain common premises exist), which suggests that they are referring to different versions of Greek skepticism and fallibilism. An analysis of this aspect is the key aim in my paper, not a detailed analysis either or Oakeshott's skepticism or Popper's fallibilism. It should also be noted that the search for these antecedents will not be based on these thinkers' literal references about Greek philosophy; rather, it will consist in recognizing a general correspondence of their thought with a given tradition of anti-dogmatic reflection. I hope that these reflections will allow for a broader look at both the notion of politics in the view of these thinkers, and at the durability of Greek ideas, above all at those that paved the way for skeptical and fallibilistic attitudes.

We should begin with Oakeshott's correspondence with Popper, supplementing it with other texts by both thinkers. In his letter to Popper from January 28, 1948, Oakeshott refers above all to Popper's conclusions from the latter's article *Utopia and Violence* (Popper 1948, pp. 109–116), which Popper had previously sent to Oakeshott. The text is divided into two parts. In the first, Popper writes: "I am a rationalist because I see in the attitude of reasonableness the only alternative to violence."[4] In his view, a rationalist solves conflicts by way of argumentation, sometimes in the form of a compromise, not by way of violence. Popper's rationalism is not dogmatic rationalism, but critical rationalism, which assumes intellectual humility; the possibility of error; a combination of allocriticism and autocriticism; the conviction of coming closer to truth, not its possession; and the awareness that most of our knowledge comes from others. Significantly, Popper declares that his rationalism "is not self-contained, but rests on an irrational faith in the attitude of reasonableness." (Popper 1968, p. 357). Critical rationalism is self-limiting, especially when it comes to reason's aspirations to finality and completeness.[5] Popper's irrational faith in reasonableness is criticized by Oakeshott, who displays an attitude of rational restraint with

---

pp. 313–338; Gerencser 2000; Tseng 2003; Botwinick 2011; Orsi 2015, pp. 575–590. Probable reasons for Oakeshott's silence on the ancient skeptical tradition and an attempt at demonstrating his views within the context of the skeptical tradition can be found in: Laursen 2005, pp. 37–55.
4 I cite the article "Utopia and Violence" on the basis of its reprint in: Popper 1968, p. 355.
5 The process of reason's self-limitation is reminiscent of the thought of I. Kant, for whom pure reason stands before the tribunal of itself, resulting in reason's self-limitation. Kant understands critique as a particular type of trial that does not end with the conviction of reason, but rather is meant to determine reason's sources, scope, and limits. Popper, on the other hand, asserts that two rules of court proceedings are to be adhered to in all disputes: hearing the arguments of both sides and not being a judge in one's own trial. It is worth noting that the tendency to compare the procedures of rational thought to court proceedings can be traced back to Greek thought, especially to the analogy between philosophical debates and forensic and rhetorical procedure (terminology).

respect to reasonableness, at least in regards to such a form of reasonableness that exhibits absolutizing tendencies and tendencies to overtake other forms of man's activeness. In the second part, Popper discusses the problem of Utopianism. This view assumes that each rational political act is preceded by and based on determining ultimate ends.[6] This view is destructive and dangerous; it is self-refuting and leads to violence, for such ends cannot be determined using scientific methods. One utopia combats another, so the principle of elimination, not conversation or – as in Popper's view – argumentation, is at work here. Ultimately, it should be said that:

> The Utopianist attitude, therefore, is opposed to the attitude of reasonableness. Utopianism, even though it may often appear in a rationalist disguise, cannot be more than a pseudo-rationalism (Popper 1968, p. 362).

In his letter to Popper, M. Oakeshott writes that he completely agrees with Popper on the subject of Utopianism. Oakeshott directs his criticism at Popper's understanding of the terms "rational" and "rationalism" contained in the first part of the article. While appreciating the role of reason in politics, Oakeshott opposes the ubiquitous – in his opinion – view acknowledging the exclusivity of reason in this sphere, i.e. the conviction that politics is fully rational, or at least should be analyzed this way. It is not enough to substitute critical reason for dogmatic reason; the practical dimension open to tradition, customs, and habits should also be taken into account. Though Oakeshott agrees with Popper's assertion that Utopianism is an enemy of reason, he also notes that Utopianism can take the form of a conviction that in seeking to solve a concrete problem, one is prepared to upset the whole of society in order to solve the problem permanently. According to Oakeshott, "*no* problem in politics is *ever* solved permanently" (OtP).[7] Popperian critical rationalism (called "true rationalism") seems to "get individual problems out of proportion." Despite this, both thinkers seem to agree that political problems are never ultimately solvable, they remain conclusively open. Instead of proposing "ultimate ends," we should agree to an "unended

---

[6] "Any rational and nonselfish political action, on this view, must be preceded by a determination of our ultimate ends, not merely of intermediate or partial aims which are only steps towards our ultimate end, and which therefore should be considered as means rather than as ends; therefore rational political action must be based upon a more or less clear and detailed description or blueprint of our ideal state, and also upon a plan or blueprint of the historical path that leads towards this goal." Popper 1968, p. 358.

[7] All citations from both letters are taken from http://www.michael-oakeshott-association.com/pdfs/mo_letters_popper.pdf. Oakeshott's letter to Popper will be abbreviated as (OtP), whereas Popper's reply to Oakeshott will be marked (PtO).

quest," to refer to the title of Popper's autobiography. In my view, this phrase ties into the Greek critical anti-dogmatic approach. It is to be critical as opposed to dogmatic, as well as zetetic, i.e. oriented towards a comprehensive understanding of the world with the simultaneous awareness of man's own cognitive limitations. Anti-dogmatic criticism in its zetetic form (zeteticism) emphasizes, on the one hand, distance in regards to the dogmatic approach (both positive and negative dogmatism, which is incorrectly, taking into account Sextus' writings, identified with skepticism), and on the other hand, the particular and rudimentary role of an active search for solutions, which is connected with the skeptic's cognitive humility.[8]

Oakeshott also accuses Popper of breaking political life into the atoms of political actions, problems that need to be solved. Meanwhile, in Oakeshott's opinion, "[t]he moral life of a man does not consist entirely in performing a number of reasonable actions, it consists in living according to certain habits of behaviour, which may be analysed into separate actions but which does not appear as separate actions except on a few occasions" (OtP). Thus, while Popper believes that particular problems need to be solved, Oakeshott emphasizes the legitimacy of conserving habits of behaviors understood holistically. Oakeshott also emphasizes that the rationality of one's behavior does not depend on the awareness that most of our knowledge comes from others, but rather on one's judgment that what he gains from others is reasonable; thus, rationality depends on one's judgment. Finally, Oakeshott questions Popper's simple assertion that reason is the only antidote for violence, as it was formulated in the essay *Utopia and Violence*. This is not so for two reasons. First, reason is not in a position to eliminate violence. Second, not only reason should be considered a potential rival of violence. For Oakeshott, a non-rational, though not irrational, form of negating violence is the politics of conversation. These politics encompass the

---

8 Here I will refer to one description of skepticism that can be found in Sextus Empiricus' *Oulines of Pyrrhonism*, namely "zetetic" (ζητητική). When describing synonyms of skepticism, Sextus writes: "Ἡ σκεπτικὴ τοίνυν ἀγωγὴ καλεῖται μὲν καὶ ζητητικὴ ἀπὸ ἐνεργείας τῆς κατὰ τὸ ζητεῖν καὶ σκέπτεσθαι, καὶ ἐφεκτικὴ ἀπὸ τοῦ μετὰ τὴν ζήτησιν περὶ τὸν σκεπτόμενον γινομένου πάθους, καὶ ἀπορητικὴ ἤτοι ἀπὸ τοῦ περὶ παντὸς ἀπορεῖν καὶ ζητεῖν, ὡς ἔνιοί φασιν, ἢ ἀπὸ τοῦ ἀμηχανεῖν πρὸς συγκατάθεσιν ἢ ἄρνησιν, καὶ Πυρρώνειος ἀπὸ τοῦ φαίνεσθαι ἡμῖν τὸν Πύρρωνα σωματικώτερον καὶ ἐπιφανέστερον τῶν πρὸ αὐτοῦ προσεληλυθέναι τῇ σκέψει." Sext., *Pyr.*, I, 7. (Sextus Empiricus 1990, I, 7). In modern debates in political philosophy, this term was used by Leo Strauss, among others: "What Pascal said with antiphilosophic intent about the impotence of both dogmatism and skepticism, is the only possible justification of philosophy which as such is neither dogmatic nor skeptic, and still less 'decisionist,' but zetetic (or skeptic in the original sense of the term). Philosophy as such is nothing but genuine awareness of the problems, i.e., of the fundamental and comprehensive problems" (Strauss 2000, p. 196).

politics of conservation. It is not only reason that connects people, because – on the one hand – there is nothing that could connect everyone, and on the other, there are more fundamental factors that determine human society, such as civilization or habits of behaviors. Near the end of his letter Oakeshott emphatically states that Popper's "true rationalism" is not so much impossible, as "it is impossible by itself" (OtP). We can see that there is clear disagreement as to the project of exchanging dogmatic rationalism for critical rationalism, which was likewise to take the place of habits, superstitions, and tradition. In Oakeshott's view, such a procedure resembles exchanging literature for literary criticism. This example is a good illustration of the essence of Oakeshott's opposition to Popper's proposal. Literature is to rationalism as literary criticism is to critical rationalism (though it would perhaps be better to say: critical literature and critical rationalism). First of all, literary criticism cannot take the place of literature, and second of all, literature has its own intrinsic value and is better understood from the perspective of the context within which it was created, including from the perspective of tradition. The same can be said about rationalism. Critical rationalism cannot be taken as the only authority explaining human action and expectations; besides, non-rational factors such as tradition and habits of behaviors cannot be omitted altogether (regardless of the fact that they can later be interpreted rationally). We can say that according to Oakeshott, the appropriate language for expressing the complexity of human behavior is not the language of rational speculation and of creating abstract models of society, but rather the language of traditions and customs, which is the most common and rudimentary. The politics of conversation is grounded in the politics of conservation, and this conservation is possible only in the language of tradition.

In response to Oakeshott's letter, Popper declaratively agrees with him on the three main issues, though Popper's theses should be treated as reformulations of Oakeshott's statements. Firstly, Popper agrees with Oakeshott that "no problem is solved permanently" (PtO), but significantly adds: "without creating a new one." Thus, both agree in advocating anti-dogmatic criticism as a lack of laying claim to permanent solutions and in treating problems as permanently open-ended. However, Popper simultaneously supplements this anti-dogmatic criticism with a processual element in the form of fallibilistically-understood procedure, which we can call zetetic-syncritic. This refers to the permanent search for better answers (zeteticism) using methods of comparing convictions (syncriticism) in order to grasp what is better, instead of dogmatically asserting that the best solution has been found. Popper's falsificationism can be interpreted as an elaboration of this method. Secondly, Popper is ready to agree with Oakeshott that the politics of conversation should take the place of his politics of argumentation. However, it should be noted that each thinker seems to understand the term "conversation" in a slightly different sense. Thirdly, Popper understands the view that reason should not take the place of habits in the sense that reason should be the "the critic of habits and behaviour" (PtO). It is worth noting that it is one thing to recognize habits and behavior as a stronger binding element between people, and another entirely to consider reason the critic of these habits and behaviors. These aspects with respect to which Popper's and Oakeshott's views diverge will be discussed later on in this article.

Popper considers the main object of disagreement between himself and Oakeshott to be their attitude toward tradition. Popper does not believe that the past is the only remedy to social problems and states: "I am against a challenge to tradition because it is tradition" (PtO). It is worth noting that both thinkers de facto accuse one another of reductionism, or more precisely, of reducing remedies to violence and suffering to one dimension. Oakeshott criticizes Popper for recognizing the exclusivity of reason (even critical reason), while Popper criticizes Oakeshott for solely appealing to "the passage of time." This leads to the more general conclusion that from a diagnostic and prospective perspective, every monomythic narration[9] gives rise to objections, and may even incur accusations of unauthorized reduction.

In the later part of his letter, Popper mentions his private Utopian dream, which he describes as "moral idealism": "I am for reforms because I believe in them, for their own sake" (PtO). In this case as well, despite their differences in approach to tradition, both think exploit the metaphor of dreaming – of *nomen omen* Heraclitean origin[10] – as a comfortable tool in their polemics with their opponent. For both thinkers, Utopianism is a dangerous dream, as a

---

9 I am referring to the terminology proposed by Odo Marquard in *Abschied vom Prinzipiellen*. Marquard believes that monomyths are always dangerous, whereas polymyths are not dangerous. He writes: "Es könnte [...] sein, daß all das nicht ohne Konsequenzen bleibt auch für die Philosophie. Es scheint mir ebenfalls fällig, daß sie ihre Kollaboration mit dem Monomythos beendet und Distanz gewinnt auch zu all dem, was in ihr selber zu dieser Kollaboration disponiert. Das ist insbesondere das Konzept der Philosophie als orthologischer Mono-Logos: als das Singularisierungsunternehmen der Ermächtigung einer Alleinvernunft durch Dissensverbote, bei dem – als unverbesserliche Störenfriede – die Geschichten apriori nicht zugelassen sind: weil man da erzählt, statt sich zu einigen" (Marquard 2000, p. 110).
10 "ὁ Ἡ. φησι τοῖς ἐγρηγορόσιν ἕνα καὶ κοινὸν κόσμον εἶναι, τῶν δὲ κοιμωμένων ἕκαστον εἰς ἴδιον ἀποστρέφεσθαι." Heraclitus D-K B 89, *Die Fragmente der Vorsokratiker. Griechisch und Deutch* von H. Diels, herausgeg. von W. Kranz, Bd. 1 – 3, Zürich 1985, hereafter cited as D-K. Heraclitus uses the term "Logos" to describe what is common and universal. Those who are asleep do not participate in what is common; for them, the world is relativized to their private view. This metaphor can also be used to describe private explanatory monomyths regarding the sources of suffering and violence. A useful statement of Heraclitus' in this context is: "οὐ δεῖ ὥσπερ καθεύδοντας ποιεῖν καὶ λέγειν." D-K Heraclitus B 73.

form of dogmatic rationalism assuming faith in ultimate ends and culminating in the *hubris* of presenting ultimate solutions. For Oakeshott, however, the absolutization of reason and simultaneous exclusion or critical control of habits and traditions is also a dream. Popper, on the other hand, as a moral idealist, is aware of the fact that his faith in reforms for their own sake falls into the category of dreaming; for him, however, it is above all Oakeshott's idealization of the "the old 'politically experienced classes' in a romantic way" (PtO) that is a dream.

Here, it is worth confronting Oakeshott's and Popper's views on the philosophy of politics by referring to both letters as well as – in the appropriate contexts – to other statements made by the two thinkers. Let us begin with the similarities. Both can be considered critics of dogmatic rationalism (especially of the Enlightenment), understood as the irrefutable authority on truth, as well as the reservoir or decisive tool sufficient to ultimately solve all of man's problems, especially within the social sphere. The critique of dogmatic rationalism as a rationalism that lays claim to indicating the formula for man's happiness is connected with the critique of Utopianism, which leads to attempts at searching for ways of eliminating suffering and violence with the awareness that this process can never be fulfilled. Both thinkers thus share a belief in the hopelessness of indicating ultimate ends; as was mentioned earlier, Oakeshott writes in his letter: "no problem in politics is ever solved permanently" (OtP), while Popper notes: "no problem is solved permanently" (PtO). The critique of Utopianism is simultaneously a critique of reason's conceit; both thinkers, aware of man's cognitive limitations, emphasize the importance of humility in human life.[11] Both Oakeshott and Popper are decisively in favor of the politics of conversation, though – as was already mentioned – both seem to understand conversation differently; in any case, Oakeshott views his politics of conversation in opposition to Popper's politics of argument. I think that in our search for essential common ground between the two thinkers we can invoke the principle that I call the "principle of *to ariston*." It refers to the Greek adjective ἄριστος, which means: "best in birth and rank," "best in any way," "morally best," "best, most use-

---

11 Popper writes: "It will be realized that what I call the attitude of reasonableness or the rationalistic attitude presupposes a certain amount of intellectual humility. Perhaps only those can take it up who are aware that they are sometimes wrong, and who do not habitually forget their mistakes" (Popper 1968, p. 356). M. Oakeshott, on the other hand, writes: "In short, if we regard these poles of our political activity as positive and negative, it is necessary to recognize that while the style of faith stands for 'everything', the complete control of the activities which compose a community, the style of skepticism stands, not for 'nothing', but for 'little'" (Oakeshott 1996, p. 115).

ful."¹² The principle of *to ariston*, i.e. the principle of what is best, played an important role in ancient philosophical debates. It assumes either the conviction that the best has been found, or heroic efforts to find the best. A belief common to both Oakeshott and Popper is the negation of the principle of *to ariston*, or at least far-reaching restraint in attempts at assuming it.¹³ Moreover, being guided by this principle in practice has led to destructive, utopian projects and actions in the public sphere. As I will try to demonstrate below, both thinkers adopt different strategies (though both are Greek in origin) of refuting the principle of *to ariston*. Oakeshott will draw near to common-sense Pyrrhonism in his politics of conservation, while Popper will replace the principle of *to ariston* with the principle of *to ameinon*.

It is also worth listing the basic differences separating the two thinkers. Popper views critical rationalism, which questions the universal and ultimate claims of reason and thus postulates mutual cooperation between scholars and intellectual humility, as an alternative to dogmatic rationalism. In reference to tradition, instead of adopting an attitude of uncritical acceptance, a critical approach should be adopted, which would consist not in the repetition or conservation of tradition, but rather in the permission to question it and, when necessary, to replace it with new solutions. Oakeshott, on the other hand, treats modern rationalism critically *in toto*, believing that such rationalism is based on a faulty notion of human knowledge, which gives priority to technical knowledge over practical knowledge. "For Oakeshott, Rationalism stems from a misplaced faith in a particular kind of knowledge – namely, technical knowledge." (Jacobs/Tregenza 2014, p. 7). Practical knowledge is rooted in customs, practices, and pre-reflective formulas of behavior, while technical knowledge encompasses petrified, purified, and abstract rules and principles of action or behavior.¹⁴

---

12 *A Greek-English Lexicon* 1996.
13 "In the latter case political action will be rational only if we first determine the final ends of the political changes which we intend to bring about. It will be rational only relative to certain ideas of what a state ought to be like. Thus it appears that as a preliminary to any rational political action we must first attempt to become as clear as possible about our ultimate political ends; for example the kind of state which we should consider the best [...]" (Popper 1968, p. 358). "There is no place in his scheme for a 'best in the circumstances', only a place for 'the best'; because the function of reason is precisely to surmount circumstances. Of course, the Rationalist is not always a perfectionist in general, his mind governed in each occasion by a comprehensive Utopia; but invariably he is a perfectionist in detail" (Oakeshott 1962, p. 5).
14 "The evanescence of imperfection may be said to be the first item of the creed of the Rationalist. He is not devoid of humility; he can imagine a problem which would remain impervious to the onslaught of his own reason. But what he cannot imagine is politics which do not consist in solving problems, or a political problem of which there is no 'rational' solution at all. Such a

Wherever they are able, rationalists search for ideal solutions, discounting extant practices and accepted models of behavior. In other words, within the framework of stipulative definitions, rationalists of this type prefer definitions discounting accepted usage of a given term, instead of formulating precising definitions. As Oakeshott notes in *Rationalism in Politics*, the politics of perfection give rise to the politics of uniformity, i. e. to a monomythic narration that projects *to ariston*. Of course, Oakeshott is not an enemy of rationalism as such; he is only an enemy of such a form of rationalism that appropriates customs and tradition through abstract forms of thinking and final designs.[15] For Oakeshott, Popper's critical rationalism, though it distances itself from ultimate solutions, is wrongly formulated, because: (1) it is treated as the sole antidote to violence, (2) it "gets particular problems out of proportion," (3) it does not take into account habits of behaviors, and (4) it treats reason as the only bonding agent between people.

The next point at which the views of the two thinkers diverge is in how each of them understands conversation. Though in his letter Popper accepts Oakeshott's formula postulating the replacement of politics of argumentation with politics of conversation, essential discrepancies are present. By "politics of conversation" Oakeshott understands the politics of cultivating order, a particular type of conversation, in contrast to the politics of argumentation characteristic of science within the framework of the open society. Popper decisively asserts: "I am a rationalist, and by this I mean that I believe in discussion, and argument. I also believe in the possibility as well as the desirability of applying science to problems arising in the social field."[16] Oakeshott, on the other hand, does not take conversation to be argumentation resulting in refutation or in convincing someone of better solutions. Thus, for Oakeshott, the politics of conversation is a politics of conservation, since it takes place with history and tradition in perspective. What is more, conversation based on conservation must be

---

problem must be counterfeit. And the 'rational' solution of any problem is, in its nature, the perfect solution" (Oakeshott 1962, p. 5).

15 "There is an ambiguity in Oakeshott's understanding of tradition, in that he often seems to imply that Rationalism (in politics, morality and religion) has come to replace traditions of political, moral or religious behaviour, and yet one of his central claims is that those in the grip of Rationalist thinking misunderstand the tradition-dependent nature of reason or reasoning. The Rationalist might think he has discovered some timeless, pure form thought uncontaminated by habit, tradition or prejudice, but for Oakeshott, no such thought exists, and the various formulae that are the products of Rationalist thinking ('codes of conduct', declarations of rights, creedal statements) are nothing but abridgements of concrete traditions of behavior. So in this sense the Rationalist's attempt to surmount tradition is as futile as the attempt of Baron von Munchausen to get himself out of the lake by pulling on his moustache" (Jacobs/Tregenza 2014, p. 7).

16 K.R. Popper, *Prediction and Prophecy in the Social Sciences*, in: Popper 1968, p. 337.

grounded in conserving in the memory past views and past forms of order (more on this below). The voice of history and tradition constitutes the foundation of politics. Oakeshott's politics of conservation are therefore an expression of totalizing reason's humility, like for Popper critical rationalism was an antidote to the *hubris* of dogmatic rationalism. In light of the politics of conversation, Oakeshott takes on the role of a conservative skeptic; Popper, meanwhile – that of a progressive fallibilist. According to Oakeshott, it is the responsibility of those who propose changes to justify their benefits: "innovation entails certain loss and possible gain, therefore, the onus of proof, to show that the proposed change may be expected to be on the whole beneficial, rests with the would-be innovator."[17] The inability to rationally prove the beneficiality of making certain changes is a sufficient reason to choose non-change. Referring back to Marquard, we can say that it is skepticism that inclines one toward conservatism. Oakeshott would surely agree with Marquard, who writes:

> Die übertribunalisierer etablieren nicht die absolute Rationalität, sondern den "Ausbruch in die Unbelangbarkeit", der für Freiheiten eintritt, die wir – vor aller prinzipiellen Erlaubnis – schon sind; dazu gehören üblichkeiten. Weil wir zu schnell sterben für totale Änderungen und totale Begründungen, brauchen wir üblichkeiten: auch jene üblichkeit, die die Philosophie ist. Die Skeptiker rechnen also mit der sterblichkeitsbedingten Unvermeidlichkeit von Traditionen; und was dort – üblicherweise und mit dem Status von üblichkeiten – gewußt wird, wissen auch sie. Die Skeptiker sind also gar nicht die, die prinzipiell nichts wissen; sie wissen nur nichts Prinzipielles: die Skepsis ist nicht die Apotheose der Ratlosigkeit, sondern nur der Abschied vom Prinzipiellen (Marquard 2000, p. 17).

Two other differences between the two thinkers' views must also be mentioned. First, in Popper's thought, social order seems to form as a result of rational reflection, whereas in Oakeshott, social order arises spontaneously. Second, as was mentioned earlier, there is the opposition between moral idealism (Popper) and the tradition of moral behavior (Oakeshott).

It is worth noting that Popper and Oakeshott identify the historical roots of conversation differently. Popper indicates early Greek philosophy from Thales to Plato, about which he emphatically writes that "it is almost too good to be

---

17 M. Oakeshott, *On being Conservative*, in: Oakeshott 1962, p. 172. Odo Marquard expressed a similar view: "Darum muß man, wenn man – unter den Zeitnotbedingungen unserer vita brevis – überhaupt begründen will, nicht die Nichtwahl begründen, sondern die Wahl (die Veränderung): die Beweislast hat der Veränderer. Indem sie diese Regel übernimmt, die aus der menschlichen Sterblichkeit folgt, tendiert die Skepsis zum Konservativen" (Marquard 2000, p. 16).

true."[18] Oakeshott, on the other hand – in his essay *The Voice of Conversation in the Education of Mankind* – points to Plato himself as the source of understanding philosophy as conversation, instead of solely as an eristic dispute.[19] Significantly, Popper mentions "the rationalist tradition, the tradition of critical discussion,"[20] while Oakeshott simply writes about conversation, which protects philosophy from dogmatism.[21]

It is worth mentioning how Oakeshott understands the philosophy of politics, as well as the basic premises of Popper's fallibilism. In his essay *Political Philosophy*[22] Oakeshott notes that all reflection assumes doubt, which nonetheless cannot be total doubt because reflection is a dialectic process, so the point of departure is already some knowledge. In this context, what makes philosophical reflection stand out is that it is radically subversive. Oakeshott invokes an evocative image comparing reflection to climbing a tower with many windows on each floor. As one climbs higher the view changes, and things successively appear that were not visible earlier. The essence of philosophical effort is the constant readiness to go further while others stop at a certain level. However, it would be a mistake to think that this is solely a metaphor for the zetetic process (Greek in origin) accenting the intrinsic value of searching and striving (an inclination toward climbing), and not for the value of reaching the end, which is out of sight during the climb (and cannot even be presumed to exist). Oakeshott significantly asserts that what differentiates the types of reflection is not the inclination towards climbing or a lack thereof, but rather the willingness or unwillingness to take the established and remembered views from lower floors (which determine the current view) upwards with oneself as one climbs

---

[18] "The early history of Greek philosophy, especially the history from Thales to Plato, is a splendid story. It is almost too good to be true. In every generation we find at least one new philosophy, one new cosmology of staggering originality and depth. How was this possible? Of course one cannot explain originality and genius. But one can try to throw some light on them. What was the secret of the ancients? I suggest that it was a *tradition – the tradition of critical discussion.*" K.R. Popper, *Back to the Presocratics*, in: Popper 1998, p. 20.

[19] See: Oakeshott 2004, p. 193.

[20] K.R. Popper, *Back to the Presocratics*, in: Popper 1998, p. 23.

[21] "What I think Oakeshott means by imputing to Plato the discovery of dialectical discussion – conversation – in this sense is that the participants in a Platonic dialogue are imbued with (or come to develop) the understanding that the phenomena they are concerned to explore and elucidate are susceptible of multiple, and even contradictory, conceptual encasements. It is the formal skepticism that they share by participating in a conversational form of interaction that enables them to think 'that each has been right all the time,' even as their substantive understandings of things deeply differ" (Botwinick 2011, p. 6).

[22] M. Oakeshott, *Political Philosophy*, in: Oakeshott 1993, pp. 138–156.

higher. Thus, a key issue becomes the attitude towards memory. As a radically subversive endeavor, philosophy, including political philosophy, cuts itself off from memory, and each new view replaces the previous one. In contrast to reflection in the service of politics and political doctrine, political philosophy, with its point of departure in political experience, allows for the subversiveness of reflection to a potentially unlimited degree. For this reason – Oakeshott notes – things are revealed in a permanent way and the continuity of the journey as the principle of unity and multiplicity is revealed. While this principle can be interpreted as the principle of unity in multiplicity, it cannot be interpreted as the principle of unity over multiplicity.[23]

It must be emphasized that political philosophy, the way it is understood by Oakeshott, i.e. as radically subversive reflection, concerns that which is permanent, and therefore not that which belongs to the sphere of practical politics. In practical politics, on the other hand, there is no room for purified ideas and philosophical doctrines that establish absolutely permanent and final plans of action. For Oakeshott, political rationalism is just such a plan, since – as he notes in *Rationalism in politics* – reason wields unlimited jurisdiction over every problem. Rationalism so-understood is reductionistic (monomythic) and desires perfectionism (the principle of *to ariston*), universalism, and certainty in a Gnostic way.[24] Such rationalism is based on the erroneous reduction of practical knowledge to technical (theoretical) knowledge. Rationalists typically do not recognize the value of practice, dogmatically absolutizing the theoretical dimension. Thus, in analyzing possible Greek skeptical antecedents of Oakeshott's views, we must keep in mind his distinction between political philosophy and practical politics. Before we move on to this issue, however, it is necessary to take a look at the main tenets of Popperian fallibilism.

Popper's fallibilism arose from his protest against the fundamentalism of not only Wiener Kreis, but also that of Descartes. Popper believed that there is no infallible source of knowledge, and no statement can ever be ultimately verified. Fallibilism presumes that scientific theories are temporary, incomplete, and unreliable, and our knowledge is fallible knowledge; however, this unreliable knowledge is knowledge. Fallibilists assert that no certain knowledge exists that would be completely secure, which distinguishes it from skepticism (modernly interpreted one-sidedly as negative dogmatism), which asserts that knowledge in general does not exist.

---

23 The problem of the relationship between unity and multiplicity was a fundamental one for Greek philosophy; an exemplary example of analyses of these categories can be found in the Platonic dialogue *Parmenides*.
24 See: Franco 2004, p. 106.

> Science is not a system of certain, or well-established, statements; not it is a system which steadily advances towards a state of finality. Our science is not knowledge (*epistēmē*); it can never claim to have attained truth, or even a substitute for it, such as probability. [...] Although it can attain neither truth nor probability, the striving for knowledge and the search for truth are still the strongest motives of scientific discovery (Popper 1959, p. 278).

It is worth noting that Popper considers his method of scientific discovery zetetic in a broad sense; such fallibilism understood as zeteticism not only questions knowledge classically understood as *epistēmē*, but also probabilism. Human cognition is finite (limited), while the zetetic process of cognition is infinite. It is for this reason that Popper emphasizes the importance of anti-dogmatic criticism, above all as learning to be self-critical. Popper develops his notion of *verisimilitude* as corroboration, as opposed to Carnap's confirmation.[25]

In my opinion, in attempting to identify the sources of Oakeshott's and Popper's views concerning political philosophy, we can look not only to the philosophical antecedents they themselves mentioned, but also to the Greek sources of skepticism and fallibilism. Let us begin with Oakeshott. As J.Ch. Laursen rightfully notes, Oakeshott's lack of direct references to the Greek skeptical tradition – to Pyrrho, pyrrhonism, Aenesidemus, Arcesilaus, Carneades, or Cicero and Sextus Empiricus[26] – is surprising at the very least, though we do find references to later thinkers associated with a skeptical approach (e.g. Montaigne, Descartes, Hobbes, Pascal, Hume). Laursen poses the following question: Why was Oakeshott's skepticism unhistorical? That is, why does he ignore the Pyrrhonian and Academic skeptical traditions?[27] According to Laursen, there are three possible reasons for this:

> One is ignorance: that he did not know much about the Pyrrhonian and Academic traditions. A second one is that he knew about the traditions, but did not respect their philosophical acumen. The third is that he knew about the traditions but saw dangers in their moral implications (Laursen 2005, p. 44).

In my opinion, there are two additional reasons why Oakeshott failed to include references to Pyrrhonian and Academic skepticism. First, we must distinguish two planes of reflection in Oakeshott's thought, and, subsequently, two types of references, namely the subversive character of philosophy (including political philosophy) and practical philosophy along with the directives linked to it. Sec-

---

[25] It is worth noting that during his studies, Popper successively departed from the idea of drawing near to truth in favor of understanding truth as a regulative idea.
[26] See: Laursen 2005, p. 40.
[27] See: Laursen 2005, p. 44.

ond, it seems that in a purely reconstructed form, no form of ancient skepticism would correspond to Oakeshott's views. At most, elements of the Greek skeptical approach can be found in his writings. In tracking these antecedents, we have to refer to his understanding of political philosophy, on the one hand, and political practice, on the other. In the first case we can refer to radically subversive thinkers, and we can certainly count the representatives of Greek skepticism among this group (regardless of the differences in their interpretations of skepticism).[28] In the second case, we can track elements of Oakeshott's understanding of political practice to certain approaches in ancient skepticism (this is what Laursen does). Finally, we can recognize in Pyrrhonian philosophy a combination of both of these approaches. Extreme radical subversion appears within it as philosophical subversion of philosophy itself in a classical sense, i.e. philosophy postulating the authority of knowledge as *epistēmē*; the consequences of this are not making judgments that lay claim to truth about the hidden nature of things, as well as ridding oneself of both perfectionism in the form of the *to ariston* principle and universal and apodictic certainty. The practical dimension of the Pyrrhonian approach, on the other hand, is expressed through the conservation of the old views, i.e. through respect for tradition, customs, and habits of behavior. This attitude simultaneously assumes appreciation for a lack of change, since the responsibility for justifying change rests on the one implementing the change. Both of these aspects can be expressed more clearly by referring to Oakeshott's tower metaphor mentioned above. Political philosophy, which for Oakeshott was to be radically subversive, is realized in severing the anchor linking the later view with the earlier one, especially in rejecting – historically-formulated – past narrations and ideas; in the theoretical dimension, Pyrrho's philosophy took on such a form. Practical politics, on the other hand, has to take into account during the climb the desire to take remembered remnants of past views upwards to higher floors, as these offer alternative ways of perceiving things and actions. This makes conversation possible, as it takes place in the language of tradition, which takes into account past views. The politics of conversa-

---

[28] The fact that Oakeshott did not mention Greek skeptics in his essay "Political Philosophy" does not mean that Pyrrho, Aenesidemus, Arcesilaus, and Carneades were not radically subversive thinkers; Oakeshott does mention Plato, Hobbes, Spinoza, and Hegel, however. A lack of direct references in this area can be compensated for with indirect references. The skeptical Platonic Academy read Plato's philosophy in this way. On the other hand, Gianni Paganini demonstrates Hobbes's borrowing from Pyrrhonism. See: Paganini, *Hobbes Among Ancient and Modern Sceptics: Phenomena and Bodies*, in: Paganini 2003, pp. 3–35; Paganini, *Hobbes and the "continental" tradition of skepticism*, in: Maia Neto/Popkin 2004, pp. 65–105. Regarding Hegel's references to ancient skepticism, see: Forster 1989.

tion is possible within the confines of politics of conservation, which presumes the conservation in memory of earlier and grounded views and habits of behaviors. Exploiting this metaphor, we can say that appreciating the practical dimension of politics boils down to analyzing the present state we are in along with the memory of past views, not beginning with reflections on the sky above the tower or on books describing such a view.

To demonstrate the possible Pyrrhonian antecedents of Oakeshott's views, it is necessary to look at several different elements. Pyrrho's skepticism should be considered a practical philosophy revealing a certain attitude toward life (Greek ἀγωγή) and oriented toward finding achievable (not abstract) happiness. The means to this end should be avoiding passing judgments that lay absolute claims to truth (ultimate solutions) concerning what is hidden. Recall that Oakeshott's critique of Utopianism is based on the assertion that "no problem in politics is ever solved permanently" (OtP). Therefore, it is recommended to develop the skill of doubting and of taking oneself out of a state of certainty, especially in the educational sphere. Lastly, Pyrrho strongly emphasizes the significant role played by customs and traditions in practical action.[29] Oakeshott's politics of conversation is possible within the framework of the politics of conservation.

As was mentioned earlier, Popper's fallibilism cannot be grasped from the perspective of radical Greek skepticism, or *de facto* negative dogmatism, which asserts that knowledge is impossible and is often fused with agnosticism. More moderate forms of ancient skepticism that prefer what Popper calls a substitute of truth, or probability, also do not correspond to Popper's position. Generally speaking, we can say that Greek skepticism, both in the Pyrrhonian and Academic traditions, understands knowledge as *epistēmē*, though it demonstrates the impossibility of achieving it, or at least the difficulties in accessing it. Popper's fallibilism does not treat knowledge as *epistēmē*, but in a doxastic sense as hypothetical opinions (conjectures); at the same time, doubt does not lead to ἐποχή, but rather acts as a stimulating factor towards further investiga-

---

[29] "καὶ ὁμοίως ἐπὶ πάντων μηδὲν εἶναι τῇ ἀληθείᾳ, νόμῳ δὲ καὶ ἔθει πάντα τοὺς ἀνθρώπους πράττειν." Diog, IX, 61, 9–10. "[...] φασὶν οἱ σκεπτικοὶ περὶ τῶν δογματικῶν ὡς δυνήσεται βιοῦν ζητήσεων ἀπέχων, οὐ περὶ τῶν βιωτικῶν καὶ τηρητικῶν· ὥστε καὶ αἱρούμεθά τι κατὰ τὴν συνήθειαν καὶ φεύγομεν καὶ νόμοις χρώμεθα." Diog., IX, 108, 6–9. This last fragment clearly shows the limitations to suspending judgment; the skeptic should suspend judgment only in reference to the dogmatic claims of philosophers, not in regards to the affairs of everyday life, in which one should act in accordance with commonly-accepted custom. A confirmation of this opinion can be found in Sextus Empiricus: "ἀκολουθοῦμεν γάρ τινι λόγῳ κατὰ τὸ φαινόμενον ὑποδεικνύντι ἡμῖν τὸ ζῆν πρὸς τὰ πάτρια ἔθη καὶ τοὺς νόμους καὶ τὰς ἀγωγὰς καὶ τὰ οἰκεῖα πάθη." Sext., *Pyr.*, I, 17, 6–9.

tions. In this sense, we can say that fallibilism is one form of the zetetic attitude, hence a form of skepticism different from negative dogmatism, agnosticism, and Montaigne's epechism. In this respect, it is difficult to consider the views of the Academics (Carneades and Philo of Larissa) the best antecedents of Popper's fallibilism, because although they were inclined toward fallibilistic solutions, they still viewed knowledge as *epistēmē*. In my opinion, however, we can look to an earlier period of philosophy before the classical notion of knowledge as *epistēmē* was formed and skepticism, in its early stages of development, had not yet taken on the form of either Pyrrhonism or Academic skepticism. Special attention is especially due to Popper's direct and indirect references to the views of Xenophanes of Colophon. Above all, it is worth taking a look at Popper's essay *The Unknown Xenophanes*, which contains the noteworthy subtitle: *An attempt to establish his greatness*.[30]

A detailed analysis of Popper's ties with and references to the views of Xenophanes would require a separate study,[31] so here I would only like to make general remarks on the most important themes. For Popper, Xenophanes is not only "the founder of epistemology," but also "perhaps the real father of history."[32] Besides this, Popper constantly emphasizes the criticism of this thinker, especially his self-criticism, which anticipated "the ideas of the European Enlightenment." Two fragments of Xenophanes (D-K B 34 and B 18 in Diels-Kranz)[33] are especially noteworthy in this context. Popper interprets the first fragment as an expression of a theory of objective knowledge; in his opinion, the fragment demonstrates the difference between objective truth and subjective certainty. The entirety of our knowledge is limited to conjectural knowledge, which will never be completely certain. Fragment D-K B 18, on the other hand, contains the view on the possibility of continually finding better solutions. Popper's interpretations

---

30 K.R. Popper, *The Unknown Xenophanes. An attempt to establish his greatness*, in: Popper 1998, pp. 33–65.
31 Select aspects of these references can be found in: Attfield 2014, pp. 113–133.
32 Popper 1998, p. 33.
33 "καὶ τὸ μὲν οὖν σαφὲς οὔτις ἀνὴρ ἴδεν οὐδέ τις ἔσται
 εἰδὼς ἀμφὶ θεῶν τε καὶ ἅσσα λέγω περὶ πάντων·
 εἰ γὰρ καὶ τὰ μάλιστα τύχοι τετελεσμένον εἰπών,
 αὐτὸς ὅμως οὐκ οἶδε· δόκος δ' ἐπὶ πᾶσι τέτυκται." Xenophanes, D-K B 34.
 "οὔτοι ἀπ' ἀρχῆς πάντα θεοὶ θνητοῖσ' ὑπέδειξαν,
 ἀλλὰ χρόνωι ζητοῦντες ἐφευρίσκουσιν ἄμεινον." Xenophanes, D-K B 18.

On the first of them, Popper writes: "To me there is nothing in the whole literature of philosophy that is so critical, so self-critical, so correct, and so true as B34," whereas he describes the second as Xenophanes' "licence to search" (Popper 1998, p. 46 and 48).

of these fragments from both a philological and philosophical perspective are at least debatable, for many scholars even controversial;[34] however, from the point of view of my analyses here, they contain two valuable bits of information. First, they allow us to recognize the antecedents of Popper's fallibilism in Xenophanes' views,[35] and second, they demonstrate sufficiently well the difference between Popper and Oakeshott within the context of the rejecting of the principle of *to ariston*. Popper suggests replacing it with the principle of *to ameinon*, in reference to Xenophanes' category of ἄμεινον (D-K B 18, 2). Only those, who seek (ζητοῦντες), i.e. critical thinkers (self-critical), can find what is better. In this case, the zetetic attitude present in fallibilism takes on the form of a syncritic procedure that consists in recognizing what is better (*to ameinon*), rather than on the dogmatic assertion that one has found what is best (*to ariston*). For Popper, Xenophanes is also the thinker who established ethical principles, such as tolerance, equality, intellectual integrity, and the value of discussion that does not necessarily lead to agreement.[36]

Even the above brief presentation of the ancient antecedents of Popper's and Oakeshott's anti-dogmatic criticism demonstrates the value and significance of ideas formulated by Greek thinkers. I think that a good summary of the above remarks can be found in a comment of Popper's concerning Xenophanes,[37] with which Oakeshott would likely concur with a large dose of certainty, *excusez-moi:* conjecture:

> Xenophanes' moralism much better characterizes the present-day situations in sciences and politics, and certainly to be preferred to the idiocy expressed by modern slogans such as 'Anything goes!', the password of some influential but irresponsible intellectuals (Popper 1998, p. 54).

---

[34] For more on the polemic against Popper's reading of Xenophanes, see: Lesher 1978, pp. 1–21; Austin 2000, pp. 239–246; Kirk 1960, pp. 318–339; Lloyd 1967, pp. 21–38. For more on my interpretation of fragments B 18 and B 34 of Xenophanes, see: Kubok 2016, pp. 31–53; Kubok 2015b, pp. 261–281.
[35] More on the topic of Xenophanes' fallibilism can be found in: Bryan 2012, pp. 48–57.
[36] See: Popper 1998, pp. 52–54.
[37] On the margin, we can add that Xenophanes' elegies suggest he was more of a conservative in the socio-political sphere. In this respect, and most likely only in this respect, his views could be treated as a selective and incomplete antecedent of Oakeshott's thought.

Bibliography

A Greek-English Lexicon (1996): Compiled by H. G. Liddell, R Scott. Revised and Augmented Throughout by Sir H.S. Jones, with the assistance of Roderick McKenzie, Oxford: Clerendon Press.
Attfield, Robin (2014): "Popper and Xenophanes". In: *Philosophy* 89, pp. 113–133.
Austin, Scott (2000): "Scepticism and Dogmatism in the Presocratics". In: *Apeiron: A Journal for Ancient Philosophy and Science* 33, pp. 239–246.
Botwinick, Aryeh (2011): *Michael Oakeshott's Skepticism*. Princeton: Princeton University Press.
Bryan, Jenny (2012): *Likeness and Likelihood in the Presocratics and Plato*. Cambridge Classical Studies. Cambridge, New York: Cambridge University Press.
Coats, Wendell John, Jr. (2000): *Oakeshott and His Contemporaries*. Selinsgrove: Susquehanna University Press.
Diels, Hermann/Kranz, Walther (eds.) (1985): *Die Fragmente der Vorsokratiker. Griechisch und deutsch*. Bd. 1–3. Zürich.
Forster, Michael N. (1989): *Hegel and Skepticism*. Cambridge, Mass.: Harvard University Press.
Franco, Paul (2004): *Michael Oakeshott. An Introduction*. New Haven and London: Yale University Press.
Gerencser, Steven Anthony (2000): *The Skeptic's Oakeshott*. London: Palgrave Macmillan.
Jacobs, Struan/Tregenza, Ian (2014): "Rationalism and tradition: The Popper–Oakeshott conversation". In: *European Journal of Political Theory* 13, pp. 3–24.
Kirk, Geoffrey S. (1960): "Popper on Science and the Presocratics". In: *Mind* 69, pp. 318–339.
Kubok, Dariusz (2015a): "Comments on the Sources of Greek Philosophical Criticism". In: *Folia Philosophica* 34. Special issue: *Forms of Criticism in Philosophy and Science*. Ed. by Dariusz Kubok. Katowice, pp. 9–31.
Kubok, Dariusz (2015b): "Allocriticism and Autocriticism in the Views of Xenophanes of Colophon". *Littera Antiqua* 10–11, pp. 261–281.
Kubok, Dariusz (2016): "Xenophanes of Colophon and the Problem of Distinguishing Between Skepticism and Negative Dogmatism". In: *Electryone* 4, Issue 2, pp. 31–53.
Laursen, John Christian (2005): "Oakeshott's Skepticism and the Skeptical Traditions". In: *European Journal of Political Theory* 4 (1), pp. 37–55.
Lesher, James H. (1978): "Xenophanes' Scepticism". In: *Phronesis* 23, pp. 1–21.
Lloyd, Geoffrey E.R. (1967): "Popper versus Kirk: A Controversy in the Interpretation of Greek Science". In: *British Journal for the Philosophy of Science* 18, pp. 21–38.
Marquard, Odo (2000): *Abschied vom Prinzipiellen. Philosophische Studien*. Stuttgart: Reclam.
Maia Neto, José Raimundo/ Popkin, Richard H. (eds.) (2004): *Skepticism in Renaissance and Post-Renaissance Thought: New Interpretations*. Amherst: Humanity Books.
Oakeshott, Michael (1962): *Rationalism in Politics and Other Essays*. London: Methuen&Co Ltd.
Oakeshott, Michael (1993): *Religion, Politics and the Moral Life*. Ed. by T. Fuller. New Haven and London: Yale University Press.

Oakeshott, Michael (1996): *The Politics of Faith and the Politics of Scepticism*. Ed. by T. Fuller. Yale University Press.

Oakeshott, Michael (2004): *What Is History? And Other Essays*. Ed. L. O'Sullivan. Exeter: Imprint Academic.

Orsi, Davide (2015): "Michael Oakeshott's Skepticism". In: *The European Lagacy* 20, issue 6, pp. 575–590.

Paganini, Gianni (ed.) (2003): *The Return of Scepticism. From Hobbes and Descartes to Bayle*. Dordrecht: Kluwer.

Popper, Karl R. (1968): *Conjectures and Refutations: The Growth of Scientific Knowledge*. New York: Harper & Row.

Popper, Karl R. (1959): *Logic of Scientific Discovery*. Transl. by K.R. Popper with the assistance of Dr. Julius Freed & Lan Freed. London: Hutchinson.

Popper, Karl R. (1998): *The World of Parmenides: Essays on the Presocratic Enlightenment*. Ed. by Arne F. Petersen, with the assistance of Jorgen Mejer. London and New York: Routledge.

Popper, Karl R. (1948): "Utopia and Violence". In: *Hibbert Journal* 16(2), pp.109–116.

Rayner, Jeremy (1985): "The Legend of Oakeshott's Conservatism: Sceptical Philosophy and Limited Politics". *Canadian Journal of Political Science* 18, pp. 313–338.

Sextus Empiricus (1990): *Outlines of Pyrrhonism*. R.G. Bury (transl.). Buffalo: Prometheus Books.

Strauss, Leo (2000): *On Tyranny*. Revised and Expanded Edition, including the Strauss-Kojève Correspondence. Chicago: University of Chicago Press.

Tseng, Roy (2003): *The Sceptical Idealist: Michael Oakeshott as a Critic of the Enlightenment*. Exeter: Imprint Academic.

Wood, Neal (1959): "A Guide to the Classics: The Skepticism of Professor Oakeshott". *Journal of Politics* 21, pp. 647–662.

http://www.michael-oakeshott-association.com/pdfs/mo_letters_popper.pdf.

Adam Grzeliński
The Critical Dimension of Locke's Epistemology

Abstract: Although renowned for its new approach to the description of mental operations (the 'new way of ideas'), the philosophy of John Locke was designed as a critique of knowledge. In the article I raise the issue of its criticism not in reference to particular standpoints the critique was aimed at, such as Aristotelianism, scholasticism, Platonism, or Cartesianism; rather, I understand it as the justification of the new cognition model emerging during the seventeenth century, i.e. of the empirical knowledge. Locke's description of constructing empirical concepts on the basis of individual experience was to guarantee the objectivity of scientific investigation results and, as such, was meant only as the introduction to his epistemology. The *Essay Concerning Human Understanding* provides a deep insight both into the conditions and the limitations of the new knowledge. The former include referring to clear sense experience, the proper and unbiased use of language, and the social functioning of knowledge; the latter are the historical character of descriptive natural sciences and the lack of scientific findings certainty. Locke does not provide the critique of knowledge in Kantian sense; however, I argue that the way he separates metaphysics and scientific investigations might be interpreted as the harbinger of Immanuel Kant's criticism.

Keywords: John Locke, critical philosophy, epistemology, natural history, philosophy of nature

In 1690, *An Essay Concerning Human Understanding* by John Locke (1632–1704), a work of crucial significance for the development of the British Enlightenment philosophy, was published. Locke's *new way of ideas* constituted the basis for many subsequent theoretical interpretations, which in turn laid the groundwork for theories within the scope of practical philosophy; it was regarded as the foundation upon which the whole edifice of human knowledge could be raised. Therefore, his famous mention of removing rubbish off the way leading to future knowledge should be treated with great attention, as the new philosophy presented by him was characterised both by a historical and systematic dimension. Although Locke's critique is aimed against previous models of knowledge represented both by scholastic philosophy and Descartes' theory, the reason behind it was to re-evaluate human knowledge which in relation to nature from this point on was to be realised not in the area of *philosophia prima* but within broadly understood natural sciences. In this sense, Locke's critique is historic in character, since it refers to Aristotle, scholastics, and Cartesians. On the other hand, the project itself "to inquire into the original, certainty, and extent of human knowledge" (E, I, 1, 2, p. 1)[1], as well as the division of sciences encompassing three basic fields (*physica*, *practica*, and *semeiotiké* – E, IV, 21, 1–5, pp. 296–298) indicates the systematic dimension of the said critique. In this case, it does not merely concern the accumulated rubbish of old theories that should be removed but the fact whether the thus prepared ground constitutes the sufficient justification for knowledge.

The purpose of this article is to attempt to answer the question regarding the extent to which Locke's philosophy can be perceived as a systematic critique of cognition. Thus, the aim is not to verify the scope and efficiency of Locke's critique of selected standpoints, but rather to examine in what sense Locke's theory fosters a new paradigm of knowledge. I am seeking to demonstrate that this critique was supported by programme objectives, as it constituted a substructure for a certain new type of knowledge and research practices. It was precisely here, in the new knowledge of nature which was to take place in the field of naturalists' vision and in experimenters' laboratories that, according to Locke, the progress of knowledge was achieved, and philosophy was to serve as its complement and justification. The thus outlined philosophical programme was to support the ongoing scientific revolution (although, as I am trying to demonstrate, it did so only partially). Ultimately, it led to a change in the role of metaphysics, i.e. a separation of the regulative use of reason that is characteristic of metaphysics from the constitutive use, typical of empirical sciences. As I will try to demonstrate later, the new cognition of nature brought along two ideas: the social functioning of knowledge and its historical development encompassing not only the accumulation of historical knowledge (in natural histories), but also falsifiable speculations concerning natural philosophy. Accordingly, Locke's position justified the possibility of creating knowledge that was largely independent of metaphysical judgements. Thus, his philosophy could justify not only the possibility of empirical sciences of nature, but also – what Locke failed to see – mathematical natural sciences. In the case of natural histories, radical and strongly sceptical conclusions were soon to be drawn from his theory by David Hume, whereas

---

[1] Quotations from Locke's *Essay* according to the following edition: Locke 1824 (henceforth E; I give the numbers of the book, the chapter, the paragraph, and the page; the first book of the *Essay* and the first six chapters of the second book are contained in the first volume of the edition).

in the case of a philosophical justification of mathematical natural sciences one had to wait for Immanuel Kant's critical philosophy.

The new model of knowledge

The task of Locke's philosophy was to provide a justification for the scientific revolution that was taking place in the seventeenth century. The new knowledge of nature developed in two principal directions outlined by the accomplishments of Galileo Galilei and Francis Bacon: mathematical natural sciences and empirical sciences. Previous speculations concerned with the structure of natural reality offered by Aristotelianism could not explain the phenomena that the New World travellers had accounted for[2] and which revealed themselves under the watchful eye of scientists using new optical and measurement instruments such as the microscope and the barometer.[3] Aristotle's complete, deliberately organised world, a combination of matter and developing forms, was being expanded with new phenomena which did not fit in the existing catalogue of species and genera. The symbolic understanding of plants and animals surrounding man which prevailed in earlier medieval and Renaissance descriptions of the world was no longer sufficient to define previously unknown species. It was also becoming evident that such a description was not concerned with nature itself but rather the human world with its phantasms[4]. These transformations made researchers more and more aware of the fact that not only did they need to describe new, previously unknown species but also to rewrite natural histories, even with regard to phenomena that appeared familiar[5]. To fulfil its task, the said description was to refer only to natural phenomena and not to human imagination, and the experience to which it referred was to be communicable, which required a new language of description. Owing to this, the results of observations and experiments could become an object of discussion[6] and verification[7].

---

2 See: Talbot 2010.
3 See e.g. Anstey 2011, pp. 136 ff, Gaukroger 2006, pp. 253–444.
4 Ashworth 1990, pp. 303–332; Eamon 1990, pp. 333–365.
5 It is worth remembering that Locke was so enraptured by fragments of John Aubrey's *Naturall Historie of Wiltshire* that he offered to cover its printing costs, see: Walmsley 2003, p. 35.
6 Not without a reason this is also the time of establishment of different scientific associations (such as German *Deutsche Akademie der Naturforscher Leopoldina* or The Royal Society of London) aimed at the promulgation of the new ideals of knowledge and constituting an arena of exchange of views and planning of new experiments.

However, to the seventeenth century naturalists, the abandonment of the organicist Aristotelian interpretation of nature was not synonymous with the abandonment of the quest to discover permanent and indispensable laws that govern it. The knowledge of nature was once more to be made possible by use of mathematical modelling, which allowed the detachment of the described phenomena from Platonic and Aristotelian substantialist metaphysics and indication of general laws. The other way to justify the order of nature was sought in natural philosophy by an attempt to reformulate the notion of substance in such a manner as to validate the said order. Hence, besides the projects aimed at the mathematisation of nature, the seventeenth-century metaphysics developed a mechanistic approach where the assumed explanatory structure was not seen in the order of reasons (as in mathematical natural sciences) but in the order of causality; however, in relation to Aristotelianism, the description of nature was ousted of the final cause. This tradition includes Descartes's concept of extended substance[8], as well as corpuscularism inherited from ancient atomism and Epicureanism[9].

Locke followed the latter direction, which was due to his early interest in medicine, anatomy, botany, and experimental sciences as well as his participation in the works of the Royal Society[10] and cooperation with Thomas Sydenham and Robert Boyle. Locke became acquainted with the main work of the new mathematical knowledge of nature, the *Principia Mathematica* by Isaac Newton relatively late, and although he did so very thoroughly[11], he was mainly able to evaluate its qualitative aspect rather than the then highly innovative and difficult mathematical calculus[12]. In addition to the developed speculative philosophy of nature, best reflected in Cartesianism, the first of the fields, empirical natural science, was essentially broken down into natural history, collecting descriptions of facts, and speculative natural philosophy, which in the second

---

[7] This difference is excellently depicted by a shift between former understanding of natural histories by Pliny, and the new guidelines presented by Francis Bacon in his *Sylva Sylvarum* (1627). The fact that Locke enthusiastically adopted the new approach towards learning about the nature, and his philosophical programme could be seen as its justification, did not stop him from being otherwise gullible and repeating quite unconfirmed opinions. From the pages of his *Essays* we learn about the existence of jumarts or animals being a result of a crossbreeding of a rat and cat that Locke had allegedly seen with his own eyes (E, III, 6, 23, p. 488), or even mermaids and sea-men, i.e. aquariuses (E, III, 6, 12, p. 483).
[8] For more on Cartesian philosophy of nature, See: Gaukroger/Schuster/Sutton 2000.
[9] Anstey 2011, p. 9.
[10] More detailed information about Locke's involvement in the works of Royal Society, see: Grzeliński 2016, pp. 255–278.
[11] See: Axtell 1991, pp. 418 ff.; idem 1965, pp. 152–161.
[12] Woolhouse 2009, p. 278.

half of the seventeenth century was dominated by such views as the Cartesian theory of vortices or corpuscularism. The interrelation between these areas of knowledge can be recognized, for instance, by Robert Boyle, living at the same time as Locke, who, on the one hand, stressed the importance of natural histories, yet at the same time was convinced of the universal nature of the corpuscular hypothesis, reaching for the essence of things. Although Locke was initially inclined to acknowledge the legitimacy of the speculative cognition of nature (at least in relation to medicine), with the radicalisation of the empiricist approach[13], where Sydenham and Bacon played an important role, the possibility of knowledge of the essence of bodies surrounding man proved questionable.

With respect to the philosophy of nature, the corpuscular theory adopted from Boyle seemed most probable to Locke. However, with the empirical knowledge moved to the foreground, the importance attributed to speculative concepts had changed: similarly to observations being a result of a generalisation, such concepts proved susceptible to falsification procedures[14]. However, since it is not possible to reach for the essence of things going beyond observations, the legitimacy of such speculations no longer resulted from their alleged truthfulness but rather their usefulness with regard to the planned observations and proposed experiments. This pragmatic dimension of speculative theories applicability causes that their validity may be justified by the possibility of their use in socially functioning practices of the experimental sciences. Useless theories – such as, for instance, the Aristotelian concept of substantial forms – from this

---

[13] Already in the early *Questions concerning the Law of Nature* Locke opposed the idea of innateness of knowledge indicating that it is the order of phenomena that proves the existence of God. However, in mid 1960s he was still divagating on the essence of biological bodies trying to reconcile the views expressed by J. van Helnont and D. Sennert. A shift in his views may be seen while comparing two medical fragments from that period, *Morbus* and *Respiratione usus*, with works written slightly later: *De arte medica* and *Anatomie*; in the latter, Locke speaks of the possibility of discovering the final structure of bodies with considerable pessimism. In the *Essay* he performs a generalisation of those views and draws conclusions from them. The detailed analysis of the medical fragments is provided by Walmsley 2008 (https://core.ac.uk/download/pdf/74250.pdf, accessed 1.7.2017).

[14] Two well-known examples of rejecting the previous speculative concepts of nature can be found in the writings by Newton and Locke. The first is concerned with the falsification of Cartesian theory of vortices by Newton – initially in the unfinished essay *De gravitatione et aequipondio fluidorum*, and eventually in *Principia mathematica*, by indicating irregularities of the mathematical calculus to which Descartes referred. The other instance is a correction made by Locke himself while he was preparing the fourth edition of his *Essay* for print, where he admitted the hypothesis of an interaction of bodies from a distance, as postulated by Newtonian theory of gravity, which did not fit in the corpuscular hypothesis allowing only for direct interaction of bodies (see E, II, 8, 11, p. 166).

perspective proved not to be theories describing the objective state of affairs but rather concepts created individually and owned by their authors. They ceased to belong to the world of nature, revealing their human provenance. Thus, the turn towards the experience visible within natural sciences was aimed at obtaining such a description of nature that would guarantee its objectivity by abandoning the world of human imagination and finding their realm in sensual reality. At the same time, however, objectivity did not mean reaching for the things themselves, independent of human cognition, but was equivalent with the constancy of laws resulting from generalisations of intersubjective experiences and research practices.

Noticeably, the change in the scientific paradigm concerned several complementary issues. *Firstly*, the possibility to verify research results provided a new criterion of objectivity: an objective element of experience was such that could be attributed intersubjectivity. This, in turn, involved the implementation of a new model of practising science – its being inscribed in the social context of institutions engaged in the accumulation of cognitive results, their dissemination, and open discussions. *Secondly*, the importance of philosophy in relation to empirical sciences changed. Although such sciences were not meant to replace it, philosophy itself was no longer to constitute merely their methodological keystone (which, in a sense, occurred in British philosophy slightly later – in David Hume's views[15]), but was also not intended to provide knowledge of nature but only justify the possibility of acquiring knowledge through empirical sciences. *Thirdly*, and finally, besides the narrow field of natural religion, a change occurred in philosophy when it comes to metaphysical concepts: material substance, spiritual substance or God began to function as regulative notions. For example, the philosophical notion of matter defined the status of an object (its objective existence, without determining its essence), whereas in the constitutive usage, it began to signify either the supposed structure of bodies or simply a set of qualities constantly manifested in experience – in this sense the notion

---

15 Hume's associationism may be seen as an expression of psychologism; thus, to a certain extent the discovery of an association between ideas and turning it into a universal tool of cognition not only explains the construction of judgements concerning the nature but also morality, and the emphasis put on *belief* and *sympathy* also forms a testimony that psychology constitutes the fundamental science when it comes to human nature, whereas other sciences that make up the system of knowledge as a whole (logic (epistemology), criticism, politics, morals) depend on it. Meanwhile, Locke makes a clear distinction between the psychological description of experience and the description of conditions for the development of knowledge, as it is demonstrated in the chapter "Of the Association of Ideas" of the *Essay*, where the associations between the ideas of imaginations are juxtaposed with logical relationships occurring between concepts (E, II, 33, pp. 419–427).

of matter belonged to speculative natural sciences. The essential characteristic of Locke's philosophy consists in bringing such features of new cognition of nature to light and examining their consequences.

Locke, his *new way of ideas*, and the danger of subjectivity

In the *Essay*, it is easy to find a confirmation of the aforementioned transition: the scepticism concerning the possibility of acquiring knowledge about real essences of bodies, Locke's theory that there is no idea of substance (in its earlier philosophical sense) but merely a function that the concept of substance fulfils in cognition (E, II, 31, 13, p. 406; II, 13, 19, p. 156), as well as the distinction between real and nominal essences, the latter of which are the result of a linguistically fixed arrangement of phenomena (E, II, 3, 15, pp. 449–450). However, the turn towards experience gave rise to the problem of the subjectivism of experience, to which Locke had to find an answer. The Lockean theory of ideas, as was soon noted by its opponents[16], assumes that the only objects with which the human mind is directly conversant is the content of its own consciousness. This, on the other hand, makes it difficult to acknowledge the adequacy of such a content both with regard to the reality existing out the mind (i.e. in relation to things) as well as to ideas present in other people minds. In other words, at least *prima facie*, from its very foundation, this theory is burdened with the original sin: the threat of solipsism.

The first of these problems, the relation between ideas and the things they represent generates a tension between the phenomenalism of ideas and the realism of knowledge in Locke's philosophy. It manifests itself in the recognition of the directness of access to ideas while at the same time accepting the corpuscular theory which presupposes the existence of non-empirical properties of the matter that makes up objects. It seems that in this way Locke is trying, so to speak, to have a cake and eat it, insisting on his theory of ideas and maintaining practical realism concerning the existence of things out of the mind; however, this alleged discrepancy disappears when the mediatory role of the scientific knowledge is recognised, situated between the psychology of ideas and metaphysics.

Quite unlike the subjective experience, scientific cognition claims the right to objectivity: it establishes laws pertaining to objects existing as if independently of the fact of being experienced. Therefore, the transition from experience to

---

[16] See: Yolton 1956, pp. 86 ff.

reality cannot be completed at a single leap; although one can say that a certain separate reality corresponds to experience, the concept of such a reality remains completely unclear. Hence, as Locke writes in one of the indicated passages on substance, "we have no idea what it is, but only a confused obscure one of what it does" (E, II, 13, 19, p. 156). This concept is then devoid of any content and only symbolises a reference to something that is supposed to be situated as if "outside" thinking. However, it is only scientific knowledge that allows us to say what the object to which experience relates is.

Along with the transition to the field of scientific cognition, the idea – substance opposition becomes particularised and gives way to another opposition: (mental) ideas – qualities (attributable to bodies). This is tantamount with no more than presupposing the existence of things endowed with knowable attributes. However, neither substances nor qualities can be completely independent of experience, since this would mean an unjustified return to metaphysics. Therefore, to be more precise, one should speak not so much about the qualities of bodies but rather the ideas of qualities; however, we should do so in a way secondarily and based on given circumstances of experience – some of them may be considered as belonging to bodies themselves (as independent of the fact of being experienced), whilst others as the way they are manifested through experience. Thus, the opposition to what is subjective (in the mind) and objective (existing regardless of the content of thought) in relation to the knowledge of bodies surrounding man gains a new articulation in the form of contrasting secondary and primary qualities of bodies.

The latter include the "extension, solidity, mobility, or power of being moved" (E, II, 21, 73, p. 273) not only because they are inherent to the existence of bodies themselves, whereas secondary qualities (such as taste, colour, or smell) sometimes cannot be detected in the experience. The example given by Locke in this instance, namely that of a grain of wheat (E, II, 8, 9, p. 112) or an almond (E, II, 8, 20, p. 116), which lose their colour or taste and yet possess a sensible extension is not convincing. As George Berkeley later argued, sensuality alone does not allow for the possibility of abstracting quantitative and qualitative characteristics[17]. Moreover, for sensuality, in a way directly reporting what is "out of the mind", it is precisely the qualitative characteristics that are considered primary[18]. Thus, the distinction of quantitative properties of bodies is not at all concerned with the primacy of experience, as Locke explicitly writes, but with the possibility of constructing the notion of things that is capacitated by a meas-

---

[17] See: Berkeley 1949, pp. 28–33.
[18] Berkeley 1948, pp. 50 ff.

urement-based scientific procedure. Suffice it to state that, in a way by definition, purely primary qualities, i.e. quantitative, as well as the ability of a mechanical interaction with one another and with the senses, would be attributed to corpuscles. Their existence may only be postulated; however, by definition they cannot be an object of experience (yet in his thought experiment concerning microscopic eyes Locke fails to notice this[19]). In the case of corpuscles, a set of qualities may be defined geometrically (with reference to their extension) and mechanically (by assuming the existence of measurable forces through which bodies interact). The justification of such a mechanical model of nature is based on the intersubjectivity of quantitative characteristics finding a reflection in research practice, development of measuring instruments, etc.

However, the mechanical model of nature is still expressed in Locke's thought in substantialist categories: what is known in quantitative categories are material particles, which has its historical justification. In fact, Locke's conception is immersed in the seventeenth-century paradigm outlined by Descartes: in both cases what is independent of thought is the substantially understood extension.[20] However, the pessimism concerned with the possibility of knowing the real essence of bodies may also be interpreted as a claim that the full knowledge of essences would mean the possibility of acquiring certain knowledge related to the entirety of things, which in connection with the cumulative character of cog-

---

19 See: "And if, by the help of such microscopical eyes (if I may so call them), a man could penetrate farther than ordinary into the secret composition and radical texture of bodies, he would not make any great advantage by the change, if such an acute sight would not serve to conduct him to the market and exchange; if he could not see things he was to avoid, at a convenient distance; nor distinguish things he had to do with, by those sensible qualities others do. He that was sharp-sighted enough to see the configuration of the minute particles of the spring of a clock, and observe upon what peculiar structure and impulse its elastic motion depends, would no doubt discover something very admirable: but if eyes so framed could not view at once the hand, and the characters of the hour-plate, and thereby at a distance see what o'clock it was, their owner could not be much benefited by that acuteness; which, whilst it discovered the secret contrivance of the parts of the machine, made him lose its use." (E, II, 23, 12, p. 297) Here Locke seems to be convinced that the possibility of knowing the real essence of bodies – the molecular structure of matter – would be useless as each such description would have to be confronted with an everyday experience. This is the same thesis that caused his pessimism regarding the possibility of learning detailed anatomy in medical practice a few years earlier (see his *Anatomia* in: Walmsley 2008, pp. 221–231). In general, this comment can be understood as a necessity of referring any model which describes nature to direct experience, which constitutes a requirement of experimental sciences.
20 One of the differences concerns the possibility of existence of a vacuum, which was denied by Descartes yet allowed by corpuscular hypothesis.

nition could be understood only as an ideal of knowledge rather than a real situation achievable with the development of sciences.

Therefore, the ultimate difference between the subjective and objective poles of cognition is concerned with the juxtaposition of the common experience expressed in everyday language and the scientific knowledge operating with clearly defined terms and based on the ability to define the quantitative qualities of bodies.[21] What is objective, is no longer an unknown substance, nor is it a substance whose qualities have been identified with a metaphysical notion, i.e. such that breaks all the ties with experience. This does not mean, however, that the scientific knowledge of nature does not require a metaphysical grounding. Since the structure of things is not available to experience, and is merely postulated as a convenient hypothesis enabling the development of empirical knowledge whose validity is reduced to prognostic power, the question of adequacy of the two orders of knowledge: a commonsensical one, based on experience and the postulated quantitative one, remains open. How is it possible that a particular experience of qualitative character corresponds to such and not other quantitative characteristics?

The reason for Locke's cognitive pessimism seems to lie in the observation that the answer to this question not only exceeds the realm of experience but also that of science. Experimental science procedures in which the hypothesis of the structure of bodies is tested through the isolation of a particular domain of nature, only allow to say that certain measurable qualities correspond to such and not another type of experience. Any question about the reason for such a state of affairs would require referring to metaphysical notions, what Locke does indeed by pointing to the actions of the Creator. However, in contrast, for instance, to Nicolas Malebranche's conception of "seeing things in God", this reference is merely of a complementary character by indicating that science is not capable of answering such questions. Nonetheless, this does not preclude its development, which is in a way realised in separation from metaphysical judgements. The purposefulness of divine Creation cannot be cognitively penetrated, it becomes a counterpart of the regulative principle of formal purposefulness of nature.

---

[21] That is why Locke points at a dual use of language – civil and philosophical. The first concerns everyday use, where there is usually no need to particularise the meaning of words by making specific references to elementary experiences; such a precision is required only in philosophical usage where words have to "convey the precise notions of things, and to express, in general propositions, certain and undoubted truths, which the mind may rest upon, and be satisfied with, in its search after true knowledge" (E, III, 9, 3, p. 7).

The assertion that experience is the source of knowledge requires yet another explanation. Namely, in negative terms, it means that knowledge cannot be innate. Although in concord with the standpoint criticised by Locke, according to which the innate nature of knowledge (or, to be precise, the innate nature of principles and impressions[22]) would confirm its universality, at the same time, every proponent of such a view must immediately confront the hard reality of the lack of a broad consensus regarding such an "innate" content. Hence, conclusively, the said innateness would have to be completely private in nature. On the other hand, the innate origin of the content of experience would mean the existence of an impression in the mind, the source of which would have to be something else than the bodies and other people surrounding a person. Although such an opportunity was provided with divine revelation, it is also essentially personal. On the positive side, Locke's assumption[23] means the possibility of deriving from experience all the concepts present in cognition, irrespective of the function[24] they may perform in it[25]. However, this is where a certain paradox occurs, since while the negation of the possibility of existence of impressions[26] constituting a source of innate ideas was to invalidate the claims of individual

---

[22] Sadly, the scope of the paper does not allow to deal with Locke's terminology in a greater detail. Nonetheless, it should be noted that Locke uses the term "impression" in its etymological sense, referring to the source of ideas.

[23] See the famous fragment of the *Essay:* "Let us then *suppose* the mind to be, as we say, white paper, void of all characters, without any ideas" (E, II, 1, 2, p. 77, emphasis – A.G.).

[24] In short, by pointing to simple ideas of sense and simple ideas of reflection, one may perform a reconstruction of the origin of all concepts. This means, in turn, that experience alone in the original state – as an object of a basic operation, i.e. perception, is not diversified but is gradually becoming more complicated and structured.

[25] Here we need to make a clear distinction between the origins of concepts and their functions. The reconstructive procedures described in Book Two of the *Essay* are designed to show how empirical concepts are formed (in this sense the reconstruction is psychological in nature and involves the division into simple and complex ideas). On the other hand, however, the division into ideas of substance, trends and relations, though having a reconstructable psychological origin, points to the different functions that these concepts fulfil in cognition (as a basis for judgments, or as definitions that can be assigned to them). In the light of the problematique of the critical character of Locke's philosophy discussed in this paper, it is important to make a distinction between the psychological origin of concepts and their epistemological function, as it partly allows us to invalidate the accusation that Locke fails to distinguish the material and formal component of knowledge, due to which Locke's concept may be regarded as a foretoken of Kantian criticism (see: Jakuszko 2011, pp. 221–223).

[26] In concord with the etymology (lat. *in-premo*), Locke understands impressions as the effect of an external action. Hence, we may speak of an impression as of corporeal effects of the activity of external bodies, or – what Locke rejects – an innate inscription, given to us from God, imprinted in the human heart (Locke 1990, pp. 138 ff.).

convictions to universal validity, the exact same allegation can be made against experience. The identification of particular components of experience, i.e. ideas, is always concerned with an experience of an individual person. However, the point is that, unlike beliefs, e.g. religious ones, in the case of experience one can point to the conditions of their communicability: certainly not in the sense that we will make certain that the same simple sensory ideas will emerge in the minds of particular people but that the right way of communicating an experience will make such ideas indistinguishable from one another. Let us refer to an example presented by Locke.

> Were I to talk with any one of a sort of birds I lately saw in St. James's Park, about three or four feet high, with a covering of something between feathers and hair, of a dark brown colour, without wings, but in the place thereof two or three little branches coming down like sprigs of Spanish broom, long great legs, with feet only of three claws, and without a tail; I must make this description of it, and so may make others understand me: but when I am told that the name of it is cassuaris, I may then use that word to stand in discourse for all my complex ideas mentioned in that description (E, III, 6, 34, p. 498).

The condition of communication is the vocabulary which makes it possible to isolate particular constituents from the whole of experience. The use of the names of colours to describe the "dark brown" shade does not mean that two people have exactly the same sensory experience. Nevertheless, the fact that they use the same word to describe what they see or that they point to the same object makes it possible to say that these experiences do not differ from each other (what, however, could be done if suitable vocabulary was introduced to define colours).

The division of ideas into simple and complex ones allows us to reconstruct the process of creation of empirical concepts by indicating basic operations of reason, i.e. simple reflective ideas. The operations consisting in the isolation of particular elements of experience and reconnecting them through the operations of human understanding allow us to demonstrate how one can achieve complex ideas on the basis of simple ones. It also means that it is possible to abandon the subjectivity of one's own experience and construct concepts whose meaning and understanding will be shared by others.

Locke on human knowledge

Unlike personal experience, knowledge must be objective. Regardless of whether it can be attributed certainty, necessity, or probability, it must contain claims whose truth may be recognised by all the people who make use of their reason.

Thus, Locke must reconcile the objectivity of cognition with the assertion that the only direct objects of the human mind are its ideas: "the mind, in all its thoughts and reasoning, hath no other immediate object but its own ideas, which it alone does or can contemplate; it is evident, that our knowledge is only conversant about them" (E, IV, 1, 1, p. 58). Knowledge, ultimately related to the relations among ideas which are expressed in a language, is therefore a construct of the human mind, whose correct reproduction by other rational humans using language properly will be possible. However, whereas we know of our existence on the basis of direct intuition and of the existence of God – based on reasoning, of the existence of bodies we are informed through our sensory experience. The certainty of senses, "an evidence that puts us past doubting" (E, IV, 2, 14, p. 76), is, however, merely a conviction of the existence of "anything without us" (ibid.). Thus, the common-sense understanding of experience is reformulated[27] as the role of senses is not to present things but merely to stimulate the activity of the mind. All that enters the mind "from the outside" is its stimulation on the basis of which the concepts of things are generated (which corresponds to the claim that perception constitutes the rudimentary operation of the mind). Therefore, one may know what exists only on the basis of subsequent operations of the human reason; the understanding of things can be achieved both through memory (collecting of observations through memory) and postulating the essence of things through abstraction. But as we have already seen, in both cases, the cognition of nature is not certain. The reduction of an interaction of bodies to a mere stimulation of understanding, the assertion concerning the participation of reason in the construction of knowledge, and finally the conviction that an explanation of the relationship between the extended bodies composed of corpuscles and ideas is not determined by experience or science, all of this demonstrates that Locke's thought is strongly embedded in Car-

---

[27] In his *Essay*, Locke operates with three complementary concepts of experience, whose distinction allows an avoidance of the implied contradictions. In concord with the commonsense understanding of experience we may speak of an experience of natural bodies, other people, and in relation to religion, probably of a religious experience. However, the individual character of experiences urges us to question this kind of understanding and replace it with psychological one, which corresponds to Locke's analysis of ideas from Book II of the *Essay*. According to it, the only objects of experience are ideas (their kinds and relations between them). Finally, in philosophical sense, experience should be seen as a source of knowledge due to the empirical origin of concepts but also because of the psychological conditioning of its certainty in the act of intuition.

tesian metaphysics.[28] Nevertheless, while knowledge requires metaphysical grounding, it constitutes a necessary premise and not an object of knowledge itself. With regard to the Cartesian model of knowledge, whose truth is guaranteed by the coherence of mathematical calculus, and which does not undergo sensory verification, the empirically oriented cognition is each time "expanded" by new facts and observations. It needs to be complemented, reformulated, thus gaining a historical dimension.

Contrary to the knowledge of nature, the two other types of cognition, moral and mathematical, are endowed with certainty. In the first case, it is the meaning of moral terms (in Locke's terminology referred to as the mixed modes) that is the result of a combination of simple ideas fixed in a language. The adequacy of these terms lies in their purely mental nature, they do not refer to any other reality, and the assurance of moral assertions is based on the possibility of their syllogistic confirmation through knowledge of definitions. Thus, in the field of morality, says Locke, it is possible to build certain knowledge which is guaranteed through precise definition of terms, a correctly applied deductive procedure, and a proper use of language. The second example of certain knowledge based on the infallibility of intuition is mathematical knowledge. Even though it only allows establishing connections between ideas and not confirming the existence of things, it constitutes a model for the knowledge of nature.

However, there exists a possibility of combining both realms of knowledge: mathematics and speculative natural science. A very interesting mention on this subject matter is found in Locke's discussion of the corpuscular hypothesis as an explanation of the causes for different shades of whiteness with the motion of light particles:

> For supposing the sensation or idea we name whiteness be produced in us by a certain number of globules, which, having a verticity about their own centres, strike upon the retina of the eye, with a certain degree of rotation, as well as progressive swiftness; it will hence easily follow, that the more the superficial parts of any body are so ordered, as to reflect the greater number of globules of light, and to give them the proper rotation, which is fit to produce this sensation of white in us, the more white will that body appear, that from an equal space sends to the retina the greater number of such corpuscles, with that peculiar sort of motion.
>
> Whether then they be globules, or no; or whether they have a verticity about their own centres that produces the idea of whiteness in us: this is certain, that the more particles of light are reflected from a body, fitted to give them that peculiar motion, which produces the sen-

---

[28] See: "the original rules and communication of motion being such, wherein we can discover no natural connexion with any ideas we have; we cannot but ascribe them to the arbitrary will and good pleasure of the wise architect" (E, IV, 3, 29, p. 123).

sation of whiteness in us; and possibly too, the quicker that peculiar motion is; the whiter does the body appear, from which the greater number are reflected, as is evident in the same piece of paper put in the sun-beams, in the shade, and in a dark hole; in each of which it will produce in us the idea of whiteness in far different degrees (E, IV, 2, 10–12, pp. 74–75).

Hence, on the one hand, Locke postulates that all the qualitative differences should be explained by turning them into purely the quantitative ones, thus allowing an accurate differentiation of experience. At the same time, however, he expresses this postulate, which is characteristic of mathematical natural science, in a substantialist manner. That is exactly why the knowledge of the particles of matter would have to be acquired through senses – the existence of bodies can be confirmed only though sense experience. Experimental knowledge can only come close to such a state and its results based on the induction procedures may only be probable. Therefore, Locke assumes the possibility of achieving scientific advancement through the development of measuring techniques, implicitly assuming that the final structure of matter can be described with the use of mathematical language. However, he does not move beyond these intuitions, and the very idea of adopting a mathematic approach to natural sciences, as developed by Galileo and then by Newton, is rather alien to him.

Instead, following Bacon's footsteps and justifying the possibility of practicing experimental natural science in its both versions, descriptive and speculative, Locke engages in the criticism of language the proper functioning of which enables the accumulation of knowledge. Since there are no grounds to believe that the known classification of natural genera and species reflects a natural, everlasting order of things, the description of nature requires re-verification. Consequently, it is necessary to describe what directly appears in experience. That explains why amongst the most common mistakes that result from an abuse of words Locke includes the use of words deprived of a meaning when they fail to represent a clear idea (E, III, 10, 1–2, p. 22), the fluidity of meaning of the words used, the use of language for rhetorical purposes and the distortion of meaning of the terms used for practical purposes, and finally – the conviction of the adequacy of language and things being out of the mind. Any classification of natural beings and bodies is made on the basis of the empirical material available to researchers. This, in turn, due to the cumulative nature of cognition, leads Locke towards a postulate of an open character of knowledge and its universal availability. It is difficult to find a better justification for a new kind of knowledge, whose existence depended on the establishment of scientific societies and specialised journals.

Conclusions

The conception of ideas presented by Locke constitutes the basis for the main purpose of the *Essay*, i.e. the critique of knowledge: it points to the autonomy of scientific knowledge developed independently of metaphysics. Several conclusions that refer to the critical function of his philosophy can be drawn.

Firstly, Locke's critique manifests itself in his emphasis of the historical and social conditioning of knowledge. "The plain, historical method" (E, I, 1, 2, p. 2) that Locke uses, presents the history of human reason on three complementary grounds: individual (the development of experience whose reconstruction is presented within the conception of ideas), descriptive natural sciences (natural histories) and speculative philosophy of nature, which, being susceptible to falsifying procedures, also develops in a historical order (in the *Essay* such subsequent concepts are the Aristotelian concept of substantial forms, the Cartesian concept, the seventeenth-century corpuscularism, and the briefly mentioned Newtonian physics). Although learning about nature aims at achieving its comprehensive description, neither cumulative natural history nor falsifiable speculative philosophy of nature can provide full and definitive knowledge. With regard to nature, cognition does not meet the requirements imposed on certain knowledge; the universal validity of natural science is historically limited.

Secondly, although what is placed in Locke's centre of interest is the descriptive natural science, still his theory opens up the possibility for criticism concerning mathematical natural sciences. This is indicated not only by his theory of corpuscles reduced to quantifiable characteristics, but also by the implication of intuitive certainty of mathematical cognition. Although Locke himself had no mathematical education and expressed the difference between Descartes and Newton's philosophy of nature in qualitative and metaphysical categories and not as a difference between classical mechanics and the new dynamics of fluids, still the criticism of mathematical cognition of nature does not so much constitute a negation of Locke's critique, as it is its supplementation and development.

Thirdly, Locke does not involve in a transcendental deduction and his empirical deduction does not allow for the separation of the material and formal elements of cognition. Thus, it cannot be said that the critique constitutes an earlier, less perfect form of Kant's critical philosophy which examines the universal validity of cognition on the example of mathematical natural science derived from Newton. Nonetheless, the distinction between metaphysical notions (such as soul, God, matter) from experience and cognition is a step forward from substantialist metaphysics towards Kantian critical philosophy. Although in this matter Locke is, at the very least, inconsistent and recognises the possibility of intuitive cognition of consciousness and the existence of God, still the distinction between a personal identity founded on experience and memory and substantive subject, as well as opening of the possibility of a transition from substantialist metaphysics (in which Locke remains) to functionalist understanding of cognition where the meaning of concepts is determined through the functions they fulfil, is the foretoken of Kant's later critical philosophy.[29]

Bibliography

Anstey, Peter (2011): *John Locke* and Natural History, Oxford, New York: Oxford University Press.
Ashworth, William B. Jr., (1990): "Natural History and the Emblematic World View". In: David C. Lindberg, Robert S. Westman (eds.): *Reappraisals of the Scientific Revolution*. Cambridge–New York–Port Chester–Melbourne–Sydney: Cambridge University Press, pp. 303–332.
Axtell, James L. (1965): "Locke's Review of the 'Principia'". *Notes and Records of the Royal Society of London*" 20, 2, pp. 152–161.
Axtell, James L. (1991): "Locke, Newton, and the 'Elements of Natural Philosophy'". In: Richard Arcraft (ed.): *John Locke. Critical Assessments*. London, New York: Routledge. Vol. 4, pp. 419–429.
Berkeley, George (1948): "An Essay towards a New Theory of Vision". In: In: A. A. Luce, T. E. Jessop (eds.)*The Works of George Berkeley Bishop of Cloyne*. London: Thomas Nelson. Vol. 1, pp. 143–239.
Berkeley, George (1949): "A Treatise concerning the Principles of Human Knowledge". In: A. A. Luce, T. E. Jessop (eds.): *The Works of George Berkeley Bishop of Cloyne*. London: Thomas Nelson. Vol. 2, pp. 3–113.
Eamon, William (1990): "From the Secrets of Nature to Public Knowledge". In: In: David C. Lindberg, Robert S. Westman (eds.): *Reappraisals of the Scientific Revolution*. Cambridge–New York–Port Chester–Melbourne–Sydney: Cambridge University Press, pp. 333–365.
Lindberg, David C., Westman, Robert S. (eds.) (1990): *Reappraisals of the Scientific Revolution*. Cambridge–New York–Port Chester–Melbourne–Sydney Cambridge University Press.
Gaukroger, Stephen (2006): *The Emergence of s Scientific Culture. Science and the Shaping of Modernity 1210 – 1685*. Oxford: Oxford University Press.
Gaukroger, Stephen/Schuster, John/Sutton, John (eds.) (2000): *Descartes' Natural Philosophy*. London – New York: Routledge.
Grzeliński, Adam (2016): "John Locke i The Royal Society of London". In: Barbara Grabowska, Adam Grzeliński, Jolanta Żelazna (eds.): *Znaczenie Filozofii Oświecenia. Człowiek wśród ludzi*. Toruń: WN UMK, pp. 255–278.

---

[29] This research was carried out as a part of a National Science Centre (NCN) grant in Poland (UMO-2012/07/B/HS1/01619).

Jakuszko, Honorata (2011): "John Locke jako prekursor krytycyzmu Kanta". In: Jolanta Żelazna (ed.): *Filozofia XVII wieku. Twórcy, problem, kontynuacje.* Toruń: WN UMK.
Locke, John (1824): *An Essay Concerning Human Understanding.* In: *The Works of John Locke*, London: Printed for C. and J. Rivington, vol. 1–2.
Locke, John (1990): *Questions concerning the Law of Nature.* Transl. Robert Horwitz, Jenny S. Clay, Diskin Clay, Ithaca, London: Cornell University Press.
Talbot, Ann (2010): *The Great Ocean of Knowledge. The Influence of Travel Literature on the Work of John Locke.* Leiden, Boston: Brill.
Walmsley, Jonathan C. (2008): *John Locke's Natural Philosophy 1632–1704* (https://core.ac.uk/download/pdf/74250.pdf, accessed 1.7.2017).
Walmsley, Peter (2003): *Locke's 'Essay' and the Rhetoric of Science.* Lewisburg, London: Bucknell University Press – Associated University Presses.
Woolhouse, Roger (2009): *Locke. A Biography.* New York: Cambridge University Press.
Yolton, John (1956): *John Locke and His Way of Ideas.* Oxford: Oxford University Press.

Tomasz Kubalica
The Old and New Critique of Pure Reason based on Immanuel Kant and Jakob Friedrich Fries

Abstract: The critical method presented by Immanuel Kant in his three most important Critiques (*Kritik der reinen Vernunft*, *Kritik der praktischen Vernunft* and *Kritik der Urteilskraft*) was to have become the basis of a new philosophy. The first *Critique* attempts to separate speculation from the contributions of pure reason to knowledge, and the other critiques show its practical and theoretical consequences. Kant's critical philosophy was to have developed into a new philosophy but quickly became the subject of criticism. This study presents one of the first philosophical revisions of his critique in Jakob Friedrich Fries' *Neue Kritik der Vernunft* and tries to compare both models of philosophical criticism. I argue that critical philosophy after Kant have begun to live its own life and manifests its own dynamics.

Keywords: critique, reason, Immanuel Kant, Jakob Friedrich Fries

In the centre of Kantian and post-Kantian philosophy, there is a critique which plays a fundamental role in contemporary philosophical thought. The idea of critical philosophy, developed from German Idealism through neo-Kantianism to post-neo-Kantianism, directly or indirectly influenced the shape of modern philosophy (cf. Noras 2012, p. 51; Krijnen 2015). Although the importance of contemporary criticism has its philosophical origins in Immanuel Kant's *Critique of Pure Reason*, it has not retained its original form and has undergone many transformations. Tracing all these transformations of the meaning of criticism is beyond the scope of this study. Instead, we will concentrate on one of the first transformations that took place in the philosophy of Jakob Friedrich Fries. Our starting point is the meaning of criticism in Kant's *Critique of Pure Reason*, and the reference point will be the meaning of critique as modified by Fries. As a result, we hope to arrive at a comparison of the two ways of understanding criticism.

Kant's Critique

Philosophical criticism is defined by Kant in his first main work *Critique of Pure Reason* as the self-criticism of reason:

> I do not mean by this [Critique of Pure Reason – T.K.] a critique of books and systems, but of the faculty of reason in general, in respect of all knowledge after which it may strive independently of all experience. It will therefore decide as to the possibility or impossibility of metaphysics in general, and determine its sources, its extent, and its limits all in accordance with principles (Kant 1929, A XII).

Kant tries to explain what philosophical criticism is and what it is not. It does not consist in the practice of analysing, classifying, interpreting, or evaluating philosophical works. Neither does it amount to the immanent or transcendent critique of other philosophical systems.

Kant offers two complementary types of the meaning of criticism, which we can identify as the epistemological and the metaphysical one. Criticism in the epistemological sense means the delimitation of rational knowledge. This type of critique relates to reason as a rule, especially to its power and ability for knowledge that is independent of experience. Kant uses universal quantifiers twice here. He refers not to any knowledge of reason but to all its knowledge. And he speaks not of knowledge independent of any experience but of knowledge independent of all experience. Kant assumes that reason is standing behind all kinds of knowledge. Nevertheless, criticism has to define the limits of rational knowledge determined by knowledge based on any experience. In other words, this epistemological concept of criticism implies the following question: May reason in general lead up to obtaining knowledge that is independent of all experience?

By contrast, criticism in the metaphysical sense implies the question of the possibility or impossibility of metaphysics in general. Kant's understanding of metaphysics was mainly influenced by Leibniz-Wolffian views, which were prevalent in Germany at that time. From this tradition comes the distinction between the *metaphysica generalis* as ontology and the *metaphysica specialis*, dealing with different realms of being, namely God, the world, and the human. Kant's problem of metaphysics had its source in the philosophy of the Enlightenment, which questioned metaphysics from the point of view of British empiricism and the natural sciences. What is important here is his second essay from 1791, entitled *What Real Progress Has Metaphysics Made in Germany Since the Time of Leibniz and Wolff?* (Kant 1983), where he comes to the conclusion that metaphysics requires a critique of pure reason. Thus, Kant's intention is to lead metaphysics from the dogmatic and sceptical phase to the critical one.

At this point, we should raise the issue of the relation between Kant's two types of meaning of criticism. I assume that they are not contradictory but complementary in such a way that epistemology determines the limits of metaphysics, especially its sources and extent, with reference to its principles. This issue, however, is beyond the scope of this paper.

Even in the title of the *Critique of Pure Reason*, the two meanings of the concept of criticism become apparent. The genitive (*der*) can be understood as both object genitive and subject genitive, so it denotes both a critique of reason and a critique by reason. This ambiguity was probably consciously introduced by Kant because reason can turn itself into the highest cognitive faculty of self-criticism. In this sense, we can find in his text the concept of the tribunal of pure reason (Kant 1929, A 751/ B 779). Kant presents the critique of pure reason as a tribunal which is to judge the illusory knowledge of metaphysics:

> It is a call to reason to undertake anew the most difficult of all its tasks, namely, that of self-knowledge, and to institute a tribunal which will assure to reason its lawful claims, and dismiss all groundless pretensions, not by despotic decrees, but in accordance with its own eternal and unalterable laws (Kant 1929, A XI / A XII).

Reason must know itself on the basis of laws that allow it to settle which claims are legitimate and which are groundless. The situation is complicated because reason has to judge reason on the basis of reasoning rules.

If metaphysics is to find "the sure road to science" (Kant 1929, B XV), it has to eliminate "a battle-field of these endless controversies" (Kant 1929, A VIII) by way of a critique of pure reason, turning to it as the true tribunal for all its disputes. The critique can become the tribunal because it "is not involved in these disputes – disputes which are concerned with objects – but is directed to the determining and estimating of the rights of reason in general, in accordance with the principles of their first institution" (Kant 1929, A 751 / B 779). The tribunal of reason refers directly not to the objects but only to the rules of reason and therefore keeps its controversies in perspective. The process of reason does not progress like war (in the polemical use of reason), with a dubious victory of one side, but consists in the critical judgment of reason.

Kant associates criticism with antinaturalistic position when he affirms that:

> In the absence of this critique reason is, as it were, in the state of nature, and can establish and secure its assertions and claims only through war (Kant 1929, A 751 / B 779).

Kant opposes the naive image of the state of nature as a state of harmony; like Hobbes, he believes that "the state of nature is a state of injustice and violence" (Kant 1929, A 752 / B 780). In the state of nature, war is the only means of recognition and acceptance of assertions and claims. Due to the above, we have to leave the state of nature and submit to law, which admittedly limits our freedom, but simultaneously enables it, as well as the freedom of other people. The antinaturalistic abandonment of the state of nature also allows for the obtaining of the common good of all.

Criticism is the opposite of the warlike state of nature, and it gives the fundament for the recognition of its own position because it can secure peace in the following way:

> The critique [...] arriving at all its decisions in the light of fundamental principles of its own institution, the authority of which no one can question, secures to us the peace of a legal order, in which our disputes have to be conducted solely by the recognised methods of legal action (Kant 1929, A 751 / B 779).

Fundamental and unquestionable principles are the basis for the critical settlement of a dispute. Criticism alone determines the principle of peaceful and legal process leading up to the settlement of a controversy. Kant believes that, contrary to the warlike state of nature, criticism can implement peaceful methods of settling disputes.

In the state of nature, a discussion ends with the defeat of one of the sides, but after such a victory, the defeated side demands revenge, and so the state of peace is only temporary. In nature, one side must lose so that the other could win, and there is no chance of eternal peace. However, criticism ensures "a judicial sentence" which gets to "the very root of the conflicts" and extinguishes them forever. In contrast to nature, only a critical culture can provide eternal peace. Moreover, Kant associates naturalism with the dogmatism of reason, as opposed to the self-criticism of reason. While nature compels reason to battle against other standpoints, criticism, which is identified with culture and civilisation, encourages reason to seek peace and harmony. Reason finds peace through criticism of itself and establishes this peace on the basis of its laws.

The interpretation of Kant's concept of critique presented above requires further comment. If we identify dogmatic conflict with the state of nature, then we must consider more types of possible interactions. In the state of nature, every organism must come into contact with other organisms. Ecology knows not only antagonistic but also non-antagonistic interactions. Kant's description refers mainly to two interactions: (1) competition, in which both organisms are harmed; and (2) predation, in which a predator feeds on its prey. Unfortunately, Kant omits the other three kinds of adversarial interactions: (3) parasitism, where the parasite benefits at the expense of the host; (4) allelopathy, a usually negative chemical effect on the growth or development of an organism of one species;

and (5) amensalism, in which one organism is harmed or inhibited while the other is unaffected. This approach also ignores non-adversarial interactions, such as (6) symbiosis, a relationship of mutual benefit or dependence; (7) commensalism, where one organism benefits from the other without affecting it; and (8) neutralism, a relationship in which neither side is affected. A reflection on the complex interactions in the state of nature could contribute a lot to the discussion on naturalistic dogmatism. This interactionist analysis could later be extended from the state of nature to the critique in order to present the types of interaction that reason enters when it appears before the tribunal of its principles.

Kant separates the critique from dogmatism and, likewise, the critique from scepticism, but not from "the dogmatic procedure of reason in its pure knowledge, as science, for that must always be dogmatic, that is, yield strict proof from sure principles a priori" (Kant 1929, XXXV). It is not the dogmatism of exact sciences that is problematic, but metaphysical dogmatism which is based on groundless claims to derive knowledge from concepts "without previous criticism of its own powers." For similar reasons, Kant rejects scepticism, which also groundlessly questions all metaphysics. Scepticism is based on "a principle of technical and scientific ignorance, which undermines the foundations of all knowledge, and strives in all possible ways to destroy its reliability and steadfastness" (Kant 1929, A 424/ B 451). Kant rejects anti-metaphysical scepticism but does not reject the sceptical method, which he presents as part of his criticism:

> For the sceptical method aims at certainty. It seeks to discover the point of misunderstanding in the case of disputes which are sincerely and competently conducted by both sides, just as from the embarrassment of judges in cases of litigation wise legislators contrive to obtain instruction regarding the defects and ambiguities of their laws (Kant 1929, A 424 B 451–452).

Criticism of reason must use the sceptical method in search of certainty. This also means, however, that the sceptical method is appropriate only in transcendental philosophy and that in other fields of knowledge it is perhaps dispensable.

In the context of Pyrrho's scepticism, Kant deals with the question of the zetetic method in metaphysics, which is understood as an activity of investigation and inquiry (Forster 2010, p. 18). In the pre-critical phase of his philosophy, Kant describes his doubts as zetetic in the following way:

> Der Zweifel den ich annehme ist nicht dogmatisch sondern ein Zweifel des Aufschubs. Zetetici (zetesin) Sucher (Kant 1998a, 175).

> The doubt that I accept is . . . a doubt of postponement. Zetetici (zetein), Seekers (Forster 2010, pp. 100–101).

Kant is aware of the problematic nature of metaphysics and undertakes to study it in a zetetic way, which means proceeding by inquiry, later transformed into a critical procedure. Likewise, in *Reflexionen* from the 1770s, he makes a similar remark about applying the equipollence method to metaphysics:

> In der Critik der Metaphysik kan man sich zweyerley methoden bedienen. Die erste ist: die Beweise zu examiniren und ihre paralogismos oder petitiones principii aufzusuchen Die zweyte: einem Beweise einen andern und zwar eben so überzeugenden des Gegentheils zu opponiren. Diese letzte methode ist die beste.

> In the critique of metaphysics two methods can be used. The first one is: to examine the evidence and to seek their paralogism or petitiones principii. The second one: to oppose two convincing proofs. This last method is the best. (Kant 1998b, 557 (Reflex. Nr. 4454), translation mine).

Thus, in the context of criticism, Kant analyses the method of examining the evidence of metaphysics and the method of equipollence, that is, Pyrrho's method. Due to the empirical non-verifiability of metaphysics, he comes to the conclusion that the sceptical approach is the best.

In the light of the above-mentioned conception, the critique does not refer to objects, but to concepts. In other words, it does not concern the objects of metaphysics, such as God, freedom, and immortality, but first and foremost the adequacy of human faculties to embrace them. Consequently, Kant focuses on the principles of a priori knowledge in order to find "an organon of pure reason," which means "the sum-total of those principles according to which all modes of pure a priori knowledge can be acquired and actually brought into being" (Kant 1929, A 11/ B 24–25). This is not "a system of pure reason," which is "still doubtful," but exactly the critique of pure reason that is only "the propaedeutic to the system of pure reason," meaning "a science of the mere examination of pure reason, of its sources and limits." In contradistinction to the doctrine (theory) of a system of pure reason, the critique can only clarify our reason and keep it free from errors. This means that the utility of the critique as the propaedeutic is only negative in speculation.

As a result, Kant clarifies that his criticism is the transcendental criticism:

> It is upon this enquiry, which should be entitled not a doctrine, but only a transcendental critique, that we are now engaged. Its purpose is not to extend knowledge, but only to correct it, and to supply a touchstone of the value, or lack of value, of all a priori knowledge (Kant 1929, A 12 / B 26).

Knowledge in Kant's meaning of the term can by transcendental only when it is "occupied not so much with objects as with the mode of our knowledge of objects in so far as this mode of knowledge is to be possible a priori." The justification of transcendental knowledge does not depend on experience because it should be general and necessary, whereas experience is neither general nor logically necessary. The transcendental critique should assess the possibility of reason to unconditionally obtain a priori-rational knowledge from mere concepts. This destructive function of the critique of reason is presented by Kant as transcendental dialectics, whose task is only "exposing the illusion of transcendent judgments, and at the same time taking precautions that we be not deceived by it" (Kant 1929, A 297/ B 354). Transcendental dialectics cannot disperse this illusion because "we have to do with a natural and inevitable illusion, which rests on subjective principles, and foists them upon us as objective" (Kant 1929, A 298/ B 354). Therefore, criticism convinces us of our natural limitations. This is the negative use of the critique: to reduce all the baseless arrogations of speculative reason if it ventures beyond the limits of experience. This negative function of the critique of the theoretical use of reason enables its positive implementation for the practical use of reason:

> So far, therefore, as our Critique limits speculative reason, it is indeed negative; but since it thereby removes an obstacle which stands in the way of the employment of practical reason, nay threatens to destroy it, it has in reality a positive and very important use. At least this is so, immediately we are convinced that there is an absolutely necessary practical employment of pure reason the moral in which it inevitably goes beyond the limits of sensibility. Though [practical] reason, in thus proceeding, requires no assistance from speculative reason, it must yet be assured against its opposition, that reason may not be brought into conflict with itself (Kant 1929, B XXV).

Kant compares the negative use of criticism to the function of the police, whose main task is to protect citizens from violence. Only when citizens are protected against abuse, can they lead their normal lives.

However, critical transcendental dialectics cannot simply avoid the semblance of transcendental judgements of rational psychology, cosmology, and theology. Therefore, criticism must be regarded as a permanent task, because there exists in the state of nature "a natural and unavoidable dialectic of pure reason," which means, "one inseparable from human reason, and which, even after its deceptiveness has been exposed, will not cease to play tricks with reason and continually entrap it into momentary aberrations ever and again calling for correction" (Kant 1929, A 298 / B 354–5). Reason is not perfect, and criticism is a constant struggle with its natural inclinations.

In the context of the Kantian notion of critique, Werner Flach raises an important question, namely, why he uses the notion of critique instead of the notion of transcendental philosophy in his three works (Flach 1967). Flach finds the answer in Chapter VII, "Idee und Einteilung einer besonderen Wissenschaft, unter dem Namen einer Kritik der reinen Vernunft" (The Idea and Division of a Special Science, under the title Critique of Pure Reason), of *Kritik der reinen Vernunft* (*Critique of Pure Reason*) (Kant 1929, A10/B24–A22/B36). On this basis, he concludes that the meaning of "Critique" was conditioned by the concept of transcendental knowledge, and thus also of transcendental philosophy, so that this kind of knowledge is subsumed in the critique. Transcendental philosophy and critique are complementary:

> Die Transzendentalphilosophie, die Prinzipientheorie des Denkens, die Wissenschaft der Letztbegründung, schließt notwendig die ‚Kritik', die Wissenschaft des Letztbegründungsgedankens als solchen selbst und nur des Letztbegründungsgedankens als solchen selbst ein.
>
> Transcendental philosophy, the principle theory of thought, the science of the ultimate foundation, necessarily includes the 'critique', the science of the ultimate foundation as such, and only the ultimate foundation as such (Flach 1967, p. 76).

Transcendental philosophy is a theory of principles of thought and contains the foundation of the science of the ultimate foundation. On the other hand, the critique is the science of the ultimate foundation as such and the realisation of the ultimate foundation.

Kant separates the critique of practical reason from the critique of theoretical reason. The concept of a "critique of pure practical reason" appears for the first time in *Grundlegung zur Metaphysik der Sitten* (1785) and later in *Kritik der praktischen Vernunft* (1788). The critique of practical reason is in fact not as urgent as that of speculative reason, "because in what is moral human reason, even in the most common understanding, can easily be brought to great correctness and completeness, whereas in its theoretical but pure use it is entirely dialectical" (Kant 2002b, 4:391); nevertheless, it needs its own critique. The task of a complete *Critique of Practical Reason* consists in the identification of the unity of theoretical and practical reason. In the second *Kritik*, there is pure practical reason, as a fact exempted from criticism:

> Hence the critique of practical reason as such has the obligation to keep the empirically conditioned reason from presuming to seek to provide, alone and exclusively, the determining basis of the will (Kant 2002a, 5:16).

In comparison to the critical theory of principles of speculative reason, the critique of practical reason positively states "the principles of this power's possibility, of its range and bounds, without particular reference to human nature"(Kant 2002a, 5:8). Here Kant presents the system of criticism rather than the system of science.

The third concept of criticism is presented by Kant in *Kritik der Urteilskraft* (1790). His *Critique of Judgment*, also translated as the *Critique of the Power of Judgment*, closes the critical project which was begun in the *Critique of Pure Reason* and continued in the *Critique of Practical Reason*. It shows that the term "critique of pure reason" has now a narrower and a broader meaning: in the strict sense, Kant designates the critique of pure understanding as the first *Critique*, and in the broad sense, as the three-part concept of the critique of pure understanding, pure judgement, and pure reason (Kant 1987, 167–168). In the first part of *Critique of Judgment*, Kant analyses the peculiarity of the judgement of taste (*Geschmacksurteil*), which claims a special form of universal validity, and in his critical justification of aesthetics, he examines the validity of aesthetic judgement:

> Hence a judgement of taste is not a cognitive judgement and so is not a logical judgement but an aesthetic one, by which we mean a judgement whose determining basis cannot be other than subjective (Kant 1987, 203).

Whoever is capable of aesthetic judgements about beauty, proves capable of the judgement of taste. With regard to the critique of taste, Kant now distinguishes between the science of transcendental criticism, which develops and justifies the a priori principle of the power of judgement itself, and the mere act of critically evaluating products of fine art according to empirical (physiological and, in this case, psychological) rules of taste (Kant 1987, 286).

With the *Critique of the Power of Judgment* Kant closes his "entire critical enterprise" and "proceeds without delay to the doctrinal one" of the "metaphysics of nature and that of morals" (Kant 1987, 170). His criticism was undertaken by his self-proclaimed successors, such as Johann Gottlieb Fichte and his critique in *Versuch einer Critik aller Offenbarung* (1792). However, Kant distanced himself from Fichte's concept of criticism in his *Erklärung in Beziehung auf Fichtes Wissenschaftslehre* (7 Aug. 1799), which he concluded on a pessimistic note with these words:

> Aber demungeachtet muß die kritische Philosophie sich durch ihre unaufhaltbare Tendenz zu Befriedigung der Vernunft in theoretischer sowohl als moralisch praktischer Absicht überzeugt fühlen, daß ihr kein Wechsel der Meynungen, keine Nachbesserungen oder ein anders geformtes Lehrgebäude bevorstehe, sondern das System der Critik auf einer völ-

> lig gesicherten Grundlage ruhend, auf immer befestigt, und auch für alle künftige Zeitalter zu den höchsten Zwecken der Menschheit unentbehrlich sey.
>
> However, this critical philosophy must feel convinced by its unstoppable tendency to satisfaction of reason in both theoretical and practical moral intention that it will be affected by no change in opinions, no improvements, nor a differently shaped edifice of knowledge, but that the system of critique rests on a completely secure foundation, fixed forever, and that it is indispensable for all future ages to the highest purposes of humanity (Kant 2008, 12:371, translation mine).

Kant was clearly disappointed with the continuation of criticism in the spirit of German idealism, and this leads to the question of the way his criticism was continued by Fries.

Fries' Conception of the Critique

Fries makes an attempt to repeat Kant's critique of reason from a different perspective as early as in 1807 in the work *Neue Kritik der Vernunft (New Critique of Pure Reason)*. His criticism has the form of "philosophical anthropology" that starts with self-observation and studies reason empirically, according to the general laws of our inner life. Like Kant's, this critique should also assess philosophical knowledge (cf. Kubalica 2017, p. 43).

Parallel to the conception of epistemology of German idealism, Fries' conception of critique – with respect to Kant's legacy – evolves in the direction that interprets knowledge as a kind of mental activity. Fries lays the foundation for this interpretation, assuming that the critique of reason can explore a priori structures of knowledge through inner experience. He describes the nature of his critical method in the discussion of metaphysics:

> Nach diesen Ansichten ist die Kritik der Vernunft eine auf Selbstbeobachtung ruhende Erfahrungswissenschaft. Unsere Methode läßt daher Beobachtung und Erfahrung an die Stelle der metaphysischen Abstractionen und deren treten.
>
> According to these views, the critique of reason is an empirical science that is grounded in self-observation. Our method therefore allows observation and experience to replace metaphysical abstractions (...) (Fries 1824c, p. 110, translation mine).

In contrast to metaphysical speculation, Fries justifies the criticism of reason with the inner experience of self-observation. Fries' critique is, in fact, a kind of psychology or anthropology, but understood as rational psychology rather than empirical psychology (Brandt 2002, p. 21).

Fries' texts provide no substantial arguments for the psychologist interpretation. He situates himself in Kantian tradition when he writes:

> Die eigentlichen Formen des Wissens selbst sind vielmehr dasjenige, was Kant synthetische Erkenntnisse a priori nennt.
>
> The appropriate forms of knowledge themselves are rather what Kant calls the synthetic knowledge a priori (Fries 1824b, p. 97, translation mine).

In this context, Fries understands the critique of reason as a systematic knowledge of the organisation of reason. Elsewhere, he speaks of psychological anthropology and observes that, as "the scientific preparation of all philosophy," it should be considered a philosophical anthropology (Fries 1824a, p. 13). However, some connections between philosophy and psychology are required, and one should ask whether this is really an expression of psychologism.

As early as in 1798, Fries publishes a text entitled *Über das Verhältnis der empirischen Psychologie zur Metaphysik*, where he shows his attitude towards psychology (Brandt 2002, pp. 19f.). He comes to the following conclusion:

> Das Erkennen und folglich die Erkenntnisse sind also selbst Gegenstände der inneren Erfahrung, und daher der Psychologie, besonders deren empirischem Teil nach.
>
> Cognition and consequently knowledge are therefore themselves objects of inner experience, and therefore of psychology, especially of its empirical part (Fries 1798, pp. 158–159, translation mine).

In this case, Fries analyses all cognitions from a psychological point of view, because they always refer to the subjective mind. Moreover, he states that an object of knowledge in this sense must be immediately cognised because it can always be an object of the subject of cognition. Fries understands Kant's turn in the philosophy of knowledge in such a way that it is no longer knowledge of an object that counts, but that it is an object that must be adapted to the subject of cognition. Thus, he interprets the Kantian turn as a rejection of the copy theory of knowledge (the pictorial theory of cognition). As a result, Fries recognises the psychological nature of the difference between an appearance and a thing-in-itself. However, he needs such an understanding of psychology only as an introduction to critical metaphysics, because its principles cannot derive from any other science by deduction or by generalisation but can only be based in inner experience that could justify the foundation of synthetic judgements a priori. Fries makes the following ascertainment:

> Transzendentale Kritik ist also eine Wissenschaft aus empirisch psychologischen Erkenntnissen und zwar die Wissenschaft von der Art und Beschaffenheit unserer Erkenntnisse a priori.
>
> Transcendental criticism is therefore a science of empirical psychological knowledge and that is the science of the nature and characteristics of our knowledge a priori (Fries 1798, p. 201, translation mine).

Thus, critical transcendental philosophy could be the basis for a priori synthetic principles of the metaphysical system of philosophy. Fries explicitly distances himself from the concept of intellectual intuition of both his teachers, Fichte and Reinhold.

In 1807, one of Fries' most important works was published: *Neue Kritik der Vernunft* (*New Critique of Reason*) (Fries 1807), whose second edition from the years 1828 to 1931 appeared under the title *Neue oder anthropologische Kritik der Vernunft* (*New or Anthropological Critique of Reason*) (Fries 1828). The similarity of the title to Kant's work should not be understood as Kantian orthodoxy, as strongly emphasised in the preface to the first edition:

> Meine Fortsetzung vorzüglich der Aristotelischen und Kantischen Untersuchungen hat ihren Werth nur in den strengsten und engsten Forderungen der Wahrheit.
>
> My continuation in relation to Aristotelian and Kantian investigations has its value only in the strictest and narrowest demands of truth (Fries 1807, p. II, translation mine).

As a result of this declaration, Fries shows Kant's philosophy in its anthropological turn and finds that:

> Kant mit seiner transcendentalen Erkenntniß eigentlich die psychologische, oder besser anthropologische Erkenntniß meinte, wodurch wir einsehen, welche Erkenntnisse a priori unsere Vernunft besitzt, und wie sie in ihr entspringt.
>
> Kant understands his transcendental knowledge as, in fact, psychological, or anthropological knowledge in which we see which cognitions our reason has a priori, and how they arise in it (Fries 1807, pp. XXXV–XXXVI, translation mine).

In Kant's position, Fries notices a rationalist superstition, which consists in the fact that Kant reduced transcendental knowledge to a priori knowledge and "misunderstood their empirical and psychological nature." In this connection, Michelet correctly observes that: "Fries wants to clearly express the subjectively-empirical, anthropological essence of transcendental knowledge" (Michelet 1837, p. 413, translation mine). Fries is therefore developing a philosophical anthropology that is aimed at the study of human cognitive abilities. For this reason, in his opinion, philosophy must be expanded to psychology so that each epistemological study should start from psychological facts (Eisler 1895, p. 33).

Not only is Fries' philosophical anthropology not empirical psychology, but also the method adopted in the *Neue Kritik der Vernunft* is not an induction method. Psychological induction is only a starting point, but it is not sufficient to the critique of reason. Fries relies on the following belief:

> Die richtige Lehre von der Schlußkraft der Inductionen führt also [...] selbst über die Erfahrungsphilosophie hinaus und zeigt, daß alle Inductionen nur durch vorausgesetzte nothwendige Wahrheiten der Mathematik und Metaphysik gültig werden.
>
> The correct doctrine of induction leads thus beyond the philosophy of experience, and shows that all inductions are valid only by the presupposed necessary truths of mathematics and metaphysics (Fries 1824c, pp. 186–187, translation mine).

These general principles of metaphysics (and also mathematics) should obtain their justification by deduction (see: Elsenhans 1902, p. 26). We must show by deduction how every principle can arise from the nature of reason. For Fries, Kant's major mistake was that he did not notice the difference between deduction and proof because of the prejudice of the Leibniz-Wolff philosophy. Kant did not think that we must first have some premises of our conclusions, such as higher truths, in order to be able to prove them; therefore, he negated the speculative validity of ideas because they cannot have transcendental evidence. For Fries, these higher truths can be grounded only by deduction (cf. Fries 1824c, p. 449). The new critique of reason is different from the old critique with regard to the understanding of deduction, which for Fries is not only anthropological in character, but also extends to the categories as well as to the ideas of reason because they cannot prove anything and should be derived from the nature of reason. The difference between the old and new critique is thus refined and methodological in nature.

According to Fries, transcendental knowledge in the critique of reason must be identical with philosophical-critical knowledge from inner experience (cf. Elsenhans 1906, p. 4). Fries accuses Kant of the following error in his understanding of the critique of reason:

> [...] liegt im Kantischen System ein unüberwindlicher Widersinn, indem durch die Apriorität der transzendentalen Erkenntnis die innere Wahrnehmung selbst zur Erkenntnis a priori gemacht wird, und so anstatt des Kantischen transzendentalen Idealismus ein absurder empirischer Idealismus herauskäme, nach welchem das Ich nicht nur Schöpfer seiner Welt, sondern sogar seiner selbst würde.
>
> [...] in the Kantian system there is an insuperable nonsense, in which the inner perception itself, by a priori status of the transcendental knowledge, becomes a priori knowledge, and

instead of Kantian transcendental idealism, there comes absurd empirical idealism, according to which the ego would be the creator not only of his world, but even of himself (Fries 1828, pp. 29–30, translation mine).

Thus, Fries accepts that the philosophical knowledge of principles must be universal and necessary. Nevertheless, he adds that the possibility of this a priori knowledge cannot come from itself, but only from inner perception.

Among the followers of Kant, Fries was the one who most definitely asserted that the task of the criticism of reason was psychological and anthropological, and that it could be solved only by inner experience (Eggeling 1875, p. 9). Fries' concept of the critique of reason demands a theory of reason based on inner experience, which can determine the fundamental elements of human knowledge to show the forms of self-activity of reason. Deduction as understood by Fries is thus to show the origin of the concepts and judgements a priori in the mind. This kind of deduction rests on the doctrine of apperception and was thoroughly developed by Fries for all a priori principles as well as for categories and ideas in his anthropological critique of reason.

Our comparison of the concepts of the critique by Kant and Fries shows the inner potential and dynamics of critical philosophy, whose assumptions were thoroughly analysed and modified shortly after their emergence. Kantian criticism, limited by the narrowly understood deduction of the category of reason, was clarified by Fries and extended to the metaphysical ideas of reason. Shortly after the first critiques, it turned out that the process of rational evaluation of the possibility of reason must be carried out once again on the basis of anthropological assumptions. The new critique of reason demonstrates that the former one was based on non-critical grounds and therefore requires a far-reaching revision. The polemic with the tradition of German Idealism, which developed the foundations of Kantian philosophy, was also an important context for the genesis of the new critique. However, an analysis of the relationship between the Friesian School and German Idealism is beyond the scope of this paper.

Bibliography

Brandt, Andreas (2002): *Ethischer Kritizismus: Untersuchungen zu Leonard Nelsons 'Kritik der praktischen Vernunft' und ihren philosophischen Kontexten*. Göttingen: Vandenhoeck & Ruprecht.

Eggeling, Heinrich (1875): *Kant und Fries. Die anthropologische Auffassung der Kritik der Vernunft in ihren wesentlichen Punkten*. Braunschweig: Westermann.

Eisler, Rudolf (1895): *Die Weiterbildung der Kant'schen Apriorita̋tslehre Bis Zur Gegenwart. Ein Beitrag Zur Geschichte der Erkenntnistheorie*. Leipzig: Friedrich.

Elsenhans, Theodor (1902): *Das Kant-Friesische Problem. Das Habilitationschrift einer hochen philosophischen Fakultät der Universität Heidelberg zur Erlangung der vania legendi.* Heidelberg: Universitätsbuchdr. von J. Hörning.
Elsenhans, Theodor (1906): *Fries und Kant. Ein Beitrag zur Geschichte und zur systematischen Grundlegung der Erkenntnistheorie.* Giessen: Alfred Töpelmann.
Flach, Werner (1967): "Transzendentalphilosophie und Kritik. Zur Bestimmung des Verhältnisses der Titelbegriffe der Kantischen Philosophie". In: Wilhelm Arnold/Hermann Zeltner (Eds.): *Tradition und Kritik. Festschrift für Rudolf Zocher zum 80. Geburtstag.* Stuttgart-Bad Connstatt: Vico, pp. 69–83.
Forster, Michael N. (2010): *Kant and Skepticism.* Princeton: Princeton University Press.
Fries, Jakob Friedrich (1798): "Über das Verhältnis der empirischen Psychologie zur Metaphysik". *Psychologisches Magazin* 3, pp. 156–202.
Fries, Jakob Friedrich (1807): *Neue Kritik der Vernunft.* Vol. I. Heidelberg: Mohr und Zimmer.
Fries, Jakob Friedrich (1824a): *Grundriß der Metaphysik. Ein Lehrbuch zum Gebrauch für Schulen und Universitäten.* Heidelberg: Christian Friedrich Winter.
Fries, Jakob Friedrich (1824b): "Reinhold, Fichte und Schelling". In: *Jakob Friedrich Fries's polemische Schriften. Bd. 1. Enthaltend eine neue verbesserte und mit neuen Beylagen vermehrte Auflage der Schrift: Reinhold, Fichte und Schelling.* 2nd ed. Vol. 1. Halle und Leipzig: Reinicke und Comp.
Fries, Jakob Friedrich (1824c): *System der Metaphysik. Ein Handbuch für Lehrer und zum Selbstgebrauch.* Heidelberg: Winter.
Fries, Jakob Friedrich (1828): *Neue oder anthropologische Kritik der Vernunft.* Vol. I. Heidelberg: Christian Friedrich Winter.
Kant, Immanuel (1929): *Critique of Pure Reason.* Translated by Norman Kemp Smith. London: Macmillan.
Kant, Immanuel (1983): *What real progress has metaphysics made in Germany since the time of Leibniz and Wolff?* Translated by Ted Humphrey. New York: Abaris Books.
Kant, Immanuel (1987): *Critique of Judgment. Including the First Introduction.* Translated by Werner S. Pluhar. Indianapolis/Cambridge: Hackett Publishing Company.
Kant, Immanuel (1998a): "Bemerkungen zu den Beobachtungen über das Gefühl des Schönen und Erhabenen, Rostocker Kantnachlass, Preisschrift über die Fortschritte der Metaphysik". In: *Akademieausgabe von Immanuel Kants Gesammelten Werken. Handschriftlicher Nachlaß.* Electronic Edition. Berlin: Karsten Worm, XX: 1–192.
Kant, Immanuel (1998b): "Reflexionen zur Metaphysik". In: *Akademieausgabe von Immanuel Kants Gesammelten Werke. Handschriftlicher Nachlaß. Metaphysik Erster Teil.* Electronic Edition. Berlin: Karsten Worm, XVII: 227–745.
Kant, Immanuel (2002a): *Critique of practical reason.* Translated by Werner S. Pluhar. Indianapolis/Cambridge: Hackett Publishing Company.
Kant, Immanuel (2002b): *Groundwork for the Metaphysics of Morals.* Translated by Allen W. Wood. New Haven and London: Yale University Press.
Kant, Immanuel (2008): *Akademieausgabe von Immanuel Kants Gesammelten Werke. Briefwechsel Band III 1795–1803.* Vol. XII. Elektronische Edition. Berlin: Karsten Worm.
Krijnen, Christian (2015): "Kritik". In: Annika Ulrich, Christian Bermes and Ulrich Dierse (Eds.): *Schlüsselbegriffe der Philosophie des 19. Jahrhunderts. Archiv für Begriffsgeschichte. Sonderheft.* No. 11. Hamburg: Meiner Verlag, pp. 267–282.

Kubalica, Tomasz (2017): *Unmöglichkeit der Erkenntnistheorie Leonard Nelsons Kritik an der Erkenntnistheorie unter besonderer Berücksichtigung des Neukantianismus*. Frankfurt a.M.: Peter Lang.

Michelet, Ludwig (1837): *Geschichte der letzten Systeme der Philosophie im Deutschland von Kant bis Hegel. Erster Theil*. Vol. 1. Berlin: Duncker und Humblot.

Noras, Andrzej (2012): *Historia neokantyzmu*. Katowice: Wydawnictwo UŚ.

Andrzej J. Noras
Criticism as It Was Understood by Hermann Cohen

Abstract: This article undertakes the problem of criticism in the philosophy of Hermann Cohen, the founder of the Marburg School of Neo-Kantianism. The Marburg School ties philosophy with mathematics, while this text is an attempt to demonstrate the evolution of Cohen's views. The most interesting trait of this evolution is the fact that while Cohen begins as an advocate of psychologism, he ends as a radical anti-psychologist.

Keywords: Hermann Cohen, psychologism, science, criticism.

In 1877, Hermann Cohen published the first edition of his book dedicated to the foundation of ethics, in which the problem of criticism explicitly appears. This problem is simultaneously connected with the conception of science characteristic of Marburgian Neo-Kantianism, as Cohen accepted that a philosophy wishing to be Kantian had to be viewed as a science. Cohen's position evolved in the years following the first publication of *Kants Theorie der Erfahrung* (1871) and in 1877 Cohen was already a declared criticist, who gradually not so much rejected Kant as began interpreting his philosophy in light of science understood in the spirit of logicism. The change that occurred in Cohen's thought is accurately described by Eggert Winter, who writes:

> In "Kants Theorie der Erfahrung" war Cohen angetreten, um den historischen, den urkundlichen Kant gegen seine "Widerleger" zu behaupten, in "systematischer Parteinahme" sollten die "Zusammenhänge geschlossener Gedanken" erhellt werden. In "Kants Begründung der Ethik" macht sich Cohen gegen den Text selbständig, unternimmt er – "unbeirrt um den Verdacht, unberufener Weise Kants Name meinen Arbeiten überzuschreiben" – "gemäß der kritischen Methode und im Anschluß an Kants Worte, die selbständige Behandlung der philosophischen Probleme" (Winter 1980, p. 119).

This rather essential change in Cohen's perception of Kant's philosophy is not, however, radical enough for us to be able to speak of an "evolution."

Cohen begins his reflections with a definition of science, which – tying into Kant's philosophy – he naturally defines within the context of idealism. As a matter of fact, it turns out that mathematics should be considered both the ideal of science and the foundation on which the entire system of science should be built. This is why Cohen states: "Denn der kritische Idealismus erhebt sich auf dem "Factum" der reinen Mathematik" (Cohen 1873, p. 55). Four years later, in his *Kants Begründung der Ethik*, Cohen still strongly emphasizes that his philosophy's ties with the philosophy of Kant, though the former had already become a different philosophy. The further evolution of Cohen's thought loosens these ties significantly; despite this, in 1877 he writes:

> Mir aber bedeutet Kantische Philosophie nichts Anderes, denn Philosophie als Wissenschaft. Und Wissenschaft muss zwar Dogmatik sein; ist aber nicht Dogma, und bleibt nicht Urkundenlesen. Wissenschaft ist Ideal des Systems auf Grund stetiger methodischer Arbeit (Cohen 1877, p. III).

Such an understanding of philosophy is meaningful due to the fact that it is evolving in the direction of what is called the logicism of the Marburg School; an expression of this can be found in the book *Logik der reinen Erkenntnis*, published for the first time in 1902. It is interesting to note that this book is a turning point in Cohen's thought. Helmut Holzhey, however, points to the second edition of *Kants Theorie der Erfahrung* (Cohen 1885), published in 1885, writing:

> Die schon für diese Rekonstruktion charakteristische besondere Akzentuierung und Weiterbildung kantischer Grundgedanken prägt sich zu einem selbständigen philosophischen System mit ausdrücklich antikantianischen Zügen aus (Holzhey 1979, p. 15).

I

As the point of departure of his reflections (which boil down to how criticism should be understood) Cohen chooses the debate between two great philosophers of his time, Friedrich Adolf Trendelenburg (1802–1872) and Kuno Fischer (1824–1907)[1], on how Kant's philosophy should be understood. The debate went through various phases, and Hans Vaihinger, citing the article *Zur Controverse zwischen Trendelenburg und Kuno Fischer* (Cohen 1871b) and the book *Kants Theorie der Erfahrung* (Cohen had published the first edition that same year), evaluates Cohen's merits as follows:

> In seiner Abhandlung in der "Zeitschrift für Völkerpsychologie und Sprachwissenschaft" [...] stellt er sich in allen Nebenfragen auf Seite von Trendelenburg; aber in "Kants Theorie der Erfahrung" [...] stellt er sich in der Hauptfrage zu Kant gegen Trendelenburgs Angriffe (Vaihinger 1922, p. 547).

---

[1] See: Noras 2012, pp. 124–154; Noras 2013, pp. 267–297.

In the preface to the first edition of his book on Kant, Cohen himself evaluates the discussion between the two philosophers as follows:

> Der Streit war ersprungen aus einer neuen Kritik der wissenschaftlichen Werthes der Kantischen Lehre, und er ist ausgelaufen in die Recension einer geschichtlichen Darstellung jener Lehre (Cohen 1871a, p. V).

Cohen's evaluation of the positions taken in the conflict results from his views on criticism and from his evaluation of Kant's philosophy. First, however, Cohen emphasizes that above all, critical philosophy boils down to a critique of experience. "Kant hat einen neuen Begriff der Erfahrung entdeckt. Die Kritik der reinen Vernunft ist Kritik der Erfahrung" (Cohen 1871a, p. 3). The object of Kant's analyses is therefore possible experience, while in the first edition of *Kants Theorie der Erfahrung* Cohen identifies criticism with the necessity of constructing a proof (Cohen 1871a, p. 93). According to Cohen, an essential role is played by the problem of synthetic *a priori* propositions, which he already noted in a paper on Kant's pre-critical philosophy that was in fact his habilitation dissertation.

> Die Natur synthetischer Sätze a priori aber, aus welcher die Sphäre der Erfahrung berechnet werden sollte, wurde aus der reinen Anschauung der Geometrie deducirt: so entstand die Kritik der reinen Vernunft (Cohen 1873, p. 13).

This intimate tie between philosophy and science is characteristic for Cohen's thought and was visible since the beginning for his philosophical journey.

Of course, critical philosophy must fulfill certain conditions. One of the first conditions for Cohen becomes the distinction between phenomena and things in themselves, which constitutes the backbone of transcendental idealism.

> Der echte Kriticismus bestehe daher in dem negativen Aufschluss: was die gemeine Erfahrung, und was alle dogmatische Philosophie als reale Dinge glaubt, das ist – Erscheinung (Cohen 1877, pp. 18–19).

At this point, Cohen stresses the fact that Kant did not consider skepticism a serious position; Cohen himself, however, affirms its weight, writing: "Das ist der einfache Sinn des Terminus Erscheinung, im Unterschiede vom Ding an sich: den Skepticismus zu entsetzen" (Cohen 1877, p. 28). At the same time, another concept (next to the thing in itself) characteristic of Cohen's understanding of criticism appears, namely, the concept of the unity of consciousness, which he considers a fundamental problem of criticism.² Kant himself, however, understands the problem of the unity of consciousness thus:

> Folglich ist die Einheit des Bewußtseins dasjenige, was allein die Beziehung der Vorstellungen auf einen Gegenstand, mithin ihre objektive Gültigkeit, folglich, daß sie Erkenntnisse werden, ausmacht, und worauf folglich selbst die Möglichkeit des Verstandes beruht (Kant 1911, p. 111; B 137).

It is already interesting that Kant titles his entire paragraph 17 in the second edition of the *Critique of Pure Reason* as follows: "Der Grundsatz der synthetischen Einheit der Apperception ist das oberste Princip alles Verstandesgebrauchs" (Kant 1911, p. 111; B 137).

In the first edition of *Kants Theorie der Erfahrung*, Cohen perceives the unity of consciousness – in the spirit of Kant's philosophy – as the synthetic unity of aperception,³ but already in *Kants Begründung der Ethik* accents the fact that it constitutes the "Grundproblem des Kriticismus" (Cohen 1877, p. 85) or condition of experience.⁴ Moreover, in *Kants Begründung der Ethik*, Cohen emphasizes that one element of Kant's criticism is the distinction between theoretical (speculative) reason and practical reason.⁵ On the other hand, in the second edition of *Kants Theorie der Erfahrung* Cohen indicates unity in the sense of systematicity and emphasizes that "Alle Einheit ist daher Einheit des Bewusstseins" (Cohen 1885, p. 141). This unity is understood as the unity of principles⁶ and according to Cohen is connected with the highest principle of synthetic *a priori* propositions.

---

2 "Diese Frage ist in der klarsten Weise beantwortet durch das Grundproblem des Kriticismus: die Einheit des Bewusstseins" (Cohen 1877, p. 85).
3 "Daher ist der letzte Grund des Gegenstandes die formale Einheit des Bewusstseins in der Synthesis des Mannichfaltigen der Anschauung. Diese formale Einheit des Bewusstseins ist die synthetische Einheit der Apperception, welche zugleich in der Kategorie entsteht, die Form derselben ist" (Cohen 1871a, p. 178).
4 "Die Einheit des Bewusstseins ist, als transscendentale Apperception, Bedingung der Erfahrung" (Cohen 1877, p. 47).
5 "Man muss daher die Unterscheidung, welche sich durch sämmtliche Schriften des Kantischen Kriticismus hindurchzieht, zwischen dem theoretischen oder dem speculativen und dem praktischen Vernunftgebrauch ernst und streng nehmen und genau einhalten" (Cohen 1885, p. 149).
6 "Der oberste Grundsatz der Apperception musste demgemäss an die Spitze der Reconstruction gestellt werden, wodurch die Ableitung der Motive des Systems strenger werden konnte, da die Einheit des Bewusstseins als Einheit der Grundsätze geltend gemacht, und jede Divergenz nach der psychologischen Seite des persönlichen Bewusstseins ausgeschlossen wurde" (Cohen 1885, p. XII).

> Das a priori der synthetischen Erkenntnisse fordert die Einheit des Bewusstseins in einer positivem Bedeutung. Der oberste Grundsatz kann daher auch als Grundsatz der "Einheit des Bewusstseins" bezeichnet werden (Cohen 1885, p. 141).

In the light of the unity of consciousness mentioned above, the problem appears of how critical philosophy is to be understood. The first serious change in Cohen's position from 1871 appears in 1883 – thus, not in *Kants Begründung der Ethik* (1877), but two years before the publication of the second, significantly revised edition of *Kants Theorie der Erfahrung*. It was then that Cohen published his book *Das Princip der Infinitesimal-Methode und seine Geschichte* (Cohen 1883). Above all, the book gives us the concept of "critique of knowledge" in place of the concept of "theory of knowledge," which is left out due to be considered as encumbered by psychological connotations. Cohen explains this illustratively, writing: "Erkenntnisskritik aber ist nicht schlechthin auf den erkennenden Geist gerichtet, sondern auf den Inhalt der Erkenntniss" (Cohen 1883, p. 10). This is significant insofar as the orientation towards content instead of towards action is an element of the battle against psychologism, though it can also be viewed as a Heglistic element in Cohen's philosophy. Elsewhere, Cohen writes as follows:

> Kritik der Vernunft ist Kritik der Erkenntniss oder der Wissenschaft. Die Kritik entdeckt das Reine in der Vernunft, insofern sie die Bedingungen der Gewissheit entdeckt, auf denen die Erkenntniss als Wissenschaft beruht (Cohen 1883, p. 6).

Moreover, Cohen emphasizes philosophy's intimate relationship with both mathematical natural science and mathematics, writing: "Die Erkenntnisskritik besteht nun also zunächst in dem Nachweis derjenigen Bedingungen, auf denen die mathematische Naturwissenschaft beruht" (Cohen 1883, p. 9).

II

The problem of science appears as soon as philosophy's relationship with mathematical natural science and mathematics is revealed. As was already mentioned, in 1902 Cohen published his work entitled *Logik der reinen Erkenntnis*, in which he writes:

> Diese Bedeutung der Kritik, die Festlegung der Beziehung zwischen Metaphysik und mathematischer Naturwissenschaft, sie ist die entscheidende That Kants, durch welche nach langer Entwicklung, in welcher er von seinen Jugendjahren an das Desiderat der Methode Newtons für die Metaphysik nur allgemein, wenngleich dringend und energisch fühlte, er

endlich zum Systematiker gereift war. Das System der Natur brachte ihn zum System der Metaphysik. Aber das Mittel lag in der Kritik, der Kritik der Principien. So wurde das System der Metaphysik zum System der Kritik (Cohen 1902, p. 8).

Nevertheless, the problem of science appears at the very beginning of Cohen's philosophical journey, when in the first edition of *Kants Theorie der Erfahrung* he points out the problem of science within the context of metaphysics and writes: "Hier giebt es nur Ein Mittel: sie ahme den Weg nach, durch den die Mathematik zu einer Wissenschaft geworden ist" (Cohen 1871a, pp. 11–12). In other words, it already becomes clear at the start of Cohen's philosophical journey that mathematics is the ideal of science, which is indirectly connected with a reference to Plato. Moreover, it is interesting that in *Kants Theorie der Erfahrung* Cohen cites Kant in reference to the latter's views on sensuality, writing: "Transscendentale Aesthetik nennt Kant die von ihm begründete Wissenschaft von allen Principien der Sinnlichkeit" (Cohen 1871a, p. 15). Thus, criticism in Cohen's understanding boils down to the idea that philosophy is the study of principles.

Since mathematics is recognized as the ideal of science, the name of Gottfried Wilhelm Leibniz cannot fail to appear. Cohen evaluates Leibniz's efforts in the following way:

> Er begeht den Fehler, die Gesetze der Logik unmittelbar und als solche auf die Probleme der Mathematik zu erstrecken; aber immerhin behauptet und betont er damit den Zusammenhang von Logik und Wissenschaft als das Problem seiner wie aller Philosophie (Cohen 1883, p. 4).

Simultaneously, Cohen himself points out the necessity of appealing to science; that is, for him, the critical nature of philosophy lies in its scientificity.

> Daher ist der Plan der transscendentalen oder der Erkenntnisskritik ein natürlicher und methodischer: was die Wissenschaft zur Wissenschaft macht, welche Bedingungen ihrer Gewissheit sie voraussetzt, von welchen Grundsätzen ihre Wirklichkeit nach ihrem angenommenen Werthe als Wissenschaft ermöglicht wird – das ist die natürliche Frage aller Philosophie; das ist das Problem der in Kant reif gewordenen Philosophie (Cohen 1883, p. 7).

The relationship between philosophy and science is indisputable, and already in *Das Princip...* Cohen explains that relationship thus:

> Die Einsicht in die solide Wissenschaftlichkeit des kritischen Idealismus wird durch das Verständniss zweier Momente bedingt, die gleichsehr constitutiv sind, aber nur schwer zusammen berücksichtigt werden. Einerseits muss der constructive Charakter des Denkens im Vordergrunde bleiben: dass die Welt der Dinge auf dem Grunde der Gesetze des Denkens

> beruht; dass die Dinge nicht schlechthin als solche gegeben sind, wie sie auf unsere Sinne einzudringen scheinen; dass vielmehr die Grundgestalten unseres denkenden Bewusstseins zugleich die Bausteine sind, mit denen wir die sogenannten Dinge in und aus letzten angeblichen Stofftheilchen zusammensetzen, und die Normen, mit denen wir die Gesetze und Zusammenhänge jener entwerfen und als Gegenstände wissenschaftlicher Erfahrung beglaubigen. Das ist das Bestimmende der Idee im Idealismus: keine Dinge anders als in und aus Gedanken. [...] dass der Raum die Bedingung der Geometrie sei. Das ist das zweite Moment, welches den kritischen Idealismus als solchen kennzeichnet (Cohen 1883, pp. 125–127).

It is nevertheless worth emphasizing that the reflections contained in *Das Princip...* concentrate on problems that were significant for science in Cohen's time, conducted against the backdrop of philosophy's scientificity. Thus, when writing about the difference between myth and science, Cohen states "[...] dass die Wissenschaft da von Materie handelt, wo der Mythos Bewusstsein sah" (Cohen 1883, p. 162). For that matter, this is how Cohen views the whole work in retrospect, when two years later in the preface to the second edition of *Kants Theorie der Erfahrung* he asserts: "Denn in dem Begriffe des Infinitesimalen werden die ‹neuen Wissenschaften› begründet, die Newton und Leibniz zum System gestalten" (Cohen 1885, p. XIII).

III

In the second edition of *Kants Theorie der Erfahrung*, Cohen analyzes the problem of science in light of the value of its validity, writing:

> So sehen wir, dass das Vertrauen in den Geltungswerth der Wissenschaft verbunden ist mit der Annahme von Grundlagen des Bewusstseins, in welchen die Wissenschaft ihren Anfang genommen und in deren Ausbau sie ihre Geschichte weiterführt (Cohen 1885, pp. 76–77).

The danger here is two-fold: first, there is the danger of implicit presuppositions (*Voreingenommenheit*), and second, there is the danger of recognizing the distinction of the elements of consciousness as final. In other words, Cohen indicates two significant issues for the understanding of science, namely the necessity of verifying presuppositions and the problem of the perpetual progress of science. In this context, Cohen emphasizes the fact that the metaphysical deduction of categories has merely provisional value. What constitutes the weakness of Kant's metaphysical deduction of categories becomes the domain of the transcendental method here.

> Diesen Ausweis bringt die transscendentale Methode, deren Princip und Norm der schlichte Gedanke ist: solche Elemente des Bewusstseins seien Elemente des Erkennenden Bewusstseins, welche hinreichend und nothwendig sind, das Factum der Wissenschaft zu begründen und zu festigen (Cohen 1885, p. 77).

The transcendental method links philosophy with science, as Cohen is convinced that its source should be sought in Newton, and more precisely in Kant's search for his philosophy's ties to the mathematical natural sciences. "Die transscendentale Methode ist in dem Nachdenken über die Philosophiae naturalis principia mathematica entstanden" (Cohen 1885, p. 67). Cohen continues accenting this connection between philosophy and the mathematical natural sciences much later as well; in *Ästhetik des reinen Gefühls*, published ten years later, he writes:

> Die Logik der reinen Erkenntnis entdeckt und begründet in den Begriffen und Methoden der mathematischen Naturwissenschaft die Grundlagen derselben als die Grundlagen der reinen Erkenntnis. Aber diese Entdeckungen kann sie und darf sie zugleich für die Probleme der Ethik verwerten (Cohen 1912, p. 69).

Thus, it turns out that an essential element characterizing the transcendental method is the fact that it is binding in all spheres of knowledge, thus not only in the theory of knowledge, but also in ethics. The method's universality simultaneously implies its bindingness, which in Cohen's thought is expressed in the conviction that it appears in Kant. Leaving aside the problems with this method, it is worth noting that Cohen also connects it with ethics.

> Die transscendentale Methode kann nicht für die Logik aufgenommen, für die Ethik aber verworfen werden. Wie die Logik in der Physik enthalten ist, so muss sie aus der Physik ermittelt werden. Und wie die Physik sonach in der Logik wurzelt, so muss auch das Recht in der Ethik seine Wurzel haben; so muss daher auch aus der Rechtswissenschaft die Ethik ermittelt und in ihr begründet werden (Cohen 1904, p. 215).

The complexity of the problem of the transcendental method can be clearly seen within the context of psychologism. Cohen perceives a problem concerning those elements of cognition, which – as permanent factors present in cognition – would exclude the possibility of any sort of change. Already in *Kants Begründung der Ethik*, Cohen characterizes the transcendental method, writing:

> Indem wir die anthropologische Art von Begründung ablehnen, verstehen wir die Aufgabe der Begründung in dem strengen Sinne, welcher die transscendentale Methode auszeichnet, und in der doppelten Forderung: erstlich das Fundament durch die Erfahrungslehre zu legitimiren, sodann aber auch die Begriffsmaterialien nach jener Methode zu untersu-

chen, die systematische Ableitung also der ethischen Sätze in Form erkenntnisstheoretischer Begründung zu vollziehen (Cohen 1877, p. 15).

Here, the problem of grounding on the basis of the transcendental method is clearly visible, and Cohen emphatically points out the difficulties with understanding this method.

> Hier stellt sich nun die andere Schwierigkeit ein, welche die transscendentale Methode zu besiegen hat. Nicht in den Grundlagen, die der Forscher voraussetzt und als solche kenntlich macht, glaubt man der wirksamen Rechtsgründe der Erkenntniss habhaft und sicher werden zu können – ist doch über die Art und Anzahl derselben Streit unter den Forschern; sondern in der Tiefe des Geistes selbst, in den Wurzeln des Denkens müsse, so meint man, dasjenige entdeckt werden, was als Quelle und Schutz der Wissenschaft soll gelten können. Damit aber entsteht der kritischen Methode die Gefahr, in eine psychologische sich aufzulösen, und anstatt die Werthe der Erkenntniss abzuschätzen, ihre vermuthlichen Anfänge und Entwickelungen zu beschreiben: von Platon zu Aristoteles abzufallen (Cohen 1885, p. 69).

The concept of "root" (*Wurzel*) is vital from the perspective of the later development of Cohen's philosophy, and it subsequently develops into the key concept of "origin" (*Ursprung*) in his thought.

Cohen points to the skepticism and dogmatism that the transcendental method has to grapple with, writing:

> Die transscendentale Methode entlarvt den Skepticismus, der gegen Elemente a priori überhaupt kämpft, als grundsätzlichen blinden Dogmatismus, und rechtfertigt den Glauben an die Wissenschaft und die Annahme von deren unauflöslichen, dem Spiel der Association entzogenen und schlechthin nothwendigen Grundlagen als die klare und reife Ueberzeugung von dem einzigen Ausgang, den die philosophische Untersuchung nehmen, und von dem aus sie zu förderlicher Einsicht gelangen kann (Cohen 1885, p. 79).

Elsewhere, he directly and matter-of-factly explains the transcendental method, asserting: "Die transscendentale Methode will nicht nur den Umfang; sie will die Grenzen der Erfahrung bestimmen lehren. So zeigt sie, wie die Kategorien in Ideen, die Erscheinungen in Noumena, die Grundsätze in Maximen münden" (Cohen 1885, p. 153). The problems with grasping this method stem from the fact that understood in such a way, philosophy becomes the sciences' "owl of Minerva," as Jürgen Stolzenberg points out, referring to the critique conducted by Max Scheler.[7]

---

7 See: Stolzenberg 1995, p. 31.

IV

As was mentioned earlier, in time, the concept of origin became a superordinate concept for Cohen. He emphasizes the fact that no superordinate concept exists for the concept of category, though the situation is completely different when it comes to the logic of pure knowledge. "Die Logik der reinen Erkenntnis hat sich auf solchem Oberbegriffe aufgebaut, auf dem des Ursprungs" (Cohen 1912, p. 240). The author's intention is radicalized further in *Logik der reinen Erkenntnis*, where Cohen speaks not only of the concept of origin, but also refers to the "Logik des Ursprungs." This is connected with his conviction as to the purity of knowledge, which Cohen expresses at the beginning of the work, writing:

> Wir dürfen, wir müssen die Logik selbst als Kritik, zur Geltung bringen. Denn sie bedeutet uns die Logik des Ursprungs. Und den Ursprung fordern wir in allen reinen Erkenntnissen. Das Denken ist das Denken des Ursprungs. Dadurch ist das Denken das Denken der Erkenntniss. Und wenn anders die Logik die Logik des Denkens ist, so ist sie, und nur sie, und sie an sich selbst die Logik der reinen Erkenntniss (Cohen 1902, p. 34).

It is here that the radical nature of the position contained in *Logik der reinen Erkenntnis* is revealed, since Cohen now speaks of a new form of philosophy. Cohen admittedly states that his book is a sharp polemic against the most important pillars of Kant's system. However, as Cohen himself emphasizes, one does not exclude the other, but rather "[...] es ergänzt sich zur Einheit einer systematischen Arbeit."[8]

Why does the concept of origin become a superordinate concept in Cohen's philosophy? Albert Görland (1869–1952), a student of Cohen and friend of Cassirer, explains this in a surprisingly simple way:

> Diese Forderung, dass dem Denken (der Wissenschaft) keine Voraussetzung gegeben sein darf, dass es aus keinem Anfange sich erheben darf, als sofern es ihn innerhalb seiner Methode selbst beglaubigen kann: diese Forderung heisst das Denkgesetz des Ursprungs (Görland 1912, p. 231).

In other words, the "presuppotionless-ness" sought by philosophers at that time is present in the concept of origin. "Origin" is the beginning of everything for Cohen, and in it he finds justification for his position. "Wir fangen – writes Cohen – mit dem Denken an. Das Denken darf keinen Ursprung haben ausser-

---

[8] Cohen 1902, p. VIII. See: Fiorato 1993, p. 5.

halb seiner selbst, wenn anders seine Reinheit uneingeschränkt und ungetrübt sein muss" (Cohen 1902, pp. 11–12). In this context, Wolfgang Marx writes:

> Der Begriff 'Ursprung' muß demnach so definiert werden, daß er der Leistung der 'reinen Denkens' genügt und entspricht: er muß verständlich machen, in welcher Weise 'reines Denken' das 'Denken in erweiternden Bestimmungsprozessen' fundiert, obwohl und weil er gerade nicht topologisch fixierbar ist in der Dimension der fiktiven Bedeutungen, als welche die Bestimmtheiten qua bestimmbare aufgefaßt werden müssen (Marx 1977, p. 129).

V

The aim of critical philosophy is to justify itself. In this context, we can speak of an evolution of Cohen's thought, which begins with the publication in 1871 of the first edition of *Kants Theorie der Erfahrung* and ultimately leads to the concept of origin (*Ursprung*). It is for this reason that Cohen's philosophy can be described as the philosophy of pure knowledge.

Bibliography

Cohen, Hermann (1871a): *Kants Theorie der Erfahrung*. Berlin: Ferd. Dümmlers Verlagsbuchhandlung. Harrwitz und Gossmann.
Cohen, Hermann (1871b): "Zur Controverse zwischen Trendelenburg und Kuno Fischer". In: *Zeitschrift für Völkerpsychologie und Sprachwissenschaft* Bd. 7, pp. 249–296.
Cohen, Hermann (1873): *Die systematischen Begriffe in Kants vorkritischen Schriften nach ihrem Verhältnis zum kritischen Idealismus*. Berlin: Ferd. Dümmlers Verlagsbuchhandlung. Harrwitz & Gossmann.
Cohen, Hermann (1877): *Kants Begründung der Ethik*. Berlin: Ferd. Dümmlers Verlagsbuchhandlung. Harrwitz und Gossmann.
Cohen, Hermann (1883): *Das Princip der Infinitesimal-Methode und seine Geschichte. Ein Kapitel zur Grundlegung der Erkenntnisskritik*. Berlin: Ferd. Dümmlers Verlagsbuchhandlung. Harrwitz und Gossmann.
Cohen, Hermann (1885): *Kants Theorie der Erfahrung*. 2. neubearb. Aufl. Berlin: Ferd. Dümmlers Verlagsbuchhandlung. Harrwitz und Gossmann.
Cohen, Hermann (1902): *Logik der reinen Erkenntniss*. Berlin: Bruno Cassirer.
Cohen, Hermann (1904): *Ethik des reinen Willens*. Berlin: Bruno Cassirer.
Cohen, Hermann (1912): *Ästhetik des reinen Gefühls*. Bd. 1. Berlin: Bruno Cassirer.
Fiorato, Pierfrancesco (1993): *Geschichtliche Ewigkeit. Ursprung und Zeitlichkeit in der Philosophie Hermann Cohens*. Würzburg: Königshausen & Neumann.
Görland, Albert (1912): "Hermann Cohens systematische Arbeit im Dienste des kritischen Idealismus". In: *Kant-Studien* Bd. 17, pp. 222–251.

Holzhey, Helmut (1979): *Die Marburger Schule des Neukantianismus*. In: Helmut Holzhey; Werner Flach (Hrsg.): *Erkenntnistheorie und Logik im Neukantianismus. Texte von Cohen, Natorp, Cassirer, Windelband, Rickert, Lask, Bauch*. Hildesheim: Gerstenberg Verlag, pp. 15–33.

Kant, Immanuel (1911): "Kritik der reinen Vernunft (2. Aufl. 1787)". In: KantsWerke. Akademie-Textausgabe. Bd. 3. Berlin: Georg Reimer.

Marx, Wolfgang (1977): *Transzendentale Logik als Wissenschaftslehre. Systemtisch-kritische Untersuchungen zur philosophischen Grundlegungsproblematik in Cohens ‚Logik der reinen Erkenntnis'*. Frankfurt am Main: Vittorio Klostermann.

Noras, Andrzej Jan (2012): *Historia neokantyzmu*. Katowice: Wydawnictwo Uniwersytetu Śląskiego.

Noras, Andrzej Jan (2013): "Debata Trendelenburg – Fischer. Problem obiektywności Kantowskich form zmysłowości". In: *Przegląd Filozoficzny – Nowa Seria* 22, Nr. 1, pp. 267–297.

Stolzenberg, Jürgen (1995): *Ursprung und System. Probleme der Begründung systematischer Philosophie im Werk Hermann Cohens, Paul Natorps und beim frühen Martin Heidegger*. Göttingen: Vandenhoeck & Ruprecht.

Vaihinger, Hans (1922): *Kommentar zu Kants "Kritik der reinen Vernunft"*. Raymund Schmidt (Hrsg.). Stuttgart–Berlin–Leipzig: Union Deutsche Verlagsgesellschaft.

Winter, Eggert (1980): *Ethik und Rechtswissenschaft. Eine historisch-systematische Untersuchung zur Ethik-Konzeption des Marburger Neukantianismus im Werke Hermann Cohens*. Berlin: Duncker & Humblot.

Beata Trochimska-Kubacka
Hermann Cohen's Critical Exposition of Kant's Critique of Taste

Abstract: This article covers Marburg Neo-Kantian Hermann Cohen's stance vis-à-vis the Kantian conception presented in the *Critique of Judgment*. Kant's thought was of prime importance to Cohen's project of systematic aesthetics. Though he shared Kant's transcendental point of departure, Cohen formulated a number of critical remarks about Kant's aesthetic thought concerning (among others) his teleology, conception of feeling, and concept of symbol. The article also discusses the differences that arise between Cohen's and Gadamer's positions regarding specific solutions in Kantian aesthetics.

Keywords: transcendentalism, aesthetics, aesthetic finality, concept of feeling.

To demonstrate the durability of the problem of systematic aesthetics, Hermann Cohen reflected on and argued against an array of conceptions in the fields of the history of philosophical thought, art history, and art theory. His critical polemic against Kant's notion of aesthetics is particularly significant for Cohen's basic conclusions in the field of aesthetics.

The aesthetic thought of the founder of Marburgian Neo-Kantianism developed gradually. In 1885, Cohen made the decision to write a third book dedicated to Kant, which appeared in 1889 under the title *Kants Begründung Ästhetik*. This intention was expressed through comprehensive research conducted in the field of aesthetic thought and through an intense interest in art, music, and poetry. Cohen also delivered a series of lectures on aesthetics at the University of Marburg.[1]

The postulate of "returning of Kant," influential at the time, did not signify an actual return to and restoration of the horizon of Kant's Critiques. This also holds in regards to Kant's aesthetic thought and the form it took in the third Critique. In *Kants Begründung der Ästhetik*, Cohen undertook the problem of Kant's

---

[1] These lectures include, among others: "Die ästhetische Prinzipien der deutsche Philosophen" for one semester in the 1885/86 academic year; a lecture dedicated to Kantian aesthetics – "Ästhetik," in the spring semester of 1887; and "Schillers philosophische Gedichte und Abhandlungen" for 4 semesters in the years 1879–1883 and 1887–1889. Aesthetics were also a permanent component of Cohen's lectures entitled "Kants System" in the years 1892/93, 1893/94, 1886/97, 1900/01, 1903/04. See: Holzhey 2009, p. 2*.

Critique of Judgment, inserting it into the framework of his (Cohen's) own interpretive perspective. Above all, Cohen considered Kant's theory of experience and morality premises, which opened up the possibility for a systematic grounding of aesthetics. Thus, Cohen presented a different understanding of "system" than the Kantian understanding. This was expressed through his narrowing of the horizon of analysis of the *Critique of Judgment* to the problem of grounding aesthetics and art, as well as through the exclusion of Kantian teleology. According to Cohen, the object of the teleological power of judgment does not belong to the sphere of aesthetics; rather, it falls within the sphere of theoretical philosophy or the theory of experience.

Despite the fact that Cohen went beyond the Kantian grounding of aesthetics, he did consider Kant of first-rate significance to the history of aesthetics. This is visible in the very structure of *Kants Begründung Ästhetik*. Cohen begins with a lengthy historical introduction. He begins by discussing the conceptions of Plato, Aristotle, and Plotinus up through the Renaissance; then, he turns toward XVIII-century views; next, arguing against the views of Winckelmann, Mendelssohn, Lessing, and Herder, he reaches Kant; finally, he ends with an even longer chapter on the continuators and opponents of critical aesthetics – thus, essentially, with the history of the reception of Kant's thought. Helmut Holzhey notes that – aside from the history of the *Infinitesimal Methode* principle – such historical outlines are something quite unique in Cohen's works (see: Holzhey 2009, p. 10*).

In *Ästhetik des reinen Gefühls*, published in 1912, Cohen presented views so different from those in *Kants Begründung der Ästhetik* that they remained only marginally related to his earlier work. In *Ästhetik des reinen Gefühls*, Cohen retained his transcendental approach to aesthetics, emphasizing the originality of the Kantian proposal. For him, it was of singular importance that thanks to Kant, aesthetics became an independent and equal part of the system of transcendental philosophy. In his view, the maturity of critical philosophy was expressed most fully in its development of systematic aesthetics. According to Cohen, the logic of the system demanded that the question of how art was possible be posed. He emphasized that Kant took into account the particularity of the aesthetic sphere, made it the object of philosophical reflection, and understood it as a systematic problem (*ein systematisches Problem*).

It is worth noting that in Kant's view, aesthetic values defined such an essential aspect of human experience that their philosophical elaboration became necessary. Avoiding both the extremity of objectivism and that of subjectivism, Kant undertook a transcendental investigation of beauty and the sublime. In doing so he transformed the rationalist tradition and initiated a new approach to beauty and art within German philosophy, rendering them valid objects of philosophical reflection. Kant contributed to the development of a new approach within the sphere of European culture, putting hope in art and seeking man's essence in the language of aesthetics.

The specificity of Kant's conception lies in its concentration on the critique of taste and on the concept of genius. Kant understood the study of the beautiful and sublime in nature and in art as the "critique of the aesthetic power of judgment." Thus, the analysis of aesthetic experience constitutes an essential aspect of Kant's accomplishments. To avoid accusations of sensualism and rationalism in regards to the critique of taste, Kant indicated "disinterested delight" as its basis. He analyzed the mental faculties that participate in an aesthetic experience and defined their range of competence and the nature of their activity. In light of his conclusions, aesthetic delight does not result from the activity of either imagination or understanding alone; rather, it follows from the cooperation of these mental faculties. Aesthetic delight is not the consequence of an impression, representation, or judgment, but of their combined activity.

Concentrating his analysis on the functions of the mental faculties led Kant to define the universal and necessary factors of the aesthetic sphere. In consequence, Kant asserted that aesthetic judgments are *necessary* because they concern objects that are built according to the subject's nature and *universal* because human minds are composed of the same faculties. In the *Critique of Judgment*, Kant uses the concept of *sensus communis*; however, in contrast to English philosophy's doctrine of "moral feeling," Kant completely separates this concept from the moral. For Kant, the power of judgment is not so much a skill, as it is a postulate set before everyone. Everyone has enough "sense of the common," i.e. the skill of judging, to make similar judgments regarding aesthetic issues on the basis of a community of feeling. This way, Kant expresses the conviction that what is universal and necessary is found not only within the sphere of cognition, or moral action, but also in that of aesthetic pleasure.

It must be emphasized that Kant aspired to an autonomous grounding of aesthetics; as a result, he was opposed to discussing the question of truth within the field of art. In the *Critique of Judgment*, Kant introduces aesthetic *a priori*, which differs from the *a priori* in his previous two Critiques. In the *Critique of Pure Reason*, *a priori* is of a formal nature, it is a feature of cognition and constitutes a condition for the possibility of cognition. Emphasizing this difference, Kant states: "For beauty is not a concept of the object, and the judgment of taste is not a cognitive judgement" (Kant 2007, § 38, p. 120).[2] Kant based the subjective

---

[2] "Schönheit ist kein Begriff vom Objekt, und das Geschmacksurteil ist kein Erkenntnisurteil" (Kant 1922, p. 141).

a priori of taste on the free play of the cognitive faculties; he transcendentally legitimated the judgment of taste and its claim to universal validity.

When Kant asks what lies *a priori* at the basis of our interest in beauty, he abandons the concept of "disinterested delight" and moves from the perspective of taste to the perspective of genius. The concept of genius serves to ground art. Genius is "the ability to represent aesthetic ideas." According to Kant, aesthetic ideas stimulate the free play of the cognitive faculties and cannot be contained within a concept. Kant does not give up the transcendental perspective. In his understanding of genius, creative flair and irrationality correlate with the creation of rules or models; the unity of these moments causes a work of art to appear unique to both the artist and its recipient. It is here that the adequacy between the notion of taste and of genius is revealed in Kant's thought. Kant based the *a priori* of taste and of genius on the free play of the cognitive faculties. Decisive importance is attributed to the free and harmonious play of the mental faculties: understanding and imagination, reason and imagination, which is accompanied by a sensation of the intensification of life. Genius is an original manifestation of this invigorating spirit.

In *Ästhetik des reinen Gefühls*, Cohen analyzes Kant's aesthetics, making references to an array of key issues. Due to the importance of Kant's aesthetics for Cohen's thought, it is essential to reconstruct Cohen's detailed findings on Kant's thought from *Ästhetik des reinen Gefühls*. What links Cohen's thought with the Kantian project is the use of the transcendental perspective in framing the problem of aesthetics. Cohen agrees with Kant that beauty is not an objective quality of an object, and that aesthetic experience does not constitute the basis for any empirical knowledge on beauty. Cohen also shares Kant's conviction that an aesthetic experience cannot be reduced to a purely personal, individual experience. In Cohen's view, such a stance would essentially preclude aesthetics as a separate field of study. Simultaneously, however, Cohen indicates certain lacks and inconsistencies in the Kant's project.

The Problem of Teleology

As mentioned earlier, Cohen's main accusation concerns the fact that aesthetic judgment (*ästhetische Urteilskraft*) is not the object of its own separate critique in Kant, but is examined in connection with teleological judgment. Kant explains the distinction between the critique of aesthetic judgment and critique of teleological judgment from the *Critique of Judgment* as follows:

Aesthetic judgement is, therefore, a special faculty of judging according to a rule, but not according to concepts. Teleological judgement is not a special faculty, but merely general reflective judgement proceeding, as it always does in theoretical cognition, according to concepts, but in respect of certain objects of nature, following special principles—those, namely, of a judgement that is merely reflective and does not determine objects. Hence, as regards its application, it belongs to the theoretical part of philosophy, and on account of its special principles, which are not determining, as principles belonging to doctrine have to be, it must also form a special part of the critique (Kant 2007, p. 29).[3]

In other words, Kant considers aesthetic judgment a part of the propedeutics of the philosophy of critique, since it does not contribute to knowledge on its object. In consequence, the second part of the *Critique of Judgment* deals exclusively with nature and its assessment in light of the concept of purpose. Cohen notes that within the framework of the whole systemic design, the aesthetic power of judgment, in its application to the beautiful and sublime in nature, has in Kant's thought a preparatory significance, to accustom understanding to applying the concept of purpose in reference to nature. According to Cohen, Kant viewed the transcendental grounding of art and the critique of taste as introductory to teleology.[4] In accordance with Kant's philosophical design, the role of the third Critique is to close the entire system by legitimating the power of judgment as the principle of teleology. By virtue of the concept of the purposiveness of nature, the power of judgment mediates between the understanding and reason, between the concept of nature and the concept of freedom.

Cohen considered this Kantian solution an essential drawback, not only due to its limitation of the aesthetic power of judgment, but also in view of systematic methodology, as the problem of teleology was not undertaken and elaborated by Kant in the first Critique. In this sense, in Cohen's view, the fact that the

---

3 "Die ästhetische Urteilskraft ist also ein besonderes Vermögen, Dinge nach einer Regel, aber nicht nach Begriffen, zu beurteilen. Die teleologische ist kein besonderes Vermögen, sondern nur die reflektierende Urteilskraft überhaupt; sofern sie, wie überall im theoretischen Erkenntnisse, nach Begriffen, aber in Ansehung gewisser Gegenstände der Natur nach besonderen Prinzipien, nämlich einer bloß reflektierenden, nicht Objekte bestimmenden Urteilskraft verfährt, also ihrer Anwendung nach zum theoretischen Teile der Philosophie gehört, und der besonderen Prinzipien wegen, die nicht, wie es in einer Doktrin sein muß, bestimmend sind, auch einen besonderen Teil der Kritik ausmachen muß" (Kant 1922, p. 32).

4 Gadamer similarly evaluates the role of Kantian teleology. Perceiving it as the core of the *Critique of Judgment*, in relation to which aesthetics plays a preparatory role, Gadamer states: "This is the systematic significance that the problem of natural beauty has for Kant: *it grounds the central position of teleology*. Natural beauty alone, not art, can assist in legitimating the concept of purpose in judging nature. For this systematic reason alone, the 'pure' judgment of taste provides the indispensable basis of the third Critique"(Gadamer 2013, p. 50).

topic of teleology was not introduced before *Critique of Judgment*, disrupts the order of the entire Kantian project.

The Concepts of Aesthetic Purposiveness and Aesthetic Feeling

Cohen also voiced a slew of accusations against specific conclusions in Kant's aesthetic conception. Most of all, he critiqued one of this conception's key concepts – the concept of "feeling." Kant ascribed to taste the ability to move from sensual pleasure to aesthetic "feeling." He described feeling as the "feeling of life" (*Lebensgefühl*), identified with the feeling of pleasure or pain, and characterized it thus:

> and this forms the basis of a quite separate faculty of discriminating and judging, that contributes nothing to knowledge. All it does is to compare the given representation in the subject with the entire faculty of representations of which the mind is conscious in the feeling of its state (Kant 2007, p. 36).[5]

In the first place, Cohen perceives an analogy between the Kantian phrase "entire faculty of representation" (*das ganze Vermögen der Vorstellungen*) and Moses Mendelssohn's phrase "all powers of the soul" (*alle Seelenkräfte*). Simultaneously, he expresses his doubts as to the accuracy of setting "entire faculty" next to "of representation." To Cohen, this phrase makes it sound as though the "entire faculty" is reduced to a relationship between imagination and understanding (as participants in the judgment of beauty), which carries the risk of narrowing the meaning of this phrase and the fear that not all powers of the soul are taken into account.

Cohen presented a list of accusations against the Kantian conception of aesthetic feeling, formulated from the perspective of systematic philosophy (see: Cohen 1912, pp. 100–116). We will conduct a general review of these, concentrating on the most important accusations.

One of Cohen's primary accusations concerns the fact that the Kantian conception of taste was formulated with a limitation of the mental faculties, i.e. with the exclusion of will. Cohen emphasizes that the Kantian conception does not

---

[5] "[...]welches ein ganz besonderes Unterscheidungs- und Beurteilungsvermögen gründet, das zum Erkenntnis nichts beiträgt, sondern nur die gegebene Vorstellung im Subjekte gegen *das ganze Vermögen* der Vorstellungen hält, dessen sich das Gemüt im Gefühl seines Zustandes bewußt wird" (Kant 1922, p. 40).

take into account the will (and thus the moral sphere), which, in his view, certainly co-creates aesthetic feeling. Though Cohen finds it understandable that Kant, in discovering the aesthetic *a priori*, had to first examine its foundation in reason, Cohen believes that this same foundation needs to be supplemented by the moral moment. According to Cohen, such a supplement is necessary to define the concept of aesthetic feeling. In his view, within the framework of a systematic formulation of aesthetic feeling, the moral should be treated as a co-active force in the play of aesthetic consciousness, remaining in force from beginning to end. Thus, Cohen did not mean for will and morality to be removed from the aesthetic sphere, but for them to be incorporated into it in a way that would accord with a systemic approach. In Cohen's view, only such a solution would enable the balance of aesthetic consciousness (*ästhetische Bewusstsein*), which was of prime importance for him and constituted something of a systemic focal point in his conception. According to Cohen, Kant's undermining of the value of pure will shook the construction of aesthetic feeling and made it unconvincing. In his view, the morality initially excluded from the Kantian project ultimately makes its way into the aesthetic sphere and the free play of the faculties, while the moral begins to co-define the aesthetic as an external, foreign principle, e.g. in the concept of symbol. As a result, the moral, instead of being gradually subject to limitation in favor of the aesthetic, gained excessive importance in Kant. This is a mistake, which in Cohen's opinion led to the connection between the aesthetic and the ethical appearing forced in the Kantian conception.

It is clear that Kant, in his conception of beauty, tried to exclude not only the participation of will and morality, but also that of cognition. Cohen critically assessed Kant's position on separating aesthetic pleasure from the sphere of cognition. As Cohen points out, the intellectual moment does ultimately make its appearance in Kantian aesthetics, in connection with the concept of purposiveness (*Zweckmäßigkeit*). Cohen recalls that in Kant, the judgment on purposiveness is essential for more than just aesthetic activity, as purposiveness is the most lawful principle within the framework of cognition. At the same time, however, Cohen emphasizes that aesthetic purposiveness is of a special nature; to grasp it properly, it will not suffice to refer to the "logical purposiveness" Kant established for the cognition of nature.

It is necessary to keep in mind that "feeling" appears in Kant in connection with the assessment of an object in light of the purposiveness of its representation, which initiates the free play of the cognitive faculties. In his reflections on the Kantian understanding of "feeling," Cohen distinguished three basic aspects: 1. feeling, 2. the assessment of purposiveness, and 3. purposiveness as the free play of the cognitive faculties. Each of these aspects is particularly significant, because each directly concerns the relationships and essential differences between cognitive consciousness and aesthetic consciousness in Cohen's thought.

With respect to the first aspect of Kant's conception of feeling, Cohen begins with general remarks. In Kant, feeling accompanies the play of the cognitive faculties, with the exclusion of will. For this reason, in Cohen's view, feeling is more recognition, than it is delight. Next, he indicates an inconsistency: on the one hand, feeling is understood as something that "does not contribute to cognition," while on the other hand, it is described as accompanying the activity of "imagination in its freedom and understanding in its conformity to law (*Gesetzmäßigkeit*)." Imagination and understanding – faculties, to which a fundamental role in cognition was ascribed within the framework of the epistemological conception in the *Critique of Pure Reason*. The Kantian solution by virtue of which understanding and imagination are granted cognitive activity in the theoretical order, only to have that activeness suspended in the aesthetic order, is not convincing for Cohen. In Kant's understanding, this was meant to demonstrate the specificity and distinctness of aesthetic feeling. In Cohen's view, it has the opposite effect – namely, when aesthetic feeling is understood as the result of the influence of two cognitive faculties (though simultaneously this function of theirs is suspended!), the distinctness of feeling cannot be maintained and the intellectualization of feeling is inevitable.

Cohen, continuing this course of deliberation, moves to discuss the second aspect of feeling – the assessment of purposiveness. Recall the basic Kantian description: the purposiveness of an object's representation constitutes a "subjective, formal condition of judgment in general," which leads to the "principle of being universally communicated." In Cohen's opinion, though the Kantian conception introduces universalization, it simultaneously increases the risk of the intellectualization of aesthetic feeling. "Aesthetic purposiveness," Cohen emphasizes, "becomes something logical, namely, the premise of all thought in general" (Cohen 1912, p. 101).[6] Within the context of justifying his interpretation, Cohen argues that though Kant excluded subsumption to given concepts in aesthetic judgments, he did not resign from subsumption as such. Cohen believed that in an aesthetic judgment, though subsumption did not refer to concepts (as it does in theoretical judgments), it does appear as an effect of the influence of the faculties of imagination and understanding. Feeling becomes the "defining assessment for this subsumption" (*Beurteilung für diese Subsumtion bestimmend*), which is directed at reflecting on "how much the former in its freedom

---

[6] "Die ästhetische Zweckmäßigkeit wird so zu einer logischen, und zwar zur Voraussetzung alles Denkens überhaupt" (Cohen 1912, p. 101).

accords with the latter in its conformity to law" (Cohen 1912, p. 101).[7] As a result – Cohen concludes – feeling so understood, instead of being a condition of judgment, becomes a judgment itself. This is because though the assessment of purposiveness was presumed to be made by virtue of feeling, it seems to be more of an intellectual judgment. In consequence – Cohen notes – we should accept that in the play of purposiveness, theoretical consciousness so understood subsequently *transforms* into feeling. Aesthetic feeling would therefore be understood as a product of transformation. Thus, feeling and aesthetic consciousness as to the content and form of its activity, are defined by the intellectual. In Cohen's view, Kant imbued subsumption with new content, just as he did with purposiveness and the free play of the cognitive faculties. It results from the presented line of argument that Cohen accused Kant of intellectualizing feeling, which in Cohen's opinion threatened to blur the specificity of aesthetic consciousness and to rid it of its distinctness in relation to cognitive consciousness. Cohen was convinced that such an outline of the intellectual basis of feeling ultimately results in the aesthetic appearing ambiguous.

Cohen takes an even more in-depth look at purposiveness. In the third point of his analysis of purposiveness as the free play of the cognitive faculties, Cohen concentrates on their agreement in play, which acts to further define purposiveness. According to Kant, the basis for evaluating purposiveness was the free play of the faculties: imagination and understanding, and agreement in this play was expressed through a feeling of pleasure, which in turn constituted the basis for judgments of beauty. According to Cohen, the strong Kantian accent on agreement in the play of the cognitive faculties leads to unexpected consequences. Agreement, in his assessment, can be interpreted as something that distances feeling from its intellectual basis and reduces it to an ordinary feeling of pleasure or pain. In reference to this issue, Cohen resorts to indirect argumentation. The point of departure of Cohen's argument is those passages in the *Critique of Judgment* in which Kant asserts that pleasure is based solely on reflection. Kant assumes the possibility of experiencing pleasure flowing from reflection, and regarding pleasure states that: "It must always be only through reflective perception that it is cognized as conjoined with this representation" (Kant 2007, p. 25)[8] of a given object. In other words, when by virtue of a given object's representation the imagination is made to agree with understanding, and the object is recognized as purposive for the reflective power of judgment, this is ac-

---

[7] "[...] sofern das erstere in seiner Freiheit mit dem letztern in seiner Gesetzmäßigkeit zusammenstimmt" (Cohen 1912, p. 101).
[8] "[...] sondern jederzeit nur durch reflektierte Wahrnehmung als mit dieser verknüpft erkannt werden muß" (Kant 1922, p. 28).

companied by a feeling of pleasure. Thus, Cohen concludes, the feeling of pleasure only accompanies reflection conducted by the power of judgment. It is in fact the power of judgment that causes the appropriateness of representations, the harmonious play of the cognitive faculties, to become the contents of consciousness, in which *in addition* a new source power of consciousness expressed in the feeling of pleasure is made manifest. Consequently, in Cohen's view, pleasure is marginalized, defined as an effect accompanying the activity of the power of judgment, and constitutes a mere symptom of the agreement in which purposiveness is expressed.

Cohen's analyses (cited above) illustrate the fact that Kant's stance on aesthetic feeling lacks precision. Kant's text opens the door to interpretations like Cohen's thanks to the use of formulations such as: "The consciousness of mere formal purposiveness in the play of the cognitive faculties of the subject attending a representation whereby an object is given, is the pleasure itself" (Kant 2007, p. 53),[9] and with some hesitation:

> The only point that is strange or out of the way about it, is that it is not an empirical concept, but a feeling of pleasure (and so not a concept at all), that is yet demanded from everyone by the judgement of taste, just as if it were a predicate united to the cognition of the object, and that is meant to be conjoined with its representation (Kant 2007, p. 26).[10]

Thus, the question remains: what is aesthetic pleasure, ultimately, in Kant's view? Is it an independent feeling of the soul, or just a manifestation of reflective consciousness, "some predicate" accompanying reflection?

In connection with the above, Cohen considers yet another consequence. In his view, in Kant's conception, the assessment of purposiveness' transformation into feeling inevitably reduces the latter to an effect. Feeling, understood as a result of the play of the cognitive faculties, merely constitutes an expression of the theoretical consciousness of purposiveness in this play. Consequently, in the Kantian conception, no active potency can be attributed to feeling. Cohen gives a negative response to the question of whether feeling, understood as a product of transformation (*Verwandlung*), can be considered equivalent to

---

[9] "Das Bewußtsein der bloß formalen Zweckmäßigkeit im Spiele der Erkenntniskräfte des Subjekts, bei einer Vorstellung, wodurch ein Gegenstand gegeben wird, ist *die Lust* selbst" (Kant 1922, p. 61).

[10] "Das Befremdende und Abweichende liegt nur darin, daß es nicht ein empirischer Begriff, sondern ein Gefühl der Lust (folglich gar kein Begriff) ist, welches doch durch das Geschmacksurteil, gleich *als ob es* ein mit dem Erkenntnisse des Objekts verbundenes *Prädikat wäre*, jedermann zugemutet und mit der Vorstellung desselben verknüpft werden soll" (Kant 1922, p. 28).

pure production (*der reinen Erzugung*). He recognizes that an insurmountable contradiction is present between feeling understood as a product of transformation, and production. In Cohen's view, Kant's subjective purposiveness, with its harmony of cognitive faculties does not suffice to describe creativity – it is impossible to recognize the original source of productivity in it. As a result, Cohen found that Kant's concept of purposiveness is too emburdened by its theoretical (cognitive) aspect, and therefore does not bring us closer to understanding the phenomenon of creativity. In other words, Cohen critically assesses the fact that Kant, in his concept of aesthetic purposiveness, began with the receptivity of feeling, instead of with its productivity (*Produktivität*). He asserts that while the aspect of receptivity should be taken into account in aesthetics, it should not be the point of departure. It is creativity that is a fundamental aesthetic problem, and the experience of art is merely an attempt at its reproduction (*Nacherzeugung*). According to Cohen, it is impossible to accept that in Kant, subjective purposiveness as a feeling becomes productive, as it does not seem to be capable of productivity. As a result, aesthetic reproduction, the reproductive experience, is also not satisfactorily explained and well grounded in Kant's thought. In Cohen's opinion, both the intellectual aspect of feeling and its volitional aspect should be methodically developed as the initial conditions of creativity, and the Kantian notion of purposiveness does not fulfill this basic task of aesthetics.

Beauty as a Symbol of the Good

Cohen's further reflections make it clear that within Kant's conception, he was particularly interested in the relationship between the aesthetic and the ethical. At the outset, Cohen notes that Kant allowed the moral to participate not only in defining the sublime, but also in defining the beautiful. This is in reference to paragraph 42 of the *Critique of Judgment*, where Kant, in comparing the beauty of nature and beauty in art, grants superiority to the beauty of nature, because it can arouse direct interest "akin to the moral" (see: Kant 2007, p. 130). In Kant's view, purpose-less accordance with our cognitive ability as such is proper to the beauty of nature; this striking purposiveness of nature tells us that we are the ultimate purpose of creation and makes us aware of our "moral vocation" (see: Kant 2007, 131).[11]

---

11 Gadamer relays Kant's position in the following words: "Precisely because in nature we find no *ends in themselves* and yet find beauty—i.e., a suitedness (Zweckmäßigkeit) to the end

According to Cohen, the Kantian understanding of beauty results in beauty's disappearing as an independent object of reflection and being reduced to the rank of a symbol of the good. Cohen cannot accept this conclusion. He asks whether, in that case, the beautiful can only be ascribed *a priori* significance on account of the moral. In his view, if this were the case, the aesthetic *a priori* would be devoid of its own content and would be abolished by the ethical *a priori* (see: Cohen 1912, p. 103).

From Cohen's point of view, this is a disastrous consequence of the fact that Kant, in defining beauty, took morality into account, which he had excluded from his earlier formulation of the conception of feeling. Cohen cites Kant's famous words: "beautiful is the symbol of the morally good," and his later elaboration, "This is the *intelligible* toward which taste looks" (Kant 2007, § 59, p. 180).[12] Cohen observes that if we consider Kant's intelligible sphere analogous to the "thing in itself," is equivalent to an "idea," then in this case it would be the moral, while beauty would be reduced to the role of a phenomenon. Moreover, this understanding threatens beauty with ambiguity. As a phenomenon, it would be an object within the framework of aesthetic experience, but it could only be properly grasped starting from the idea of the moral. As a result, beauty loses its autonomy; it ceases to define an independent value. Cohen perceives the risk of Platonism in the Kantian conception. Beauty taken as a symbol would merely be an expression or manifestation of an idea.

According to Cohen, this way of thinking is confirmed by the Kantian definition of symbol, in which a symbol is distinguished from the scheme and always signifies a lack in the presentation (*Darstellung*). This lack is inevitable; since the moral is to be revealed in the aesthetic presentation, a lack results from the presence of a foreign problem. Cohen also points out that within the framework of the Kantian understanding of symbol, the moral aspect does not have a chance to be fully expressed. What is moral in the symbol always gains a limited, narrow presentation; as a result, it becomes vague and less meaningful. Cohen critically assessed the Kantian concept of symbol; in his opinion, it

---

(Zweck) of our pleasure, nature gives us a 'hint' that we are in fact the ultimate end, the final goal of creation. The dissolution of the ancient cosmological thought that assigned man his place in the total structure of being and assigned each entity its goal of perfection gives the world, which ceases to be beautiful as a structure of absolute ends, the new *beauty* of being purposive for us" (Gadamer 2013, p. 47). In Gadamer's opinion, the Kantian comparison and distinction of the beauty of nature from the beauty of art in essence pushed the aesthetic problem forward and in consequence contributed to the emancipation of art.

12 "das Schöne ist das Symbol des Sittlichguten [...] Das ist das Intelligibele, worauf der Geschmack hinaussieht" (Kant 1922, § 59, p. 213).

undermines the intellectual basis of the conception, making it vulnerable to accusations of inconsistency. The concept of symbol is the undoing (*Verhängnis*) of aesthetics, Cohen concludes (see: Cohen 1912, p. 104).

The question arises: is Cohen right to blame Kant for the lack of consistency in resolving this issue, and does the statement "beauty is a symbol of what is ethically good" really do away with beauty's independence by subordinating it to an external principle? In paragraph 59 of the *Critique of Judgment*, Kant discusses, perhaps too succinctly, his understanding of symbol. According to this discussion, the symbolic manner of the presentation is always intuitive (*intuitive Vorstellungsart*) and based on analogy. The lack characteristic of a symbol that Cohen mentions is due to the fact that no intuition directly corresponds to a given rational concept – despite this such a presentation is ascribed to it *a priori*. This is done by virtue of analogy, which occurs "between the rules of reflection upon both and their causality" (see: Kant 2007, § 59, p. 180). According to the Kantian example, a coffee grinder can be considered a symbol of a despotic state and an organism a symbol of a monarchic state. Next, Kant lists the moments of analogy between beauty and morality, e. g. that both beauty and morality are directly and disinterestedly appealing, that their judgments are universally valid and independent from empirical laws, that they bring the mind into similar states, and so on. Kant does not therefore claim that beauty is similar to good, as he does not claim that the coffee grinder is similar to a despotic state. The analogy concerns the ways in which they are perceived and the internal causal relations in their representations, which are achieved through reflection. We can therefore say that beauty as a symbol in Kant's conception does not manifest the ethical; rather, like the ethical, it refers to the supersensible sphere. In this sense, the Kantian symbol, rather than the unequivocally indicating the moral, referred to a certain higher reality and a certain spiritual content.

Consequently, it seems that in relation to the above problem, the distinctiveness of art and aesthetics from the moral is maintained in the Kantian project. Naturally, it should be borne in mind that the solutions from the *Critique of Judgment* indicated by Cohen outline possibilities for reconciling the aesthetic and moral spheres that were, in time, undertaken and developed by Schiller. However, most commentators of Kant's aesthetic thought are inclined to emphasize the importance of his thought for the process of emancipating the aesthetic from foreign principles.

Cohen's uncompromising position on Kant's concept of symbol was an expression of the fact that, in principle, Cohen was strongly critical of symbolism in art and aesthetics. He perceived symbolism as a real threat to art. This was due to his negative assessment of Schelling's notion of symbol and of romanticism due to its close, vital correlation with metaphysics. According to Cohen, symbolism brings traditional forms of thinking about morality (especially in its religious variant) to art and its reception. He argued that the place for symbols was in forms of religious worship, where they played the role of raising cognition to the divine, towards a supernatural being. Cohen's critical attitude is the result of the belief that the notion of symbol abolishes the specificity and autonomy of a work of art; the beautiful ceases to be an independent aesthetic problem and instead becomes a symbol of the moral (see: Cohen 1912, pp. 103–104). Cohen believed that the independence and freedom of aesthetic consciousness lay in its liberation from mythical-religious ties. Presumably not without significance for Cohen's negative assessment is also the fact that Kant attributed an intuitive character to the symbolic approach. Meanwhile, according to Cohen's position, not only is there no such thing as intuitive cognition but, moreover, nothing can be decided on the basis of intuition.

The Concept of the Sublime

Let us now return to Cohen's further accusations against Kantian aesthetics. The principle of agreement established by Kant within the framework of the play of cognitive faculties has an opposite. A lack of purposiveness is joined to purposiveness, pain is joined to pleasure, and in the course of Kant's reflections the sublime is joined to beauty. Cohen wonders whether this correlation is only a formal aspect of purposiveness and agreement, or whether it is something more. Cohen is interested in the reasons that led Kant to accept the distinction between beauty and the sublime. In his opinion, this solution has opened up the possibility of reconciling contradictions: purposiveness with a lack of purposiveness.

In Cohen's opinion, it is also essential that with sublimity taken into account, the scope of subjectivization was broadened significantly. The subjectivization that manifested itself in the process of defining feeling (in distinguishing the subsumption of an aesthetic judgment from subsumption under a defined concept) and in the concept of genius, received full expression only after the sublime was taken into account. In Cohen's opinion, the sublime in Kant is not dependent on an object, but solely on the subject, not on nature, but on a person. According to Cohen, this Kantian reference of the sublime to man is the result of the conviction that it is closely correlated with the moral. Consequently, the ultimate subordination of the aesthetic to the ethical occurs in Kant within the framework of his conception of the sublime. In Cohen's opinion, this is a fundamental error in the Kantian project. Sublimity and beauty should be understood as moments of aesthetic consciousness, aesthetic feeling; they should be considered exclusively as aesthetic content, without mediation through the moral.

Further objections from Cohen are elicited by the fact that in Kant's opposition of pleasure (beauty) and pain (sublimity), there seems to be a qualitative advantage on the part of pain, of disharmony. Cohen emphasizes that this is a consequence of the Kantian conception of the sublime and the relationship – in this case not of understanding, but of reason and imagination – presumed to underlie it. Ultimately, in Kant's description of the sublime, the disharmony in the play of reason and imagination is overcome, giving way to a sense of deliberate adaptation of the cognitive powers to one another. Cohen expresses his doubts as to the methodical correctness of this solution, just as he had previously done with respect to beauty. In his opinion, the assessment of purposiveness in this case does not fulfill the function assigned to it any better than it did in regards to beauty; thus, it is difficult to consider it a satisfactory grounding of the aesthetic feeling of sublimity. In addition, Cohen again calls into question the sense of separating beauty and sublimity. Since both the feeling of pleasure and the feeling of pain are grounded in the assessment of purposiveness, the validity of this distinction must raise methodical doubts. The concept of aesthetic feeling itself does not, in his conviction, sufficiently justify this distinction.

The Ideal of Beauty and the Normative Idea

Cohen also opposes the teleologism of feeling on the basis of paragraph 17 of the *Critique of Judgment*, in which Kant distinguished the ideal of beauty from the normative idea (*Normalidee*), discrediting the normative idea with respect to the ideal of beauty. In Kant, we read: "But the normal idea is far from giving the complete *archetype* of *beauty* in the genus. It only gives the form that constitutes the indispensable condition of all beauty, and, consequently, only *correctness* in the presentation of the genus" (Kant 2007, p. 65).[13] The normative idea in Kant is therefore an individual presentation that constitutes a common "measure" or canon (e.g. the Doryphoros of Polykleitos, Myron's cow), enabling the assessment of a specimen on the basis of its belonging to a particular genus. The canon, in Kant's understanding, is important insofar as it defines the initial condition of the aesthetic, though it is not the prototype of beauty, but merely correctness.

---

[13] "Sie ist keineswegs das ganze Urbild der Schönheit in dieser Gattung, sondern nur die Form, welche die unnachläßliche Bedingung aller Schönheit ausmacht, mithin bloß die Richtigkeit in Darstellung der Gattung" (Kant 1922, p. 76).

Only the ideal of beauty, which is also a presentation, and thus the ideal of imagination, brings perfection, and that is because it is based on the rational idea that *a priori* defines a being's purpose. Thus, in the case of the ideal of beauty, the assessment is based on the concept of objective purposiveness. In other words, Kant concluded that only the human figure is fit for the ideal of beauty, for only man, by virtue of his reason, can, on the basis of concepts, set goals for himself; only he is capable of the beauty established by the concept of purpose. At the same time, Kant makes clear that an assessment based on the ideal of beauty cannot only be a judgment of taste; it "must be one *fixed* by a concept of objective purposiveness. Hence it cannot belong to the object of an altogether pure judgement of taste, but must attach to one that is partly intellectual" (Kant 2007, p. 63).[14]

Considering paragraph 17 of the *Critique of Judgment* concerning the purposiveness assumed for the ideal of beauty, Cohen wonders: is the normative idea merely an initial condition because it gains less purposiveness in the play of the cognitive powers than the ideal? According to Cohen, the intellectual interest attributed to the ideal of beauty (the ideal of beauty is, after all, determined by the ideas of reason) was understood by Kant as akin to the moral. In his opinion, an ideal grounded in the moral distorts the aesthetic problem. In Cohen's view, appealing to moral interest when intellectual interest is present undermines the autonomy of aesthetic pleasure and throws doubt on its grounding in the purposiveness of the cognitive faculties.

Ultimately, Cohen, concentrating in his discussion on the negative effects of Kant's solution for the conception of art, recognized the separation of the normative idea from the ideal of beauty as incompatible with systematic method, since the ideal of beauty was reduced to "the expression of the moral" (*Ausdruck des Sittlichen*). Cohen observes that the moral is a complex problem, and all its manifestations in religion, law, and art constitute questionable signs of culture. In his opinion, the artist would not be able to properly fulfill his task were he to create under dictation from a morally-conceived symbol. According to Cohen, objections to conditions such as these have led to the appearance of an equally disturbing phenomenon under the slogan of "art for art."

In the next step, Cohen points out that Kant's ideal of beauty excludes the lawfulness of nature and emphasizes the difference of this approach to that proposed by Winckelmann. According to Cohen, Winckelmann's "ideal of a line"

---

[14] "[...] durch einen Begriff von objektiver Zweckmäßigkeit fixierte Schönheit sein, folglich keinem Objekte eines ganz reinen, sondern zum Teil intellektuierten Geschmacksurteils angehören müsse" (Kant 1922, p. 73).

(*Ideal der Linie*) is the ideal of nature; the ideal of a methodical reproduction of nature in line, and as such constitutes the initial condition of the aesthetic reproduction of nature in a work of art. In Cohen's opinion, in such an approach, the ideal does not oppose the lawfulness of nature, and the cognition of nature expressed in the canon is not subject to being discredited in favor of an ideal grounded in morality. In his opinion this is the correct solution, because an ideal should not be perceived as being in opposition to nature. Winckelmann saw the source of the aesthetic problem in the concept of the ideal, Kant, on the other hand, asserted that the ideal: "can never be purely aesthetic." In Cohen's opinion, this approach made it impossible for Kant to properly recognize the concept of ideal; instead of subjecting the content of the ideal to methodical examination and grounding in the field of aesthetics, he excludes it from this field. In Cohen's opinion, the ideal, if understood as a mixed concept, becomes useless for the purity of aesthetic consciousness. Unlike Kant, Cohen believes that the ideal should be grasped "purely aesthetically" and only as such may belong to the aesthetic consciousness.

Cohen is well aware that almost every artistic representation of nature, whether it is a landscape or a still life, can express moral ideas. He would also agree with the assessment that in such cases the expression of the moral is "borrowed," and that only man expresses these ideas in full, because he is what he is. But according to Cohen, cognition and will, when they share in aesthetic pleasure, create a unity with it. The absence of this unity, in his opinion, is a basic shortcoming of the Kantian approach to the ideal of beauty, in which intellectualized and interested pleasure attaches itself as additional, external content to the aesthetic delight. From the perspective of the purity of the aesthetic, Cohen considers this state of affairs unacceptable. In his opinion, this is a consequence of grounding critique in the field of taste and simultaneously refusing taste any cognitive significance and moral interest.

In connection with paragraph 17 of the *Critique of Judgment*, Gadamer formulated an opinion opposite to Cohen's. According to Gadamer, Kant had to be convinced that such intellectualized and interested delight as in the case of the presentation of the ideal of beauty does not differ from aesthetic pleasure and constitutes a unity with it, that the representation of the human figure and artistic content of this representation are one and the same, that they simultaneous express their object. At the same time, Gadamer notes that though Kant first excluded, as a vain and internally contradictory task, the possibility of defining beauty by means of concepts, beauty for the ideal of beauty is determined by the concept of objective purposiveness.

Ultimately, Gadamer positively assessed the Kantian removal of "dry pleasure" beyond the aesthetics of taste, beyond formalism (see: Gadamer 2013, p. 45).

He considered conceiving of a work of art as more than just what satisfies the feeling of taste to be valuable. Gadamer emphasizes that in Kant, we are dealing with on the one hand, an undermining of the rationalism of aesthetics due to the indication that beauty pleases non-conceptually, and on the other, a discreditation of the concept of imitation in art, due to the distinction between the normative idea and the ideal of beauty. Thanks to this, according to Gadamer, within the framework of Kant's conception, art gained autonomy – its task was no longer to imitate perfect nature, but for man to meet with himself in nature and in history. Thus, in Gadamer's view, the doctrine of the ideal of beauty leads to a proper definition of the essence of art, which, according to the hermeneutical perspective, means the valorization of the sense, of the meaning of a work of art. In Gadamer's conviction, combining the ideal of beauty with the human figure, with the "expression of the moral," finds its consistent continuation in the doctrine of aesthetic ideas and beauty as a symbol of morality.

The above juxtaposition of two contrary interpretations of Kant's doctrine on the ideal of beauty is interesting. Without a doubt, paragraph 17 is among the most important and most controversial fragments of the *Critique of Judgment*. Both Cohen and Gadamer perceive the weight that the moral carries in Kant's aesthetic thought. However, where Gadamer perceives an aspiration to the independence of art and indication that a work of art is in the first place a carrier of meaning, there Cohen sees a threat to the autonomy of art and an incomplete, aggressively didactic realization of the moral.

The Concept of Genius

Cohen emphasizes that though Kant grounded the concept of art in the concept of genius, which fulfils a transcendental function, in justifying his aesthetic conception he started with receptivity, rather than with the artist's creative activity. Kant based the concepts of taste and genius on the same transcendental foundation; the faculties of the mind, whose combination (in a given proportion) accounts for genius, are also imagination and the understanding. Ingenious art is the ability to convey states of mind, the pleasure aroused by the free play of the cognitive faculties. Genius achieves this by virtue of the aesthetic ideas contained in a work of art. Taste also refers to this play of the cognitive faculties, as it assesses the state of mind resulting from this play. In Cohen's view, it is the doctrine of taste that constitutes the core of the Kantian conception. In his opinion, compared with the concept of genius, the aesthetic delight of taste is of greater systemic significance and can be applied both to the beauty of nature and to the beauty of art.

"Free" and "Dependent" Beauty

In Kant's view, taste does not come to know objects evaluated as beautiful, but is also not merely a subjective reaction of the senses in contact with a beautiful object. Taste is reflective and this allows it to fulfill its transcendental function. In his line of argument, he demonstrates that these conditions are only fulfilled by the "pure" judgment of taste. For this reason, Kant undertakes reflection on the difference between "pure" and "intellectualized" judgments of taste, and this distinction is reflected in his doctrine of "free" and "dependent" beauty. Among the objects that fall under the pure judgment of taste, Kant lists the free beauty of nature, in the field of art – ornaments, music (without a theme), as well as e.g. patterned rugs. In the case of free beauty, aesthetic delight is not subject to limitation by the concept of purpose. Kant counts all other cases, those in which the concept is involved, i.e. a majority of works of art (representative art), as belonging to "dependent" beauty. "Dependent" beauty encompasses the "intellectualized" judgment of taste, which is muddled and limited. In other words, a pure aesthetic judgment is a judgment made according to "what he has present to his senses," not according to "what he has present to his thoughts." Simultaneously, Kant adds that one and the same object can be grasped from both points of view: the free, and the dependent.

In interpreting the above stance, Gadamer recognizes that distinguishing a pure judgment of taste is an attempt at describing a model and an artificial, purely methodological procedure. Gadamer also asserts that "Kant regards the resulting diminution of aesthetic pleasure as, from the moral point of view, a gain" (Gadamer 2013, p. 42). In Gadamer's view, Kant, in not insisting on the purity of aesthetic judgments, signals that taste does not exhaust the essence of the power of judgment and thus prepares the basis for introducing the concept of genius. In his reading of the *Critique of Judgment*, Gadamer attempts, on the one hand, to demonstrate the consistency and order of Kant's line of argument, and on the other, indicates those aspects of Kant's project that are valuable from a hermeneutic perspective. For this reason, he positively views every departure beyond the subjectivism and formalism of the aesthetics of taste. At the same time, Gadamer considers the Kantian aesthetic project a closed chapter belonging to the past, as Gadamer's own thought is directed toward the hermeneutic meaning and ontology of a work of art.

Cohen read and interpreted the *Critique of Judgment* from a completely different perspective. For the most part, Cohen accepted Kant's transcendental point of departure and search for the *a priori* foundation of art and aesthetics. At the same time, however, Cohen's ambition was to creatively continue the transcendental perspective in art and aesthetics, which entailed a critical attitude towards an array of specific aspects of Kant's conception. The problem of the "purity of the aesthetic" was of utmost significance for Cohen, and seems to constitute the vital source of the dissimilarity of the two aesthetic conceptions. For this reason, the Kantian idea of a "pure" and "intellectualized" judgment of taste and its elaboration had to meet with a negative assessment from Cohen.

Summary

The above analyses demonstrate that Cohen's attitude towards Kant's aesthetical conclusions was not uncritical. In the first place, this concerns the concepts of teleology, aesthetic feeling, and symbol, which Cohen considered problematic. His assessment of the Kantian concept of purposiveness, which was connected with the teleological concept of feeling, was especially negative. Cohen emphasized that in Kant's thought, the feeling of beauty was grounded in the judgment on purposiveness, as a judgment of beauty is always a judgment of purposiveness. Cohen did not accept the identification of the aesthetic power of judgment with the teleological power of judgment, and critically evaluated correlating aesthetic *a priori* with subjective legislation. In Cohen's view, this Kantian idea contributed to the dissemination of the conviction that no objective principle of taste exists. From Cohen's perspective, such a foundation of aesthetics constitutes a threat towards recognition of the methodic nature of aesthetic *a priori*. He considered referring to subjectivity justified in reference to the teleological feeling of harmony, but could not accept that it constitutes the basis for aesthetic *a priori*. To aesthetic consciousness Cohen ascribed apriority, which is irreducible to the apriority of a teleological judgment.

Above all, however, Cohen thought that purposiveness did not accurately accentuate the creative nature of the activity of aesthetic consciousness. Purposiveness proceeds from the receptivity of aesthetic feeling, rather than from its productivity. Cohen negatively viewed Kant's understanding of feeling, which reduced feeling to the sensations of pleasure and pain. Taking this road, one could at most explain aesthetic experience; it did not allow for the moment of creation to be grasped, nor, in consequence, for a grasp of the methodical condition of pure production. In Cohen's view, aesthetic consciousness, instead of being cognition, should produce cognition, as only in this way can it confirm its sovereignty. Activity itself does not suffice; everything original and unique comes about by virtue of *creative* activity.

Bibliography

Akindinova, Tatiana (2010): "Die systematische Ästhetik von Cohen und ihre Ausstiege zu der Philosophie des 20. Jahrhunderts". In: *Divinatio* 32, pp. 71–77.

Cohen, Hermann (1912): *System der Philosophie. Teil III: Ästhetik des reinen Gefühls.* Bd. 1. Berlin: B. Cassirer.

Gadamer, Hans- Georg (2013): *Truth and Method.* Transl. J. Weinsheimer and D. G. Marshall. London, New Delhi, New York, Sydney: Bloomsbury Academic.

Holzhey, Helmut (2009): *Einleitung.* In: Cohen, Hermann: *Kants Begründung der Ästhetik.* In: Cohen, Hermann: *Werke.* Hermann-Cohen-Archiv am Philos. Seminar der Univ. Zürich. Bd. 3. Holzhey, Helmut (Hrsg.). Hildesheim: Olms Verlag, pp. 1* – 12*.

Horstmann, Rolf- Peter (2008): "Hermann Cohen on Kant's Transcendental Aesthetic". In: *The Philosophical Forum* 39 (2), pp. 127 – 138.

Kant, Immanuel (2007): *Critique of Judgement.* Transl. James Creed Meredith. New York: Oxford University Press.

Kant, Immanuel (1922): *Kritik der Urteilskraft.* Karl Vorländer (Hrsg.). Leipzig: Felix Meiner Verlag.

Kinkel, Walter (1924): *Hermann Cohen. Eine Einführung in sein Wert.* Stuttgart: Verlag von Strecker und Schröder.

Renz, Ursula (2002): *Die Rationalität der Kultur. Zur Kulturphilosophie und ihrer transzendentalen Begründung bei Cohen, Natorp und Cassirer.* Hamburg: Felix Meiner Verlag.

Ryszard Kleszcz
Criticism and Rationality in the Lvov-Warsaw School

Abstract: The Lvov-Warsaw School was founded in Lvov in 1895 by Kazimierz Twardowski, a student of Franz Brentano. In this paper I discuss the problem of criticism and rationalism as the methodological foundation of Twardowski's school. Criticism (scientific criticism) protects us against dogmatism and skepticism. For Twardowski, the language of philosophy should respect the postulates of clarity, precision, and accuracy. For this reason, his philosophical program assigns a significant role to logical tools and the semiotic method of analysis. Another important feature of Twardowski's school was rationalism, called anti-irrationalism in the Lvov-Warsaw School. Anti-irrationalism (rationalism) valued knowledge with intersubjective traits: communicability and controllability. The author takes into consideration the value of the meta-philosophical program accepted by the Lvov-Warsaw School.

Keywords: criticism, Kazimierz Twardowski, Lvov-Warsaw School, Kazimierz Ajdukiewicz, anti-irrationalism, rationality, logical tools in philosophy.

> "...to say of someone that she is a dogmatist is to say that she holds her views more strongly than is appropriate, more strongly than the evidence warrants, for example; alternatively, it is to say that she holds her views uncritically, without paying sufficient heed to objections and alternatives, or to the limitations of human reason..."
> **Alvin Plantinga**

> "The essential characteristic of philosophy, which makes it a study distinct from science, is *criticism*. It examines critically the principles employed in science and in daily life; it searches out any inconsistencies there may be in these principles, and it only accepts them when, as the result of the critical inquiry, no reason rejecting them has appeared"
> **Bertrand Russell**

1. The Lvov-Warsaw School is a Polish school of analytic philosophy founded by Kazimierz Twardowski in 1895 in Lvov, where he was the Head of Lvov University's Department of Philosophy. From the very beginning, Twardowski, a student of Franz Brentano, wished to give his philosophical reflection a scientific, but simultaneously nonpositivistic character. To achieve this, he adopted two important postulates: criticism and rationalism. In this text, I would like to examine what Twardowski said on this matter and what was later adopted by his students in the Lvov-Warsaw School (hereinafter LWS). The problems of criticism and its opposite, dogmatism, as well as the tools necessary for the realization of the postulates of criticism in philosophical activity can be found in various texts of Twardowski. They are present in Twardowski's programmatic speech, which opened the first session of the Polish Philosophical Society in Lvov on the 12th of February 1904. The postulate of criticism, as well as its realization, requires a recourse to methodological tools, especially those provided by logic. The problem of criticism, of utilizing logic in the field of philosophy, also relates to the issue of rationality in the domain of belief. Therefore, criticism involves the usage of tools (logic) which simultaneously enable it, as well as the fulfillment of the requirements of rationality.

2. The philosophy Twardowski postulated was supposed to be a scientific-philosophy, critical of the models of the German idealistic philosophy.[1] Twardowski's critical assessment of German idealism was almost as negative as Franz Brentano's.[2] However, this does not mean that Twardowski directed his path towards the positivism he was also so critical of. He writes:

> There are numerous objects with which metaphysics could busy itself; there is a lot of material for work and only the narrow horizon of positivists does not allow them to correctly evaluate the significance of these issues (Twardowski 1994, p. 229).

For Twardowski, criticism was the opposite of dogmatism, because criticism ("scientific criticism") was meant to protect us from prejudices and preconceived arbitrary notions. Embracing the spirit of criticism makes our way of thinking critical; furthermore, it guards us against a bias, which is a threat posed by dogmatism, on the one hand, and by skepticism, on the other. In Twardowski's opinion, the spirit of criticism protects us against the narrow-mindedness of dogmatism and skepticism, contributing to the creation of proper cognitive and personal virtues. This also requires criticism, since:

---

[1] See: Twardowski 1904, p. 242. Also see: Dąmbska 1948, pp. 14–25.
[2] See: Brentano 1968, pp. 11–14.

> [...] only with criticism can a man protect himself against overconfidence and disregarding the opinion of another, and at the same time keep the proper balance between rampant emotionality and barren curtness (Twardowski 1965, pp. 346–348).

Criticism can be associated with the postulate of impartiality and with not submitting to the dominance of a methodological or national tradition in philosophy. Hence Twardowski's appeal, which still seems to be relevant:

> We should not succumb to the biased influence of such and such trend, or even of such and such nation [...] (Twardowski 1904, p. 242).

It was Twardowski's intention that criticism be combined with independence of thought and seeking that which could provide a lasting support for philosophical reflection. The independence he postulated should become an attribute of both individual thinkers and of philosophy as a whole. Criticism, which is essential to all thinking, is particularly crucial in the field of philosophy, as it not only protects us from dogmatism, but also from mistakes (see: Russell's words in the second motto). The specific nature of philosophy is the reason why difficulties encountered in this area easily lead to errors. Kazimierz Twardowski noted this fact, stating the following about philosophical teachings:

> These teachings, remaining in the area of the furthest reaching abstractions and dealing with issues directly or indirectly, but always and without exception, linked to the spiritual life of human beings, make its workers most easily exposed to the numerous errors and mistakes that arise most often in places where grasping the actual state of affairs and thus verifying hypotheses, is the most difficult (Twardowski 1904, pp. 240–241).

Thus, it is clear that the unique situation of philosophy is related to its unique character, which can be described as follows:
a) Philosophical teachings refer to the most abstract issues, in contrast to the **specialty** sciences,
b) Issues touched upon by various branches of philosophy always relate, directly or indirectly, to the spiritual life of human beings,
c) These subject- and object-related issues may lead to errors more often than in the case of other sciences,
d) This risk of errors mainly results from the fact that in philosophy, grasping the real state of affairs and verifying formulated hypotheses is especially difficult.

Hence the particular importance of criticism in philosophy, because especially restrictive means should apply within its sphere to protect against dogmatism, but primarily, against errors which are much easier to make there than in other disciplines. The special role of criticism in philosophy has been stressed by numerous thinkers, especially, although not solely, by those continuing a tradition initiated by Twardowski or, more generally, representing the analytical trend.

According to Twardowski, the postulate of criticism is related to that of precise thinking. This precision is indispensable not only in theory, but also in practice. As Twardowski points out, this was already noted by David Hume, who indicated the practical benefits arising from the cultivation of philosophy, which nurtures the spirit of precision in us:

> Besides, we may observe, in every art of professions, even those which most concern life or action, that a spirit of accuracy, however acquired, carries all of them nearer their perfection, and renders them more subservient to the interests of society. And though a philosopher may live remote from business, the genius of philosophy, if carefully cultivated by several, must gradually diffuse itself throughout the whole society, and bestow a similar correctness on every art and calling (Hume 1778, p. 10).

The postulates of criticism should have consequences and their implementation requires an appropriate level of precision in the texts (speeches) of their authors. For Twardowski, as I mentioned earlier, it was of the utmost importance that the language of philosophy should respect the postulates of clarity, precision, and accuracy, when it comes to both the presentation of a problem, and to the proposals of solutions. All of Twardowski's works demonstrate this implicitly, while explicitly this desire was best expressed in his article *O jasnym i niejasnym stylu filozoficznym* (*On Clear and Unclear Philosophical Style*).[3] Twardowski was one of those philosophers who were not inclined to accept the thesis that the level of complication of a philosophical issue must entail its lack of clarity. He rejected such an opinion in the article mentioned above, associating the lack of clarity in style to a lack of clarity and vagueness of thought. Therefore – according to Twardowski – clarity of thought is also linked to clarity of writing. Twardowski asks whether the acceptance of an unclear philosophical style can be allowed, and gives a negative answer. It does not seem justifiable to suppose that a lack of clarity, at which German thinkers in particular seem to excel, is caused by the complexity of certain problems. Two arguments speak against this:

a) it cannot be proved that all written texts on a given complicated philosophical issue are unclear;

---

[3] See: Twardowski 1965, pp. 346–348.

b) it is easy to prove that some issues, perceived as difficult and complex, are expressed by some philosophers clearly.[4]

Twardowski points out that thought and speech are closely related; it is not possible to think about a given philosophical issue and only afterwards put it into words. An abstract form occurs instantly in verbal form. Thus, it is not possible to think about something clearly and later have difficulties clearly expressing these thoughts. Therefore, a lack of clarity never results from difficulties caused by the nature of the issues studied, but is always the result of a lack of clarity and vagueness in a given author's way of thinking.[5] Twardowski ends his deliberations with the conclusion that it is not worth racking one's brain about what was written by an author using an unclear style.

3. In general logic, the relation between clarity logic skills is easy to grasp. Knowledge, and especially training in this area, gives us abilities that allow us to cope with difficulties related to research and work in the field of philosophy. The work of Twardowski himself provides us with good examples in this regard. He stresses the fact that the language we use is not a perfect tool and requires hard work to improve; hence, the attention that should be paid to the analysis of language, including the analysis of philosophical notions used. Twardowski's philosophical program assigns an important, even key, role to the semiotic method of analysis. Numerous disputes, including those significant for philosophy, have their origin in linguistic misunderstandings.

Thus, the use of logical tools can protect us against errors, which requires paying attention to the place and meaning of logic in Twardowski's though. In speaking of the use of logic, we mean logical tools in the broadest sense of the word. In short, it boils down to logic perceived as general logic, including semiotics, formal logic, and general methodology. Kazimierz Twardowski appreciated the role of logic so understood, and thought that some general preparation in the field of logic was indispensable for all educated human beings. In his opinion, one could speak of a logical education if one possessed certain indispensable knowledge and some developed abilities. Thus, logical competency is a matter of knowledge and some training in the field of logic. Such training should provide a person with knowledge on what drawing conclusions is, and with some logical sensitivity that should protect against falling into the trap of logical inconsistency. According to Twardowski, in his times, logic was not well developed among educated people. It was therefore important to him to ed-

---

4 See:Twardowski 1965, pp. 346–347.
5 See: Twardowski 1965, p. 347.

ucate teachers, because various logical inconsistencies could also be found in scientific works. Thus, besides teaching and holding seminars, he also wrote a textbook for teachers. This textbook, *Zasadnicze pojęcia dydaktyki i logiki do użytku w seminariach nauczycielskich i nauce prywatnej* (*The Main Notions of Dydactics and Logic for Use in Pedagogical Schools and in Private Learning*), was published in 1901.[6]

A separate, significant, and especially interesting issue is the role of logic in philosophical education and in philosophical research. When it comes to logic as science, Twardowski stressed changes that took place in this regard during the second half of the 19th century.[7] These changes, which gave it a new shape, lead to the present state (the beginning of the 20th century) in which it became clear that Kant's statement about logic defining it as a complete science to which nothing new can be added, could no longer be supported. Twardowski writes:

> As a result of such a lively interest in logic by scholars a review – so to say – of almost all theses appropriate for this science and submitted by a many-century tradition sanctioned by Kant's statement on the permanency of the logic of Aristotle took place. Today, nobody believes in this permanency and the one who proclaimed it, forgot that mathematics, based no less than logic on a priori data, has always developed and develops still today (Twardowski 1996, p. 156).[8]

According to Twardowski, at the beginning of the 20th century, some logical issues were well developed (e.g. the theory of induction), while others were still the subject of disputes, as it was with the theory of judgments. Logic was perceived by Twardowski from a psychologistic perspective for some time. Even in the above-mentioned text entitled *Theory of Judgments*, which was primarily a lecture, logic is still perceived psychologistically, or at least psychologically. This visible psychologism is, however, overcome by Twardowski during this period.[9] Appreciating the role of logic, Twardowski was nonetheless moderate

---

[6] In this book, in six chapters devoted to logic, the following issues are discussed: issues in the theory of judgments, their validity, the issue of reasoning and its forms, deduction and proofs, the theory of notions (along with the issue of definitions, logical division, and classification), as well as methodological issues along with a short description of the empirical and deductive sciences. See: Twardowski 1901, pp. 13–92.

[7] See: Twardowski 1996, p. 156. It seems that the issue of Twardowski's perception of logic and its meaning requires consideration of the influence his teacher Franz Brentano had on him. In Twardowski's archives, notes from Brentano's lectures on logic were found. On this matter, See: (Dąmbska 1978, pp. 117–129; and: P. Simons 2004 *passim*, especially pp. 63–64).

[8] This text by Twardowski was presented during lectures in Lvov University, probably during the 1902/1903 academic year.

[9] See: Kleszcz 2009, pp. 163–170.

about the use of such methods. In his article *Symbolomania i pragmatofobia* (*Symbolomania and Pragmatophobia*), he clearly warns against their inappropriate use.[10] He means that while using this tool one should not forget the meaning of a given symbolism. One could say that Twardowski's concerns are evoked by analyses of a purely syntactic nature without any attempt to establish if the gained results are compatible with reality. Thus, his intentions can be read as a will to appreciate the semantic area and at the same time research of this type.

An analysis of Kazimierz Twardowski's works and the place he ascribed to logic attests to the significance he ascribed to it. His appreciation for logic (*sensu largo*) is not limited to the declarative ascription of a certain place in philosophy to it. Without using the tools of logic, one cannot achieve the goals set by philosophical analysis. This does not mean that Twardowski personally carried out research in the field of logic that was compliant with the newest trends (i.e. logistic research according to the terminology of the day). He did not carry out and did not apply any sophisticated logical tools in philosophy. Kazimierz Ajdukiewicz, extremely well acquainted with this area, describes this accurately.[11]

Twardowski was the first philosopher to acquaint students in Lvov with the new logic. From the beginning of his activity as a teacher in Lvov, i.e. since 1895, he held lectures on general logic, and in the winter semester of 1898, i.e. from the third year of his activity as a professor, he held lectures on algebraic logic entitled *O dążnościach reformatorskich na polu logiki formalnej*.[12] These classes initiated by Twardowski in the academic year of 1899/1900 were continued in mathematical logic (logistics), starting in 1906, by his student Jan Łukasiewicz – later a world renowned logician.[13] Thus, although Twardowski himself did not carry out innovative formal and logic research, he attached great importance to general logic and methodological culture, and he directly contributed to its popularization. This highly positive attitude towards logic was common at LWS. At the same time, among Twardowski's students, a specialization could be distinguished and a group of his students chose logic as their main area of

---

10 See: Twardowski 1965, pp. 354–363.
11 See: Ajdukiewicz 1934, pp. 400–401.
12 However, in his list of Twardowski's lectures and seminars, Ryszard Jadczak enumerates a one-hour lecture entitled *O dążnościach reformatorskich na polu logiki formalnej* in the winter semester of the 1899/1900 academic year. See: Jadczak 1991, pp. 60–61.
13 In P. Simons' opinion: "Twardowski, Brentano's last important Viennese student, taught a course on the reforms logic at Lwów, and his lectures ... were attended by or at least known to later stars of the Lwów – Warsaw School such as Łukasiewicz and Leśniewski" (Simons 2004, p. 63).

interest (Stanisław Leśniewski, Jan Łukasiewicz). Others focused their research on psychology (Władysław Witwicki) and other philosophical disciplines (Kazimierz Ajdukiewicz on epistemology and methodology). However, all of them underwent training in the area of broadly-understood logic.

4. Aside from criticism, another significant distinguishing feature of LWS was rationalism, which, following the publication of a famous article by Kazimierz Ajdukiewicz, was called anti-irrationalism.[14] The way Twardowski perceived philosophy and its methods was close to models referring to notions of some type of rationalism and of an approach requiring rationality from philosophical reflection and philosophical beliefs. The notion of "rationality" itself sometimes appears *expressis verbis* in his texts and speeches. Kazimierz Twardowski speaks about it in his subsequent text, in a speech for the 25th anniversary of the Polish Philosophical Society in Lvov (1929). Twardowski employs three notions there, namely: rationality, irrationality, and non-rationality.[15] Thus, in his reasoning there is no simple dichotomy of beliefs into rational ones and those deprived of rationality. This allows us to classify human beliefs, within the scope of this proposal of Twardowski, into three groups:

A) Rational beliefs, characterized by the fact that in their case the methods of gaining beliefs as well as their justification are obtained from the arsenal of science. Rationality according to Twardowski seems to be a synonym of science.

B) Irrational beliefs, which differ from rational beliefs as to the source from which they are obtained. In this case, one can refer to various (sources) which science does not use, such as intellectual observation or intuition, special experiences, etc. However, if one analyzes such beliefs from the perspective of the content, they do not have to be in conflict with rational beliefs and thus with scientific theses.

C) Non-rational beliefs, whose specificity consists in a lack of compliance with the content of data provided by science. Thus, in terms of evaluating their cognitive quality, not the way they are obtained is important, but rather the fact of the lack of the content compliance with the scientific data.

Twardowski concludes that in a human being's belief set, a majority constitute beliefs which, according to the above-mentioned terminology, have to be included into the second group of beliefs defined as irrational and which do not have to be in conflict with beliefs defined as rational ones. Such are, according to Twardowski, beliefs of the area of general worldview.

---

14 See: Ajdukiewicz 1934, pp. 399–408; 1935, pp. 151–161.
15 See: Twardowski 1965, pp. 379–384.

When the notion of worldview appears in the context of Twardowski's philosophy, it is necessary to keep in mind the metaphilosophical assumptions visible when one analyzes his philosophical thought. Twardowski differentiates between scientific philosophy and a philosophical (metaphysical) view on the world and life. Scientific philosophy is, first of all, a theory of knowledge (although not solely because there also is a general theory of the subject). These methodological assumptions accepted by Twardowski may only be used within a limited field of research – one that remains available for research carried out with the use of scientific tools and methods. One cannot refer to it if one wants to answer some final questions about the human being which remain beyond scientific philosophy. According to Twardowski, one cannot prove the correctness of one or another point of view within the scope of a worldview by way of scientific argumentation. Twardowski postulates the separation of scientific philosophy from worldview.[16] This point of view later became typical for LWS. For Twardowski it was obvious that people have beliefs in area of worldview. He did not underestimate this area because according to him, the practical value of these beliefs was huge. In his opinion:

> Philosophical views on the world and life are of a great value for their advocates making signpost for their opinions on the world, human environment, and themselves (Twardowski 1965, p. 381).

Due to them one can obtain guidelines as to one's views on the world, one's surroundings, and oneself. Beliefs in this area which are not scientific beliefs are not classified as rational according to this concept. However, as Twardowski stresses, they do not have to be non-rational (in Twardowski's terminology) and thus need not be in conflict with scientific theses.

In 1934, in the above-mentioned article by Kazimierz Ajdukiewicz, first published in Polish and then in German, LWS can be characterized in the following way.[17] It is characterized by the following methodological traits: **1) anti-irrationalism; 2) the postulate of notional clarity and linguistic precision; 3) acquisition of the devices of modern formal logic.**[18] Rationalism, called anti-irrationalism by Ajdukiewicz (these notions can be used interchangeably), is a point of view valuing the scientific cognition provided by mathematics and the natural sciences. Scientific cognition should, as Ajdukiewicz indicated a dozen years later in *Zagadnienia i kierunki filozofii* (*Problems and Trends in Phi-*

---

[16] For a more detailed analysis, see: Kleszcz 2016, pp. 135–151.
[17] See: Ajdukiewicz 1934, pp. 399–408; German version in: Ajdukiewicz 1935, pp. 151–161.
[18] See: Ajdukiewicz 1934, p. 399.

losophy, 1949), fulfil two conditions: intersubjective communicability and intersubjective verificability.[19] The condition of intersubjective communicability requires that a given content of thoughts be submitted literally, i.e. without any metaphors, comparisons, and other means of submitting thoughts. Intersubjective verificability, in turn, is the possibility of (an intersubjective) control allowing to convince each appropriately prepared person about the correctness / incorrectness of a given thesis. This point of view of Ajdukiewicz is often presented, not without reason, as typical for the characteristics of rationalism (anti-irrationalism) at Twardowski's School. Anti-irrationalism (rationalism), valuing cognition with intersubjective traits (communicability, controllability), is juxtaposed with the irrationalistic position. Such rational cognition comes at a price, however. It has a schematic, abstractive character and, as Ajdukiewicz expresses it, loses "its intimate contact with the subject." Thus, for anti-irrationalism one has to pay a price and not every philosopher is willing to do it.

5. Criticism and anti-irrationalism as a program strongly popularized by the above-mentioned philosophers refer to, as it has been proved, to scientific knowledge and acknowledge the value of science. However, such a program does not have to be scientism, and it definitely does not have to be radical scientism. The value of the anti-irrationalistic program would be protection it offers against vagueness and voicing unfounded views, i.e. against what Twardowski called declamation. It allows us to ascribe the appropriate cognitive values to our beliefs. Both cognitive and ethical arguments are in favor of accepting this program. It does not have to be scientism and its basis does not need be a single defined metaphilosophy. The anti-irrationalistic program is attractive for philosophers placing value on the mind, however, its implementation and materialization can be a subject of a debate. In the case of such a debate it is worth recalling the words of Kazimierz Twardowski:

> [...] searching for the truth, no one wants to discover the whole truth alone, or to claim that its discovery was due to his own merits (Twardowski 1994, p. 236).

Philosophy is a joint endeavor of more and less important philosophers who always create this work independently, on their own and at their own risk.

---

19 See: Ajdukiewicz 2004, pp. 49 ff. Ajdukiewicz also notes that although philosophers, e.g. of the 18th century, often referred to rationalism, this notion has never been clearly formulated.

Bibliography

Ajdukiewicz, Kazimierz (1934): "Logistyczny antyirracjonalizm w Polsce" [Logistic Irrationalism in Poland]. In: *Przegląd Filozoficzny* 3, pp. 399–408.
Ajdukiewicz, Kazimierz (1935): "Die Logistische Antirrationalismus in Polen". In: *Erkenntnis* 5, pp. 151–161.
Ajdukiewicz, Kazimierz (2004): *Zagadnienia i kierunki filozofii* [*Problems and Trends in Philosophy*]. Kęty – Warszawa: Wydawnictwo Antyk.
Brentano, Franz (1968): *Über die Zukunft der Philosophie*. Hamburg: Verlag Felix Meiner.
Dąmbska, Izydora (1948). "Czterdzieści lat filozofii we Lwowie" [Forty Years Philosophy in Lvov]. In: *Przegląd Filozoficzny* 1–3, pp. 14–25.
Dąmbska, Izydora (1978): "François Brentano et la pensée philosophique en Pologne; Casimir Twardowski et son école". In: *Grazer Philosophische Studien* 5, pp. 117–129.
Hume, David (1778): *An Enquiry Concerning Human Understanding*. In: D. Hume: *Philosophical Essays Concerning Human Understanding*: London: A. Millar.
Jacquette, Dale (ed.) (2004): *The Cambridge Companion to Brentano*, Cambridge (UK): Cambridge University Press.
Jadczak, Ryszard (1991): *Kazimierz Twardowski. Nota biobibliograficzna*, [*Kazimierz Twardowski. Bibliographical Note*]. Toruń: PTF.
Kleszcz, Ryszard (2009): L'antipsychologisme en logique. Twardowski et Łukasiewicz. In: A. Horecka (ed.): *Logic, Methodology and Philosophy of Science at Warsaw University*. Vol. 5, pp. 163–170.
Kleszcz, Ryszard (2016): "Kazimierz Twardowski on Metaphysics". In: Anna Brożek, Alicja Chybińska, Jacek Jadacki, Jan Woleński (Eds.): *Tradition of the Lvov –Warsaw School: Ideas and Continuations. Poznań Studies in the Philosophy of Sciences and the Humanities*. Vol. 106. Leiden: Brill/Rodopi, pp. 135–151.
Simmons, Peter (2004): "Judging Correctly: Brentano and the Reform of Elementary Logic". In: D. Jacquette (ed.): *The Cambridge Companion to Brentano*. Cambridge (UK): Cambridge University Press, pp. 45–65.
Twardowski, Kazimierz (1897): *Psychologia wobec fizjologii i filozofii* [Psychology against Physiology and Philosophy]. In: Twardowski (1965), pp. 92–113.
Twardowski, Kazimierz (1901): *Zasadnicze pojęcia dydaktyki i logiki do użytku w seminariach nauczycielskich i w nauce prywatnej* [The Main Notions of Dydactics and Logic for the Use in Pedagogical Schools and in Private Learning]. Lwów.
Twardowski, Kazimierz (1904): "Przemówienie na otwarciu Polskiego Towarzystwa Filozoficznego we Lwowie" [A Speech Delivered During the Opening Session of the Polish Philosophical Society in Lvov]. In: *Przegląd Filozoficzny* 2, pp. 239–243.
Twardowski, Kazimierz (1913): *O psychologii, jej przedmiocie, zadaniach, metodzie, stosunku do innych nauk i jej rozwoju* [On Psychology, Its Object, Aims, Method, Relation to the Other Sciences and Its Development]. In: Twardowski (1965), pp. 241–291.
Twardowski, Kazimierz (1919–1920a): *O jasnym i niejasnym stylu filozoficznym* [On the Clear and Unclear Philosophical Style. In: Twardowski (1965), pp. 346–348.
Twardowski, Kazimierz (1919–1920b): *Filozofia w szkole średniej* [Philosophy in High School]. In: *Ruch Filozoficzny 1919/1920*, I, pp. 1–6.
Twardowski, Kazimierz (1923): *O naukach apriorycznych, czyli racjonalnych (dedukcyjnych), i naukach aposteriorycznych, czyli empirycznych (indukcyjnych)* [On a priori or Rational

(Deductive) Sciences and on a posteriori or Empirical (Inductive) ones]. In: Twardowski (1965), pp. 364–372.

Twardowski, Kazimierz (1931): Przemówienie wygłoszone na obchodzie dwudziestopięciolecia Polskiego Towarzystwa Filozoficznego we Lwowie [A Speech Delivered During the Twenty Fifth Anniversary of the Polish Philosophical Society]. In: Twardowski (1965), pp. 379–384.

Twardowski, Kazimierz (1965): *Wybrane pisma filozoficzne* [Selected Philosophical Writings], Warszawa: PWN.

Twardowski, Kazimierz (1994): "Wykład wstępny w Uniwersytecie Lwowskim" [Introductory Lecture in Lvov University]. In: *Principia* VIII – IX, pp. 227–236.

Twardowski, Kazimierz (1996): "Teoria sądów" [Theory of Judgements]. In: *Filozofia Nauki* 4, pp. 155–173.

Adam Jonkisz
Rationality and Criticism in the Views of the Philosophers of the Lvov-Warsaw School and K.R. Popper

Abstract: The article contains a comparative analysis of the Lvov-Warsaw School's and K.R. Popper's views on rationality and criticism. The analysis is preceded by clarifications of the notions of rationality and criticism – what they refer to and the relationship between them – to justify the aspects in which these views are compared in the article, i.e. testability, objectivity, and the critical attitude. The results of these analyses lead to the conclusion that in each of these aspects, Popper's views had better, though lesser known, antecedents in the output of the School's philosophers; and to a more general assessment: Popper's views evolved in the direction of the programs and conceptions elaborated by the Lvov-Warsaw School philosophers.

Keywords: Lvov-Warsaw School, Popper, rationality, criticism, testability, objectivism

1 Introductory Remarks

1. Despite the order listed in the title, I will present the views of the Lvov-Warsaw School philosophers against the backdrop of K.R. Popper's views. Though such an order of analysis reverses the chronological order in which these philosophers published their philosophical conclusions, it is justified by the fact that Popper's views on rationality and criticism are much better-known than those of the Lvov-Warsaw School philosophers. Moreover, though Popper's views evolved over the course of his lifetime – this is described in the history of the philosophy of science and systemized in its metaphilosophy[1] – it is easier to look for parallels to elements of his theory of rationality in the conceptions voiced by the Lvov-Warsaw School, than it would be to reconstruct a coherent whole from the views of the School's many representatives, scattered throughout many philosophical publications.

---

[1] I. Lakatos, a student and continuator of Popper, elaborated such an ordering: Lakatos 1968, pp. 149–186, Lakatos 1970, pp. 96–103, 180–189, Lakatos 1974, p. 244.

2. In accordance with the title of these reflections, I will only take into account those of the School's philosophers, whose views are significant to the problem of rationalism and criticism – not all of them, however. In the comparative analysis I will almost exclusively discuss those results published independently of Popper's views; above all, therefore, those that were contained in works published before the first edition of *Logik der Forschung*. References to later publications will only be made if they are rooted in views from before 1934. An important reason for selecting only certain philosophers of the School and their views is the fact that I am not familiar with its entire output – regardless of the criteria used to determine which philosophers are representatives of the School. Hence, regarding this matter, I accept what has been established in studies of this output,[2] making use of select conclusions for my own comparative analyses.

3. I will preface the comparison of Popper's and the School's representatives' views with distinctions concerning the notions contained in the title, i.e. rationality and criticism. My goal is not to undertake an in-depth analysis, but rather to indicate their references and the conditions implicit in their content – and only to the extent in which I will use them in comparing K. Popper's views with those of the School's philosophers.

2 The Concepts of Rationality/Rationalism and Criticalness/Criticism

1. The terms *rationality* and *rationalism* are often used interchangeably, despite the fact that their respective referents are located on different levels. Rationality refers to an action – specifically, to the decisions and actions of scientists, while rationalism refers to a conception of rationality. In other words, rationality is located on the objective level, while rationalism (rationalisms) is situated on the metalevel upon which conceptions of rationality (e.g. scientific rationality) are formulated. A failure to distinguish between the objective level (e.g. of science) and the level of metascience (e.g. the philosophy of science) is even more frequent in regard to the terms *criticalness* and *criticism*. The first of these terms

---

[2] The following works constitute the basis for most of my reflections: Zamecki 1977, Woleński 1985, and Woleński 1997.

The conclusions contained in the works mentioned above are either used directly in this article or treated as indications of where significant views from the point of view of my analyses can be found in the publications of the Lvov-Warsaw School philosophers.

is rarely used. The phrases *critical view* and *critical attitude* are often used in place of it to emphasize that one is speaking about a feature of scientific actions, rather than about postulates or conceptions formulated in the philosophy of science. Most often, however, the term *criticism* is used in reference to both scientific attitudes and metascientific conceptions.[3]

2. Regarding conceptions formulated in the philosophy of science, the opposition rationalism-irrationalism can be understood as based on either a contradiction or a contrary. According to the first understanding, every philosopher – as long as he or she makes statements within the context of this opposition – is either an advocate of rationalism, or an advocate of irrationalism. In contrast, the second interpretation allows the possibility of a conception that is neither rationalistic, nor irrationalistic, but lies somewhere in between the two extremes. An analogous ambiguity is present in the opposition rationality vs. irrationality.[4] To disambiguate my analyses concerning the philosophers mentioned in the title, especially those of the School, I take the terms *rationalism* and *irrationalism* to be contradictory terms, in accordance with the most common understanding of the relationship between these concepts. Therefore, if someone is not an advocate of rationalism, or more precisely – if that person rejects rationalism, then he or she is an advocate of irrationalism; analogously, if an action is not rational, then it is irrational. It is worth noting that such an understanding of this opposition opens up the possibility of distinguishing variants of irrationalism and degrees of irrationality.

Because the opposition rationalism-irrationalism, understood as contradictory, encompasses all possible positions on this issue, anti-irrationalism, as the contrary of irrationalism, is coextensive with rationalism. We can say that it is the polemic version of rationalism. Thus, from the critique of irrationalism, we can explicate the components (content) of the rationalist stance called anti-irrationalism. Moreover, in cases where rationalism's program was put into practice rather than declared, we can identify the components of the rationalist attitude on the basis of a style of philosophizing. Both of these methods of reconstruction – i.e. on the basis of a critique of irrationalism, and on an implemented program of scientific philosophy – will be used in presenting the views of the School's representatives.

---

[3] The title of this article also contains the term *criticism*; however, because it is used in the context of "the view of philosophers ....," it refers to the level of scientific attitudes, with which the postulates formulated in philosophy are concerned.

[4] Changing "ir-" to "non-" does not disambiguate the terms formed with these prefixes, since there remains a difference between being non-rational in the sense of not being rational and in the sense of being irrational.

3. In these reflections, distinctions often used in studies on rationality – e. g. rationality of thought vs. rationality of action,[5] as well as those used in descriptions of variants of irrationalism, e. g. logical, epistemological, metaphysical, psychological,[6] will not be needed. In comparing Popper's conception with the views of the Lvov-Warsaw School philosophers, I will limit myself to what concerns the rationality of action, or more precisely – the rationality of actions concerning the products of science, e. g. scientific sentences (questions, hypotheses, statements), theories, methods, etc. Such an approach will also allow us to take into account actions like declaring and justifying statements (usually considered as belonging to the field of the rationality of thought), and limits analyses to the context of justification – which is accurate with regard to both Popper's views, and those of the School's philosophers.[7]

4. Broadly-understood scientific rationality boils down to the recognition of products of science on the basis of reasons justifying their acceptance, or more precisely – to recognizing, stating, and advancing scientific claims and theories in a degree appropriate to their degree of justification. This includes cases of rejecting claims and theories that are unjustified or less justified than competing claims and theories. The components of rationality so understood, or more precisely – its necessary conditions, are testability, objectivity, and criticism. Testability and the requirements it posits must be fulfilled by products of science; the objectivity condition can refer to both products and scientific actions; while criticism is an indispensable trait of the scientific attitude, and thus a component of the scientific method, or more precisely – it constitutes the pragmatic and axiological aspect of this method.

3 The Pattern of Scientific Rationality

The analyses conducted in accordance with the remarks formulated above concern methodological rationality, i. e. patterns of the scientific method proposed

---

[5] See e. g. Szaniawski 1994, p. 532, first printed in: Szaniawski 1983.
[6] The variants of irrationalism listed above are described in: Dąmbska 1937/38; reprint in: Perzanowski/Janik 2009.
[7] The division of sciences according to their method of justification, rather than discovery, can already be found in a work by K. Twardowski published in 1923. See: Woleński 1985, pp. 48–49; Zamecki 1977, pp. 125–126. Thus, the source of this division should be sought not in H. Reichenbach's 1938 publication, but rather – at least with regard to Polish philosophy – in the views of the School's philosophers.

or implemented by philosophers of the Lvov-Warsaw School and Popper.[8] Simultaneously, these patterns will be compared mainly from the perspective of the presence of the postulates of testability, objectivity, and criticism.

3.1 Testability

The preliminary condition of testability is sensefulness, i.e. the possession of meaning. Testability is connected in a positive way with a good formulation or articulation of sense: good means precise, while precise means unambiguous, sharp, and clear. And, what is known, often only the degree of precision of expressions can be compared. Testability also favors generality, i.e. a wider range of the formulated statements and theories, as well as their richer content (which is connected with precision). The requirements of sensefulness and testability are expounded in the empirical sciences: statements and theories must by empirically testable, which in turn requires them to have empirical meaning, empirical content.

1. Despite the visible evolution in Popper's views on scientific rationality, one permanent component is the falsificationalist conditions of testability of hypotheses and theories. Empirical testability is understood as falsifiability, i.e. the possibility of refuting through the results of experience. A theory (claim, hypothesis) is falsifiable when it has empirically refutable logical consequences, i.e. when empirically testable statements that may turn out to be false follow from it, when – in Popper's terminology – the class of its potential falsifiers is not empty. Not only theories lacking testable empirical content are unfalsifiable; theories that are logically inconsistent, i.e. internally contradictory, are also unfalsifiable.[9]

Popper maintains a demarcational understanding of falsifiability,[10] i.e. as the criterion distinguishing science from non-science: unfalsifiable statements and theories are not scientific.[11] In time, Popper exhibited the demarcational un-

---

[8] Because Popper's philosophy was the object of many studies, the main conclusions of which are known, in this article I will refer only to three works of his that well illustrate the evolution of Popper's views on rationality and criticism: Popper 1959, Popper 1963, Popper 1974.
[9] Popper 1959, pp. 91–92.
[10] See: Popper 1959, pp. 34, 37, 313; Popper 1963, pp. 33, 37, 39, 197, 255–256; Popper 1974, pp. 963, 976, 981, 984, 989.
[11] In his remarks on the demarcation criterion, Popper also discusses separating: the expressions of the empirical sciences from other expressions (Popper 1963, p. 39; Popper 1974, pp. 963, 989); scientific systems from prescientific, pseudoscientific, and metaphysical systems

derstanding of falsifiability increasingly weakly. This is visible in later formulations of the demarcation criterion, in which Popper uses the term "testability" (empirical testability) in place of "falsifiability."[12] However, in treating falsifiability demarcationally, he always emphasizes that falsifiability is not a test of theorems' empirical meaningfulness.[13] Among empirically testable theories, the more falsifiable a theory is, the more valuable it is. The degree to which a theory is falsifiable is positively correlated with its empirical content, to which the generality, precision, and simplicity of the theory contribute. Generality and precision influence the degree of falsifiability (testability) directly: the more general (broader) and more precise a theory is, i.e. the more accurately, and thus more it says about phenomena (richer content), the more falsifiable it is.[14] On the other hand, a theory's simplicity is dispositional quality, so to speak – it appears in the procedure of drawing the consequences of a theory: the simpler a theory is, the easier it is to draw empirically testable consequences from it. A valuable quality of theories, one which also appears in their empirical content and raises their degree of falsifiability, is independent testability – independent, i.e. in the scope of phenomena foreseen only on the basis of a particular theory. This quality attests to the fact that a theory (hypothesis) is not extemporaneous, is not *ad hoc*.[15]

2. The postulates concerning testability, understood by Popper in the way described above, are also contained in the works of the Lvov-Warsaw School philosophers. Despite the fact that these postulates were typically formulated with philosophy in mind, interpreting them as describing a pattern of scientific rationality is obvious within the context of the scientism advocated by the School.[16] Though this scientism is admittedly a metaphilosophical view, the postulates concerning (scientific) philosophy that it posited were advanced against the backdrop of the pattern of rationality attributed to science.

(Popper 1963, p. 39; Popper 1974, pp. 963, 976, 981); the empirical sciences from mathematics and logic, as well as metaphysics (Popper 1959, p. 34; Popper 1963, p. 255); and science from metaphysics (Popper 1959, p. 313). This last understanding of the aim of the demarcation criterion is closest to the intention behind the School's representatives' formulation of postulates concerning the scientificity of philosophy, though their intention was not to reject metaphysical problems, but metaphysical methods (scientific philosophy cannot be speculative).

12 Popper 1963, pp. 37, 197, 256.
13 See: Popper 1963, pp. 257–258; Popper 1974, pp. 978–983.
14 See: Popper 1959, pp. 112–113, 121–123, 126–145, 170–173, 189–190, 198–205, 286–286; Popper 1963, pp. 217–256.
15 See: Popper 1959, pp. 82–83; Popper 1963, p. 241; Popper 1974, p. 985.
16 See: Woleński 1985, pp. 72–76; Zamecki 1977, p. 64.

A component of rationality (scientificity) common to all philosophers of the School was the postulate of good articulation, i.e. precision and clarity of utterances.[17] This is attested to not only by the clearly posed postulates scattered throughout many works, but also – even to a greater degree – by the method of philosophizing practiced by the School. The source of many postulates formulated in this regard and directly discussed was K. Twardowski's article *O jasnym i niejasnym stylu filozoficznym*, published in 1919.[18] In a text on Twardowski's program of scientific philosophy, S. Łuszczewska-Romahnowa asserts that: according to Twardowski's intentions, accepted by his students, the concept of clarity refers to "formal qualities, such as precision, logical correctness, unambiguity, and the like"; that "the cult of the clarity in thought and speech was one of the main characteristics of Twardowski's school"; and that the philosophers of the School "always aspired to the clearest possible formulation of their views; moreover, they considered spreading and promoting the skills and practice of clear thought and clear speech to be one of the tasks of philosophy."[19] The postulate of clarity is also present in the program for philosophy outlined by J. Łukasiewicz (in a presentation given in 1927 and article published a year later[20]), who rejects the cognitive value of unclear statements and postulates their removal (as metaphysical) from scientific philosophy.[21] T. Czeżowski emphasizes the significance of clarity and precision in philosophical argumentation,[22] while K. Ajdukiewicz (in an article from 1934) considers the postulate of conceptual clarity and linguistic precision a characteristic trait of the Lvov-Warsaw School's philosophers' methodological approach.[23]

Regarding the requirement of empirical testability, this postulate – formulated for scientific philosophy – can already be found in the writings of K. Twardowski. On the basis of his analysis of Twardowski's work from 1897, J. Woleński writes: he was convinced "[...] that every philosophical problem could be solved empirically"; "He intended [...] to formulate the problem of philosophy's scientificity as the possibility of empirically solving its problems"; that he condemned so-called metaphysicism, i.e. the aspiration "[...] to erect constructs lacking suf-

---

17 See: Woleński 1985, pp. 75–76; Woleński 1997, p. 90; Zamecki 1977, p. 6.
18 See: Woleński 1985, pp. 42–43; Woleński 1997, pp. 85–96; Zamecki 1977, pp. 43–47.
19 Qtd. in Zamecki 1977, pp. 45–47, trans. L. Fretschel.
20 Woleński 1997, pp. 124–130.
21 Zamecki 1977, p. 45, fn. 18. Despite the hint of Popperesque demarcationalism present in the last line, Łukasiewicz's postulate can only be understood as a necessary condition for the scientificity of concepts and claims.
22 Woleński 1985, p. 71.
23 Zamecki 1977, pp. 54, 59.

ficient foundation in the sphere of facts."[24] Analyzing Ajdukiewicz's views from the period in which Ajdukiewicz was an advocate of radical conventionalism, J. Woleński directly points to the analogies between the "tendencies" in the progress of science (the procedures applied in science) listed by Ajdukiewicz, and Popper's recommendations regarding scientific rationality (favoring more falsifiable theories).[25]

Representatives of the School also made statements coinciding with Popper's conception of the degree of falsifiability/testability/corroboration. They were formulated in analyses of theories of induction – evidently by T. Czeżowski. In summarizing Czeżowski's views on the confirmation of hypotheses by their consequences, J. Woleński asserts that according to Czeżowski: "The strength of confirmation is greater the less probable a consequence is *a priori*, the more precisely it is formulated (quantitatively), the less similar it is to consequences previously taken into account"; and that those hypotheses should be chosen, which explain "more without taking on additional presumptions" (according to J. Woleński, K. Ajdukiewicz and J. Kotarbińska drew the same conclusions from the theory of induction).[26] The analogies with Popper's conception of the degree of falsifiability/corroboration are clearly visible.

3.2 Objectivity

The comparison of Popper's views and those of the School's philosophers with regard to objectivity will be ordered according to senses of the term "objectivity" that appear in Popper's works. These include objectivity understood pragmatically, epistemologically, and ontologically.

---

[24] Woleński 1985, pp. 37–38, trans. L. Fretschel.
[25] Woleński 1985, p. 196. He also perceives in Ajdukiewicz's views awareness of the difference, later made prominent by T. Kuhn, between the falsification and elimination of a theory. We can add that in the work analyzed by Woleński, there are statements similar to the Duhem-Quine thesis.
[26] Woleński 1985, p. 267 trans. L. Fretschel. J. Woleński also emphasizes the novelty and value of the results achieved in inductive logic by philosophers of the School, especially by J. Hosiasson-Lindenbaum (Woleński 1985, pp. 259–272, 278–279). It is worth noting (Woleński 1997, pp. 38–40) that the arguments Popper formulated against induction were critically analyzed by J. Kotarbińska (already in her review of *Logik der Forshung*, written in 1935).

3.2.1 Objectivity in a Pragmatic Sense

I speak of the pragmatic sense to emphasize that this variant of objectivity always refers to the active side of science, i.e. to scientific practice. Popper uses various terms to refer to objectivity so understood, including impartiality, openness to discussion, nonarbitrariness, conventionality, rule-based objectivity, and consensuality. An accurate representative of this family of terms is "intersubjectivity" – and this term will be applied here, as it also appears frequently in the writings of the School's philosophers.

1. The requirement of intersubjectivity already appears in Popper's views within the context of falsificationism. The falsification and elimination of theories from science is not possible without the intersubjectivity of the theories themselves and of the procedures for testing them. The condition of intersubjectivity is even more visible within the context of Popper's fallibilism. The view that all statements in the empirical sciences are refutable also encompasses so-called basic statements. Even if such statements are confirmed in many independent observations, they cannot be considered irrefutable (to emphasize this, Popper uses the term "basic statements" in quotation marks). The empirical foundation of science is the result of the agreement and cooperation of scientists: each "basic" statement can be refuted, but in order for the empirical testing of theories to be possible at all, certain statements describing the results of experience are consensually recognized as irrefutable.[27]

2. In an article from 1912 on the role of creativity in science, J. Łukasiewicz expressed the view that there are no naked untheorized facts, that no empirical base aside from the "empirical base" of science exists: "All facts expressed in words are already, however primitively, elaborated by man. A 'raw fact,' untouched by the mind, seems to be a borderline concept."[28] We can also find the idea of the theorization of all observation, as it is known today, in Ajdukiewicz (in a publication from 1938), when he asserts e.g.: "[...] statements based directly on experience are not [...] imposed solely by experience [...]"; they "also contain a certain dose of convention," since, being "conceptually formulated," they are based on accepted principles and definitions.[29] Meanwhile, in characterizing the irrationalist attitude (in 1934), he formulates the postulate of "rec-

---

27 See: Popper 1959, pp. 49–56, 97–111; Popper 1974, pp. 976–984, 1010.
28 Quoted from Łukasiewicz 1961, p. 74; trans. L. Fretschel; the bibliographical information on the first print of the cited text was included.
29 Quoted from Ajdukiewicz 1985, p. 305; trans. L. Fretschel; the bibliographical information on the first print of the cited text was included.

ognizing only those statements that are justified in a controllable way."[30] Ajdukiewicz also originated the definition of valuable knowledge as intersubjective – i.e. communicable and independently testable knowledge – definition which was representative for philosophers of the School and remains in use today.[31]

3.2.2 Objectivity in an Epistemological Sense

In this sense, objectivity refers to the reality of products of science, to their reference to reality; in the empirical sciences, therefore – to empirical theories' reference to physical reality.

1. Initially, Popper did not connect the reality of a theory with its truth. A sign that the theory reaches reality is the theory's usefulness, understood evolutionistically. Theories, and more generally – knowledge, are to increase the human species' chances in its fight for survival: the source of knowledge-generating action is a problem situation, solved by the method of trial (hypothesis) and error (falsification).[32] To separate himself terminologically from verificationism, and more broadly – justificationism, which refer to the concept of truth and degree of probability, he introduces the terms *corroboration* and *degree of corroboration:* an unsuccessful attempt at empirically refuting a theory does not raise its degree of probability, but rather, its degree of corroboration – the more so, the higher the degree of falsifiability of the theory subjected to empirical tests.[33]

Popper announced the truth interpretation of a theory's realism after acknowledging that A. Tarski's definition of truth accurately clarifies the previously obscure notion of correspondence between a statement's content and reality. The degree of corroboration, which indicates the theory's epistemological value, becomes the degree of verisimilitude, i.e. the indicator of the theory's approximation to truth.[34] Despite the fact that all empirical theories are, or will turn out to be false, they may differ in their degree of approximation to truth.[35] The goal of science is truth, while the ultimate goal is the all-embracing truth.[36]

---

30 Qtd. in Zamecki, p. 54.
31 Woleński 1985, p. 65.
32 See: Popper 1959, pp. 32–34; Popper 1963, pp. 42–46; Popper 1974, pp. 1013–1014.
33 Popper 1959, pp. 265–273. Though Popper emphasizes the difference between the degree of confirmation, probability, and the degree of corroboration (e.g. ibid., pp. 269–270), common problems with defining (the measure of) both of these degrees point to a purely terminological difference.
34 Popper 1963, pp. 228–233.
35 Popper 1963, pp. 233–235.

2. Łukasiewicz's views coincide with Popper's antiverificationism (more broadly: his antijustificationism). In an article from 1909, Łukasiewicz argued that confirming hypotheses' logical consequences did not increase their degree of probability.[37] In terms of Popper's views reconciled with the concept of truth, similar statements expressing a vision of science aspiring to the ultimate goal, can be found in Ajdukiewicz: "[...] the ultimate developmental phase of all the empirical sciences seems to be a theory explaining – with the help of few hypotheses and principles – the entirety of statements dictated by experience against the backdrop of these principles" – though, as is worth noting – Ajdukiewicz does not speak of a true theory.[38] Objectivism understood in terms of truth is clearly visible in the vision of science's progress outlined by Czeżowski (in a work from 1936): the trait of judgments essential for science is their truth, while the goal of science is a system of all true propositions accessible to cognition.[39]

Generally speaking, we can say that the School's philosophers took from Twardowski (and through his mediation, from Brentano) "[...] realism, objectivism, and the correspondence theory of truth oriented absolutistically [...]."[40]

3.2.3 Objectivity in an Ontological Sense

Objectivity understood this way is an ontic property. Ontological objectivism thus indicates a way of existence that is beyond subjective. In regards to scientific cognition, this refers to the existence of products of science beyond the cognizing consciousness.

1. Summarizing Popper's vague and incoherent statements, we can say that in his view, the intersubjective results of cognition, including scientific statements and theories, exist in a so-called third world, one that differs from the physical world (first world) and world of psychic processes (second world).

---

36 Such an view of the ultimate goal of science is suggested by Popper's (unsuccessful) attempts at determining the degree of approximation to truth, which are consist in comparing (subtracting) the number of false and true consequences of theories. See: Popper 1963, pp. 223–225, 245–246. However, Popper himself admits that approaching truth may be an object not of knowledge (measure, criterion), but of faith. See: Popper 1963, pp. 51, 234; Popper 1974, pp. 1025–1030. He already makes a similar remark in Popper 1959, p. 270, fn. 3*.
37 Woleński 1985, p. 260. J. Woleński perceives the idea of the hypothetical-deductive method and statements made in a falsificationist spirit in Łukasiewicz's article (as well as in S. Zawirski). Cf.: Woleński 1985, pp. 260–261, 296; Woleński 1997, pp. 37–38.
38 Qtd. in Ajdukiewicz 1985, p. 306; trans. L. Fretschel.
39 Zamecki 1977, p. 102.
40 Zamecki 1977, p. 50; trans. L. Fretschel.

Such objectivity is not ascribed to concrete formulations of sentences, theories, rules of the scientific method, or problems, but to their objective contents. The objects of the third world are genetically dependent on scientists and their cognitive actions, but in their objectified form exist independently from them. The influence of the third world's contents on the remaining two worlds testifies to this existence.

2. Despite the terminological differences, it is clear that the ideas of K. Twardowski (presented in a work published in 1911[41]) constitute a precedent for Popper's conception of the three worlds. In the mentioned work, Twardowski speaks of the products of cognitive actions fixed in language. He distinguishes between the concrete contents of a cognizing consciousness induced by linguistic expressions (linguistic signs), and the meaning of expressions abstracted from these concrete contents[42] (in Popper's terminology we would say – the objectified meaning). Twardowski's conception is superior not only to Popper's conception of the three worlds, but also to many later ideas by both the School's philosophers and others concerning the ontological status of scientific statements and theories.[43]

The idealistic view of propositions is clear in Czeżowski's thought. In a work from 1936, he distinguishes concrete convictions, as subjective psychic phenomena, from their impersonal content, and concrete sentences, in which convictions are expressed, from the meaning of these sentences. He also situates propositions in the sphere of ideal objects: "[...] scientific propositions are products of abstraction in relation to concrete thoughts and spoken or written sentences; they are **ideal objects**, completely different from empirical, individual, concrete objects of the positive world"; simultaneously, "**For science, an essential trait of propositions is their truth** [...] – a trait completely independent of whether or not the proposition constitutes the content of

---

[41] Zamecki 1977, pp. 85–90.
[42] J. Woleński, following I. Dąmbska, indicates the difficulties with such a conception of meaning and the correlated doubts as to whether it is free from psychologism (Woleński 1985, pp. 41–42).
[43] A good illustration of the latter are attempts conducted within the framework of the so-called structuralist approach at eliminating Platonism from J. Sneed's concept of a theory, which constitutes the point of departure of this approach. Such attempts were undertaken by W. Stegmüller, among others, whose ultimate conclusion was nihilistic: scientific theories do not exist; only scientists using the theories exist (Stegmüller 1979). It is worth noting that this "nihilistic" solution was already present in the School much earlier, namely, in the reism of T. Kotarbiński: science, theories, and scientific statements do not exist; what do exist are scholars researching concrete things and expressing their thoughts, which are fixed in the concrete sentences of a given language. See: Zamecki 1977, pp. 112–113.

someone's conviction [original emphasis – AJ]."⁴⁴ The idealism of such a conception is indubitable (and directly declared); however, Czeżowski's statements cannot be interpreted in a Platonic spirit, because the article cited states that the system of true propositions is enriched along with the progress of science, which ultimately aspires to a system of all true propositions accessible to cognition.⁴⁵ The ontological description of the sphere of abstract senses – "impersonal" in Czeżowski's nomenclature, objectified in Popper's terminology – is therefore the same as that of the third world: they exist ideally, though they are genetically dependent on scholars and their actions (i.e. on objects in the first and second worlds).

3.3 Criticism

1. The postulate of criticism is most clearly visible in Popper's first model of scientific rationality, whose main components are hypotheticism and falsificationism. The critical attitude is revealed in the drive toward falsifying hypotheses/theories that were formulated to solve scientific problems. This results in the rejection of irrefutable hypotheses (the initial demarcation of scientific hypotheses from unscientific ones), followed by the selection of the most falsifiable hypothesis. This initial selection of hypotheses is to be conducted before they are tested empirically.⁴⁶ The next step is to subject the theories to reliable empirical tests, i.e. such tests that aim not to confirm the theories, but to refute them. Falsificationally-oriented criticism precludes the application in scientific practice of procedures aiming to confirm theories and protect them from being refuted. For example, it prohibits the persistent rejection of results of experience that are incompatible with a theory (e.g. explaining away such results by blaming the disruptive influence of some unknown factor) and the artificial adaptation of theories to the results of experience, e.g. through changing the value of the constants postulated in the theory or through the addition of hypotheses, whose only goal and consequence is the immediate restoration of the theory's compatibility with empirical data.⁴⁷ The more stringent the tests a theory survives – and the stringency of empirical tests depends on the theory's degree of falsifiability –

---

44 Qtd. in Zamecki 1977, p. 100; trans. L. Fretschel.
45 Zamecki 1977, pp. 101–102. It is worth noting that Czeżowski's remarks on the progress and goal of science are made in the spirit of positivist conceptions – insofar as cumulativism is considered a component of the positivist model of the progress of science.
46 Popper 1959, pp. 42, 50. 81–82, 85, 97–111.
47 See: Popper 1959, pp. 42, 54, 83, 104–105; Popper 1974, pp. 985, 1035–1039, 1186–1187.

the greater its reliability (degree of corroboration), though, like with all earlier theories, it, too, will someday be rejected.[48]

A weakening of this primary model of rationality and criticism is visible already in the model referring to verisimilitude. The metascientific postulate to select theories with a higher degree of verisimilitude is inapplicable, because it is not based on any effective criterion, as it is not possible to compare the sets of true and false consequences of theories; one can only have faith that a recognized theory is closer to truth.[49] An even less criteria model is the one that emerges from Popper's later statements, formulated in reply to critiques of his earlier models of rationality. The model of scientific rationality is reduced to the postulate of retaining the critical attitude – both in regards to proposed theories and critiques of (attempts at refuting) theories; in science, there should be room for debate, for attacks and defenses, so long as the defenses are not dogmatic.[50]

2. Regarding the School's philosophers, seeds of criticism in the form of hypotheticism and falsificationism are present in the writings of J. Łukasiewicz. In his article *O twórczości w nauce* from 1912, he recognizes hypotheses as a permanent, non-imitative, constructive component of knowledge. Hypotheses are incorporated into science not because they are true – since "Demonstrating [...] only, that the *consequences* of hypotheses are in accordance with facts, does not mean changing hypotheses into truth. The truth of a consequence does not imply the truth of its premises" [cursive from the original – A.J.]. "Despite this we incorporate them into science, insofar as they are connected by a relation of implication with propositions of the first category [i.e. "reconstructing facts given in experience" – A.J.] and they do not lead to consequences incompatible with the facts." In Popper's terminology, we can say: as long as they are falsifiable and have not been falsified. The role of experience, on the other hand, boils down to the fact that it *"is to be a stimulus for creative ideas and grant material for testing them"* [cursive from the original – A.J.].[51] Using terms that were popularized later, we can say that in the text of Łukasiewicz cited earlier, there are statements incompatible with the components of the positivist model of science, i.e. statements undermining inductionism and verificationism. In the writings of the School's philosophers – Ajdukiewicz, Zawirski, Kotarbińska – arguments undermining the original version of falsificationism and the falsificationist pattern

---

[48] Cf. Popper 1959, pp. 265–275.
[49] See: Popper 1963, pp. 42, 50, 81–82, 85, 97–111; Popper 1974, pp. 1025–1030.
[50] Popper 1974, p. 986.
[51] Łukasiewicz 1961, pp. 72–74; trans. L. Fretschel. In his later works on this subject, Łukasiewicz replaces the term "proposition" with the term "statement" (cf. Zamecki 1977, p. 91).

of criticism are more common. In these arguments, the difference between falsification – understood logically, as deductive reasoning – and the elimination of hypotheses in the empirical sciences is emphasized.[52]

On the other hand, parallels (precedents) of later versions of Popper's criticism can be found in postulates formulated by many of the School's philosophers. In a speech given on the occasion of the twentieth anniversary of the Polish Philosophical Society in Lvov (on February 12, 1929), Twardowski emphasized that "a scientific society, dedicated solely to methodical research work" cannot undertake problems excluded by scientific criticism, "metaphysical" problems, i.e. such problems whose solutions cannot be "justified with scientific methods."[53] In regards to this program of scientific philosophy, in the part concerning the separation of philosophy from worldviews, J. Woleński emphasizes that "[...] according to Twardowski, a special responsibility to criticism and self-criticism rested on the shoulders of philosophers."[54] Thus, in his later statements on rationality and criticism (summarized above), Popper postulates what is contained in those views of Twardowski that formed the foundation for the School's philosophical program and were elaborated in the writings of Twardowski's students. For example, Czeżowski postulated that scientific research be guided by methodological rules of reliability (recognizing theorems that flow from justifying reasons), objectivity (the critical attitude, i.e. taking into account arguments for and against recognized theorems), and impartiality (in disputes, the attitude of an arbiter guided solely by what is right).[55]

4 Comparative Conclusions

The evolution of Popper's views is visible in nearly every component of rationality distinguished in these analyses, i.e. testability, objectivity, and criticism.

1. In terms of views on the testability of scientific statements and theories, the evolution of Popper's views can be illustrated by the following sequence of terms: falsifiability, testability, corroborability. Despite Popper's declarations, the accent moves from refutability to the confirmability of hypotheses and theo-

---

[52] Woleński 1985, pp. 268, 271–272.
[53] As cited in Zamecki 1977, p. 47; trans. L. Fretschel. The analyses in (Woleński 1985, pp. 36–38) demonstrate that similar postulates were already contained in Twardowski's work from 1897.
[54] Woleński, 1985, pp. 39–40; transl. L. Fretschel.
[55] I am summarizing the results of analyses of Czeżowski's views contained in Woleński 1985, p. 67.

ries. At the same time, Popper increasingly emphasized the fact that the effective falsification and elimination of theories depends on reliability, impartiality, criticism, and so on, that is, he moved the accent from the logical qualities of scientific products (statements, hypotheses, theories) to the components of the scientific method necessary for their testability. Such an understanding of scientificity, i.e. from the point of view of method instead of statements and theories, is present in the views of the School's philosophers from the outset.

2. In terms of objectivity, a permanent component of Popper's conception is objectivity understood as intersubjectivity and the later-elaborated objectivity as non-subjective existence (the notion of the third world). There are parallels to these views in the views of the School's philosophers; the postulate of intersubjectivity was part of the School's program, and the conception of objective knowledge is better (and earlier) justified than it is in Popper's thought. There is a visible change in Popper's views regarding objectivity understood as realism: from evolutionary instrumentalism to realism (successive theories are closer to truth, truth is the goal of science). Realism so-understood, i.e. assuming a classical understanding of truth, was present in the views of the School's philosophers from the outset – though diverging views were also present (Łukasiewicz, Ajdukiewicz) – and it was additionally strengthened and justified by Tarski's semantic theory of truth.

3. The evolution of Popper's views is also clearly visible in terms of criticism understood as a component of the pattern of scientific rationalism regarding scientific procedure and the scientific approach. Popper gradually weakens the postulated model: from falsificationist criticism (*Logic of Scientific Discovery*), through rational criticism (*Conjectures and Refutations*), he ultimately reached critical rationalism (*Replies to My Critics*). The postulates that critical rationalism can be reduced to are already present in K. Twardowski's program of scientific philosophy and were realized in the anti-irrationalistic philosophizing of subsequent generations of the School's representatives.

4. Thus, comparing only the content of the views advocated by Popper with the core of the conception of rationality of the School's philosophers – i.e. omitting the real or possible influences, inspirations, borrowings – we can say that Popper's views evolved in the direction of the program of rationality and criticism advocated and realized from the outset by the philosophers of the Lvov-Warsaw School.[56]

---

[56] J. Woleński formulates and justifies an analogous conclusion concerning the relationship between the School's philosophy and the logical empiricism of the Vienna Circle philosophers. See: Woleński 1985, pp. 296–305.

Bibliography

Ajdukiewicz, Kazimierz (1985): *Język i poznanie. Tom I. Wybór pism z lat 1920–1939.* Warszawa: Państwowe Wydawnictwo Naukowe.
Dąmbska, Izydora (1937/38): "Irracjonalizm a poznanie naukowe". In: *Kwartalnik Filozoficzny* 14, z. 2, pp. 83–118 and z. 3, pp. 185–212; reprinted in (Perzanowski/Janik 2009), pp. 195–256.
Lakatos, Imre (1968): "Criticism and the Methodology of Scientific Research Programmes". In: *Proceedings of the Aristotelian Society* 69, pp. 149–186.
Lakatos, Imre (1970): "Falsification and the Methodology of Scientific Research Programmes". In: Imre Lakatos/Alan Musgrave (eds.): *Criticism and the Growth of Knowledge.* Cambridge: Cambridge University Press, pp. 91–197.
Lakatos, Imre (1974): "Popper on Demarcation and Induction". In: Paul Arthur Schilp (ed.): *The Philosophy of Carl Popper.* La Salle, Illinois: Open Court, pp. 241–273.
Łukasiewicz, Jan (1912): "O twórczości w nauce". In: *Księga Pamiątkowa ku uczczeniu 250 rocznicy założenia Uniwersytetu Lwowskiego.* Lwów: Nakładem Uniwersytetu Lwowskiego, pp. 1–15; reprinted in (Łukasiewicz 1961), pp. 66–75.
Łukasiewicz, Jan (1961): *Z zagadnień logiki i filozofii. Pisma wybrane.* Wyboru dokonał, wstępem i przypisami opatrzył Jan Słupecki, Warszawa: Państwowe Wydawnictwo Naukowe.
Perzanowski, Jerzy/ Janik,Piotr (eds.) (2009): *Rozum – serce – smak. Pamięci Profesor Izydory Dąmbskiej (1904–1983).* Kraków: Wyższa Szkoła *Filozoficzno-Pedagogiczna "Ignatianum,"* Wydawnictwo WAM.
Popper, Karl (1959): *Logic of Scientific Discovery.* London: Hutchinson.
Popper, Karl (1963): *Conjectures and* Refutations. London: Routledge and Kegan Paul.
Popper, Karl (1974): "Replies to My Critics". In: Paul Arthur Schilp (ed.): *The Philosophy of Carl Popper.* La Salle, Illinois: Open Court, pp. 961–1197.
Stegmüller, Wolfgang (1979): *The Structuralist View of Theories. A Possible Analogue of the Bourbaki Programme in Phisical Science.* Berlin, Heidelberg, New York: Springer-Verlag.
Szaniawski, Klemens (1983): "Racjonalność jako wartość". In: *Studia Filozoficzne* 5–6, pp. 7–15; reprinted in (Szaniawski 1994), pp. 531–539.
Szaniawski, Klemens (1994): *O nauce, rozumowaniu i wartościach. Pisma wybrane.* Wybrał i opracował Jan Woleński, Warszawa: Wydawnictwo Naukowe PWN.
Woleński, Jan (1985): *Filozoficzna szkoła lwowsko-warszawska.* Warszawa: Państwowe Wydawnictwo Naukowe.
Woleński, Jan (1997): *Szkoła Lwowsko-Warszawska w polemikach.* Warszawa: Wydawnictwo Naukowe SCHOLAR.
Zamecki, Stefan (1977): *Koncepcja nauki w szkole lwowsko-warszawskiej.* Wrocław, Warszawa, Kraków, Gdańsk: Zakład Narodowy Imienia Ossolińskich, Wydawnictwo Polskiej Akademii Nauk.

Christoph Demmerling
More than Words: from Language to Society. Wittgenstein, Marx, and Critical Theory

Abstract: The present article discusses the relationship between the critique of language and social philosophy—in particular, with reference to the philosophy of Ludwig Wittgenstein. The opening section starts with an explanation of what it means to understand philosophy as critique. A variety of forms of language criticism is distinguished. It is against such a background that Wittgenstein's philosophy is interpreted as a form of critique of language, which aims at an analysis of the mechanisms of linguistic reification and may be related to socio-philosophical analyses of reification. Wittgenstein's understanding of philosophy as therapy may, in turn, be related to the emancipatory dimension of critical social philosophy. Finally, using the comparative example of our linguistic and real-life interaction with time, the argument comes to a close with a reflection concerning the extent to which criticism of language may manifest its potential as an apt tool serving the purpose of the critique of society.

Keywords: Enlightenment, emancipation, criticism, Marx, critique of language, therapy, Wittgenstein

"All philosophy is 'Critique of language,'" Wittgenstein noted in his *Tractatus logico-philosophicus*, published in 1921.[1] In the reflections that follow, I am not concerned with a representation of Wittgenstein's philosophy in terms of its immanent ideas, but rather—on the basis of his concept of philosophy—I would like to establish an understanding of philosophy as critique, a critique that, in particular, takes into consideration that it is not only people's individual lives, but also their social and political lives that are entangled in the network of language. In this context, language is to be viewed from the outset in terms of its performativity, in terms of the effects it leaves in the world and not primarily (or not only) as an instrument or medium through which we make our thoughts transparent, communicate them to others, describe reality or make it accessible. We use words and sentences not only to describe objects or processes in the world: in itself the use of words and sentences constitutes a type of action

---

[1] Wittgenstein 1922, 4.0031.

that has its own effectiveness. This is particularly clear in the case of expressions in which the so-called performative verbs occur, as in the statement "I promise you to clean up the apartment by tomorrow evening." In the course of such speech operations, words generate expectations. With a promise, I commit myself to carry out what I have promised to the person to whom I made the promise. Promises, but also other forms of performative speech, have implications that produce institutional and moral liabilities. Yet, the results of the work of language cannot be limited only to its effects associated with explicitly performative utterances: basically, language causes effects whenever it is used. It does so by creating spaces for thought and perception; it lets certain things be seen, blurs others, and lends specific forms to things and their context. Words shape the appearance of things, they change the world and, last but not least, they may also change us. A word can be liberating, redeeming or even annihilating,[2] and even the seemingly simplest and most trivial communications affect us—often inconspicuously—by directing our gaze.

Even these few hints suggest that language plays an important role in the formation and development of social conditions. For this reason, language is to be analyzed not only from the point of view of logic or semantics but also from the outset in the light of its concrete relation to historical and social circumstances. In the following sections, I will deal with the practical sense of the philosophical critique of language and address the question of whether—and to what extent—the critique of language may also be understood as a critical philosophy of the social.[3] Therefore, the first part of the essay opens with the formulation of the most relevant questions connected with philosophy understood primarily as critique (I). Against such a backdrop, I address Wittgenstein's reflections on the critique of language in the second part, referring to considerations that enter the domain of the critical philosophy of the social (II). The third part illustrates the way in which a critique of language may be related to the critique of ways of life and ideology by means of an example (III).

---

[2] In particular it is the extent to which language can be used to violate persons that have been the subject of a heated discussion in recent years and decades. Among many titles, see, for instance: Kuch/Herrmann 2007, pp. 179–211.

[3] The reflections in this essay are partly based on sections of my book (Demmerling 1994), as well as parts of my essay (Demmerling 2014, pp. 19–36). For an alternative take on Wittgenstein and Adorno, see also Wiggershaus 2000. The latter study offers a philosophical vision that differs from that offered in my book (or in the mentioned essay), but it shows to what extent Wittgenstein's reflections can be related to the concept of philosophy as developed by representatives of Critical Theory.

1 Philosophy as Critique

Since its inception, philosophy has understood itself in terms of "enlightenment"; as such, it has primarily been concerned with distinguishing legitimate knowledge claims from unjustified conjectures, real knowledge from mere faith. It was already as early as antiquity that the effort of the enlightenment would be directed towards the rational penetration of the mythical images of the world. This process has continued within the frames of the European Enlightenment: To this day, scientific worldviews increasingly replace religious formulas of self-understanding. Hence, the idea of philosophy as a critical activity is firmly linked to the ideals of enlightenment.

One of the culminating points of the Enlightenment era is the birth of Kant's critical philosophy, which aims at revealing, in the form of a critique of knowledge, the categorial presuppositions of knowledge that rational beings have of themselves and of the world. Kant's formula "*Sapere aude!* Have the courage to use your mind without the guidance of another" is the formula with which he (epigrammatically) answers the question, "what is enlightenment?" In essence, the fundamental issue of his philosophy is liberation: liberation from religious (and other) prejudices as well as from the constraints and suffering that these prejudices may cause. Kant is guided by the ideals of autonomy and rationality. These ideals are fulfilled when human beings live according to the rules and laws that they themselves have created (or, at least, could have created), and if the beings concerned are able to provide good reasons to justify their actions and convictions. However, the ideals of autonomy and rationality seem to presuppose that people understand themselves correctly and that they can live their lives within a framework that allows them to align themselves as far as possible with the ideals concerned.[4] Yet, there are social and psychological barriers that may prevent such an autonomous orientation. People sometimes misunderstand themselves and misinterpret their situations; they often cultivate practices that can run counter to their own interests and they do so in a manner that is not (or at least not fully) comprehensible. At this point, an understanding of philosophy as critique comes into play in the narrower sense, namely that of philosophy as critique of ideology, critical social philosophy or a critical theory of society.

Even if one could regard it as commonplace, it does not hurt to recall that a critical philosophy, as a critical theory, is directed towards the mediation of knowledge that primarily relates to social reality. On the whole, it is the matter

---

[4] See also: Tetens 2006, pp. 17 f.

of analyzing phenomena on the premise that all facts are socially preformed. Critical theories pursue the purpose of changing this social reality for the benefit of man.[5] They are never concerned solely with the analysis or description of social reality. Rather, from their very outset, they involve a direct approach to action and strive for a change for the better. Critical theories represent a form of *intervening thought*, to use Bertolt Brecht's expression. They aim at the enlightenment of individuals and social groups alike, with a view to enabling them to recognize their true interests and allowing them to distinguish these interests from the pressures that they themselves have adopted and those imposed upon them by someone else. Thus, a critical theory may be claimed to have emancipatory force. Moreover, critical theories try not to comprehend their topic in a purely objectivized manner. Instead, they exercise self-reflexivity in that they repeatedly bring the assumptions of their own formation or convictions into critical focus and thus engage the subjects of the emancipation process in a particular way.[6] Therefore, methods and intentions of critical theory are sometimes understood in analogy to the methods and goals of psychoanalysis.[7]

Meanwhile, a multifaceted discussion continues about the conditions of the possibility of critique and its limits: be it social criticism, the critique of society, or the critique of ideology. On what grounds can social conditions be criticized? Is such a critique about the differences in the levels of education or income? Is it about the arbitrary administration of justice? The marginalization or impoverishment of certain social groups? Where do the standards and norms of critique come from and how can they be justified? In the case of the critique of ideology, further questions arise. If we understand an ideology as a system of beliefs that translates into both practical consequences and social effects—and thus, non-transparently, or outright opaquely, determines one's views as well as one's perceptions—a question arises as to how theorists can unmask ideologies at all—and thus, what allows them to criticize them.[8] In other words, how does the critic know that it is the others who suffer the consequences of self-deception, and not himself? From what point of view is critique performed and what is the relationship between critique and its addressees? To resolve this problem, philosophy and sociology have adopted quite different approaches, devising, accordingly,

---

[5] A classic contribution to this theoretical tradition is Horkheimer 1937, pp. 162–216.
[6] See: Geuss 1981, pp. 1f.
[7] This is particularly clear in Habermas 1981, pp. 262ff; see also Celikates 2009, pp. 195–216. Celikates also makes it clear that this option does not necessarily involve a connection to the particular content of psychoanalysis.
[8] See also Jaeggi 2009, pp. 266–295, who attempts to modify—and thus rescue—the project of a critique of ideology.

quite different intellectual tools. It seems to be clear that the critic and the criticized cannot simply be juxtaposed; they are not completely separate from one another. If this were the case, critique would lose ground, drawing conclusions out of thin air, which—as such—could no longer be related to any event or object. Basically, if this were so, everything could be criticized, and criticism itself would become vulnerable to the accusation of arbitrariness. Under such assumptions, criticism would lose its legitimacy: it would be possible to accuse the critic of taking issue with a given state of affairs or its developments, which in the eyes of others is rather unproblematic. Yet, at the same time, it seems clear that criticism must be able to dissociate itself in some way from entanglements with quotidian life experience and the practices adopted by social actors.[9] Criticism requires distance. It cannot be practised beyond those criticized; it cannot be performed if a critic adopts a purely external perspective. But—at the same time—it is not enough for the critic simply to reproduce the self-conceptions and self-interpretations of social actors and to adopt a purely internal perspective. Criticism is then at risk of unreflectively taking over the inner perspectives of social groups and communities affected by particular circumstances. Thus criticism also becomes arbitrary by addressing matters that, in the worst case, arise solely from the subjective perspectives of concerned people. Therefore, a certain theoretically motivated distance from life practice is probably indispensable.

Ultimately, a concept that is likely to prove viable is one in which the perspective of the observer and that of the participant are intertwined. Criticism must be applied to the manifestations of falsity—manifestations that, from an immanent perspective, must at least be perceived as symptoms, but that must also be more or less clearly perceivable from an external viewpoint. Criticism is only possible if at least a trace of discrepancy exists in the practices and belief

---

9 See: Celikates (2009), who distinguishes a *model of fracture* from *a model of symmetry*. According to the model of fracture, a critical theorist must break away from the perspective adopted by social actors in order to be able to present a social science-based critique from a perspective that is both theoretically and methodologically privileged. As a paradigm of such a conception, Celikates discusses the sociology of Pierre Bourdieu. Within the frame of the model of symmetry, on the other hand, analysis, interpretation, reflection and critique are understood as dimensions entailed in everyday practices, Celikates refers to forms of ethnomethodology, enlightened by phenomenology and hermeneutics, and especially to Luc Boltanski's sociology of critique and that proposed by the *Groupe de Sociologie Politique et Morale*. Celikates favors an understanding of critical theory as reconstructive critique, which attempts to avoid the disadvantages of the concepts outlined above and to make the most of their advantages. For this purpose, he essentially refers to the early work of Jürgen Habermas, construing critical theory as reconstructive critique.

systems under scrutiny—a discrepancy that can be felt by those who are affected and that should be both comprehensible and systematically analyzable from the viewpoint of the critic. Since in this paper I do not presume to thoroughly investigate this central methodological question—a question pertaining to every critical endeavor—an example may be helpful to at least sketchily explain the idea outlined above.

Let us imagine the situation of a part-time journalist. Occasionally, he receives short-term and underpaid stand-in employment contracts with a local newspaper and, often, as a self-employed person, has to do his very best to keep afloat by delivering freelance contributions to whoever will have them. He is always under pressure to produce quickly; the competition is enormous and he cannot afford to do extensive in-depth research. He is thus forced to work in a superficial manner, and pressed into opportunism with respect to those who would commission his work. Having long abandoned his original idea of what good journalism is, he is no longer sure if he knows what the real purpose of his work is. He rushes through life, his income barely sufficient to make ends meet. On the one hand, he deems his situation intolerable since it always exposes him to intellectual insults and makes him vulnerable to humiliation, but, on the other, he is also somewhat glad to receive temporary contracts and small assignments. There is no doubt that such an activity must inevitably lead to exhaustion and resignation, leaving no room for professional and personal self-realization. There are no prospects for freedom of choices of possibilities for self-development. Surprisingly often, life situations of this kind are simply accepted, both by those directly concerned and by other actors in the social environment. "Such is life," one would rationalize; "things are as they are, and they could be worse." A situation of this kind—and the social conditions that enable it—may be criticized in a variety of ways. One may look at it "from the outside" referring to a certain ideal of human activity, an ideal of a successful rhythm of human life, and point out that in this case this ideal has not been taken into account or realized, and that our journalist, albeit not an assembly-line worker, is an alienated laborer whose work ultimately serves to maximize the profit of others. But one may also look at it "internally" and identify the traces of inconsistency, even if the journalist himself has already come to terms with his fate by imagining that his situation could be an outcome of even worse scenarios. There is resignation, a feeling of discomfort, exhaustion, the sense of impotence, the looming specter of poverty; there is life under the yoke of self-exploitation imposed by circumstances. Such inconsistencies can be identified if the practice sketched above is to be put to the test of criticism. The immanent perspective can then be combined with an enlightened perspective that, for example, uses sociological and psychological concepts in order to present a critical diagnosis of our times.[10] In this way one can explore misleading ways of life and their causes with a view to effecting a change in circumstances.

After these preliminary considerations concerning the understanding of philosophy as critique and the methodological questions that this understanding of philosophy entails, in the following parts of this paper I would like to turn to the subject of a critique of language. I distinguish between three kinds: *genuinely philosophical forms* of language criticism, primarily *socially and politically motivated* language critique, and a kind of *language-immanent critique* of language. The immanent critique of language is based on certain norms of speaking and writing, primarily those originating from historically informed, highly cultured, and educationally middle-class milieus. With such norms as its starting point, immanent critique of language serves to criticize language uses, which the critic may perceive as "deviant." Thus, one may voice displeasure when observing that in the practice of the German language today the dative case is widely used in sentence constructions with "wegen" ("because of"), even though the proper form would be that of the genitive. However, this form of language criticism—often associated with complaints about the "decay of language"—is of lesser interest to us and therefore will not be discussed in the following sections. Likewise, socially and politically motivated forms of language criticism, which often go hand in hand with proposals for a political regulation of language usage (for example, when proponents of gender equality argue for the mandatory use of both the feminine and the masculine forms of salutation or when advocates of political correctness call for the avoidance of derogatory expressions in reference to particular groups), are of no central importance to my argument. I am primarily concerned with the *genuinely philosophical form* of the critique of language, which is based on my reflections on the understanding of philosophy as both *enlightenment* and *criticism*. This type of critique of language rests on the assumption that people often fail to correctly grasp the words and sentences they use and thus allow themselves to be led into linguistic misunderstandings, ending up with false images of the world which is ultimately conducive to self-misunderstanding.

Historically, the roots of philosophical language criticism can be traced back to the Early Modern period, the formula developing intensively in the 18th and 19th centuries.[11] It is already Francis Bacon who points to the "idols of the market", "which have entwined themselves round the understanding from the associations of words and names. For men imagine that their reason governs words,

---

10 About exhaustion see: Ehrenberg 2010.
11 See: Cloeren 1988.

while, in fact, words react upon the understanding; and this has rendered philosophy and the sciences sophistical and inactive".[12] Similar complaints are later to be found in the work of philosophers representing the tradition of empiricism, such as Locke, Berkeley, or Hume. Time and again, indications recur that words devoid of clear or specific meaning are used and that such practice only leads to bickering over vocabulary, that words do not point to things or present objects in a false way. Rigorous consequences of the misuse of language are later drawn by Frege when, in connection with his findings, he observes that in developing his conceptual notation he intended "to break the domination of the word over the human spirit by laying bare the misconceptions that through the use of language often almost unavoidably arise concerning the relation between concepts and by freeing thought from that with which only the means of expression of ordinary language [...] saddle it".[13]

Frege's reflections on the development of language-critical thought within the framework of analytical philosophy have proven most significant to the philosophical millieu, including Wittgenstein. At first sight, Wittgenstein's critique of language appears to be merely a critique of philosophy aimed at reining in its occasional free language acrobatics. He wanted to bring words back from their metaphysical to their everyday use. Understanding has to be protected in order to avoid injury from running one's head up against the limits of language. The imagery to which Wittgenstein resorts in his attempts to describe the effects of the critique of language is not unlike the imagery one finds in the discourse of the classical German philosophy energized by the attempt to critique the language of Kantian pure reason (e. g. Herder). While in Wittgenstein a whole cloud of philosophy condensed into a drop of grammar,[14] Herder's critique of language is supposed to ultimately disperse the "transcendental vapor."[15] However, I do not intend to explore such historical references here. Rather, the next section discusses the extent to which Wittgenstein's reflections—especially their critical dimension with respect to language—can be related to the understanding of criticism in the sense of a critical theory which is concerned not only with *analysis* but also with *emancipation*.

---

[12] Bacon 1863, I, LIX.
[13] Frege 1972, p. 7.
[14] Wittgenstein 1953, part I, xi, p. 222.
[15] Herder 1955, p. 305.

2 Wittgenstein, Marx, Critical Theory

It is true that Wittgenstein's explicit remarks about the language-critical dimension are primarily directed against the philosophical misuse of language. It is, however, characteristic of Wittgenstein's understanding of philosophy that he does not regard it merely as a theoretical effort, but considers it an activity that is always related to human life and human coexistence. He focuses on the analysis of the mechanisms of linguistic hypostatization and reification, which do not ony play important roles in philosophy, but also affect human life. On the one hand, his analyses aim to rectify certain concepts of the philosophy of language (such as those advocated by the thinkers of the Vienna Circle milieu) but, on the other hand, they also serve the purpose of liberating reified understandings of human life—understandings that have, in fact, been suggested or approximated by means of, or perhaps owing to, mistaken interpretations of language. Thus, on the one hand, Wittgenstein's philosophy is critical in that it offers *a critique of philosophy*; on the other, it is critical because it *offers a critique related directly to human life*. Doubtlessly, however, Wittgenstein's philosophy is a form of critique of language that is not related to historical or social situations in the narrow sense of these notions.

According to Wittgenstein, philosophy is first and foremost a description of the functions of our language. If so, then it is capable of rectifying misunderstandings conditioned by the (mis)use of language, which often lead to philosophical frictions. A thus conceived philosophy makes it possible to recognize erroneous or problematic language uses. They can be identified as such and consequently rejected. It is the language-critical dimension of Wittgenstein's philosophy that led him to the formulation of his famous adage that "the philosopher's treatment of a question is like the treatment of an illness." The aim of philosophy is to banish magic from language and thus to eliminate what may be regarded as the chief cause of philosophical, as well as "everyday", maladies. [16]

Language can be bewitching in a variety of ways: established and often unquestioned distinctions—such as those between "the inner" and "the outer" to characterize the difference between "the mental" and "the physical"—can impose a certain direction on one's thought and lead it astray. Thoughtless use of jargon may suggest "depth" and "complexity" where the matter at hand is really simple. Philosophy understood as a critique of language is intended to curb the diseases caused by inadvertent usage of language. In this sense, Wittgenstein's philosophy is regarded as a therapy aimed at one's liberation from

---

[16] Wittgenstein 1953, § 255.

thought constraints and language habits. It succeeds in its liberatory efforts by dispelling questions and collapsing distinctions that have repeatedly been forced upon us by the philosophical tradition and established theories, but also by the idle talk of institutionalized science and cultural business, as well as other discourses, approved, legitimized and authorized over and over again. In his *Tractatus logico-philosophicus* Wittgenstein writes:

> Most propositions and questions, that have been written about philosophical matters, are not false, but senseless. We cannot, therefore, answer questions of this kind at all, but only state their senselessness. Most questions and propositions of the philosophers result from the fact that we do not understand the logic of our language [...] And so it is not to be wondered at that the deepest problems are really no problems (Wittgenstein 1922, 4.003).

A little later he adds: "Philosophy is not a theory but an activity. [...] The result of philosophy is not a number of 'philosophical propositions', but to make propositions clear."[17] With such formulations, he offers his readers a clear statement concerning his concept of the function of philosophy. Philosophy is a critique of language, primarily committed to the goal of clarity. Although the focus of Wittgenstein's reflections shifts over the years, the idea of a philosophical critique of language remains the basic pillar of his thinking. [18] In his *Tractatus*, Wittgenstein understands critique of language in the sense of an analysis of the logic of language, while in his *Philosophical Investigations* his argument concerns a broader reflection on the meaningful use of expressions.

In *Philosophical Investigations*, *all* philosophical problems are repeatedly attributed to a misunderstanding—not to say to the wrong use of language. Wittgenstein sees philosophical theorizing as having committed a significant mistake in releasing words from their everyday contexts of familiar use and embedding them in particular philosophical and theoretical contexts, in which they are no longer meaningful—and which, irritatingly, evoke unanswerable questions.

---

17 Wittgenstein 1922, 4.112.
18 Wittgenstein's concept of philosophy and his views on the contrast between philosophy and science do not change in the course of the development of his thought, despite the fact that differences between his early work and his late work are easy to indicate. An important element in his early works is the emphasis on the philosophical problems of logic, while in the later works it is the diversity of the different openings to address language that gains importance. This, however, does not alter the fact that questions concerning the nature of language and the status—and method—of philosophy form brackets that hold Wittgenstein's early and later works together. For example, Gordon Baker and Peter Hacker write: "[H]is view of the status of philosophy changes very little. This is one of the main threads of continuity in Wittgenstein's opera" (Baker/Hacker 2004, p. 265). For support of the thesis that in his early works Wittgenstein also pursued therapeutic aims, see the introduction to Crary/Read 2000, pp. 1–18.

Such contexts arise when we ask about the essence of something, for example about the "the *essence* of language, of propositions, of thought."[19] If such questions are asked, according to Wittgenstein, "it may come to look as if there were something like a final analysis of our forms of language [...] as if there were something hidden in them that had to be brought to light."[20] It is to such an appearance that therapeutic philosophizing would be opposed. The mystery or myth of final forms of language which purportedly contain hidden, yet philosophically revealing, treasures is revealed by the return of words from their philosophical use to their everyday use. The method aims at clarifying and resolving philosophical problems by means of a description of our use of language.

> When philosophers use a word—"knowledge", "being", "object", "I", "proposition", "name"—and try to grasp the essence of the thing, one must always ask oneself: is the word ever actually used in this way in the language-game which is its original home? What we do is to bring words back from their metaphysical to their everyday use (Wittgenstein 1953, § 116).

Wittgenstein's reflections occasionally sound as if they were to suggest that a mere consideration of the everyday use of words might lead to the resolution of philosophical problems, or that everyday language use is *per se* clearer than philosophical or scientific use. It is with good reason that one may question whether the everyday use of words is indeed the measure of all things. In terms of philosophical standards, the sense of words used in a quotidian context is often unclear and ambivalent. Moreover, everyday uses of words are not untouched by the perspectives, attitudes or images suggested by metaphysical usages. Rather, corresponding self- and world-understandings trickle into everyday language, and thus "language-critical therapy" must be recommended not only as a move to heal the diseases of professional philosophers but also as a means serving the purpose of elucidating everyday speech with all its preconditions and implications. Let us, for example, return to the distinction between the "inner" and the "outer" already mentioned in connection with the attempt to say something about the relation between "mind" and "body." This distinction is not only widespread in philosophical theories concerning the mind-body problem but also an integral part of many quotidian self-understandings: in neither case is this distinction less misleading than in the other.[21]

---

19 Wittgenstein 1953, § 92.
20 Wittgenstein 1953, § 91.
21 The extent to which this "inner/outer" image has spread within and outside of philosophy is accentuated by the reflections of Hubert Dreyfus and Charles Taylor presented in: Dreyfus/Taylor 2015.

Quite independently of exegetical questions arising from the discussion of Wittgenstein's work, I am inclined to understand the instruments of language criticism in such a way that it not only aims at correcting philosophical and metaphysical (mis)uses of linguistic expressions but also serves to uncover false images and errors in everyday language. The recourse to everyday use of precarious words such as "knowledge," "sentence," or "name" does not, therefore, constitute a solution to problems associated with their metaphysical uses. Rather, a compilation of the instances of the use of expressions in everyday language may be perceived as a *corrective measure*. It may serve the purpose of identifying meanings of expressions incorporated into everyday speech and quotidian reasoning in order to gain insight into the usage of such expressions with the aim of bringing order into philosophical questioning.

According to Wittgenstein, the task of philosophy understood as therapy is *grammatical* analysis. Wittgenstein's understanding of the word "grammar" clearly goes beyond the usual sense of this expression, where the word "grammar" denotes the totality of the syntactic and morphological rules by means of which expressions of a language and parts thereof are formed or organized into syntagms. Wittgenstein's use of the term "grammar" is also connected with an analysis of the rules and regularities concerning expressions of language that determine their actual use in practice. In any case, in the widest sense, these rules and regularities also involve a semantic dimension. In that dimension, the concept of "grammar"—in this particular sense—becomes the "successor" to the discourse of the logic of a language.[22] Therefore, statements that concern the grammar of language in the Wittgensteinian sense are to be strictly distinguished from empirical propositions. They do not elucidate the world but deal with presuppositions and conditions of our thinking, speaking and acting. In the context of a grammatical analysis of expressions, it is always a matter of denuding the inferential relations in which the expressions function (or might function) in order to make clear to what one is committed by the use of words and expressions and what such uses imply.

With the onset of therapeutic philosophizing and the development of the method of grammatical analysis, philosophy does not necessarily come to rest: rather, philosophy's work changes its locus. The philosophical theorist whose work rests on the model developed by strict sciences is replaced by the philosophical grammarian who investigates language habits and rules of our lan-

---

[22] A short overview of Wittgenstein's concept of grammar is presented by Hans Johann Glock (Glock 2000, pp. 154–157) and Joachim Schulte (Schulte 1989, pp. 112–118). For the role of the concept of a philosophical grammar in the history and development of Wittgenstein's thought, see Gebauer 2009, pp. 107 ff.

guage use in order to get a glimpse of philosophical problems manifest in such use and to trace falsities and misconceptions into which the language of philosophy may drive us. More specifically, different mechanisms potentially leading to errors in the understanding of language are emphasized. Among those are the projection of linguistic structures onto the world, analogies in the surface grammar of words and sentences, which, to give an example, may tempt us to interpret emotive vocabulary as if it described things, prejudices resulting from long-established language habits, images and metaphors that have been "deposited," or ingrained, in the language to such an extent that they are no longer recognized as such, and are unreflectively taken for granted, as well as many other, equally important, processes. All of these mechanisms may be subjected to language-critical reflection: in many cases, it is possible to demonstrate that linguistic misunderstandings go hand in hand with misguided cultural practices.

Regarding philosophy as therapy, Wittgenstein also recognizes its *emancipatory* function. Philosophy's task is to *liberate* man from misunderstandings—of both himself and his language. Therapeutic procedures can be understood as paradigmatic for emancipatory practices, especially in the light of methods developed by psychoanalysis. We remember: it was the early Habermas who developed the relevant considerations in this context.[23] The emancipatory aspect of therapeutic treatment remains limited to individuals. If so, I should pose the question of whether the therapeutic dimension of philosophy in a Wittgensteinian sense includes in its scope the dimension of social critique, even if only in the widest sense of the term? Does it have the potential for a critique of society?

Furthermore, is critique of language *not* a form of philosophical therapy, which must only be recommended to the philosopher, who, groping in the darkness of his linguistic hypostasis, leads himself astray? Inasmuch as one would be inclined to hastily give a positive answer to this question, one should emphasize the fact that language also conditions the interpretations of reality and practices of everyday life. The range of distortions and deformations resulting from false readings of the language we use is significant. Therefore, the critique of language in its therapeutical function is by no means limited in its concerns to philosophers alone: even everyday belief systems are exposed to the power of language.

At first sight, one might find it surprising that a form of critique of language highly similar to that conceptualized by Wittgenstein may already be found in Marx, where it is directly connected with social criticism.[24] According to Marx,

---

[23] Once again I refer to Celikates 2009, pp. 195–216.
[24] In more recent bibliography, studies addressing Marx's work from the perspective of the philosophy of language, or from the point of view of theory, are rather rare. See, for instance, Le-

language hypostatizations are to be viewed as a result as well as an expression of social relations having acquired independent existence, as he asserts proposing his alienation theorem and offering his diagnosis of commodity fetishism. Marx writes:

> All relations can be expressed in language only in the form of concepts. That these general ideas and concepts are looked upon as mysterious forces is the necessary result of the fact that the real relations, of which they are the expression, have acquired independent existence. Besides this meaning in everyday consciousness, these general ideas are further elaborated and given a special significance by politicians and lawyers, who, as a result of the division of labour, are dependent on the cult of these concepts, and who see in them, and not in the relations of production, the true basis of all real property relations (Marx/Engels 1976a, p. 365).

As Wittgenstein would later do, Marx recommends that those who fall into the trap of the "cult of concepts" should revert these notions to their everyday use:

> The philosophers have only to dissolve their language into the ordinary language, from which it is abstracted, in order to recognize it as the distorted language of the actual world and to realize that neither thoughts nor language in themselves form a realm of their own, that they are only manifestations of actual life (Marx/Engels 1976a, p. 447).

With these remarks, Marx applies his basic conception—a conception that he first developed paradigmatically along with his analysis of the commodity—to language. Just as commodities—as products of human practices—do not "live" an individual life in their own realm (from which they only seem to be detached if an object-oriented perspective is applied), language must also be rooted in the real world, and should not be separated from the everyday practice in which it is used by its speakers.

The parallel with the Wittgensteinian critique of language notwithstanding, Marx's ideology and his social criticism as a whole can also be understood as a therapeutic measure. His critique of political economy diagnoses social diseases, which should be cured by means of philosophy—through enlightenment and criticism. The correspondences between institutional restrictions at the social level and neurotic compulsive behavior at the individual level are striking: in both cases, patterns of behavior that cause suffering are reproduced.

---

cercle 2006. A classical work on the subject by V. N. Vološinov was published in Russian as early as 1929, but it was only in 1973 that it was published in English (Vološinov 1973). For a comparative analysis of Marx and Wittgenstein, see: Rossi-Landi 1972.

According to Wittgenstein, philosophy is an instrument for solving difficulties. The thinker is not simply concerned with the dissolution of theoretical riddles; rather, he understands philosophy as practical work towards our liberation from misconceptions suggested by the language we use. As a form of therapy, philosophy itself is a practice. As a thus understood therapeutical practice, it must orient itself towards (the restitution of) the autonomy of the individual. It is a practice of an essentially emancipatory nature which aims at enlightenment. The therapeutic measures of philosophy are directed at freeing people from their own products. The entanglement of human beings in the network of language cannot, of course, be eliminated; what can be resolved, however, are the deformations that may result from such entanglement. "What is your aim in philosophy?—To shew the fly the way out of the fly-bottle."[25] This image most efficiently expresses the emancipatory claim of Wittgenstein's philosophy: the fly in the bottle is not only the philosopher who misunderstands the language; it also stands for all those who are caught in the darkness of their linguistic hypostases. The escape from the fly-bottle is tantamount to liberation from false understandings of oneself and of the world, from understandings suggested by—or resulting from—misinterpretations of language. But can this form of language criticism be understood at all in terms of a critique of ideology? Is it conceivable to connect it with, or relate it to, Marx's analysis of alienation and commodity? The next section addresses this question by discussing an example that suggests a positive response.

3 Language, Society, Ideology

In connection with his analysis of commodity in terms of its fetish-like nature, Marx draws one's attention to the problem of *reification*. Reification, above all, refers to a process in the course of which *a thing is made of something that is not a thing*. Thus, the concept of reification can be used to describe a process in which relationships or properties are addressed as if they were independent entities. In social philosophy, the term often serves as an expression for the instrumentalization of human relationships and the treatment of people as objects. The term may also refer to the fact that products of human action or results of historical developments appear as natural phenomena. This applies, for example, to commodities that are not what they are *by nature:* what they are is determined within the framework of certain social forms of production and certain

---

25 Wittgenstein 1953, § 309.

modes of human life. Authors, who—in the broadest sense of the term—represent Critical Theory, sometimes assume that the commodity form permeates all the manifestations of the life of a society, which leads to the comprehensive reification of different spheres of human life.[26] This kind of view is sometimes also used as a general instrument for the analysis of modern philosophy and science. As such, reification functions as the basic concept of the theory of rationality and of a socially founded critique of reason. It serves as a means to criticize formalistic conceptions and fundamentalist interpretations of notions in philosophy, and is also used to question the orientation of science towards the study of isolated facts.[27] Following Lukács, the concept of reification, next to the concept of alienation, has been used in the context of a variety of attempts to create outlines for a critique of society, culture and science—essentially attempts inspired by Hegel and Marx—but it also plays an integral role in the analysis of the normative foundations of modern societies.[28]

Wittgenstein's philosophical considerations of language can also be read as a critique of reification. So, it is possible to relate it to the more classical variants of a critique of ideology and a critique of social circumstances. In various sections of his work, Wittgenstein points to our tendency to look for things that correspond to respective words as their meanings—a tendency caused by unreflective language use. Such a tendency leads to linguistic hypostatizations, which may further lead to social (and individual) pathologies such as those discussed by Marx in the context of his critique of political economy. The example below might help to illustrate the point I have in mind.

What is time? It is already in the very asking of a question of this kind that Wittgenstein sees a tendency towards reification. The noun "time" suggests the presence of a particular entity, of a *thing* that corresponds to this *word*. In a question thus formulated, "time" appears as an entity independent of the action of man. The formulation of a question such as "What is time?" allows to expect a response in terms of a general definition which will give one information concerning what time is. Such a definition, however, also invokes a certain mode of our dealing with time. Because of the linguistic structure of the interrogative mood, the question concerning time is formulated just as any other question about the nature of an object would be: "What is the thing?" In answering such questions, we are often oriented towards physical reality and such an orientation becomes a dominant trait of our thinking. Structurally, the surface

---

[26] See: Lukács 1986, p. 96.
[27] See: Lukács, pp. 19ff.,121f., 198ff.
[28] For a discussion of the problem of reification in contemporary philosophy see: Honneth 2005. An updated reading of the alienation theorem can be found in: Jaeggi 2005.

grammar does not distinguish between "time" and any other physical object. The idea of "time" as a "thing" suggests such a quantified conception.

How can we characterize a physics-oriented perception of time? The physical time is time that can be measured by clocks. Time is usually depicted as a line or as an arrow pointing in a certain direction in which context one must think of the centrality of the metaphor of the "run of time". The past, the present and the future may be presented in the form of a "timeline". Our physical conception of time corresponds to a particular understanding of time as adapted to the technical demands of the world. Outside of this broader technical framework, however, the limitations of the physical concept of time are readily visible. For example, the phenomenon of differently experienced duration is not at all taken into account. Time, in accordance with such a model, is always "equal in length." Human life in its temporal constitution does not appear in such a discourse at all. Nevertheless, the physical conception of time coins many of our everyday interpretations of it. A glance at various situations in which we deal with time may quickly shed some light on the issue:

- What time is it? It's already 9.30; now I have to hurry, since I have no more time.
- I'll be working for a few more hours to make the most of the remaining time.
- If we drive to Jena tomorrow instead of taking the train, we can save time.
- One who has time has money.
- Don't waste your time!

The examples make clear that it could be the idea of "time as a thing" that leads to its quantification. Naturally, it is not all the kinds of quantification of time that result in the deformations of human life. Many contexts, however, reveal that it is the quantification of time that makes the distortions possible in the first place. You may "have time," or you may "not have it"; time can be "saved," "lost" or "wasted." It is no coincidence that it was not only Wittgenstein who dealt with the reification of time from a language-critical perspective. The reification of time was also discussed by Marx and by other thinkers representing the milieu of broadly conceived Critical Theory.[29] This, again, is an indication that the philosophy of language and critical social theory may yield similar results when analyzing phenomena. The saying "time is money" draws our attention to the possibility of a theoretical analysis of time in terms of value and money. In capitalist, production-oriented relations, "time" is fully quantified as "working

---

[29] See, for example: Rosa 2010.

time." Related to working time as a mere quantum of labor, Marx writes in his discussion of Proudhon's *Philosophy of Poverty:*

> that the pendulum of the clock has become as accurate a measure of the relative activity of two workers as it is of the speed of two locomotives. Therefore, we should not say that one man's hour is worth another man's hour, but rather that one man during an hour is worth just as much as another man during an hour. Time is everything, man is nothing; he is, at the most, time's carcass. Quality no longer matters. Quantity alone decides everything; hour for hour, day for day (Marx 1976b, p. 127).

As working time, time solidifies into a quantitatively measurable thing, especially where it serves to measure the value of the work in the sense of a specific and purposeful action. The reification of time into working time can be seen in correspondence to the hypostatization of the concept of time. The quantification of time, however, is not limited to the time of labor alone: it penetrates all spheres of human life and organizes the biographies of individuals. The experience of time-during-work becomes a paradigmatic experience of time.

Time, misunderstood as a "thing," and then "forced" into the categories of manageability and availability, gives rise to a variety of forms of reified relations in life. Since time is "precious," it can be "saved." Life is brought into dependence on an economically and linguistically quantified time. It is reduced to a "time factor" with no qualitative references funded on the basis of experience. Both language-critical analysis and Marx' theory may criticize the dominant misunderstandings and trace their origins. Wittgenstein's language-critical analyses do not lead directly to elements of social theory but they can be philosophically related to problems addressed by it. But the possibility of relating the critique of semantic hypostatizations to an economically based critique of reification is sufficient to assert the compatibility of language criticism with the theory of society. Examples such as the one discussed above can be regarded as building blocks for a critical theory transformed by means of the critique of language.

The example shows that the critique of language may be incorporated into a socio-theoretical framework, even if not every form of language criticism manifests the potential for social criticism and a critique of ideology. It seems clear that the criticism of social pathologies and ideologies can be supported by means of an analysis of the pathologies in our language usage. With the growing importance of language as the medium of social reproduction in a world developing towards a postindustrial society—an issue frequently addressed by the social sciences—language-critical analysis may gain particular importance in the context of critical theory. A philosophical critique of language has a practical sense: whoever speaks a language does more than just "use words." His or her language leaves behind tangible effects in the world; his or her thinking and perceptions are never "out of the box" but always locked within language, a fact that may lead to pathologies at the individual and social levels.

Many questions remain open. In particular, further clarifications are required with respect to problems connected with the concept of critique as well as with regard to the question of the social-philosophical foundations of the critique of language. Other important questions include the following: what is the basis on which language use can be criticized? To what extent—and at what points—do misunderstandings manifest themselves in the social fabric? Do more general connections between the critique of language and social philosophy prove viable also beyond the example discussed in this text? How can the links between the critique of language and social philosophy be sketched in greater detail? These questions should be examined in the course of more detailed investigations in the future.

A critical philosophy of language would also have to trace a more detailed connection between language and historically developed and socially-shaped practices. This is a further task. Max Horkheimer expressed this aspect of the critical philosophy of language with a beautiful, if perhaps a little romantic, adage:

> Philosophie muß empfindlicher werden für die stummen Zeugnisse der Sprache und in die in ihr aufgehobenen Erfahrungsschichten sich versenken. Jede Sprache bildet eine geistige Substanz, in der sich die Denkformen [...] ausdrücken, die in der Entwicklung des Volks, das sie spricht, ihre Wurzeln haben. Sie ist der Behälter der wechselnden Perspektiven des Fürsten und des Armen, des Dichters und des Bauern (Horkheimer 1985, p. 155).

Translated from German by Paweł Jędrzejko.

Bibliography

Bacon, Roger (1863): *Novum Organum*. In: R. Bacon: *The Works*. Transl. James Spedding, Robert Leslie Ellis, and Douglas Denon Heath. Boston: Taggard and Thompson.
Baker, Gordon/Hacker, Peter Michael Stephan (2004): *Wittgenstein: Meaning and Understanding*. Oxford: Oxford University Press.
Celikates, Robin (2009): *Kritik als soziale Praxis. Gesellschaftliche Selbstverständigung und kritische Theorie*. Frankfurt am Main: Campus Verlag.
Cloeren, Hermann J. (1988): *Language and Thought: German Approaches to Analytic Philosophy in the 18th and 19th Centuries*. Berlin/New York: De Gruyter.
Crary, Alice/Read, Rupert (eds.) (2000): *The New Wittgenstein*. London: Routledge.
Demmerling, Christoph (1994): *Sprache und Verdinglichung. Wittgenstein, Adorno und das Projekt einer kritischen Theorie*. Frankfurt am Main: Suhrkamp.
Demmerling, Christoph (2014): "Philosophie als Therapie. Die Auflösung philosophischer Dualismen". In: Chr. Barth/D. Lauer (eds.): *Die Philosophie John McDowells. Ein Handbuch*, Münster.

Dreyfus, Hubert/ Taylor, Charles (2015): *Retrieving Realism*. Cambridge/Mass.: Harvard University Press.
Ehrenberg, Alain (2010): *The Weariness of the Self: Diagnosing the History of Depression in the Contemporary Age*. Montreal & Kingston, McGill-Queen's University Press.
Frege, Gottlob (1972): "Conceptual Notation". In: G. Frege: *Conceptual Notation and related Articles*. Transl., ed. bibliogr., introd. T.W. Bynum. Oxford: Clarendon Press.
Gebauer, Gunter (2009): *Wittgensteins anthropologisches Denken*. Munich: Verlag C.H. Beck.
Geuss, Raymond (1981): *The Idea of a Critical Theory. Habermas and the Frankfurt School*. Cambridge: Cambridge University Press.
Glock, Hans Johann (2000): *Wittgenstein-Lexikon*. Darmstadt: Wissenschaftliche Buchgesellschaft.
Habermas, Jürgen (1981): *Erkenntnis und Interesse*. Frankfurt am Main.
Herder, Johann Gottfried (1955): *Metakritik zur Kritik der reinen Vernunft*. Hrsg. von F. Bassenge. Berlin: Aufbau-Verlag.
Honneth, Axel (2005): *Verdinglichung. Eine anerkennungstheoretische Studie*. Frankfurt am Main: Suhrkamp.
Horkheimer, Max (1937): "Traditionelle und kritische Theorie". In: M. Horkheimer: *Gesammelte Schriften*. Band 4. Schriften 1936–1941. Frankfurt am Main: S. Fischer.
Horkheimer, Max (1985): *Zur Kritik der instrumentellen Vernunft*. Frankfurt am Main.
Jaeggi, Rahel (2005): *Entfremdung. Zur Aktualität eines sozialphilosophischen Problems*. Frankfurt am Main: Campus Verlag.
Jaeggi, Rahel (2009): "Was ist Ideologiekritik?". In: R. Jaeggi/T. Wesche (eds.): *Was ist Kritik?*. Frankfurt am Main: Suhrkamp.
Kuch, Hannes/Herrmann, Steffen Kitty (2007): "Symbolische Verletzbarkeit und sprachliche Gewalt". In: S. Krämer/S. Kitty Herrmann/H. Kuch: *Verletzende Worte. Die Grammatik sprachlicher Missachtung*. Bielefeld.
Lecercle, Jean-Jacques (2006): *A Marxist Philosophy of Language*. Leiden: Brill.
Lukács, Georg (1986): "Die Verdinglichung und das Bewußtsein des Proletariats". In: G. Lukács: *Geschichte und Klassenbewusstsein. Studien über Marxistische Dialektik*. Darmstadt/Neuwied, pp. 170–355.
Marx, Karl/Engels, Frederick (1976a): "The German Ideology". In: Karl Marx/Engels, Frederick: *Collected Works (Vol. 5)*. London: Lawrence & Wishart.
Marx, Karl (1976b): "The Poverty of Philosophy". In: Karl Marx/Engels, Frederick: *Collected Works (Vol 6)*. London: Lawrence & Wishart.
Rosa, Hartmut (2010): *Alienation and Acceleration. Towards a Critical Theory of Late-Modern Temporality*. Aarhus: NSU Press.
Rossi-Landi, Ferrucio (1972): *Sprache als Arbeit und als Markt*, München: Carl Hanser Verlag.
Schulte, Joachim (1989): *Wittgenstein. Eine Einführung*. Stuttgart: Reclam.
Tetens, Holm (2006): *Kants "Kritik der reinen Vernunft". Ein systematischer Kommentar*. Stuttgart: Reclam.
Vološinov, Valentin Nikolaevich (1973): *Marxism and the Philosophy of Language*. London: Seminar Press.
Wiggershaus, Rolf (2000): *Wittgenstein und Adorno. Zwei Spielarten modernen Philosophierens*. Göttingen: Wallstein.
Wittgenstein, Ludwig (1922): *Tractatus Logico-Philosophicus*. London: Kegan Paul, London: Harcourt.

Wittgenstein, Ludwig (1953): Philosophische Untersuchungen/Philosophical Investigations. Oxford: Blackwell.

Peggy H. Breitenstein
Reflexive Social Critique.
On the Dialectical Criticism of Ideology According to Marx and Adorno

Abstract: For a long time philosophers would avoid addressing the subject of ideologies, steering clear even of the critique of ideology. In the last few years, however, positions attempting to implicitly or explicitly revive this method have been on the rise again. The criticism of ideology has been rediscovered and is now practiced as a means of social criticism—among others, by thinkers such as Luc Boltanski and Ève Chiapello, Sally Haslanger, Nancy Fraser or Slavoj Žižek, and also by some representatives of the younger generation of the Frankfurt School, such as Rahel Jaeggi, Robin Celikates or Titus Stahl. However, to date, hardly any of the existing analyses of the assumptions and claims of this particular method of social critique, or clarifications if how it works exactly, prove to be satisfactory.

The present article aims at shedding light upon these questions by referring back to Marx and Adorno. More specifically, the dialectical concepts of "ideology" and of the "critique of ideology"—which both thinkers employ, but which neither of them specifically explicates—are hereby clarified and subjected to methodological reflection.

Keywords: ideology, criticism of ideology, social criticism, critical theory, the Frankfurt School, Marx, Adorno, emancipation, dialectics

The word "ideology," as it is used in public discourse, seems outright inflated—and that appears to be the case irrespective of whether the debate focuses on the "ideology of national socialism," the "right-wing" or "left-wing populists," whether "identitarian," "religious" or "gender ideologies" are criticized, or whether the issue at stake is the "ideology of financial markets" or even "technology and science as ideology". The list could go on forever. As these examples demonstrate, however, if the label of "ideology" can simultaneously be attributed to worldviews, attitudes, socio-political measures, institutions, or systems of social organization—whether it is done for descriptive, analytical or critical purposes or whether the underlying intention is to depreciate the object of the debate—it seems obvious that in each such case the sense of the central concept is understood differently. Furthermore, the problem is not limited to the public space alone: In the various disciplines of the humanities and social sciences the concept is used equally ambiguously.[1]

In view of this confusing variety, and bearing in mind that central to this essay is the frequently misunderstood, rather complex and quite specific concept of ideology as proposed by the advocates *dialectical criticism of ideology*, it seems appropriate to open these reflections by introducing order to the debate by delineating the core meaning of the term—a meaning which those who choose not to use the term "ideology" carelessly would agree upon.

The first clarification should probably concern a variety of notions which, in themselves, seem to rest upon other, alternative, concepts: Concepts, whose sense the attribute "ideological" seems to best approximate. Worldviews, political programs or ideational systems obviously cannot be classified as ideological *per se*. Strictly speaking, they cannot be considered ideological insofar as *they are simply false*—and their falsehood may be *proven* in the light of recent, better knowledge. Not all errors are ideologies, although all ideologies are, in particular respects, errors. Thus, not even the irritatingly explicit false information, such as the currently omnipresent fake news and "alternative facts," may be considered to be ideological, but—at most—means of deliberate manipulation or propaganda. In a somewhat simplified way, one can claim that neither the traits of a given *Weltanschauung* (alone), nor the content of a political program or a concrete organizational form of an institution, etc., are ideological in themselves. Rather, their ideological dimension depends on their implicit or explicit *validity claim*, or, more precisely, it is the function of the *aspect of validity* itself. Whatever such a claim of validity is based on, and irrespective of what it appeals to—be it the pure facticity of the obvious/self-explanatory, or the "test of time," tradition, authority, political power, or established structures of domination—that which can be considered "ideological" is knowledge in its broad sense (i.e., understood as a system of beliefs and desires or interests associated therewith), as long as it comes with a *presumption of, or claim to, universality*, even though such knowledge simply does not lend itself to being generalized, and hence, on reasonable grounds, can be regarded as one-sided or restricted. One could probably expand on this subject much further. Even this brief reflection upon the interdependence between *ideology* and *validity* may, however, shed some light on the criticized claims that ideologies should purportedly be "true and false at the same time," or that they constitute "errors of thought of a higher

---

[1] Cf. Balibar 2013, p. 75; Haslanger 2011, p. 180. An attempt at creating a clear typology may be found, for instance, in: Næss/Kjell 1956, pp. 161 ff.; Larrain 1979, p. 13; Eagleton 1991, p. 1 f.

order"—claims as frequent as they are erroneous, or perhaps even absurd.² The above notwithstanding, this opening clarification only serves as a point of departure for the present essay, whose central objective is to explain what dialectical criticism of ideology is (as Adorno, in particular, conceived it, building on Marx's social critique), and wherein the source of its potential for social criticism lies.³

I begin my explanations by posing a series of questions which, in my opinion, any ideological criticism should be able to answer if it simultaneously considers itself to be *social* criticism, i.e.: Criticism that—on the one hand—is more than mere sociology of knowledge, and—on the other—wishes to be more than just criticism of ideas (I). These questions can be answered within the framework of dialectical criticism of ideology, as it was practiced, above all, by Marx and Adorno: To demonstrate this is the ultimate objective of the present study. Since, however, both thinkers carry out their acts of ideological criticism within the conceptual limits of critical theory, the characteristics of the latter also need to be explored. In step two (II), I focus on how Marx and Adorno develop their concept of ideology and the method of ideological criticism, offering the reader a more detailed interpretation of relevant texts. In conclusion (III), I recapitulate the results of this interpretation and close my argument by proposing answers to the questions formulated at the outset of the text.

I

After a lull of several decades, the dialectical criticism of ideology as developed by the Frankfurt School of Critical Theory has now returned to the forefront of academic attention.⁴ To this date, it has, however, not been satisfactorily clarified what dialectical criticism of ideology *is* or how it actually *works*. There is certainly a consensus about the fact that it is applied with the purpose of analysing

---

2 Alternative attempts at the explanation thereof may, for instance, be found in studies by Rahel Jaeggi or Titus Stahl (Jaeggi 2009, Stahl 2013).
3 It is only marginally that I allude to theories of ideology (such as those proposed by the Althusser School), which have developed as definitely divorced from the real or assumed premises of the dialectical criticism of ideology and thus in opposition to economism, the base and superstructure scheme, dogmatism and elitism, truth claim, etc. For the distinctions between the *theory of ideology* and *criticism of ideology*, see, above all, Rehmann 2004; as well as Rehmann 2008, pp. 10 ff.
4 See, among others, Boltanski/Chiapello 2006, Fraser 2009 and Slavoj Žižek, who explicitly refers to Adorno (Žižek 1989; Žižek 1997; Žižek 2009). Furthermore, the number of methodologically oriented studies constantly increases (see, for instance, Jaeggi 2009; Jaeggi 2013; Celikates 2006; Stahl 2013, Ng 2015).

social grievances or pathologies, or, in a broader sense, that the issue at stake is an answer to the question of a better life. Beyond this, however, there is a lack of clarity, especially with regard to the following questions:

(1) What may be regarded as the carrier or the medium of the ideological? Is the ideological realized in social or scientific *discourses* or *party programs*, in "hand-held" social or individual practices, or is the ideological rooted in prior thinking or behavioral patterns?
(2) What exactly is the subject of criticism? Is it the inadequacy of certain *descriptions*, *explanations*, or *justifications* of social reality, or even the possible *reproduction* of social practice itself, supported by these discursive practices? Or is it both?
(3) Which constitutive elements—or structures—of social practice are ultimately to be modified by criticism? Are these *institutions?* Codified or informal *normative systems?* Or perhaps *convictions* and *self-perceptions of the actors* reproducing this social practice?
(4) What is the status of socio-critical analyses and statements? Are they *descriptive* or *normative?* And, if the latter, what are their *axiological frames* and where do the *values* underlying such an axiology come from?
(5) How can dialectical criticism of ideology function as *a social critique?* Does it require an elaborate theory of society as its theoretical background?

In my opinion, these five complex questions lend themselves to being coherently answered with reference to the work of the Founding Fathers of dialectical criticism of ideology if it is truly to be regarded as a serious philosophical method of social critique. So far, however, these issues have been clarified only partially, and the present short article is only a first sketch, aimed at a primarily systematic clarification.[5] The ambivalence surrounding these questions may have something to do with the fact that the Founding Fathers themselves—especially Marx and Adorno—would usually only practice criticism of ideology, rarely analyzing or explaining the theoretical foundations of their work in greater detail.[6] This, in turn, may be due to the thinkers' awareness that they represented the type of theory that most directly contradicts many traditional beliefs, including self-evident distinctions underlying theory of science as well as academic pat-

---

[5] For instance, see also sketches by Geuss 1981 and Detel 2007; they refer to important methodological features of ideological criticism by means of the term of "the reflexive social theories method."

[6] At this point, it seems worth recalling Adorno's adage: "Philosophisches Ideal wäre, daß die Rechenschaft über das, was man tut, überflüssig wird, indem man es tut" (Adorno 1970a, p. 58).

terns of thought.⁷ Such a surmise can be made because ever-since its inception "Critical Theory"—as a type of theory—does not only leave ossified prejudices with regard to the relation between *theory* and *practice*, *thinking* and *action*, *concept* and *reality* behind, but also cuts itself off from the convictions concerning the allegedly clear distinction between *expert* and *lay knowledge*, between *first-person* and *third-person* perspective, as well as between *normative* and *descriptive statements*, traditionally taken for granted. The radical break with the fundamental assumptions of traditional theories might perhaps be traced back to the fact that "Critical Theory" has always attempted to understand *society* and/or *social practice* as a *set of complex interrelationships* and, simultaneously, to comprehend both the everyday and the scientific understandings themselves *as a practice* within *this social practice*. In light of this, theory is precisely *not an area removed from practice*, but nor is it merely an autopoietic functional system of self-referential acts. And such a "theoretical practice" is always "in progress"—it always take the form of "working" social, political, economic theories and theories addressing everyday systems of beliefs and convictions. Critical Theory, therefore, sees such a practice as both *an expression* and as *a source* of "objective forms of thought." As such, it is simultaneously *the starting point, the object*, but also *the medium of criticism*. More precisely, such theory criticizes these "forms of thought" immanently: "Als dialektische muß Theorie – wie weithin die Marxische – immanent sein, auch wenn sie schließlich die gesamte Sphäre negiert, in der sie sich bewegt. Das kontrastiert sie einer bloß von außen herangebrachten und [...] dieser gegenüber ohnmächtigen Wissenssoziologie."⁸ And that is precisely what obligates critical theories to embrace ideological criticism—but, as is understandable, such a gesture is tantamount to the adoption of further (basic) assumptions, to lending the critical formula a particular set of characteristics, and yields an effect in terms of the development of the theory's unique self-understanding.⁹

Thus, critical theories (i) claim to be reflexive in several ways: They are aware of their own multifaceted dependence on social practice, which they attempt to understand and criticize. The point of departure for subsequent critical steps within such theories is defined by the already existing, effective, descriptions and explanations developed within the broadly understood area of the social sciences (sociology, political science, law, economics). These definitions and

---

7 Cf. Horkheimer 1988.
8 Adorno 1970a, pp. 197 f.; Adorno puts the criticism of the impotent, defused use of important ideological concepts, effected by means of the sociology of knowledge, into practice as early as in his *Antrittsvorlesung 1931* (Adorno 1986, p. 341).
9 See also: Geuss 1981, pp. 2ff.

explanations, however, are only effective insofar as they characterize the self-descriptions and self-understanding of the actors, as well as their experiences. At the same time, they reflect a historically conditioned necessity and, thus, the validity of the concepts, distinctions, and models adopted within the systems of description pertinent to these disciplines—including concepts, distinctions and models serving the purpose of self-description and those worked out by each of the above disciplines. It is against such a backdrop that one should interpret Adorno's well-known speech on the "temporal core of truth" ("Zeitkern der Wahrheit"), which alludes to Walter Benjamin's truth-oriented reflections[10]. Regardlessly, however, the eponymous "truth" cannot be understood in terms of a correspondence theory: Rather, it is to be shown that in relying upon existing descriptive systems, such correspondences fail in the face of current experiences and tendencies. The reflection itself has a negative dialectical structure. Moreover, it is not end in itself, but rather it is social responsibility (ii) that drives critical theory towards criticizing the social practices that it itself reproduces with a view to shedding light upon the phenomenon, thereby (iii) also to contributing to their emancipation. In this context, however, the notion of "emancipation" differs from the concept developed in the tradition of the Enlightenment in terms of its somewhat more modest connotations: It is not about autonomy, or about individual freedom in the emphatic sense, but rather about *critical self-reflection* and *liberation*. Specifically, emancipation is liberation from *self-reproduced social pathologies*, which are either experiencable or experienced as *suffering*.

Accordingly, both the Founding Fathers of the Frankfurt School and Marx felt obliged to enlighten those who suffer. To those wishing to escape the suffering, experienced either as a result of being locked in (or committed to) the current social practice, or as a consequences of its dominance, the Enlightenment is tantamount to the realization that this is only possible if they themselves change the social practice they currently abided by.

With its emancipatory claim, critical theory thus also relates to a *dependency* by acknowledging—on behalf of certain social actors and actresses, who are the addressees of the theoretical discourse—the plight of the degraded, the oppressed, the despised.[11] Such an *acknowledgment* does not, however, simply ensue from the fact that those affected find their suffering adequately represented and explained in theories: An acknowledgment would itself be an act of an *emancipated* and *emancipatory practice*. "Reconciliation" is only a possible

---

10 Adorno 1977d, pp. 471f.; Benjamin 1991, p. 578.; see also: Horkheimer 1988, p. 208 u. 212.
11 Marx 1956, p. 385.

name for the corresponding regulative idea, which may guide this open practice: A practice, which can only be conceived as a process, not a state.

If the above, simplified characterization of "Critical Theory" as a type of theory, may suffice as a general introduction, it does not yet explain what exactly Adorno and Marx understand by ideology and ideology criticism.

II

In this section, I will concentrate on offering an interpretation of and a commentary on a small, but (in my opinion) largely underestimated contribution to the doctrine of ideology—"Beitrag zur Ideologienlehre"[12]—in which Adorno explicates his concept of ideology, while simultaneously presenting a masterpiece of ideological criticism. On the basis of two excursuses, I will also demonstrate that Adorno's concept of ideology, as well as his understanding of ideological criticism, is largely identical with that proposed by Marx.[13]

Adorno's contribution is revealing in several respects. Not only does it actually bring some clarity into the ambiguous concept of ideology, but his explanation of the central notion also consists of a reconstruction of the dialectical transformations of the meaning of ideology and—along with the transformation of "the thing itself"—outlines its structure and function.[14] In doing so, Adorno also demonstrates what he means by "philosophical work on the concept," which goes beyond the established projects of the history of the *concept* and the evolution of the *problem:* He is concerned with the elaboration of a general, but *critically sound* core of meaning, which makes it possible to show the truth and falsity of both present and past interpretations of the term, although the sense of this historically conditioned concept and the transformations of its

---

12 The article is based on a lecture by Adorno at the 12th German Sociology Day in Heidelberg, which, among others, raised the issue of the ideology. It was first published as "Beitrag zur Ideologienlehre" in the 1953/54 issue of the *Zeitschrift für Sozialforschung,* and then was also included in his *Gesammelte Schriften.* In 1956 an slightly revised version appeared in *Soziologische Exkurse* (see: Institut für Sozialforschung 1991, pp. 162–181), although it is not clear if Adorno was the author of the revisions.

13 Among others, it may already be seen in Kuhne's work (see Kuhne 1998). Kurt Lenk, on the other hand, offers a most comprehensive insight into the dependence of Marx's concept of ideology on Hegel's theory of alienation (Lenk 1986, pp. 114 ff.; see also Larrain 1983; Siemek 2007); yet, more frequently than not, this connection is denied or neglected (see, among others, König 2011).

14 "Was Ideologie heiße und was Ideologien sind, läßt sich ausmachen nur so, indem man der Bewegung des Begriffs gerecht wird, die zugleich eine der Sache ist." (Adorno 1977c, p. 458).

meaning have always been dependent on specific social conditions.[15] In accordance with this understanding, the "philosophical work on the concept" aims at reconstructing the change of concepts as a function of collective learning processes and experience.

Adorno's starting point, however, is a critique of the concept of ideology as it was coined by the sociology of knowledge, established as a subdiscipline of social sciences at the time—a critique, more precisely, concentrating on the implications and effects of the application of the term.[16]

> Der Begriff der Ideologie ist allgemein in die wissenschaftliche Sprache eingegangen. [...] Durch Beziehung auf Motivationszusammenhänge werden geistige Gebilde von der Erkenntnis in die gesellschaftliche Dynamik hineingezogen. Der unabdingbare Schein ihres Ansichseins ebenso wie ihr Anspruch auf Wahrheit wird kritisch durchdrungen. Die Selbständigkeit geistiger Produkte, ja die Bedingung ihrer Verselbständigung selbst wird im Namen Ideologie zusammengedacht mit der realen geschichtlichen Bewegung der Gesellschaft. In ihr entspringen die Produkte und in ihr üben sie ihre Funktion aus. Sie sollen willentlich oder unwillentlich im Dienst partikularer Interessen stehen. Ja ihre Absonderung selbst, die Konstitution der Sphäre Geist, seine Transzendenz, wird zugleich als gesellschaftliches Resultat der Arbeitsteilung bestimmt.[17]

It is clear that Adorno here identifies the concept of ideology as developed by the sociology of knowledge and that pertinent to a trivial historical-dialectical materialism, to which he himself, as well as Marx, succumb all too often.

According to this understanding, ideologies are beliefs or images of the world which come into existence as a result of certain concrete interests, or interest areas (social class standpoints) or of limited knowledge. The transformations of such beliefs or images of the world go hand in hand with those of the social circumstances which, generally, determine ideologies.

This is the well-known doctrine of base and superstructure, against which the equally well-known accusations of determinism, economism, etc. have been levelled. Furthermore, in Adorno's eyes, the doctrine is ahistorical and thus the function and structure of ideology itself are assumed to be unchangeable. The central motive behind Adorno's critique is, however, that such a con-

---

15 In his *Negative Dialektik* Adorno talks of "substance" ("Substanz") or "participation" ("Teilhabe") in a "Typology" ("Typik"), which can capture an interpreter by bringing the various historical meanings into constellation; without this "substance" the change of the concept—and of the object—would not be detectable at all. See: Adorno 1970a, pp. 163f.

16 Adorno worked out a first more comprehensive critique of Mannheim's concept of ideology in 1937; but it appeared for the first time in 1953 in the magazine *Aufklärung*, then in 1955 in Adorno's volume of essays Prismen (Adorno 1977a).

17 Adorno 1977c, p. 457.

ceptual assumption leads the project of "the critique of ideology as a social critique" *ad absurdum:* It implies the impossibility of *any* social criticism which claims to represent more than just the position of class-specific interests. Nonetheless, the hereby criticized trivial understanding of ideology (and thus also of the critique of ideology), continues to be influential to this day. It is also to this day that the base-superstructure scheme has, ultimately, been the reason why materialist criticism of society continually confronts the following apparent dilemma: Critics can only criticize in earnest, objectively or universally, insofar as they claim not to be determined by personal or class interest, but if that is the case, they themselves cannot identify their own position. Alternatively, if they acknowledge the determinacy and narrowness of their standpoint or their interests, then they cannot perform critical acts in earnest, objectively or universally. One may, however, resolve this dilemma quite successfully by looking at the problem through the prism of a dialectical concept of ideology and with reference to the corresponding alternative interpretations of theory. Such a concept is already present in Marx—a concept that does not directly stem from the simple base-superstructure determinism. In fact, passages which might suggest otherwise all lend themselves to being read either as criticism, or can easily be interpreted in an alternative fashion. This is especially the case with texts commonly celebrated (or frowned upon) as founding documents of "historical materialism".

A brief excursus may illustrate this claim. Marx would use the term "ideology" in his early writings in a manner quite typical for his time, and he retained this use in his later works.[18] In the Germany of the 1830s, the term stood, above all, for *unrealistic theorizing*, or for the *propagation of ideals meaningless for the political practice.*[19] Marx, however, defines the concept more differentiated, and formulates hypotheses in search of a genetic explanation of the *alienation* of reality, or the *confusion* between the idea and reality. It is already in his "Zur Judenfrage" (1843) that he explains this disparity by reference to self-contradictions in man and by the split (or decomposition) of the ego, which, in turn, may be traced back to antagonisms within social practice. As long as people act as *private individuals* in a bourgeois society, i.e. as long as they make their self-interested contribution to the system of mutual satisfaction of needs, while independently acting as *citizens* of the political community, participating—or sharing—in *the*

---

18 I thus assert against the prevalent view that Marx's concept of "ideology" was contradictory, and that in his later work (positivist in spirit) he deliberately avoided its use (see Bohlender 2010, p. 41; Dierse/Romberg 1976, p. 164; Projekt Ideologie-Theorie: *Theorien über Ideologie*, p. 7), and hence—I argue that the core meaning of the term is also visible in Marx.
19 This is also how Napoleon uses the expression. See: Dierse 1987, p. 147.

public use of reason, they lead "nicht nur in Gedanken, im Bewusstsein, sondern in der Wirklichkeit, im Leben ein doppeltes, ein himmlisches und ein irdisches Leben."[20] It is, however, "the present world order" itself that corresponds to the "division of man into public persons and private individuals."[21]

In the text quoted here Marx accuses Bruno Bauer of an outright "ideological distortion," which consists of the fact that the latter *mistakes* the freedom of religion—politically guaranteed by law, and practically boiling down to the liberation of the state from religion—for human emancipation, thereby validating the division of men into private and public persons. This, however, is precisely the factor preventing the "real emancipation of man," the *sine-qua-non* condition of which would be the abolition of the division itself.[22] In this way Marx demonstrates how Bauer's claims contradict the actual intention of his criticism and, at the same time, serve the existing status quo.

This classic argument pattern of the critique of ideology is present in all the texts of his Early Period (*Die heilige Familie, Die Deutsche Ideologie*), in which Marx criticizes the *critical Criticism* of the Young Hegelians. Here, however, the thinker is not (only) concerned with the explanation of the genesis of *false representations*;[23] moreover, he also does not simply stop at showing that these ideas are wrong in the sense that they contradict their own critical motivations. Rather, Marx is already practicing the ideological-critical method here, the mastery in which he demonstrates later in *Das Kapital* and in his preparatory work to it. As a dialectical critique, the critique of ideology is a "double critique": a *critique of circumstances* attained by means of the *critique of representations*—and *vice versa*. The fact that it is possible to describe the *binaries*, such as "practice" and "consciousness," "relationships" and "productive forces," or the "base" and the "superstructure" as *contraries*—as is rarely observed—is in itself the object of criticism: It is not a mere basis for an explanatory model. and insofar as such criticism is plausible, so is, at the same time, the need for the overturning of the conditions which such contradictions made possible in the first place. This stance is documented in a key passage:

> Und endlich bietet uns die Theilung der Arbeit gleich das erste Beispiel davon dar, daß solange die Menschen sich in der naturwüchsigen Gesellschaft befinden, solange also die Spaltung zwischen dem besondern & gemeinsamen Interesse existirt, solange die Thätigkeit also nicht freiwillig, sondern naturwüchsig getheilt ist, die eigne That des Menschen

---

20 Marx 1976, p. 355.
21 Marx 1976, pp. 356 f.
22 See: Marx 1976, p. 370.
23 This, for example, is suggested by Tilman Reitz (Reitz 2004, p. 694).

ihm zu einer fremden, gegenüberstehenden Macht wird, die ihn unterjocht, statt daß er sie beherrscht.[24]

Returning to Adorno, it is, however, worth noting that on the basis of the affirmative use of the term central to our reflections—a use which in his day was already prevalent—the thinker outlines a history of semantic and functional transformations of the concept of ideology, in which he attempts to show the simultaneity of truth and falsehood in the respective iterations of the notion. Adorno's history of "ideology" may be organized into its prehistory, its "real" history and its posthistory.[25] Moreover, Adorno distinguishes between a *pre-dialectical* and a *dialectical* concept of ideology, the latter primarily serving as a heuristic purpose, while the former is revealed in the perspectives of pre- and post-historical theories, and is subjected to criticism. Adorno's "prehistory" includes the subjective and psychological concept as put forth by Bacon and the French idéologues as well as the subjective-sociological concept proposed by the French Encyclopaedists and Napoleon. These notions of ideology may be called subjective, insofar as they regard the subjective reason as a source of errors and also as a corrective instance. Whether these errors are attributed to man's limited ability to reason, to his dependence on language or abstract concepts and ideas (Bacon), or to sensory perception (Idéologues), whether they are attributed to concrete interests of power (Encyclopaedists) or to illusions detached from reality (Napoleon), all these positions rely upon the assumption that "es genüge, das Bewußtsein in Ordnung zu bringen, um die Gesellschaft in Ordnung zu bringen."[26] In a nutshell: The "material life-process of society" is still not sufficiently taken into account: The concept of ideology remains naïve.[27]

---

24 Marx/Engels/Weydemeyer 2004, p. 20. Another revealing passage is the following: "Warum die Ideologen alles auf den Kopf stellen. Religiösen, Juristen, Politiker. Juristen, Politiker (Staatsleute überhaupt), Moralisten, Religiöse. Für diese ideologische Unterabteilung in einer Klasse, 1. Verselbständigung des Geschäfts durch die Teilung der Arbeit; jeder hält sein Handwerk für das Wahre. Über den Zusammenhang, worin ihr Handwerk mit der Wirklichkeit steht, machen sie sich um so notwendiger Illusionen, da dies schon durch die Natur des Handwerks selbst bedingt wird. Die Verhältnisse werden in der Jurisprudenz, Politik etc. – im Bewußtsein zu Begriffen; da sie nicht über diese Verhältnisse h[in]aus sind, sind auch die Begriffe derselben in ihrem Kopf fixe Begriffe; der Richter z. B. wendet den Code an, ihm gilt daher die Gesetzgebung für den wahren aktiven Treiber. Respekt vor ihrer Ware; da ihr Geschäft es mit Allgemeinem zu tun hat. Idee des Rechts. Idee des Staats. Im gewöhnlichen Bewußtsein ist die Sache auf den Kopf gestellt" (Marx/Engels/Weydemeyer 2004, p. 99).
25 He could draw his inspiration from Barth's study, *Wahrheit und Ideologie*, first published in 1945.
26 Adorno 1977c, pp. 464f.

This changes with the dialectical concept of ideology, in light of which one may first pose the question "nach der Wahrheit und objektiven Verbindlichkeit der Ideen [...], und ebenso die nach objektiven geschichtlichen Tendenzen, von denen die Gesellschaft sowohl in ihrem blinden ‚naturgesetzlichen' Verlauf wie auch im Potential ihrer bewußten vernünftigen Ordnung abhängt."[28]

Adorno's *real history of ideology*, and at the same time the history of the opening of the possibility of understanding it within the framework of a socio-philosophical/sociological doctrine of ideology, begins with the establishment of bourgeois society: "das Wesen von Ideologie selbst [...] ist bürgerlich."[29] Even though he does not mention the names of Hegel and Marx at this point, it is obvious that Adorno is referring to these two Founding Fathers of dialectical criticism of ideology, to whom— not quite by chance— theorists of bourgeois society, its essence, its genesis, its dynamism and *its ideologies* also refer at the same time. In this context, Adorno also explains (more or less clearly) how the establishment of the bourgeois society impacts truth, falsity, and the inevitability of ideologies—and to what extent these can be criticized at all.

Before exploring this further, let me first shed some light upon the *post-historical* end of ideologies as suggested by Adorno. Its beginnings are marked by the regression to the thought preceding the dialectical concept of ideology that could be observed in the sociology following Max Weber and Vilfredo Pareto. Adorno accuses Weber of neutralizing the concept of ideology by reducing it to "merely a prejudice to be tested" ("ein je zu überprüfendes Vorurteil"), while for Pareto "all that is spiritual is ideology," whose task is to rationalize and justify all possible interests and claims.[30] In particular, Adorno accuses Pareto of not posing questions about the element of the truth of ideologies which can be grasped only in relation to the objective conditions.[31] It is, however, precisely this theory of ideology that truly reflects its time:

> Indem Pareto sich blind macht gegen die Vernunft in den Ideologien, wie sie im Begriff der historischen Notwendigkeit hegelisch mitgedacht war, begibt er sich zugleich des Rechtsanspruchs der Vernunft, über Ideologien überhaupt zu urteilen. Diese Ideologienlehre taugt trefflich selber zur Ideologie des totalitären Machtstaates. Indem sie vorweg alles Geistige dem Propaganda- und Herrschaftszweck subsumiert, bereitet sie dem Zynismus das wissenschaftlich gute Gewissen.[32]

---

27 See: Adorno 1977c, p. 464.
28 Adorno 1977c, p. 464.
29 Adorno 1977c, p. 465.
30 Adorno 1977c, p. 467.
31 See: Adorno 1977c, p. 467.
32 Adorno 1977c, p. 467.

Adorno also levels similar accusations at Max Scheler and Karl Mannheim, although, indeed, the philosopher admits that "Mannheim fühlte wohl, daß der Begriff der Ideologie nur als der eines falschen Bewußtseins sein Recht hätte, aber ist eines solchen Begriffs inhaltlich nicht mehr mächtig und postuliert ihn lediglich formal, als angeblich erkenntnistheoretische Möglichkeit."[33] Yet, through the back door, his theory of ideology justifies the replacement of ideology by propaganda. This, however, would mean the end of ideology. Such practices are indeed put into effect in totalitarian regimes, but they also pose a serious peril in times of the dominance of the cultural industry.[34] How so?

Adorno's forecast may be explained against the backdrop of what has already been mentioned with regard to the constitutive aspects of the validity of ideology. Only those convictions or views to which the claims to truth and universal validity are attributed can fail to live up to these claims—and in that sense they can be ideological. As is well known, Adorno's critique of the cultural industry aims at reproaching its producers and its products, who explicitly deny that claim. The products of the cultural industry are deliberately meant only to entertain and amuse—and thereby, in Adorno's eyes, they lose the property of "spirituality," the quality of independence, and thus also their authenticity: In this sense they cannot be true.[35] In the time of "fake news" and "alternative facts," Adorno's predictions and warnings may be considered most valid and topical. That to which Adorno wants to draw particular attention is the following: If, from the outset, it is questionable whether any adequate representations of events can exist, and when "facts" are understood as arbitrarily produced, when political attitudes and beliefs can be changed as the wind blows, if arbitrariness, non-bindingness and non-commitment are publicly acknowledged as regulative principles—or even goals—of social and political practice, then one can no longer talk of truth and lies, and ideologies can no longer be discussed. At the same time, however, every political discourse becomes superfluous or impossible, for any request for reasons, or for a corresponding justification of a given position one adopts or given measure one takes must inevitably prove pointless, because no such justification can ever be provided. In Adorno's understanding, politics is thus nothing more than cultural industry. This, in turn, sheds some light on the meanings of the dialectical concept of ideology, as Ador-

---

33 Adorno: Adorno 1977c, p. 472.
34 This goes to support one of the theses of the *Dialektik der Aufklärung* that totalitarianisms are not just "operational accidents" ("Betriebsunfälle") of history (see: Adorno 1977b, p. 264; Horkheimer/Adorno: *Dialektik der Aufklärung*).
35 See: Adorno: Adorno 1977c, pp. 474 ff.

no holds is. What then does it consist of? And how does dialectical critique of ideology work?

As already indicated, according to Adorno, the real (social, economic, political and legal) conditions for the emergence of ideologies only surface in the "age of the bourgeoisie." Ideology understood as "objektiv notwendiges und zugleich falsches Bewußtsein, als Verschränkung des Wahren und Unwahren" belongs to "einer entfalteten städtischen Marktwirtschaft [...]. Denn *Ideologie ist Rechtfertigung*. Sie erheischt ebenso die Erfahrung eines bereits problematischen gesellschaftlichen Zustandes, den es zu verteidigen gilt, wie andererseits die Idee der Gerechtigkeit selbst, ohne die eine solche apologetische Notwendigkeit nicht bestünde, und die ihr Modell am Tausch von Vergleichbarem hat. Wo bloße unmittelbare Machtverhältnisse herrschen, gibt es eigentlich keine Ideologien."[36] This passage carries the central premise of the concept of dialectical ideology. Adorno himself made this clear by means of italicization: The only instance of the use of this typeface in the whole text emphasizes that *ideology is justification*. Ideologies are justification discourses. That is to say, in all cases, ideologies are *discursive practices* in which certain social or political conditions, structures, institutions (power relations, distribution of goods, positions, prospects, etc.) that are straightforwardly problematic in the eyes of ideological criticism—are justified. Implicit or explicit as their justification might be, they are, in any case, formulated in the context of the actors to whose needs they (directly or indirectly) cater, and whose claim to such a justification is fundamentally recognized.[37] According to Adorno, the recognition of this claim on the part of all the participants of the culture and their corresponding self-understanding, along with the very sociopolitical conditions which require justification were only born in the context of the bourgeois society with its antagonistic dynamics—a society, which *de jure* and *de facto* is no longer governed by personal dependencies (as in corporate or caste societies); a society, which consists of self-interested, simultaneously competing and cooperating individuals, in each case dependent upon the fundamental social context of the so-called "system of needs" so aptly defined by Hegel; a society where, owing to advances in technology and productive forces, a previously unimaginable, but most unevenly distributed affluence and immense *know-how* have been generated. In Adorno's view, it is specifically texts such as manifestos or programs, whose declared goal is to convince and to

---

36 Adorno 1977c, p. 465.
37 The speech of "hidden" ideologies in practices (cf. Jaeggi 2009, p. 268) resp. ideological background as "Ensemble von Apparaten und Praxisformen", like in Gramsci, Althusser or Haug (cf. Rehmann 2004, p. 720; Haug 1993), would be certainly inaccurate in the eyes of Adorno.

persuade, but also—or perhaps particularly—*philosophical and scientific theories* that arise with the claim of objective knowledge of the world, that chiefly deliver discourses of justification. It is in this sense that Adorno speaks of "the spiritual," which is not merely a "manipulative means of rule[ing]," as the discourse of the "Ideologies of National Socialism," or the theory of deception by priests, would suggest.[38] He refers to the spiritual, which itself "stems from the social process" and can—in this sense—be attributed to the sphere of the objective mind.

This clarification points to the truth that, according to Adorno, is constitutive of ideologies, and it shows that he actually reverts to the critical claim found in the works of Marx, i.e, the latter's critique of philosophical criticism (the Young Hegelians' or Feuerbach's), [39] of philosophical legal theories and theories of the state (Hegel),[40] of the explanations of the world as offered by the humanities (e. g. German historiography), of the theories of political economy (from the early *Ökonomisch-Philosophische Manuskripte* to *Das Kapital*),[41] and finally, also of particular political programs (*Kritik des Gothaer Programms*)[42]. Marx also criticizes—as has been shown above—all these very different types of texts because they serve to justify and thus reproduce a flawed social practice. Marx, however, can only attribute these effects to texts insofar as he does not consider them simply as carriers of expert knowledge. Such texts provide the vocabulary and arguments with which people reflectively describe themselves and their practice, or with which they articulate and justify their claims and self-interpretations. Directly or indirectly, whether by becoming familiar with particular uses of language or through public discourse, the actors themselves revert to these theories: It is visible in their interpretations of their own practices, in their self-descriptions, as well as in their explanations, including the formulation of background beliefs and norms, as well as higher-level practices of justification and substantiation.

Thus, for example, we evidently understand and describe ourselves as actors in the labor market—as employees who face an employer in a mortgage case, who receive a wage for work which we convulsively, often in vain, try to reconcile with family life, while homemaking, care and education are not regarded as legitimate work in the labor market. This example is only intended to demonstrate

---

38 Adorno: Adorno 1977c, p. 465.
39 See: Marx 1957; Marx/Engels/ Weydemeyer 2004.
40 See: Marx 1956.
41 This is especially clear in Marx 1990, as well as in his critique of Proudhon in Marx 1964.
42 See: Marx 1962.

that such self-perceptions and descriptions are evidently based on certain theories—in this case, economic ones.

In this sense, theories can be viewed as the resources off which political/ practical as well as everyday discourses feed. *In this sense*, theories are at the same time an expression of the knowledge and of the consciousness of their time: They orient themselves towards social practice and serve its reproduction. *In this sense* they can also be regarded as true, according to Adorno and Marx. Wherein, then, lies their falsehood? Just like "independent" visions, which contain a "spiritual" component manifest double-characteristic, so, according to Adorno, do the theories describing social practices and attempting to understand them. They are both "*fait social*" and "autonomous," both features they share with authentic art.[43]

This "spiritual" is socially conditioned, as Marx explains, insofar as it is in accordance with the actual, concrete *praxis*, manifest in a variety of concrete discursive and non-discursive practices, the objectivized knowledge, implicit and explicit normative systems, self-understanding, etc. Insofar as these "factual" practices are also the subject of observation, description and reflection in the "spiritual," it also arrives at an autonomous moment, whereby the "spiritual" may also distance itself from, and transcend, the concrete, local, socially-situated practices. In the form of advances theories—according to Adorno—the "spiritual," with its claim to the capacity of the recognition of the essentials of social practice, does not merely represent surface phaenomena, and this is precisely what substantiates its claim to the truth.[44] Referring to "essentials," Adorno does not refer simply to what is obvious: Under this term, the philosopher understands the unique capacity of social practices, including their potential and tendencies, which can either be positively utopian or negatively dystopian, and thereby lend themselves to thematization.

It is, however, exactly here that Adorno finds the source of the falsity of ideologies: In his eyes, it is precisely the blatantly uncritically affirmative theories that tend to demonstrate proper, positively connoted potentials, which, as present in practice in the form of concrete desires and longings, are simultaneously connected to real possibilities—as if they were already realized, or, at least —in light of given social relations—possible to realize. This is also where the dialectical problem of ideologies manifest itself: "Unwahr werden eigentlich Ideologien erst durch ihr Verhältnis zu der bestehenden Wirklichkeit. Sie können ‚an sich' wahr sein, so wie die Ideen Freiheit, Menschlichkeit, Gerechtigkeit es sind,

---

[43] For the dual character of art see Adorno 1970b, pp. 16, 334 ff., 340, 374 f.
[44] Cf. Adorno 1977c, pp. 464, 474.

aber sie gebärden sich, als wären sie bereits realisiert."[45] Theories, whether empirical or normative, are misunderstood if they are not regarded as *ideal theories*. As such, they function as a resource for "conceptual fetishes," which simply conceal the fact that their implementation is impossible—or that it is impossible under given circumstances. This "non-truth" too can be explained with an excursus on Marx. Within the frames of his early ideological criticism, Marx, as has already been shown above, accuses some theories—and criticizes their objectives—for their onesidedness, as manifest in their falling into a perverse relationship with the social reality and relying in their assessments upon their own, more general, claims and intentions. He sees one of the causes thereof in the given circumstances themselves—the social practice of the division of labor, and the public/private split imposed upon man—unless these circumstances are specifically recognized and reflected upon. In his major works dedicated to the critique of the economy, Marx's criticism becomes even sharper: He points out that this rift is related both to the inability of political parties (or initiatives) to initiate a fundamental improvement in social practice, as well as to the inability of theories to *intrinsically grasp the existing conditions*. In his eyes, the categories of the bourgeois political economy remain "social hieroglyphs" or "crazy forms."[46] In the famous "fetish chapter" of the first volume of *Das Kapital*, Marx also offers an elaborate structural analysis of this "insanity," which relates both to the ideological content of economic theories and to the everyday understanding of the actors, which, at the same time, is the confirmation and reinforcement of the ideology itself. If one understands Marx's concept of fetishism very generally, as "Sichfestsetzen der sozialen Tätigkeit, [...] Consolidation unsres eignen Produkts zu einer sachlichen Gewalt über uns, die unsrer Kontrolle entwächst",[47] it is also possible to comprehend and criticize quite different, both discursive and non-discursive social practices as "fetishistic." In the "fetish chapter" of *Das Kapital* Marx asserts, for example, that the "Geldform der Warenwelt" disguises "den gesellschaftlichen Charakter der Privatarbeiten und daher die gesellschaftlichen Verhältnisse der Privatarbeiter".[48] In other words, the monetary form obscures the fact that the *work of an individual and the time of his life that he dedicates to it* are always reduced to some common denominator, always measured or evaluated according to some uniform standard of abstract work and thus an investment must be made accordingly. But the "categories

---

45 Adorno 1977c, p. 473.
46 See also: Marx 1972, pp. 86, 88, 90, 562.
47 Marx/Engels/ Weydemeyer 2004, p. 21.
48 Marx 1972, p. 90.

of bourgeois economics" themselves can also be regarded as *conceptual fetishes or fetish theories*, insofar as they are "socially valid, i.e. objective, forms of reflection" within this practice.[49] As such, they not only express fetishism: They also describe it rather adequately. The claim to scientific objectivity and truth of such forms of thinking also conceals the fact that they are man-made as concepts, theories, and intellectual properties, and thus that their categories—refering to a practice that is historically and geographically concrete—have only limited validity. Furthermore, all of the above goes hand in hand with the blurring of the real conditions through representation.

It is, however, the *reproduction of the formation of the capitalist society* itself that depends on such concealment. For example, Marx illustrates this by describing the "value of labor" with reference to the abstract concept of the "wage":

> Man begreift daher die entscheidende Wichtigkeit der Verwandlung von Wert und Preis der Arbeitskraft in die Form des Arbeitslohns oder in Wert und Preis der Arbeit selbst. Auf dieser Erscheinungsform, die das wirkliche Verhältnis unsichtbar macht und grade sein Gegenteil zeigt, beruhen alle Rechtsvorstellungen des Arbeiters wie des Kapitalisten, alle Mystifikationen der kapitalistischen Produktionsweise, alle ihre Freiheitsillusionen, alle apologetischen Flausen der Vulgärökonomie.[50]

Just how profoundly such fetishisms are grafted the thought and the practice, the self-understanding and the understanding of other human being, is illustrated by a passage in which Marx characterizes the world of the capitalist circulation of goods as the "Eden of the innate human rights":

> Was allein hier herrscht, ist Freiheit, Gleichheit, Eigentum und Bentham. Freiheit! Denn Käufer und Verkäufer einer Ware, z.B. der Arbeitskraft, sind nur durch ihren freien Willen bestimmt. Sie kontrahieren als freie, rechtlich ebenbürtige Personen. Der Kontrakt ist das Endresultat, worin sich ihre Willen einen gemeinsamen Rechtsausdruck geben. Gleichheit! Denn sie beziehen sich nur als Warenbesitzer aufeinander und tauschen Äquivalent für Äquivalent. Eigentum! Denn jeder verfügt nur über das Seine. Bentham! Denn jedem von den beiden ist es nur um sich zu tun. Die einzige Macht, die sie zusammen und in ein Verhältnis bringt, ist die ihres Eigennutzes, ihres Sondervorteils, ihrer Privatinteressen. Und eben weil so jeder nur für sich und keiner für den andren kehrt, vollbringen alle, infolge einer prästabilierten Harmonie der Dinge oder unter den Auspizien einer allpfiffigen Vorsehung, nur das Werk ihres wechselseitigen Vorteils, des Gemeinnutzens, des Gesamtinteresses.[51]

---

49 Marx 1972, p. 90.
50 Marx 1972, p. 562.
51 Marx 1972, pp. 189f.

Whether this is still applicable today or not, this ideology-critical satire shows the truth and the un-truth of ideologies in the Adornian sense. Marx, however, developed the economic theory of society employed here on his own. Adorno, on the other hand, only uses this as his "background theory," even where he elaborates it as a critique of the cultural industry. Marx developed his *Kritik der politischen Ökonomie* as an anatomy of the formation of bourgeois or capitalist society, working on it for several decades (unfortunately, without a proper finale), including his still unmatchable *Theorie des Mysteriums der Warenform*, which to this date remains the basis of the conception of ideology as a critique of the fetish. It demonstrates that activities and products—be they tables, skirts, services, or the fruits of intellectual creativity—become mysterious as commodities as soon as they are produced solely for profit-oriented exchange, driven by an anonymous need. [52] According to Marx, these requirements, which are necessarily associated with the private ownership of the means of production, already relate to goods before they are produced and in production, yet in reference exclusively to commodities other than those to be produced: labor, raw materials, other goods. In this context, they are reduced to an abstract and their exchange value is expressed in terms of a general equivalent—"money."[53] Adorno adopts Marx's basic concepts and follows his analyses: Even the form of the critique of the conceptual fetishes of political economy finds a correspondence in his works. The critique of ideology follows the path of the immanent criticism of theories, which claims to have grasped the essence of the society (or individual areas thereof); yet it is precisely through that claim that it criticizes the social condition itself. The critique of ideology is "im Hegelschen Sinn bestimmte Negation, Konfrontation von Geistigem mit seiner Verwirklichung, und hat zur Voraussetzung ebenso die Unterscheidung des Wahren und Unwahren im Urteil wie den Anspruch auf Wahrheit im Kritisierten."[54] In this exact sense Adorno's criticism may also be understood as an emancipatory theoretical practice: In its critique, it offers a theoretical set of instruments that make it possible for

---

52 Cf. Marx 1972, p. 87.
53 In the so-called "service society" or "knowledge society," the tendency to reduce individual activity to abstract human labor has not diminished; what is even more obvious is that—precisely because much of the labor and the time of one's life must be dedicated directly to consumption—fetishism has come to affect every activity, every free minute of each individual can afford. The corresponding discourses of justification are particularly clearly embodied in work-life balance initiatives or in slogans such as "compatibility of life and work," "Are you still working or have you started to live?" All this also obscures the fact that it is still geographically, culturally, or professionally random *whether, for how much, when and for how long an individual will be able to sell himself.*
54 Adorno 1977c, p. 466.

the thought to reach beyond the present state of affairs—whether within concretized frames of a counterfactual scenario called "communism" (as in Marx), or with the view to emphasizing the dystopian moments of the present (as in Adorno).

And thus we have arrived at the point at which the fundamental questions concerning the critique of ideology as the critique of the society—posed in the introductory part of this text—have been answered. It is now time to recapitulate these reflections in the form of a brief summary.

III

The primary object of dialectical criticism of ideology are the discursive practices that support other discursive as well as non-discursive practices. It fulfils this function, insofar as it feeds the systems of convictions and beliefs at the individual, as well as collective, levels, which—in turn—simultaneously serve as the resource base for the rationalization, and thus also legitimation of social norms, rules, and practices (question 1).

As such, systems of beliefs—which include knowledge of the facts of the primeval social world (Vorwelt), contemporary social world and social environment (Mitwelt), and of the natural and cultural environment, as well as the knowledge of the corresponding norms regulating the respective worlds and environments—serve to reproduce social practice in all individual areas (questions 2 and 3). Dialectical criticism of ideology, in turn, is reflected in the mirror of these systems of beliefs and convictions—again, on individual and collective levels—but it is through the immanent, yet socially induced inconsistencies that such criticism is capable of showing people—laymen and experts alike—that their first or third-person interpretations, their self- or external descriptions—that is, in principle, what they think and say about what they think and do—their beliefs can be self-contradictory and deceptive and that laymen and experts alike could change the state of affairs if only they were aware of the existence of the underlying system of beliefs (questions 2 and 3). Such a formula of criticisms indicates that these are deceptions—or errors—of a "higher order," that is, errors regarding the validity of beliefs, including norms, purposes, values, which the actors themselves consider abiding by and which they actually abide.

In this respect, criticism remains immanent; at the same time, however, it is normative. It is assumed that profound, latent or open self-contradictions or even conflicts are the cause of suffering, which—in turn—is intrinsically evil and should therefore be prevented or at least minimized (question 4). More specifically, self-deception—or, in other words, false consciousness—may manifest itself in a variety of ways and may be driven by different causes: As a rule, the chief cause lies in the concealment of direct, lasting and profound (existential) contradictions, triggered and perpetuated by the adoption of specific social roles, self-interpretations and claims corresponding thereto. For example, the opposition between the self-interpretations of an individual as a mother or father, as a politically engaged, committed citizen, as a self-fulfilled person—and as an employee (even in our prosperous society) is striking. It seems to be just as difficult to be a good consumer and an end-user concerned about the sustainability, and—at the same time—to remain conscientious and responsible with respect to the present and future producers. Still, there exist higher-level beliefs that allow the individual to conceal the associated inner rift, or to attribute the sense of such incompatibility to one's own inability. For example, a belief that looms particularly large is the conviction that all these roles must be played and juggled all at once—a conviction that dispenses with the need to ask for the real justification of such an imperative or for the appropriate basis for such an imbalance. For example, the imperative of "reconciling family and career", commitment and self-realization—supported by economic theories, the pension and social security systems, reinforced by habits, political slogans, etc., can become so, seemingly, self-evident that it is taken for granted. The outcome of such a self-deception is the accelerated pace of human life and, inevitably, the exhausted self.[55]

Dialectical criticism of ideology may also serve to analyze the extent to which the limited systems of beliefs and claims that allow the actors involved in the specific functional areas of their historically specific society (labor and merchandise market, politics and public life, family-oriented welfare sector) to cooperate and thereby to reproduce the social practice. In this respect, the self-deceptions of the higher order are not simply false or corrigible, like other simple errors; nor—in their fallacy—are they necessary or necessarily false: Contradictions and self-adopted illusions are likewise self-induced as a result of social practice. The explanation of the above, however, is the task of sociological theorems (question 5). Criticism of ideology, as social critique, is thus dependent on social theory, even if it, in itself, cannot be developed into a "major theory" matching the format of Marx's critique of political economy. Furthermore, it must be observed that Marx's *Fragment* may still prove to have enough explanatory and interpretive potential to apply to modern capitalist societies.

The final point is that even the illusions themselves which are the subject of ideological criticism always can be identified (and prove deceptive) against the

---

[55] See: Rosa 2010 und Ehrenberg 2010.

background of concrete social practices that have induced them in the first place. Likewise, the criticism of ideology also functions as nothing other than an immanent critique: The convictions and beliefs concerning norms, values and claims can be mediated (and habituated) only by the social practices themselves—for example, in the family life, at work, in political initiatives or in consumption, which, by revealing these antagonisms make criticism possible. Therefore, in order for authentic life to possible within falsity, the falsity must be experienced—this is the *sine-qua-non* condition of the critique.

Translated from German by Paweł Jędrzejko.

Bibliography

Adorno, Theodor W. (1986): "Die Aktualität der Philosophie". In: *Philosophische Frühschriften*. Frankfurt a.M.: Suhrkamp, pp. 325–344.
Adorno, Theodor W. (1977a): "Das Bewusstsein der Wissenssoziologie". In: *Kulturkritik und Gesellschaft I*. Frankfurt a.M.: Suhrkamp, pp. 31–46.
Adorno, Theodor W. (1977b): *Minima Moralia*. Frankfurt a.M.: Suhrkamp.
Adorno, Theodor W. (1977c): "Beitrag zur Ideologienlehre". In: *Soziologische Schriften I*. Frankfurt a.M.: Suhrkamp, pp. 457–477.
Adorno, Theodor W. (1977d): "Wozu noch Philosophie". In: *Kulturkritik und Gesellschaft II*. Frankfurt a.M.: Suhrkamp, pp. 459–473.
Adorno, Theodor W. (1970a): *Negative Dialektik*. Frankfurt a.M.: Suhrkamp.
Adorno, Theodor W. (1977e): "Marginalien zu Theorie und Praxis". In: *Kulturkritik und Gesellschaft II*. Frankfurt a.M.: Suhrkamp, pp. 759–782.
Adorno, Theodor W. (1970b): *Ästhetische Theorie. Gesammelte Schriften*. Bd. 7. Frankfurt a.M.: Suhrkamp.
Althusser, Louis (2010): "Ideologie und ideologische Staatsapparate". In: *Gesammelte Schriften*. Bd. 5/1. Hrsg. von Frieder Otto Wolf. Hamburg: VSA.
Althusser, Louis (2012): "Über die Reproduktion, Ideologie und ideologische Staatsapparate". In: *Gesammelte Schriften*. Bd. 5/2. Hrsg. von Frieder Otto Wolf. Hamburg.
Balibar, Étienne (2013): Marx' Philosophie. Übers. und eingeleitet von Frieder Otto Wolf. Berlin: b_books.
Barth, Hans (1974): *Wahrheit und Ideologie*. Frankfurt a.M.: Suhrkamp.
Benjamin, Walter (1991): "Das Passagen-Werk". In: Gesammelte Schriften V. Frankfurt a.M.: Suhrkamp.
Bohlender, Matthias (2010): "Die Herrschaft der Gedanken". In: Harald Bluhm (ed.): *Die deutsche Ideologie*. Berlin: Akademie, pp. 41–57.
Boltanski, Luc/ Chiapello, Ève (2006): *Der neue Geist des Kapitalismus*. Konstanz UVK.
Breitenstein, Peggy H. (2013): *Die Befreiung der Geschichte. Geschichtsphilosophie als Gesellschaftskritik nach Adorno und Foucault*. Frankfurt a.M.: Campus.
Celikates, Robin (2006): "From Critical Social Theory to a Social Theory of Critique: On the Critique of Ideology after the Pragmatic Turn". In: *Constellations* 13, No. 1, pp. 21–40.

Detel, Wolfgang (2007): "Habermas und die Methodologie kritischer Theorien". In: Rainer Winter/ Peter V. Zima (eds.): *Kritische Theorie heute*. Bielefeld: Transcript, pp. 177–203.
Dierse, Ulrich (1987): "Ideologie". In: Otto Brunner/ Werner Conze/ Reinhart Koselleck (eds.): *Geschichtliche Grundbegriffe. Historisches Lexikon zur politisch-sozialen Sprache in Deutschland*. Bd. 3. Stuttgart, pp. 131–169.
Dierse, Ulrich/ Romberg, Reinhard (1976): "Ideologie". In: Joachim Ritter (ed.): *Historisches Wörterbuch der Philosophie*. Bd. 4. Basel, pp. 158–186.
Eagleton, Terry (1991): *Ideology. An Introduction*. London: Verso.
Ehrenberg, Alain (2010): *The Weariness of the Self: Diagnosing the History of Depression in the Contemporary Age*. Montreal & Kingston: McGill-Queen's University Press.
Fraser, Nancy (2009): "Feminismus, Kapitalismus und die List der Geschichte". In: Rainer Forst, u. a. (eds.): *Sozialphilosophie und Kritik*. Frankfurt a. M.: Suhrkamp, pp. 481–505.
Geuss, Raymond (1981): *The Idea of a Critical Theory*. Cambridge: Cambridge University Press.
Haslanger, Sally (2011): "Ideology, Generics, and Common Ground". In: Charlotte Witt (ed.): *Feminist Metaphysics: Explorations in the Ontology of Sex, Gender and the Self*. Dordrecht 2011, pp. 179–208.
Haug, Wolfgang Fritz (1993): *Elemente einer Theorie des Ideologischen*. Hamburg: Argument.
Horkheimer, Max (1988): "Traditionelle und kritische Theorie". In: M. Horkheimer: *Gesammelte Schriften*. Bd. 4. Frankfurt a.M.: Fischer, pp. 162–225.
Institut für Sozialforschung (1991): *Soziologische Exkurse*. Hamburg: EVA.
Jaeggi, Rahel (2009): "Was ist Ideologiekritik?" In: Rahel Jaeggi/ Tilo Wesche (eds.): *Was ist Kritik?* Frankfurt a.M.: Suhrkamp, pp. 266–295.
Jaeggi, Rahel (2013): *Kritik von Lebensformen*. Frankfurt a.M.: Suhrkamp.
König, Helmut (2011): "Historischer Materialismus und Antisemitismus. Ideologiekritik bei Marx, Adorno/Horkheimer und Kurt Lenk". In: Henrique Ricardo Otten/ Manfred Sicking (eds.): *Kritik und Leidenschaft. Vom Umgang mit politischen Ideen*. Bielefeld: Transcript, pp. 199–220.
Kuhne, Frank (1998): "Marx' Ideologiebegriff im Kapital". In: Hans-Georg Bensch, u. a. (eds.): *Das automatische Subjekt bei Marx*. Lüneburg: zu Klampen, pp. 9–24.
Larrain, Jorge (1979): *The Concept of Ideology*. Athens: The University of Georgia Press.
Larrain, Jorge (1983): "Ideology". In: Tom Bottomore, u. a. (eds): *A Dictionary of Marxist Thought*. Cambridge, MA, pp. 219–223.
Lenk, Kurt (1986): *Marx in der Wissenssoziologie. Studien zur Rezeption der Marxschen Ideologiekritik*. Zweite, verbesserte und mit einem neuen Vorwort versehene Auflage. Lüneburg: zu Klampen.
Marx, Karl (1976): "Zur Judenfrage (1844)". In: Marx-Engels-Werke 1. Berlin 1976, pp. 347–377.
Marx, Karl (1990): "Auszüge aus James Mills Buch 'Éléments de l'économie politique' (1844)". In: Marx-Engels-Werke 40. Berlin, pp. 445–463.
Marx, Karl (1998): "1) ad Feuerbach (aus: Notizbuch aus den Jahren 1844–1847)". In: MEGA IV/3. Berlin, pp. 19–21.
Marx, Karl (1957): "Die heilige Familie (1845)". In: Marx-Engels-Werke 2. Berlin.
Marx, Karl (1972): "Das Kapital. Erster Band (1867/90)". In: Marx-Engels-Werke 23, Berlin.
Marx, Karl (1962): "Randglossen zum Programm der deutschen Arbeiterpartei (1875)". In: Marx-Engels-Werke 19. Berlin, pp. 13–32.

Marx, Karl (1956): "Zur Kritik der Hegelschen Rechtsphilosophie. Einleitung (1843)". In: Marx-Engels-Werke 1. Berlin, pp. 378–391.
Marx, Karl (1964): "Das Elend der Philosophie (1847)". In: Marx-Engels-Werke 4, Berlin.
Marx, Karl/ Engels, Friedrich/ Weydemeyer, Joseph (2004): *Die Deutsche Ideologie. Artikel, Druckvorlagen, Entwürfe, Reinschriftenfragmente und Notizen zu I. Feuerbach und II. Sankt Bruno*. In: Marx-Engels-Jahrbuch 2003. Hg. v. der Internationalen Marx-Engels-Stiftung. Berlin: Akademie.
Næss, Arne/ Christophersen, Jens A./ Kjell Kvalø (1956): *Democracy, Ideology, and Objectivity: Studies in the Semantics and Cognitive Analysis of Ideological Controversy*. Oslo- Oxford: B. Blackwell.
Ng, Karen (2015): "Ideology Critique from Hegel and Marx to Critical Theory". In: *Constellations* 22, No.3, pp. 393–404.
Projekt Ideologie-Theorie (1979): *Theorien über Ideologie*. Berlin: Argument.
Rehberg, Karl-Siegbert (2011): "Von den großen Mobilisierungsideologien zur ideologischen Verdeckung". In: Henrique Ricardo Otten/ Manfred Sicking (eds.): *Kritik und Leidenschaft. Vom Umgang mit politischen Ideen*. Bielefeld: Transcript, pp. 277–295.
Rehmann, Jan (2004): "Ideologietheorie". In: Wolfgang Fritz Haug (ed.): *Historisch-kritisches Wörterbuch des Marxismus*. Bd. 6/I. Hamburg, pp. 717–760.
Rehmann, Jan (2008): *Einführung in die Ideologietheorie*. Hamburg: Argument.
Reitz, Tilman (2004): "Ideologietheorie". In: Wolfgang Fritz Haug (ed.): *Historisch-kritisches Wörterbuch des Marxismus*. Bd. 6/I. Hamburg, pp. 690–717.
Rosa, Hartmut (2010): *Alienation and Acceleration. Towards a Critical Theory of Late-Modern Temporality*. Aarhus: NSU Press.
Siemek, Marek J. (2007): "Hegel und das Marxsche Konzept der Ideologie". In: Andreas Arndt (ed.): *Das Leben denken* (= Hegel Jahrbuch 2007). Teil 2. Berlin, pp. 182–190.
Stahl, Titus (2013): "Ideologiekritik als Kritik sozialer Praktiken". In: Rahel Jaeggi/ Daniel Loick (eds.): *Nach Marx*. Frankfurt a.M.: Suhrkamp, pp. 228–254.
Žižek, Slavoj (1997): "The Spectre of Ideology". In: Slavoj Žižek (ed.): *Mapping Ideology*. 3. ed. London/New York, pp. 1–33.
Žižek, Slavoj (2009): *Violence*. London: Polity.
Žižek, Slavoj (1989): *The Sublime Object of Ideology*. London: Verso.

Renata Zieminska
Skepticism and Atheism.
Three Types of Relationships

Abstract: In the history of skepticism there are three types of a relationship between skepticism and atheism: (1) skepticism is beyond the atheism-theism debate (Sextus Empiricus); (2) skepticism is the way to fideism (Montaigne); and (3) skepticism is the way to atheism (Hume). Skepticism lead to all possible practical options in religious matters so it has no practical power and can be combined with all practical choices. In like vein, contemporary skepticism is sometimes neutral towards religion, sometimes hostile to religion and sometimes sympathetic towards religion. However, the irreligious or anti-religious skepticism is dominating in our times. Neutral skepticism is typical for epistemology and the skepticism that is sympathetic towards religion is preserved in some type of the philosophy of religion (Schellenberg). Religious people usually dislike skepticism because they see it as first step towards atheism. But some religious people make radical distinction between reason and faith and in such a case skepticism can be good introduction to faith and religion. Typical skeptic is hesitating about the concept of God, typical atheist has conceptualized God in some way and s/he has determined view that God conceptualized in this way does not exist. The different conceptualizations allow that even atheism of some kind (as negation of theism and personal God) can be connected with the religious attitude (Schellenberg's skeptical and a-theistic religion).

Keywords: religious skepticism, atheism, fideism, Montaigne, Hume, Schellenberg

In the history of skepticism there are three types of a relationship between skepticism and atheism: (1) skepticism is beyond the atheism-theism debate (Sextus Empiricus); (2) skepticism is the way to fideism (Montaigne); and (3) skepticism is the way to atheism (Hume). In every case skepticism concerning the knowledge about God brings some problems for theism as a rational view. Theism is replaced either by suspension of judgment, or by blind faith or by accepting the opposite view. Let us first look at three philosophers-skeptics: Sextus Empiricus, Montaigne, Hume (they represent Antiquity, the Renaissance, and the Enlightenment) and ask if skepticism, according to them, is something good, wrong or neutral towards the religious beliefs. I claim that those three relationships are preserved in contemporary thought. The third is dominating in common thinking, the first is used in epistemology, the second appears sometimes in the philosophy of religion.

1 Sextus Empiricus – skepticism is beyond the atheism-theism debate

Sextus' ancient (2nd century AD) texts are stocked with arguments against gods or God, but they also contain some arguments for the existence of the object of worship. He remarks the disagreement among philosophers concerning the concept of god (is god corporeal or not, anthropomorphic or not, in space or not, within the universe or outside, sentient or imperishable, comprehensible or perfect, omnipotent or good). Canvassing the conflicting theories of god, Sextus suggests that the human spirit is incapable of acquiring a concept of god, because "we posses neither an agreed substance for him nor a form nor a place" (PH 3.3).

Yet, even granting that god is conceivable, conceivability does not translate into a proof of existence. Rather, Sextus gives reasons to convince us that it is necessary to suspend judgment about whether gods exist or not. The first is the dispute among philosophers that shows that the existence of gods is not-evident and in need of proof (cf. PH 3.6).The second is the lack of valid arguments, which Sextus proves by surveying existing arguments and showing that they are invalid. Having rejected the self-evidence of divine existence, Sextus then deploys, as his third reason, the positive arguments against their existence. The most space is devoted to the argument of evil. (PH 3.9–10) According to it god allowing for evil is weak or malign. "If they say that the gods provide for everything, they will say that they are the cause of evil; and if they say that they provide for some things or even for none at all, they will be bound to say either that the gods are malign or that they are weak" (PH 3.12).

According to Sextus, it is impious to say that gods are cause of evil or that they are weak and malign. This leads to the paradoxical assertion that those who say that the gods exist are being impious. Thus, it is more pious to say that they do not exist (or at least that they have no providence for the world). But, Sextus is not an atheist, he does not accept the conclusion that gods or God does not exist. It would be negative dogmatism. Sextus' position is not any thesis but suspension of judgment about gods.

To counter the arguments against the existence of gods, Sextus then turns to atheism and its negative results. He refers to ancient atheists, Diagoras of Melos, Euhemerus, Prodicus of Ceos, Theodorus of Cyrene or Critias (M 9.51), and tries to argue against atheism. For instance we can find this weak argument: "if god does not exist, neither will piety, since piety is the knowledge of service to the gods; but piety does exist; so, too, do the gods" (M 9.123). Sextus juxtaposes the opposite claims (atheism and theism) and suspends judgment about gods (concerning both concept and existence). The skeptic will not believe either side on the question of whether the gods exist or not. He is neither a theist nor an atheist.

But if skeptic suspends judgment, what is his/her everyday activity? Does he attend religious ceremonies or not? We expect that disbeliever will be rather inactive in religious matters. But Sextus surprisingly says: "following ordinary life without opinions, we say that there are gods and we are pious towards the gods and say that they are provident" (PH 3.2). "We accept, from an everyday point of view, that piety is good and impiety bad" (PH 1.24). Skeptics suspend judgment about the existence of gods but in practice are pious and say that gods exist. They do not actually believe that the gods exist but they take part in religious ceremonies. Sextus does not mean hypocrisy but sincere religious activity without any religious beliefs.

It is a very strange to modern reader view that presupposes the radical gap between beliefs and practice and the possibility of human practice without any theory, for instance the religious practice without any religious beliefs. This presupposition and Sextan psychology of managing all beliefs seems unacceptable today (and it was criticized in his times by the Stoics, Galen and others). The only reasonable way out is the distinction between strong and weak religious beliefs but it was contradicted by Sextus (PH 1.226). So, we are forced to conclude that Sextan skepticism was pragmatically inconsistent (Zieminska 2017).

Skeptical position even interpreted in consistent way as the thesis with weak assertion, is still hopeless in practical life that requires some decision: religion or irreligion. But there are persons hesitating, in the process of making decision, and skepticism is good for this period. In the longer period of time a skeptic tips in favor of some position. Practical life, sooner or later requires some decision: to pray or not to pray, to take part in religious ceremonies or not.

2 Michel de Montaigne – skepticism is the way to fideism

Montaigne's (1533–1592) modern *Essays* are full of arguments against certainty of our knowledge about the nature of God (E II.12). However, there is no arguments against the existence of God. Only the human description of God is doubted. "We prescribe limits to God [...] we want to enslave him to the vain and feeble approximations of our understanding, him who made both us and our knowledge" (Montaigne 2007, p. 97). "When we say that the infinity of the centuries both past and to come is to God but an instant, that his goodness, wisdom, power, are the same thing as his essence – our tongue says it, but our intelligence does not apprehend it" (Montaigne 2007, p. 97). Human mind, both senses and reason, seems unable to apprehend God. Such thesis is a kind of skepticism about religious knowledge. Montaigne is one of those Christian thinkers that have read and embraced skeptical arguments collected by Sextus Empiricus in his *Outlines of Pyrrhonism*, translated into Latin and published in 1562.

Pyrrhonism, in Montaigne's opinion, is a very good preparation to religion. "It presents man naked and empty, acknowledging his natural weakness, fit to receive from above some outside power; stripped of human knowledge, and all the more apt to lodge divine knowledge in himself, annihilating his judgment to make more room for faith[1] [...]; a sworn enemy of heresy, and consequently free from the vain and irreligious opinion introduced by the false sects. He is a blank tablet prepared to take from the finger of God such forms as he shell be pleased to engrave on it" (Montaigne 2007, p. 96). Skepticism questions human knowledge about God as the product of human imagination and misuse. It removes false prejudices and that is why it is the first step towards truth.

According to Montaigne, the unknown God exists and blind faith is the only proper relation to God. "It is not by reasoning or by our understanding that we have received our religion; it is by external authority and command. The weakness of our judgment helps us more in this than its strength, and our blindness more than our clear-sightedness. It is by the mediation of our ignorance more than of our knowledge that we are learned with the divine learning. It is no wonder if our natural and earthly powers cannot conceive that supernatural and heavenly knowledge; let us bring to it nothing of our own but obedience and submission" (Montaigne 2007, p. 95). Montaigne was a skeptic about reason who accepted following faith in religious matters. Skepticism was for him the good tool to reveal the weakens of our rational prejudices about God but also the good tool to show the need of faith.

We can describe Montaigne as both skeptic and fideist. Ann Hartle sees Montaigne's Catholic faith as the contradiction of his skepticism or as inconsistency in his philosophical position (Hartle 2005, p. 200). There is a lot of discussion among the scholars concerning Montaigne's superficial insincere fideism and hidden atheism. "Montaigne has been read both as a total sceptic, doubting everything, even the religious tenets he pretended to defend, and more recently as a serious defender of the faith" (Popkin 2003, p. 56, p. 320). In my view he was

---

[1] "anéantissant son judgment pour faire plus de place à la foi" (Montaigne 1965: 226).

the man of his times and Christianity was interior element of his thinking. He was a Christian pyrrhonist who reconciled ancient skeptical arguments and Christian revelation (following Arnobius, Lactantius, John of Salisbury, Nicholas of Cusa, Erasmus of Rotterdam, Giovanni Pico della Mirandola and others). Christian pyrrhonism/skepticism is a broad movement in the Renaissance. Montaigne's skepticism can be seen as "mildly religious" (Popkin 2003, p. 56) or as circular movement of thought "from simple inarticulate belief he ascends through doubt to autonomous rationality and then descends through doubt to the truth of faith" (Hartle 2005, p. 203). Christian skeptic may in practice either believe without reason or submit to custom.

3 David Hume – skepticism is the way to atheism

David Hume's (1711–1776) had the reputation of unbeliever and persisted in disbelieving "even when he had death before his eyes" (Bell 1990, p. 1). But he did not identify himself with the outright atheism, for example, Baron d'Holbach, Hume was rather doubting skeptic than outright atheist. He dissociates himself from atheism: "The ill use, which Bayle and other libertines made of the philosophical scepticism of the Fathers and first Reformers" caused that "it is now in a manner avowed, by all pretenders to reasoning and philosophy, that atheist and sceptic are almost synonymous" (Hume 1990, p. 49). This passage confirms that in Hume times these two words were taken as synonymous. George Berkeley was more determined than Hume and connected skepticism with atheism.[2]

In *Dialogues Concerning Natural Religion* Hume shows many superstitions in popular religion but he also rejects deism as purged natural and rational religion independent on revelation and faith (deists have no rational grounds as well). According to Hume, people are not usually led to religion by reasoning. As far as the matter of bringing someone to religion is considered "a talent of eloquence and strong imagery is more requisite than that of reasoning and argument" (Hume 1990, p. 103).

---

[2] See the titles of his works: *A Treatise concerning the Principles of Human Knowledge. Wherein the chief causes of error and difficulty in the sciences, with the grounds of **Scepticism, Atheism, and Irreligion**, are inquired into* and *Three Dialogues Between Hylas and Philonus. The design of which is plainly to demonstrate the reality and perfection of human knowledge, the incorporeal nature of the soul, and the immediate providence of a Deity: in opposition to **Sceptics and Atheists**.* See: Berkeley 1948.

Also philosophers cannot come to religion by reason alone. First of all they have no adequate idea of God or divine nature, because they have no experience of God. According to Hume every idea is a copy of some vivid and forceful impressions. "Our ideas reach no farther than our experience: We have no experience of divine attributes and operations" (Hume 1990, p. 53). So we have no adequate idea of God's nature and attributes. His skeptical discussion with some arguments for the nature and existence of God can be interpreted as arguments from the possibility of error (they are only conjectures) or as arguments from his empirical presuppositions (we have no experience of God's activity and we cannot establish any existence a priori).

Hume declares that he does not doubt in the existence of God (Hume 1990, pp. 38, 51). He develops many doubts about the human descriptions of God's nature. Putting aside Hume's sincerity here, those doubts are enough to question the natural theology. Even if we feel the existence of God, we do not know what we mean. So, we know about God nothing. Some attempts at describing God's role, for instance the design argument and the cosmological argument, are pure conjectures.

The design argument generates some anthropomorphic notion of God's mind (intelligence with human sentiments like gratitude, love or pity). It is an absurd to believe that deity has human passions, that is "delighted with entreaty, solicitation, presents, and flattery" (Hume 1990, p. 137). Such analogy is weak and prone to "error and uncertainty" (Hume 1990, p. 54), it is "no more than a guess or conjecture" (Hume 1990, p. 55). The problem of evil (both natural and moral) is especially difficult for omnipotent and morally perfect loving God. Is our world, asks Hume, what we can "expect from a very powerful, wise, and benevolent deity?" (Hume 1990, p. 115)

The alternative to cosmological argument (God as a necessary cause of the world) is eternal blind nature. Hume writes that the first cause of the world can be perfect goodness, perfect malice, both goodness and malice or neither goodness nor malice. According to him the fourth is the most probable (Hume 1990, p. 122). Additionally no argument a prori can demonstrate the existence of any being (Hume 1990, p. 99).

In fact, the thesis that the God's nature is incomprehensible is similar to skeptic's and atheist's stance that God is unknown. We have two options of describing divine nature: irrational mysticism or rational anthropomorphism (Hume 1990, p. 69). Hume rejects both options and takes the attitude of a skeptic: "a total suspense of judgment is here our only reasonable resource" (Hume 1990, p. 97). Sometimes it is only methodological skepticism; he writes about being cautious and modest in conclusions (Hume 1990, p. 121).

Religious person can only believe that arguments for the existence of God exceed the objections against it. "Some astonishment indeed will naturally arise from the greatness of the object: Some melancholy from its obscurity: Some contempt of human reason, that it can give no solution more satisfactory with regard to so extraordinary and magnificent question." (Hume 1990, p. 138) But reason is our nature. Both total skepticism and religion is exceeding the nature.

Sometimes Hume writes like a skeptical fideist. "To be a philosophical sceptic is, in a man of letters, the first and most essential step towards being a sound, believing *Christian*" (Hume 1990, p. 138). Hume makes in this context the reference to Bayle fideistic confession and to the other skeptics that were fideists. But he himself is not a fideist. He divides human mind into two parts: reason and instinct. Skepticism is on the side of reason. Religion is on the other side. Skepticism is hostile towards rational grounds for religion, and in Hume's case leads to practical atheism.

According to Hume "religion originates in our emotional responses to the uncertainties of life, in our feelings of insecurity and vulnerability in a hostile world" (Bell 1990, p. 8). We are "not satisfied with life, afraid of death" (Hume 1990, p. 107). Both fear and hope enter into religion (Hume 1990, p. 136). People need religion to comfort their fears and express their hopes.

Most people need some creeds and ceremonies. Few, like Hume, can cope with the mystery of nature alone. Hume is not anti-religious, but he takes religion as something natural for many people. Both theist and atheist go beyond the reason. Theist exaggerates the dissimilarity between nature and God, atheist exaggerates the similarity in nature. Hume prefers skepticism as the theoretical option beyond theism and atheism. But he concedes that in practice skepticism is helpless and we need some course of action. Hume chooses the atheist attitude but he thinks that most people prefer religious superstitions. So, skepticism is his theory, and atheism is his practice. Skepticism can lead to practical atheism but it is open to religion (fideism).

According to Paul Russell, Hume is an atheist rather than a skeptic. The atheist interpretation provides coherent way of reading Hume's *Treatise* and "a very different picture of the unity of Hume's philosophical thought as a whole" (Russell 2008, p. 275). On Russell's account, Hume uses extreme Pyrrhonian skepticism to question a religious conception of philosophical anthropology and ethics and uses moderate, Academic skepticism to develop new science of human nature. He employs skeptical principles in an attempt both to discredit a religious world view and to construct a systematic, naturalistic alternative. I disagree with this interpretation. My earlier analysis shows that atheism was rather practical attitude taken by Hume on the ground of his theoretical skepticism than basic presupposition taken before skeptical conclusions (skepticism was basic and atheism was its consequence and not the reverse).

4 Contemporary concepts of skepticism

I have enlisted three relationships between skepticism and atheism in the history of skepticism: skepticism is beyond the atheism-theism debate (Sextus Empiricus); skepticism is the way to fideism (Montaigne); skepticism is the way to atheism (Hume). So, skepticism in its history lead to all possible practical options in religious matters. It is the argument that skepticism has no practical power and can be combined with all practical choices.

Contemporary skepticism supports this conclusion, because it is sometimes neutral towards religion (Unger 1973), sometimes hostile to religion (Dennett 1995) and sometimes sympathetic towards religion (Schellenberg 2013). It seems however, that the irreligious or anti-religious skepticism is dominating in our times. Neutral skepticism is typical for epistemology and the sympathetic towards religion skepticism is preserved, even if as something unusual, in some kind of the philosophy of religion.

First, most general concept of contemporary skepticism, the epistemological skepticism as the thesis that knowledge does not exist, is neutral towards religion. Skepticism concerning the nature and existence of God is a kind of local skepticism. From the perspective of contemporary epistemology, skepticism about God is suspending judgment in religious matters and it is beyond atheism and theism debate. There are no sufficient reasons for both atheism and theism. We have a right to believe and disbelieve by faith. The burden of proof is on both sides. It is the standard epistemic status of theism and atheism. Religious skepticism is a kind of theoretical stance towards religion. In practice such skepticism is rare. We can doubt sometimes but in a longer period of time, a skeptic accepts some religion or not, becomes fideist or atheist. Epistemological skeptics can be both believers and disbelievers (religious and irreligious persons).

The dominate concept of contemporary skepticism, the irreligious or anti-religious skepticism, is connected with the practical perspective. It is the most popular since the Enlightenment and it has formed contemporary common notion of skepticism. According to it, a skeptic (assuming that there is no knowledge about God) is a disbeliever, close to more determined agnostic (God is unknowable) and even more determined atheist (God does not exists). This third meaning is dominating in our culture. So the term *skeptic* is connected or equaled with the term *atheist*. The epistemological neutral meaning of the term *skepticism* is typical for philosophical vocabulary but in common thinking it is minor.

The third, religious (sympathetic towards religion) concept of skepticism, typical for the Renaissance, seems to be out of date now. The roads of skepticism and fideism are branched in different directions. But such approach is preserved in contemporary philosophy of religion. We can hear a very interesting voice of skeptical religion and religious atheism by John Schellenberg. In my view Schellenberg's religious skepticism is similar to Montaigne's Christian pyrrhonism and fideism.

5 Schellenberg's religious skepticism and atheism

According to Schellenberg we have many reasons to doubt about the world, and especially about God. Theism has no rational justification and is even falsified on the ground of available evidence (divine hiddenness, horrendous evil, free will problem; Schellenberg 2013, p. 144). The result of falsifying theism is atheism. After destructing theism he formulates a deeper and basic religious proposition called by him *ultimism* ("there is a reality triply ultimate – metaphysically, axiologically, and soteriologically"; Schellenberg 2013, p. 145). Ultimism is a thesis that there is the ultimate, the deepest metaphysical fact that is also greatest value and the source of our salvation; the ultimate is inexhaustible and not qualified as personal. Ultimism is distinct from theism even if entailed by it and by most religions. According to Schellenberg we should withhold also the belief whether the ultimate exists and so whether ultimism is true or false. Withholding is the skeptical attitude. But such atheism and religious skepticism does not need to be an irreligious worldview, like Daniel Dennett's naturalism. "I am an atheist but not a metaphysical naturalist" (Schellenberg 2013, p. 143).

Between theism and irreligious naturalism there is a third way: religious skepticism and skeptical religion. Skeptical religion is grounded on critical examination of religious beliefs. Neither belief nor disbelief in ultimism is rationally justified. "Reason justifies no more than scepticism about ultimism even if it justifies disbelief of theism" (Schellenberg 2013, p. 145).

But even if we cannot have rational beliefs in religious matters, we can have skeptical faith. Faith, according to Schellenberg, is something different than belief. Faith is non-doxastic and imaginative (Schellenberg 2013, p. 144). Faith is voluntary assent to a proposition when belief is involuntary. "Propositional faith is a voluntary imaginative attitude rather than a believing one" (Schellenberg 2013, p. 147). Faith like belief is divided on faith-that (propositional) and faith-in (operational). Faith is some acceptance with ability to investigate.

Faith seems to be uncertain and weak. It is assent with doubt, open to further investigation. According to Schellenberg only such weak faith is rational answer to religious questions."I am a defender of faith but not a believer" (Schellenberg 2013, p. 144).

Schellenberg writes that religious skepticism is the opportunity for development of our religious beliefs, the first step towards finding truth about the ultimate and the source of a new kind of religion, skeptical religion. "Propositional faith focused on ultimism, and operationalized, is an unnoticed form of religion – sceptical religion" (Schellenberg 2013, p. 147). Skeptical faith is better justified than all sectarian religious beliefs. People with skeptical faith are going to be more open to the description of the ultimate in all religions and so, to be in better situation to seek the truth about the ultimate. Schellenberg trades belief for imagination and theism for ultimism. Skeptical religion is also compatible with atheism.

Theism is a thesis that the personal God exists. Atheism is the thesis that personal God does not exist. Atheism as negation of theism (a-theism) can be consistent with religious faith, for instance ultimistic imaginative faith. Atheism is a particular claim about personal God that does not exclude more sophisticated religion. Skepticism and atheism are "only the starting point for the path leading back to religion – though a somewhat different brand of religion than any extant" (Schellenberg 2013, p. 144). This new religion is a stance of hope in our times. "The new evolutionary religion, touched by sensitivity to our place in time, can be a vehicle of highly positive cultural evolution" (Schellenberg 2013, p. 149).

In my view Schellenberg's position is a kind of fideism, proposing religion grounded on irrational imagination, without reasons. It is close to Montaigne, but closer to Erasmus, Pascal or Kierkegaard. They connected fideism with skepticism. But as we remember the discussion between Erasmus and Martin Luther, there is also big divide between religion and skepticism. Religion entails strong conviction, certainty and personal commitment. "You are either the Christian or a skeptic, you cannot be both" – Luther replies to Erasmus. Religious skepticism was popular in early modern philosophy, but after Spinoza and especially in the Enlightenment, skepticism started to work with irreligion.

Schellenberg makes some confusion by using terms in nonstandard meaning. Religious atheism appears like round square. But such view is important as far as it shows how our opinions depend on our concepts. And the concept of personal God seems out of date today, suffering from anthropomorphic fallacy, like Greek polytheistic gods. We are persons but it is very suspicious that the absolute being is a person as well, disembodied absolute mind, the idealized human soul. In my view Schellenberg tries to preserve religion after rejecting such anthropomorphic concept of God. Because he is in opposition to theism (as rational view about personal God), Schellenberg can say that his view is modest atheism (a-theism). As a result it is a kind of religious atheism.

An example of standard irreligious atheism is given by Daniel Dennett (1995). "The kindly God who lovingly fashioned each and every one of us and sprinkled the sky with shining stars for our delight – that God is, like Santa Claus, a myth of childhood, not anything a sane, undeluded adult could literally believe in. That God must either be turned into a symbol for something less concrete or abandoned altogether" (Dennett 1995, p. 18) According to Dennett religion is irrational but it is good to comfort people. It is psychologically useful but intellectually wrong. In the case of Dennett his skepticism lead him to a kind of stronger agnostic view and to practical atheism.

6 Conclusions

Skeptical views are usually moderate and cannot reject any consistent view. That is why skepticism can lead both to religious fideism and anti-religious atheism. Religious people usually dislike skeptics because they see it as first step towards atheism. But some religious people make radical distinction between reason and faith and claim that their religion is grounded on the faith alone (*sola fide*). And in such a case skepticism can be good introduction to faith and religion.

What is the difference between a skeptic and an atheist? Typical skeptic is hesitating about the concept of God, typical atheist has conceptualized God in some way and s/he has determined view that God (conceptualized in this way) does not exist. The different conceptualizations allow that even atheism of some kind (as negation of theism or negation of personal God) can be connected with religious attitude (Schellenberg, Buddhism, pantheism).

I accept religious skepticism about the notion of God. But, in my view we have no way to reject the absolute in general. Something must exist. We do not know what it is but we feel that there is some source of our being. Religion is the longing to this source. All religious doctrines and ceremonies are probably very funny. They are relative to the particular time and culture, constructed by human imagination. Some people need them to express the longitude for unknown absolute. Some others, like atheists, prefer empty nature, that is mysterious and is going to be sacred itself. That is why even atheism can be a religious position. Atheism is just an attempt to make corrections in human description of the absolute. The real theoretical problem is the weakness of our concept of God/the absolute. The problem of the existence of God/the absolute is secondary because we know this existence without any concepts. We feel the absolute and this is the source of all religions.

Table 1. Past and contemporary skeptics about religion.

	Rational justification for religious beliefs?	Religious faith?	Is skepticism good for religion?
Sextus	No, skepticism	No, but religious practice	Neutral
Montaigne	No, skepticism	Yes, fideism	Yes
Hume	No, skepticism	No, atheism	No
Schellenberg	No, skepticism	Yes, fideism, a-theism	Yes

Bibliography

Bell, Martin (1990): "Introduction". In: David Hume: *Dialogues Concerning Natural Religion*. London: Penguin Books, pp. 1–32.
Berkeley, George (1948): *The Works of George Berkeley, Bishop of Cloyne*. Ed. by A.A. Luce and T.E. Jessop. Vol. 1–9. London: Thomas Nelson and Sons Ltd. 1948–57.
Dennett, Daniel (1995): *Darwin's Dangerous Idea*. New York: Touchstone.
Hartle, Ann (2005): "*Montaigne and skepticism*". In: Ullrich Langer (Ed.): The Cambridge Companion to Montaigne. Cambridge: Cambridge University Press, pp. 183–206.
Hume, David (1990): *Dialogues Concerning Natural Religion*. Ed. by Martin Bell. London: Penguin Books.
Hume, David (1896) : *A Treatise of Human Nature*. Ed. by Lewis Amherst Selby-Bigge. Oxford: Clarendon Press (http://oll.libertyfund.org/title/342/55255; access 2011–04–30).
Montaigne, Michel de. (1965): *Essais*. Paris: Gallimard.
Montaigne, Michel de. (1965a): *The Complete Essays*. Translated by Donald M. Frame. Stanford, CA: Stanford University Press.
Montaigne, Michel de. (2007): *The Apology for Raymond Sebond*. Translated by Donald M. Frame. In: Richard H. Popkin, José Raimundo Maia Neto (Eds.) 2007: *Skepticism. An Anthology*. Amherst NY: Prometheus Books, pp. 93–105.
Popkin, Richard M. (2003): *The History of Scepticism from Savonarola to Bayle*. Oxford: Oxford University Press.
Russell, Paul (2008): *The Riddle of Hume's Treatise: Skepticism, Naturalism, and Irreligion*. New York: Oxford University Press, 2008.
Schellenberg, J.L. (2007): *The Wisdom to Doubt: A Justification of Religious Skepticism*. Ithaca NY: Cornell University Press.
Schellenberg, J.L. (2009): *The Will to Imagine: A Justification of Skeptical Religion*. Ithaca NY: Cornell University Press.

Schellenberg, J.L. (2013): "My stance in philosophy of religion". In: *Religious Studies* 49, pp. 143–150.
Sextus Empiricus (2000): *Outlines of Scepticism*. Transl. by J. Annas and J. Barnes. Cambridge and New York: Cambridge University Press (quoted as PH).
Sextus Empiricus (2005): *Against the Logicians*. Translated by R. Bett. Cambridge and New York: Cambridge University Press (quoted as M 7 or M 8).
Unger, Peter (1975): *Ignorance. A Case for Scepticism*. Oxford: Clarendon Press.
Ziemińska, Renata (2017): *The History of Skepticism. In Search of Consistency*. Peter Lang Edition. Frankfurt am Main.

Piotr Świercz
Criticism in Political Philosophy.
On the Advantages of Pragmatism over Ideologized Politics in Light of the Works of Witold Gombrowicz

Abstract: The main goal of this article is to indicate the possibility of analyzing the works of Witold Gombrowicz from the perspective of political philosophy. Special emphasis is placed on the particular critical method used by the author of *Ferdydurke*. The essence of this criticism is the idea of the "equal-strength of opposites," understood as the rejection of arbitrary and dogmatic ("ideological") justification. My analysis encompasses three main themes found in Gombrowicz's works: Ojczyzna versus Synczyzna (Fatherland versus Sonland), *Cogito* versus the Interhuman Church, and Polishness versus Europeanness.

Keywords: W. Gombrowicz, criticism, political philosophy, *Cogito*, Interhuman Church, Polishness.

I Introduction. Gombrowicz and Politics. Criticism as the Equal Strength of Opposites.

Because my choice of topic for this article may seem controversial to many – criticism in the works of Gombrowicz within a political context? – I consider it necessary to justify this choice. Thus, before I move to my analysis of the problems mentioned in the title, I will explain my understanding of the place of politics/the political in the works of Gombrowicz, as well as my understanding of criticism.

I understand politics from the perspective of political philosophy, which I take as reflection on the essence of the political and on its first principles. Thus, it is not about the analysis of concrete political events, nor specific legal issues (though, of course, the problem of the first principles, of the "spirit of the laws," would fit within the scope of political philosophy so understood). At the same time, I understand the political in the broadest possible way: "the political" refers to the nature of collective human life organized under and according to some sort of *władztwo*. By *władztwo* I do not mean any particular form of ruling power or even rule (pol. *władza*) as such. Both rule and the particular forms it takes are merely consequences of *władztwo*. What, then, is *władztwo*? It is the principle or idea of a "central point of reference" inherent in man, either in his biological nature ("instinct") or intellectual nature ("thought").

I think that with such a definition of the "the political" and "political philosophy,"[1] the thesis that W. Gombrowicz's works may be analyzed from the perspective of political philosophy may be considered admissible.[2] The main metathemes found in Gombrowicz – "pure form," the Interhuman Church, Ojczyzna versus Synczyzna, and the facilitated life with its corollary problem of the archetype of Polish political culture – largely fit into the subject matter of political philosophy. They all deal with the issue of "władztwo" and the problem of the principles of community life.

The issue of criticism may raise significantly more doubts – both the understanding of it, and its manifestations in the work of the author of *Ferdydurke*.

The problem of understanding the notion of "criticism" and its role in philosophy is an extremely complex and difficult matter. Unfortunately, due to space constraints, I can only include a general outline of the problem here. Above all, I would like to emphasize that I treat the meaning and role of criticism in light of its Greek source – my point of departure is the meaning and understanding of criticism in Greek philosophy.

From an etymological perspective, "criticism" refers back to the Greek κρίνω, κρίσις, κριτικός. According to the LSJ, the basic meaning of κρίνω is "to separate," "to put asunder," "to distinguish," and also "to decide," "to judge," or "to choose"; the basic meaning of κρίσις – "separating," "distinguishing," "decision," "judgment"; while that of κριτικός – "able to discern," "critical," as well as "separated," "picked out," "chosen." In reference to the etymology of the concept of criticism, Dariusz Kubok states: "philosophical criticism in the broadest

---

[1] For different definitions of political philosophy, see: e.g. Bird 2006, pp. 3–4; Brennan 2016, pp. 1–6; Cohen 2001, pp. 1–3; Harman 2003, pp. 415–425; Knowles 2001, pp. 14–21; Larmore 2013, pp. 276–306; Miller 2003, pp. 1–18; Warren 1989, pp. 606–612; Bruin and Zurn 2009, pp. VII–XIV.

[2] "It began promisingly. *The Marriage*, in his opinion, is closely bound to the historical cataclysms of our times, it is a 'chronicle of history gone crazy,' the action of *The Marriage* is a grotesque parody of real events. But then? Goldmann makes the Drunkard into the rebellious masses, Henry's fiancée into the nation, the King into the government, and me into a 'Polish squire' who contained the historical drama in these symbols. I timidly protested, yes, I do not deny that *The Marriage* is a wild version of a crazy history; in the dreamy or drunken becoming of this action is mirrored the fantasticality of the historical process, but to make Molly the nation and Father the state…??," (Gombrowicz 2010, p. 670). In the very rich secondary literature concerning W. Gombrowicz's works and topics, the political aspect (or, better, meta-political aspect) is not very popular. In terms of exceptions, see: Kulas 2012; Szymankiewicz 2017.

and, as it turns out, also (historically) earliest, and (conceptually) most rudimentary sense, is tantamount to the ability to differentiate, distinguish, separate. [...] This broadest form of criticism may be described as *source-separative criticism*."³ Referring in turn to Sextus Empiricus' classification of the trends in ancient philosophy,⁴ Kubok specifies a narrower meaning of the term "criticism": "In a narrow sense, [...], criticism may be understood as a certain cognitive approach in opposition to dogmatism, which consists in constant inquiry, involves a ceaseless search for truth, and requires the most comprehensive analysis possible of any issue subjected to study, yet without claiming to have achieved any final, irrefutable truth. [...] In this sense, criticism corresponds with the source Greek understanding of skepticism as zetetic anti-dogmatism. [...] I propose to call this type of criticism *anti-dogmatic criticism*."⁵

As Kubok points out, the trend which should be considered the most representative for anti-dogmatic criticism in ancient philosophy is skepticism. For our considerations it will be extremely fruitful to take a closer look at the fundamental arguments of the Pyrrhonian School.

Taking into account the so-called skeptic tropes, it is doubtless that the key skeptical argument is the argument from relativity (πρός τι) – everything in the reality we are investigating remains in relation to something else; in consequence, it is impossible for us to come to know anything in itself. In addition, all of our cognition is tangled up in a complicated web of relations in which changing just one factor can completely change the outcome of one's investigation. In other words: in light of the great variety in the world, a dogmatic attitude (whether positive or negative) must involve disregarding a great deal of data, disregarding many possible and equally justified ways of interpretation. Such an attitude is not fitting for a philosopher, as it is a denial of reason.

One of the most significant arguments used by the skeptics, especially in an ethical, legal, and political context, is the argument from the multiplicity of persuasions, customs, and laws. This argument is used in essentially the same form by Socrates and the sophists.⁶ The essence of this line of argument can be stated thus: in regard to every formulated or possible to formulate opinion referring to every ethical, legal, political problem, an opposite opinion can be formulated. The opposing opinion will be just as justified as the initial opinion. It is impossible to determine which of these opinions is true and which is false on the basis of a rational, philosophical method of justification. We may call this the principle

---

3 Kubok 2015, pp. 14–15.
4 See: Sextus Empiricus, Πυρρώνειοι ὑποτυπώσεις, I, 1–2.
5 Kubok 2015, p. 15.
6 See e.g. Gorgias, *Peri tou me ontos e peri physeos*.

of the equal strength of opposing opinions. Consequently, the basis for criticism in regard to ethical, legal, and political matters must be an impartial analysis of opposing opinions. It is precisely such an understanding of criticism that can be found in the works of Gombrowicz.

Above, I mentioned the metathemes present in the works of the Polish author. Each of these is formulated within the framework of opposing opinions, conceptions, and paradigms. Thus, the problem of "pure form" is shown in confrontation with the problem of content. The relationship between "Ojczyzna" and "Synczyzna" itself contains opposing ideas. The background for reflections concerning the "Interhuman Church" is always the Cartesian *Cogito*. The conception of the "facilitated life" and corollary problem of the Polish archetype of political culture are formulated within the context of reflection on the political culture of Europe. The object of this article is precisely an analysis of the mentioned metathemes and the particular opposing ideas that constitute their context.

To conclude these introductory remarks, I would like to clarify one more terminological issue regarding how I will be using the terms "ideology" and "ideologization." By "ideology" I understand a dogmatic system of political convictions (overwhelmingly in the sense of positive dogmatism), rooted in a dogmatic understanding of justice and the good. Within the context of the above understanding of criticism – as a method of analysis based on the "equal strength of opposites" – I understand "ideology" as the arbitrary siding with one of these opposites. I take "ideologization" to refer to the method of either decision making and political action, or analyzing and explaining political matters on the basis of ideology. The relationship between "ideology" and "ideologization" thus understood remains in the same relation to criticism in philosophy, as dogmatism to criticism in philosophy.

II The Main Themes – "Pairs of Opposites" – in Gombrowicz's Reflection within the Context of Politics.

The topic I have undertaken is, of course, very broad. In a single article it would be impossible to exhaust even one of the topics discussed here. My goal here is simply to outline Gombrowicz's approach to the problems he undertook; therefore, the reflections contained in this article are merely *prolegomena* to the problem mentioned in the title. I will concentrate on three pairs of opposites: Ojczyzna versus Synczyzna, *Cogito* versus the Interhuman Church, and Polishness versus Europeanness. The problem of "Pure Form" versus "Content" will be a recurring theme throughout these reflections, but will not be treated separately here. Let us also note that all of Gombrowicz's metathemes are intimately connected; they are interpenetrating and complementary. Their separation in these analyses is somewhat artificial, but justified in that it facilitates a clear presentation.

1 Ojczyzna versus Synczyzna (Fatherland versus Sonland).

The problem of Synczyzna appears in many of Gombrowicz's works. Already in his first story, *Ferdydurke*, we can find a foretaste of the analyses Gombrowicz later dedicates to this problem. We can also find Synczyzna in *Trans-Atlantic*, *Pornography*, the *Diary*, and in a way that is especially interesting to philosophers of politics, also in the play *Marriage*.Gombrowicz created the neologism "Synczyzna" as a contrary of "Ojczyzna." According to Gombrowicz, the latter's despotism, its complete subordination, almost enslavement, of what is younger and dependent on it, requires a proper reaction. Synczyzna should be able to express itself independently: for itself, through itself, and in view of itself. Under Ojczyzna's despotism, Synczyzna is treated solely as an extension of Ojczyzna, as an instrument serving the despot's need for grounding, self-expression, and self-realization. But how does Ojczyzna justify its privileged position? Two things: precedence and causation. However, this argument is not so certain and unambiguous. Ojczyzna is the cause of Synczyzna, but only in the Natural order, so to speak. In the social order, things are quite the opposite: it is Synczyzna that is the cause of Ojczyzna, since children grant their parents the status of "parent"; it is thanks to youth that maturity becomes what it is. Moreover, childhood and youth are also first in the natural order from the perspective of the individual; childhood and youth are the causes of maturity, not the opposite. Therefore, the dominance of Ojczyzna seems to be a usurpation, based more on the law of the jungle, than on justice.

In many places in his works, Gombrowicz indicates a need for the "emancipation" of Synczyzna, a need for rebellion, so Synczyzna can come to power and take control of the socio-political order.

But is what Gombrowicz writes really so unambiguous? Is he really an uncritical glorifier of Synczyzna? Certainly not. The "heroes" of Synczyzna always suffer defeat. This is the case with Henryk in the *Marriage*, whole downfall is even more painful because it occurs on the grounds of principles established in the order of Synczyzna. Henryk's defeat and helplessness are best illustrated by his own words from the last scene of the play directly preceding his warrant for his own arrest:

> "I am innocent.
> I declare that I am as innocent as a child, that I have done
> Nothing, that I am ignorant of everything...
> No one is responsible for anything here!
> There is no such thing as responsibility! [...]
> No, there is no responsibility
> Still, there are formalities
> To be attended to..."[7]

The New Order introduced by Henryk, which seems to be a realization of Synczyzna, constitutes a radical negation of freedom.[8] The enslavement of everyone and everything, including oneself – is a greater defeat even conceivable?

In *Pornography*, likewise, *Synczyzna* suffers a defeat that is no less severe. An innocent pair of sixteen year-olds – Karol and Henia – is manipulated into murder, which is only the culmination of an ongoing, perverse, "purely Formal" manipulation on the part of Ojczyzna – Witold and Fryderyk. Their manipulation finds exceptionally fertile ground. The shocking description of the innocently sadistic crushing of the bug reveals the true (?) face of Synczyzna. Its innocence is just as real as its perverse sadism.

How, then, does the real relationship between Ojczyzna and Synczyzna, between maturity and youth, look in the thought of Gombrowicz? Let's take a look at two significant quotations from the *Diary:* "to pass the world through youth; to translate it into language of youth, that is, into the language of attraction...To soften it with youth...To spice it with youth – so it allows itself to be violated,"[9] and a little later, "And here one comes upon extreme formulas: maturity *for* youth, youth *for* maturity."[10]

Thus, we see that this relationship is decidedly more complicated than it seemed at first glance. Synczyzna and Ojczyzna interpenetrate – they mutually shape one another. However, Gombrowicz avoids easy one-sided constructions. At no point does his analysis or way of presenting the problem take on the form of ideologization. We are not dealing with an unjustified tilt of the relation-

---

7 Gombrowicz 1998, p. 199.
8 "There is peace. All the rebellious elements are/Under arrest. Assembly has also been taken into custody along/With military and civilian circles, vast segments of the popula-/tion, the High Court, the Joint Chiefs of Staff, Boards and/Departments, all public and private authorities, the press,/Hospitals and orphanages. All the Ministries have been placed/Under arrest, and everything else besides; in short, Your Maj-/esty – everything. The police have likewise been imprisoned./There is peace. Quiet. It's humid" (Gombrowicz 1998, p. 155).
9 Gombrowicz 2010, p. 372.
10 Gombrowicz 2010, p. 373.

ship between the opposites toward the side of either one of them. This is due to the relationship being grasped in a critical-dynamic manner. This theme will appear once more in this article, in the context of Gombrowicz's formulation of the Polish archetype of political culture.

2 *Cogito* versus the Interhuman Church.

The context of the entirety of Gombrowicz's creative output is the Cartesian *Cogito*. As he states in one of his works: "I am certain that this is in my consciousness but does not correspond to reality. For example, the centaur. Systematic doubt. Puts the world in doubt, in parentheses: 1. the object. 2. everything involving the object. The only certainty is that they exist *in my consciousness*. [...] the sciences which relate to reality (supposedly objective): sociology, psychology, except for the abstract sciences; mathematics and logic, because they do not concern the outside world, but are laws for my own consciousness."[11] From the perspective of political philosophy, the consequences of *Cogito* are huge. *Cogito* is necessarily an indivisible unity. Its world is completely closed and impenetrable. This is a double impenetrability: on the one hand, *Cogito* is not able to go beyond itself; on the other, nothing external to *Cogito* is able to enter into the world of *Cogito*. How, then, is political philosophy possible at all within the context of *Cogito*? The basic categories of political philosophy – the state, power, justice – are conditioned upon multiplicity and divisibility. Therefore, the key question is: how can we derive this multiplicity and divisibility from *Cogito*? Gombrowicz suggests an original way of thinking about this issue in his play *The Marriage*.

It is *dubito* – "systematic doubt" – that lies at the basis of *Cogito*. Doubting the reality of any representation of the mind leads to one's recognizing *Cogito* as the only certainty. However, the certainty of *Cogito* does not imply certainty as to the unreality of any of its representations. Therefore, what remains for certain-of-its-existence Cogito is an attitude of uncertainty, both with regard to the reality and unreality of representations. It is from these doubts, from this uncertainty, that the multiplicity and divisibility mentioned above are "born" (or "created"). A passage from the beginning of *The Marriage* serves as a great illustration of this reasoning:

---

[11] Gombrowicz 2004, p. 2. For more analyses on *Cogito* as a context of Gombrowicz's works, see: Margański, 2001.

> "A void. A desert. Nothing, I am alone here
> Alone
> Alone
> But perhaps I am not alone; who knows what is behind me,
> perhaps...something...someone is standing here alongside
> me, off to the side, off to the side, some id...some insuperable,
> ungovernable, idiotized, idiotouchable idiot, who can touch
> and...(*With alarm*) I'd better not move...no, don't move,
> because if we move...he'll move...and touch...(*With
> growing uneasiness*) Oh, if only something or someone would
> come out from somewhere...Aha! There's something...
> JOHNNY *emerges from the shadows.*"[12]

In this way, multiplicity and divisibility are created and justified. And it is in this context that political philosophy, as reflection on the relationship between *Cogito* and the world of "others" it has "created-dreamed up,"[13] must be analyzed.

However, *Cogito* is not only the creator of the world – it is also an actor. It plays roles and gets masks-faces – *gęby*. What is very important – it also plays before the audience of itself:

> "And yet if I, I, I alone am, why then
> (Let's try that for effect) am I not?
> What does it matter (I ask) that I, I am in the very middle, the
> very centre of everything, if I, I can never be
> Myself?
> I alone.
> I alone.
> Now that you're alone, completely alone, you might at least
> stop this incessant recitation
> This fabrication of words
> This production of gestures
> But you, even when you're alone, pretend that you're alone
> And you go on [...]
> Pretending to be yourself
> Even to your very self. [...]
> Such are the
> Attitudes I might adopt...in your presence
> And for your benefit! But not for my own! I'm not
> in need
> Of any attitude! I don't feel

---

12 Gombrowicz 1998, p. 87.
13 The aspect of dreamy-creative relationship between *Cogito* and "the others" appears in *The Marriage* frequently, e.g. Gombrowicz 1998, p. 97.

Other people's pain! I only recite
My humanity! No, I do not exist
I haven't any 'I,' alas, I forge myself
Outside myself" (pp. 180–181).

This game, the role-playing before oneself and before the "others" one has created shapes both *Cogito* and these "others." This mutual shaping is what Gombrowicz calls the Interhuman Church.[14] The world, the reality of *Cogito* is set in opposition to the Old Order understood as "Real Reality," which is subject to an Objective and Absolute Criterion. In reality, of course, *Cogito* is lacking this Criterion. The Interhuman Church becomes something of a substitute. Gombrowicz writes in *The Diary:* "'People' are something that must organize itself every minute – nevertheless, this organization, this collective shape, creates itself as the by-product of a thousand impulses and is, in addition, unforeseen and does not allow itself to be ruled by those who make it up. We are like tones from which a melody issues – like words forming themselves into sentences – but we are not in control of what we express, this expression of ours strikes us like a thunderbolt, like a creative force, it arises from us unrefined. [...] Doesn't this phenomenon possess divine attributes, which are a result of interhuman power, that is, superior and creative, in relation to each of us separately?"[15]

Again, we are faced with a situation, in which Gombrowicz's critical-dynamic manner of writing renders it impossible to "pigeonhole" him and his reflection, to force it into an ideological, quasi-ideological, or systemic framework. His thought constitutes such an inspiring intellectual "charge" precisely because it is not blind in its passion. It does not aim at closing and resolving problems at all costs; instead, it always critically weighs both sides of every opposition. When indicating proposed approaches to a given problem, Gombrowicz always leaves them anti-dogmatically open. The above theses can be illustrated most convincingly by referring to how Gombrowicz understood the Polish archetype of political culture against the backdrop of the European archetype thereof.

---

14 It is necessary to emphasize that the conventional context of the Interhuman Church is not the only, nor the most important one. Gombrowicz states in *The Diary*: "As long as you understand *Ferdydurke* as a battle with convention, it will trot calmly down the well-beaten path; but if you understand that man creates himself with another man in the sense of the wildest debauchery, *Ferdydurke* will neigh and leap forward as if you had jabbed it with a spur, carrying you off into the realm of the Unpredictable. *Ferdydurke* is more a form-element (here, Polish "żywioł" could be better translated as untamed "passion," "energy," "force," "dynamism" – P. Ś.) than a form-convention" (Gombrowicz 2010, p. 288).
15 Gombrowicz 2010, pp. 357–358.

3 Polishness versus Europeanness.

The discussion on Poland's place in Europe and on the relationship between the Polish and Western European archetype of political culture goes back to the late XV century.[16] The XVI century brought a "solution" decisive for the development of Polish political culture, the essence of which is revealed in the debate between Andrzej Frycz Modrzewski and Stanisław Orzechowski.[17] Presenting its conclusion in the most synthetic way possible: the archetype of Polish political culture is different from the Western European archetype. Though "Polishness" belongs to "Latinness," this "Latinness" is different than Western European "Latinness" – Poland does not belong to "Europeanness." Freedom lies at the heart of "Polishness," though this freedom – referring back to Benjamin Constant's conception – is different from both "ancient" and "modern" freedom; it constitutes something of a synthesis of these two types of freedom, though its aim – a particular form of conviviality – is specific to Polishness.

Irrespective of the aforementioned resolution, the discussion has continued and continues today. The modern approach to the problem was expressed in the subsequent great debate between the historical school of Joachim Lelewel, on the one hand, and the Kraków historical school, on the other hand.[18] This discussion has become the basis for a key distinction concerning the main trends in Polish historiography: the "optimists" and the "pessimists."[19]

In my opinion, Witold Gombrowicz's stance on the problem of the Polish archetype of political culture is the crowning achievement of formulations of this problem found in Polish literature. It should be noted that though Gombrowicz is commonly perceived as a critic of "Polishness" (which would imply proximity to the Kraków School and the "pessimists"), a careful analysis of his works decidedly falsifies this assessment of the author of *Trans-Atlantic*'s reflection.

There can be no doubt that Gombrowicz took for granted "Polishness'" distinctness from "Westernness": "Our Slavic attitude to artistic matters is lax. We are less involved in art than the Western European nations and so we can afford a greater freedom of movement. This is exactly what I often said to Zygmunt Grocholski, who takes his Polishness (which is very elemental in him and is crushed by Paris) very seriously. His struggles are as hard as those of so many Polish artists, for whom the one rallying cry is 'Catch up to Europe!' Unfortunately they

---

[16] Pawiński 1884, pp. 123–181; Baczkowski 1989, pp. 26–32.
[17] Frycz Modrzewski 1953; Orzechowski 1984.
[18] Lelewel 1855; Bobrzyński 1987.
[19] Sobieski 1908; Adamus 1958, 1961, 1964; Kaute 1993; Świercz 2002, pp. 17–32.

are impeded in this pursuit by their being a different and very specific type of European, born in a place where Europe is no longer fully Europe."[20]

It is also undeniable that in many places in his works, Gombrowicz takes an extremely critical stance towards "Polishness." As he states in the *Diary:*

> I, who am terribly Polish and terribly rebellious against Poland, have always been irritated by that little, childish, secondary, ordered, and religious world that is Poland. I attributed Poland's historical lack of dynamism as well as Poland's cultural impotence to these characteristics because God led us around by our little hand. I compared this well-behaved Polish childhood to the adult independence of other cultures. This nation without a philosophy, without a conscious history, intellectually soft and spiritually timid, a nation that produced only a 'kindly' and 'noble-minded' art, a languid people of lyrical scribblers of poetry, folklorists, pianists, actors, in which even Jews dissolved and lost their venom... My literary works guided by the desire to extricate the Pole from all secondary realities and to put him in direct confrontation with the universe. Let him fend for himself as best as he can. I desire to ruin his childhood (Gombrowicz 2010, p. 31).

Gombrowicz's interpretation of the archetype of Polish political culture is grasped within the context of the aforementioned problem of the relationship between Ojczyzna and Synczyzna, between maturity and immaturity. As in the case of that problem, Gombrowicz nuances his position in the discussion on the Polish archetype. Although his point of departure lies in a critique, not only does Gombrowicz not stop there, but he also goes so far as to note the valuable aspects of what he initially criticized:

> Ruin a childhood? In the name of what? In the name of a maturity that I myself can neither bear nor accept? It is the Polish God, after all (in contrast to Weil's God), who is that splendid system that has maintained man in a sphere of indirect being, who is that veering away from the ultimate that is demanded by my insufficiency. How can I desire that they not be children if I myself, per fas et nefas, want to be a child? A child, yes, but one that has come to know and has exhausted all the possibilities of adult seriousness. This is the big difference. First, push away all the things that make everything easier, find yourself in a cosmos that is as bottomless as you can stand, in a cosmos at the limits of your consciousness, and experience a condition where you are left to your own loneliness and your own strength, only then, when the abyss which you have not managed to tame throws you from the saddle, sit down on the earth and discover the sand and grass anew. For childhood to be allowed, one must have driven maturity to bankruptcy. I am not bluffing: when I pronounce the word 'childhood,' I have the feeling that I am expressing the deepest but not yet roused contents of the people who gave me birth. This is not the childhood of a child, but the difficult childhood of an adult (Gombrowicz 2010, p. 219).

---

20 Gombrowicz 2010, p. 31.

I will venture the thesis that in his critical approach based on the "equal strength of opposites," Gombrowicz transcended the "optimism" – "pessimism" opposition. In choosing either of these dominant ways of interpreting the Polish archetype of political culture, one runs the risk of falling into dogmatism, into ideology, at least in certain respects. In a sense, supporters of both the apologists and the critics went down this road. Studies in XIX- and XX-century political thought (especially up until 1939) reinforce this conviction. There is no room here to elaborate on this issue in depth, but I will indicate one important feature of a majority of formulations of the problem of the Polish archetype of political culture. Each of these formulations points to a certain quality, deeming it a "virtue" or a "vice." However, the justification for this is often, if not always, arbitrary. Consequently, the assessment of the Polish archetype and attitude of given trends or thinkers to it is reduced to the sum of partial, arbitrary resolutions. In contrast, Gombrowicz shuns easy and arbitrary assessments. His approach is entirely different: each aspect of the analyzed problem can be perceived negatively or positively. This depends entirely on the context and on the way a particular attitude is justified. Deepened consciousness of a particular aspect of the archetype plays a key role here. If an apparently unambiguously positive feature is not fully considered, if it does not result from in-depth reflection but is instead the result of personal preferences, stereotypes, class biases, and the like, then it is essentially something negative – it constitutes an expression of the superficiality of intellectual life. On the other hand, what may initially seem like a negative element – if it constitutes the culmination of in-depth reflection on the context and conditions of the archetype – may turn out to be a great creative force allowing for the harmonization of the national culture with the requirements of progress and modernization.

Bibliography

Adamus, Jan (1958): *Polska teoria rodowa*. Łódź: Zakład Narodowy im. Ossolińskich.
Adamus, Jan (1961): *Monarchizm i republikanizm w syntezie dziejów Polski*. Łódź: Zakład Narodowy im. Ossolińskich.
Adamus, Jan (1964): *O kierunkach polskiej myśli historycznej*. Łódź: Łódzkie Towarzystwo Naukowe.
Baczkowski, Krzysztof (1989): *Rady Kallimacha, [Consilia Calimachi]*. Kraków: Krajowa Agencja Wydawnicza.
Bird, Colin (2006): *An Introduction to Political Philosophy*. Cambridge-New York: Cambridge University Press.
Bobrzyński, Michał (1987): *Dzieje Polski w zarysie*. Warszawa: Państwowy Instytut Wydawniczy.

Brennan, Jason (2016): *Political Philosophy. An Introduction.* Washington: Cato Institute.
Bruin, Boudewijn de; Zurn, Christopher F. (Eds.) (2009): *New Waves in Political Philosophy.* New York: Palgrave Macmillan.
Cohen, Martin (2001): *Political Philosophy. From Plato to Mao.* London–Sterling: Pluto Press.
Frycz Modrzewski, Andrzej (1953): *O poprawie Rzeczypospolitej.* Transl. Edwina Jędrkiewicz. Warszawa: Państwowy Instytut Wydawniczy.
Gombrowicz, Witold (1998): *Three Plays.* London and New York: Marion Boyars Publishers Ltd.
Gombrowicz, Witold (2004): *A Guide to Philosophy in Six Hours and Fifteen Minutes.* Transl. Benjamin Ivry. New Haven & London: Yale University Press.
Gombrowicz, Witold. (2012): *Diary.* Transl. Lillian Vallee. Orwigsburg. Pennsylvania: Yale University Press.
Harman, Gilbert (2003): "Three Trends in Moral and Political Philosophy". *Journal of Value Inquiry* 37 (3) 2, pp. 415–425.
Kaute, Wojciech (1993): *Synteza dziejów Polski Michała Bobrzyńskiego.* Katowice: Wydawnictwo Uniwersytetu Śląskiego.
Knowles, Dudley (2001): *Political Philosophy.* London: Routledge.
Kubok, Dariusz (2015): "Comments on the Sources of Greek Philosophical Criticism". In: Folia Philosophica, vol. 34. Special issue: Forms of Criticism in Philosophy and Science. Ed. by Dariusz Kubok. Katowice, pp. 9–31.
Kulas, Piotr (2012): "Gombrowicz i problem teologiczno-polityczny". *Przegląd Polityczny* 114, pp. 147–152.
Larmore, Charles (2013): "What Is Political Philosophy?" *Journal of Moral Philosophy* 10 (3), pp. 276–306.
Lelewel, Joachim (1855): "Uwagi nad dziejami Polski i ludu jej". In: idem: *Polska, dzieje i rzeczy jej.* T. 3. Poznań: Księgarnia J. K. Żupańskiego.
Margański, Janusz (2001): *Gombrowicz. Wieczny debiutant.* Kraków: Wydawnictwo Literackie.
Miller, David (2003): *Political Philosophy. A Very Short Introduction.* Oxford: Oxford University Press.
Orzechowski, Stanisław (1984): *Policyja Królestwa Polskiego na kształt arystotelesowych Polityk wypisana i na świat dla dobra pospolitego trzema księgami wydana.* Przemyśl: Towarzystwo Przyjaciół Nauk.
Pawiński, Adolf (1884): *Jana Ostroroga żywot i pismo o Naprawie Rzeczypospolitej. Studyum z literatury politycznej XV wieku.* Warszawa, Drukarnia S. Olgebranda synów.
Sobieski, Wacław (1908): *Pesymizm i optymizm w historiografii polskiej.* Lwów: Ateneum Polskie, t. II, nr 2.
Szymankiewicz, Błażej (2017): *"Ślub" Witolda Gombrowicza jako dramat egzystencjalno-dziejowy (Witold Gombrowicz's "The Marriage" as the existential and historical drama),* https://www.academia.edu/22259445/Slub_Witolda_Gombrowicza_jako_dramat_egzystencjalno-dziejowy; access: 10.03.2017.
Świercz, Piotr (2002): "Polska i Polacy w polskiej myśli politycznej XIX i XX wieku". In: Tadeusz Godlewski, Wojciech Jurkiewicz (eds): *Polacy – Polska – Europa. Interpretacje idei politycznych.* Bydgoszcz: Wydawnictwo Akademii Bydgoskiej, pp. 17–32.
Warren, Mark E. (1989): "What Is Political Theory/Philosophy?" *Political Science and Politics* 22, No. 3, pp. 606–612.

Agnieszka Woszczyk
Consolatio or Critical Methods? Reflections on Philosophical Counseling

Abstract: This article outlines the role of reason within the practice of philosophical counseling, viz., two questions related to this practice. Firstly, that of rationalization as a potential threat to the speculative use of reason and an alienation from further existential engagement. Secondly, that of normalization in relation to the professional aspects of philosophical counseling. In particular, the subjection of this practice to regulations which may be linked to other fields of development or care. Criticism remains an integral component in preserving the autonomy of philosophy, here understood as in internal standard for its application in the form of philosophical counseling. Such a critical stance during philosophical counseling allows for an acknowledgement and respect for the personal boundaries between "I" and "You." It likewise leads to a rapport based upon partnership in dialogue, thereby avoiding one-sided, arbitrary counseling.

Keywords: philosophical practice, philosophical counseling, rationalisation, criticism, normalization.

Introduction

Since the publication of Boethius's work, the motif of *consolatio* brings to mind hardship, suffering, and the ill hand of fate. All of these serve as a reminder that philosophy is a practice of life, based upon the observance of a certain set of rules that, collectively, lead to happiness. At the least, they steer us clear from its antithesis (Boethius 2005). Philosophy is thus a haven and a reassurance in distressing situations; though certain problems cannot be avoided, one can always learn to tolerate them (Tukiainen 2010). Episodes of pain, suffering, loss, mourning, existential angst, along with a lack of confidence or life perspective, were all legitimate reasons to consult a philosophical counselor. However, the question arises as to whether such counseling was meant to provide *consolatio*, or simply to make use of philosophical works as if through a collection of prescriptives, recommendations, or exercises, that delineate a specific life course. Or, was counseling meant to be a critical reflection, which neither directly presupposed nor excluded any consolatory aims? Despite the discrepancy within the title, *consolatio* was not thought of as disjunctive, but more acutely, as a way of nuancing the understanding of philosophical practice and a prevalence in attitudes – either closer to one element (*consolatio*) or to the other (critical methods). The latter, *therapeia* or critical methods, has deliberately been eschewed since it could also be a form of a [philosophical] healing of the soul.[1]

I would like to consider those questions in relation to two problems: firstly, that of rationalization as a potential threat to the speculative use of reason, which can likewise distance it from existential engagement. Secondly, the normalization of issues related to the professional practice of philosophical counseling, specifically, those that appear to regulate this practice. Related to these issues are questions associated with critical reflection and not simply an adoption of its guidelines and standards.

Does philosophical counseling, despite being a subject still in its infancy as a pre-paradigmatic development (Padin 2013), satisfy the requirements of philosophical criticism? How does such a criticism function? Driven by self-criticism which managed to place even the philosopher's reason on trial through a history of transformations, conceptual pluralism, discussions and polemics – does philosophy allow itself to become a critical practice?

Rationality or Rationalization?

The titular subject of *consolatio* suggests that philosophy might provide solace in suffering, because the strength of reason is capable of managing mental states.

---

[1] Any explanation will encounter the question of nomenclature, in that philosophical counseling or counselling is distinct from philosophical therapy. The latter has been understood to mean a different form of psychotherapy: as a possible alternative (Achenbach 1995), pastoral counseling (Padin 2013), or a related form of psychological therapy (Allen 2002). In outlining the various stances concerning counseling's relationship with therapy (Brown 2010), Shlomit C. Schuster uses the name philosophical practice as an umbrella term for philosophical counseling, philosophical consultation, and philosophical psychoanalysis. She underscores the gap between psychological consultations and psychotherapy (1999). These questions can be considered along with the relationship between philosophical practice's ancillary and developmental aims. The name would suggest, at least theoretically, something to do with *consolatio* belonging to philosophical therapy; whereas critical methods falling under counseling. In practice, however, the solution appears somewhat difficult. Firstly, that would require the introduction of artificial distinctions between the characteristic features of critical reflection and its therapeutic effect. Secondly, it assumes that therapy could not carry the title "philosophical" if it did not, at the bare minimum, satisfy critical requirements as a *contradictio in adiecto*. Therefore, I will use the term philosophical counseling when referring to philosophical practice/philosophical therapy. I will occasionally reference other authors and their positions, using their respective terminological distinctions. I will not, however, make any fundamental distinction between the two forms.

Lydia B. Amir, espousing this critical approach in relation to philosophical counseling, tackles the problem of philosophical practice as a means to solve or alleviate the counselee's problems. She notes that philosophical reflection can not only help, but can [conversely] aggravate a situation, e. g., through an exaggeratedly complicated "exit strategy" or perhaps even through a disparity between the theoretical understanding of a problem and its impossible resolution (Amir 2004). She shares this view with other scholars (Schuster 1991, Achenbach 1995).

There is yet another issue, one related to the unconscious mechanisms of human behavior. It could be argued that such practices based on rational reflection aim to strengthen mechanisms that eliminate the *pathos* of experience through rational interpretation. In other words, the true domain of philosophical counseling of the spiritual (self-awareness, autonomy of the will) can paradoxically distance one from an understanding of oneself, to the extent that the counselee will be unable to reach an adequate level of self-criticism vis-à-vis the measure of reason. It may of course then lead to a state of self-deception.

In the understanding of modern psychoanalytic theory, rationalization is an unconscious defense mechanism, which, akin to intellectualization, is a form of the more elementary process of "isolation of affect." These mechanisms belong to the "secondary defensive processes," themselves being considered, depending on the form, as being capable of having a beneficial, adaptive, or dysfunctional meaning (see: McWilliams 2011, pp. 232–247). As Nancy McWilliams states, "the cultural tendency to admire the capacity to isolate affect from intellect" (McWilliams 2011, p. 255), which can be understood as a self-alienation of reason that does not indeed serve reason, but manipulation. Numerous scholars of critical thought have similarly remarked upon on this social phenomenon, demonstrating the influence of instrumental rationality on the formation of the human character (Horkheimer 2004, Fromm 2001).

These mechanisms – beyond their literal and psychological definitions – can be viewed as not only a means to deal with a particular situation, but also as a more fundamental process, through which communication with the self and a more wholesome participation in existence, are hindered. Reason plays the role of "alienator," since it performs a function of pseudo-control over the experiences that do not correspond with the interpretation or the self-image of the object. One could interpret the aforementioned mechanisms as the dogmatic use of reason. Without examining the rationale behind such a choice, reason cuts off contact with whatever may hinder its functioning and assumes an autonomous role. Though these mechanisms owe their names to *ratio* and *intelectus*, the respective processes create an opposition in behavior by closing reflective capacities, fixating the object on a particular interpretation, without the knowledge that this indeed is the correct interpretation. Thus, fear underlies the process of recognizing threats to the object or limitations of conscious choice. Such threats are different types of ambivalences, ambitendencies, or even the uncertainties of the internal and external world. Accepting such an understanding of rational mechanisms would seem to reverse the Socratic-Platonic *epimeleia heautou*, as the process of forming an object through a movement of the spirit that relates to itself, thereby attempting to uncover its own nature (Foucault 2005). Likewise, similar threats are especially visible in philosophical practices that attempt to form the individual based on proposed resolutions within the framework of one philosophical concept. Rationalization can also be a conviction of the sufficient role of rationalization itself. Time and again, such a conviction stems from the philosophical arrogance of reason vis-à-vis other interpretations of reality, particularly, when inclined to accept aporetic exaggerations about the state of things or as a result of the inability to recognize the limitations of one's competencies.

The above argument serves to justify the postulate that the practice of philosophical counseling should be a critical part in the search for understanding and openness toward the uncertain, not just the use of reason in the hopes of creating a tell-all formula. In the latter case, the accusation that the problem is merely rationalized here, remains in force because reason would not so much serve an explanatory function, as it would one of mastering experience. Through the creation of a thought process, immanent logic would not necessarily accede to the complexity of being or the experiences of the individual seeking philosophical counseling. Critical philosophy can also exacerbate escapist strategies, which one can interpret as belonging to categories of broadly understood rationalization. In that way, these strategies would not be used so much to deepen understanding as to create a comfortable world of detached reflection, thereby creating an alternative for existential engagement. It is important to remember that pure theorization is not something which succumbs to a negative valorization even when it serves to tear the counselee (by his own volition) away from the mundane, everydayness. In order to make such a judgment, one would need an objective assessment of human behavioral values and the regularity of development. Regarding the danger of escapism, it has less to do with the primacy of engagement, i.e., acting on theorization, but more to do with the choice of philosophy instead of another activity, as a substitutive, non-conscious choice. Therefore, the task of the counselor is to examine the intentions of his client as to whether philosophical practice will indeed satisfy critical requirements, not just as *consolatio*.

Ran Lahav signals that the counseling process serves as a long-range transformation of the subject and not just of the thought process. It can thus be compared to exiting Plato's cave "towards a fuller, freer, deeper life. In the course of the counseling, counselees learn to understand this potential fullness – not only in words, but mainly through their emotions, behaviors, and entire range of attitudes" (Lahav 2013, p. 97). The philosophical counselor who maintains a critical sensitivity will have the opportunity to counteract the usage of philosophy solely to create alternative universes in relation to the client's own life – assuming he does so in a holistic manner by not limiting himself to intellectual contact through thought constructs. In this context, counseling based on the examination of emotive experiences is particularly valuable so as to attain a more profound understanding of them – as a hermeneutical approach to emotions (Raabe 2000) or as a unification of body-mind perspectives in the spirit of the Buberian dialogic (daVenza Tillmanns 2013).

The distinction between philosophical counseling and psychological psychotherapy remains a matter of discussion (Falikowski 2012, Knapp/Tjeltveit 2005). Such debate is nonetheless unfounded, in light of the aforementioned reasons and because the philosopher's task would have to become purely intellectual, disregarding the person as a whole. Conversely, the task of the psychotherapist would be limited to the emotive. The depreciation of psychotherapy as an "overwhelmingly focused" science of emotions, stems from an underestimation of the number and diversification of psychotherapeutic methods or even levels of disability and illness (which might exceed the limits of philosophical counseling)[2] (Knapp/Tjeltveit, 2005).

In a slightly different context, the problem of rationalization appears in Lou Marinoff's PEACE model – both the process and model illustrated by Vincent's case study (Marinoff 1999).[3] Firstly, this case demonstrates that the philosophical therapist does not give in to critical considerations simply by virtue of the nature of the client's visit. Furthermore, he does not actively seek out ways to access the attitude and character of the client's state of emotional turmoil, which may come to a head between his [the client's] private worldview versus the norms of social interaction. According to the client's own interpretation, his suffering is a result of injustice. And yet, this interpretation was not analyzed as attempt to accept an alternative version of events. The philosopher's key intervention, apart from the other elements shown in the model that measure the emotional state of the client, is based on the necessity of differentiating the meanings of *mental state* and *hurt*. This purely intellectual exercise, employed to demonstrate the active role of allowing oneself to get upset, decisively presented the possibility for the client to

---

[2] With exceptions, which will be the discussed in the next subheading on professionalization, criticism, and standardization.
[3] For further reading see: Schuster (2004).

function without undue, inhibitive emotions. Additionally, Marinoff critiques both psychiatry and psychology as being disciplines that focus too heavily on emotions, having nothing to say about injustice. When addressing philosophical problems, he recommends that one consult a philosopher. Marinoff further propounds, though indirectly, an economic argument. The client's problem had been solved in as little as one session.

One can assume that the client's problem may reappear at a later date, not through an unsympathetic (not necessarily one of justice) interpretation, but rather through the client's inability to cope with emotions. Therefore, in that one session, the client learned how to apply Stoic ways of separating dependent and independent variables from a subject. There is still some doubt as to whether such a philosophical practice is the only source of instant relief, and thus, some form of *consolatio*. Has it reached a moment of in-depth understanding, a critical questioning of conventional ways of thinking, or has the client received a tool that allows him not to worry about emotional signals and to ignore them as a potential source of self-knowledge? It seems that the shortness of Marinoff's description does not allow for the formulation of one-sided conclusions. Rather, there is an intellectual separation from deeper self-examination. On the one hand, this may be partly due to the reason behind the client's visit. On the other hand, one can surmise that the decision may be based off the choice of method and criteria provided by the counselor, securing positive results with easily applicability. Unfortunately, neither of the above have been the subject of critical discussions – whether as definitions, accepted assumptions, or normative implications.

Lech Ostasz presents yet another problem related to philosophical criticism. For him, philosophical therapy is shown to be on par with psychotherapy as a helpful aid in cases of light to mild disturbances. The term "mental therapy," for philosophical psychotherapy, highlights its function as an intellectual, organizational tool of the mind. Thus, mental therapy sets goals just as advice and directives had done before, but *not* as ready-made solutions for improving the functioning of the mind, avoiding errors in reasoning, extreme emotions, the valorization of neutral positions, and attaining happiness. Mental therapy draws upon ancient philosophical concepts, by accentuating what is developmentally desirable but also moderating the harmful. The intention is to integrate the subject under the aegis of the mind. According to this author, certain philosophical trends impede in accomplishing such an aim. By directly invoking the subject of "soul healing," this philosophical practice likewise implies normative judgments about the internal state of man (without having subjected this question to critical consideration). This is not so much thanks to the authority of the ancient practitioners of life philosophy, but rather to the mental-therapist's personal vision and preferences. If so, what is the point of such a practice; wherein lies the threat? Can the answer be found in philosophies that disrupt inner harmony or perhaps in those which prevent an openness to critical thought, thereby compromising dubiety and a lack of confidence?

Regarding this last question, it might be useful to reference Elliot D. Cohen's Logic-Based Therapy, "a relatively new psychological counseling modality that uses philosophical and logical methods and theories" (Cohen 2013, p. 2). In this model, Cohen juxtaposes Stoic theories of emotional states and cognitive interpretations, found in Albert Ellis's Rational Emotive Therapy. The linguistic theory of emotions maintains that "fallacies of emotions always involve the use (or misuse) of certain types of language in the premises (especially in the major premise rule) of one's emotional reasoning, which tend to promote destructive and self-defeating emotional responses" (Cohen 2009, p. 275). Both propositions demonstrate various ways of dipping into the philosopher's thesaurus of concepts in practice. Yet by placing them on a firm theoretical grounding, these propositions become more along the lines of practices that provide *consolatio* as opposed to an open-ended search for their premises. In particular, Otasz's idea of giving advice contradicts the Socratic spirit of questioning (Fastvold 2015, p. 11). Even if Cohen's proposition is derived from secondary gains of Stoic practices confirmed by psychology, at least as far as the discipline's methodology permits. Yet the question remains as to the nature of certain premises within this approach. Cohen illustrates how to deal with hesitation resulting from doubt (Cohen 2015). He writes that "the practice of LBT attempts to liberate us from such self-imposed prisons and chains." Whether someone ought to regulate hesitation via a change of mindset (and therefore a higher degree of rationalization), remains doubtful.

While evaluating the practical consequences of philosophical counseling from a critical methods standpoint, it would seem more beneficial to include a greater receptivity and appreciation when approaching hesitation. From the onset, the client will have a broader spectrum of choices in terms of goals and the process to be followed. This would allow him either to eliminate or accept a specific emotion or emotional state. Indeed, hesitation may not always need to be eliminated. Rather, it may contribute to a greater degree of self-understanding, for example, toward a higher level of internal integration (Dąbrowski 2015) or by building a more heroic, existential attitude (Tillich 1980). Nonetheless, it would be inadvisable to choose one course of treatment based upon the client's hesitation or anxiety, inasmuch as the philosophical counselor might find himself constrained by one theoretical approach of the phenomenon. If so, his role would become more of a paternalistic, dogmatic expert.

Professionalization: acceptance of the *status quo* or critical distance?

When speaking about practical philosophy as a profession, the former must already be somehow related to established professional standards and therapeutic advising. However, this raises the issue of market value, i.e., as a legitimation of services. Professionally, it must not only be measured by the subjective criteria of customer satisfaction and overall utility, but also by a recognition of the status of the specialists themselves, especially psychologists and psychotherapists. The latter have their own, often varied, standards of professional training and practice. Nonetheless, gathering evidence as to the efficacy of such treatments or counseling practices can be somewhat problematic (Hansen 2014), in that varying schools of thought establish very different criteria and set very different goals. This undoubtedly complicates questions of conceptualization and operativity, not to mention other elements involved in methodological investigations of efficacy. James T. Hansen therefore proposes that counselors should think about whether truths are created relationally or whether they are discovered thanks to such a relationship, hoping that a "consideration of the question might open up new intellectual and practical possibilities for counselors" (Hansen 2014, p. 95). These issues draw attention to the fact that, at first glance, a client may develop a belief that he is the end goal of the whole process in which he partakes. Secondly, the objective language used to evaluate counseling services is built on cause-and-effect assumptions in which a given type of practical intervention produces a specific result, which may be one possible way of interpreting a complex process rather than a real-life scenario.

Marinoff (2002) mentions the ambivalent situation associated with a lack of regulation in the field of professional philosophical counseling at the end of the twentieth century. He likewise notes that the economy had influenced the need for such measures, so much so, that he entitled the fifth chapter of *Philosophical Practice* as the *Politics of Political Practice* (Marinoff 2001), wherein the author identifies the forces that both threaten and support philosophical practice. This perspective, as a legitimization of philosophical counseling, highlights a type of client-provider relationship. Conversely, as with other pragmatist-instrumentalist approaches, Marinoff's claim has certain limitations. In questioning the advantages of "harmlessness" (or lack thereof, from a minimalist perspective) in the practice of philosophical counseling, it becomes an indisputable point of reference. Furthermore, it likewise implies economic categories and useful measurements taken from socially pervasive beliefs about desirable mental health and developmental goals.[4] A philosophical approach must also recognize these elements in terms of their originality, and therefore, their arbitrariness, as elements that require critical elaboration.

The above signifies a readiness to question how modern normative narratives function. Aside from just subverting and replacing them with other content, narrative norms become subject to discussion, for example, by using tools supplied by the "masters with suspicion" and their disciples (Ricoeur 1970). Yet critical philosophical practice cannot go so far as to debate the standards of mental health brought on by the wave of antipsychiatry (Szasz 1991, Van Deurzen 2010). Even if this position espouses a certain extreme position, the presence of such types of voices in the discussion produces a valuable dialectical tension with respect to well-established beliefs about the value of diagnostic criteria grounded in empirical science. The very awareness of the ambiguity of those positions is important for an understanding of the socio-cultural determinants, wherein the philosopher-practitioner finds himself.

Understanding the conventional nature of standards and institutions does not, however, make it easy to reject them in the name of indefinableness – such a stance would inevitably give way to arbitrary resolutions in opposition to that convention. Keeping a critical distance is one aspect of functioning under specific circumstances. It is not an independent sphere, in the sense that fulfilling the high standards of criticism would put an end to the possibility of action. The noncritical approach would also involve the depreciation of psychotherapy's accomplishments and the norms therein. In spite of appearances, this would not serve as a validation of philosophical practice. Indeed, in order to remain critical, the practice must also recognize the boundaries of its own competencies in the context of established forms of advisory and developmental work. Sam Brown rightfully notes that philosophical practice has a limited scope: "a skilled and responsible practitioner should be capable of recognizing when the service is unlikely to be constructive" (Brown 2010, p. 115). He further remarks that students of philosophy may not possess adequate knowledge of psychiatric illnesses.

The question then arises as to whether contemporary diagnostic criteria should become the reference point for philosopher-practitioners, operating out-

---

4 Chris Megone (2017) notes that in antiquity, validation of philosophical therapeutic practices took the form of health and wellbeing standards for individuals and even society as a whole. The contemporary case is somewhat more complicated. Philosophers are no longer the ones who exaggerate their knowledge about medicine or the harmony of the soul, thereby discovering the inner workings of man, the required methodology, or *paideia*. Nevertheless, they must still reckon with the institutionalization and standardization of interpretations.

side the mental health fields.[5] Cohen shares this position, by arguing that a separation between philosophical counseling and psychology would be objectionable, considering that the former has a hybrid character as a psychological process that makes use of philosophical theories (Cohen 2013). This demonstrates that a pure philosophical approach must yield to the requirements of the counselor's expertise. Philosophy is applied as either a method or a tool in a concrete relationship with the client, who is ruled by certain psychological regularities. Likewise, the client functions on various levels and not simply as a theoretical, abstracted reason, which necessitates a broader knowledge base. The aforementioned fears, associated with inadequate diagnostic knowledge of psychiatric disorders, reaffirm this line of argument.

There are nonetheless possible counter-augments: firstly, in lieu of seeking professional help, one may opt instead to listen to either friends or loved ones about the difficult life situation. Secondly, the philosophical counselor, who without the requisite medical knowledge, could just as well collaborate with a psychotherapist or refer the client to another specialist or psychiatrist. It has less to do with the philosophical counselor's knowledge of nosology and more to do with recognizing the limitations of his own practice. Thirdly, in reference to the hybrid nature of the philosophical counseling services based on psychological truths, one can argue on the principle of *reductio ad absurdum* that every human relationship is, somehow, psychological in nature. Especially within close relationships, at least one party should have an adequate background in psychology. *Ergo*, relationships with non-psychologists run the risk of overlooking both diseases and mental disorders. Figures such as Plato, St. Augustine, Kierkegaard, Nietzsche, were endowed with brilliant psychological intuition that both preceded and, indeed, inspired later findings of scientific psychology. To this list, one could add writers such as Dostoyevsky or Tolstoy. In sum, psychological "intuition" does not always go hand-in-hand with a psychotherapeutic education.

The counter-arguments presented above, serve to emancipate philosophical practice from a psychological or psychopathological context. Conversely, one could qualify them as naive, a misunderstanding of the problems' complexity, and, above all, a lack of ethical responsibility. They create, nevertheless, a dialectical tension during the dispute, protecting against a dogmatic acceptance by either party. And yet, the client who discusses his deep-seated problems cannot

---

[5] The National Philosophical Counseling Association accepts this resolution. The NPCA explicitly outlines the types of problems philosophical counselors can treat and those which only medically-qualified consultants of mental illness are able to handle: (http://npcassoc.org/practice-areas-boundaries/ [12.05.2017]).

ignore this aspect by limiting himself to purely intellectual work (Zinaich 2013, Mills 2013). Rather than trapping followers of the psychological approach in logical pitfalls, it would behoove the philosopher-practitioner to train and develop a broader knowledgebase of psychology (particularly in soft and communicative skills and understanding the mechanisms of transference and countertransference).[6] The conscientious practitioner should be critical. However, critical does not mean to ignore the psychological regularity of the counseling relationship, but to take a psychosocial approach to psychological knowledge by understanding its probabilistic nature.

In summarizing his study on philosophical counseling, Jon Mills calls for an "external review" and a field specific self-critique: "with systematic critique, revision, and experimentation, philosophical counseling may perhaps enjoy future recognition as a behavioral science" (Mills 2013, p. 108). Mills's observation points to the peculiar status of research in philosophical counseling, which, in order to validate the discipline, must associate the methodology of philosophy with the methodology of social research. Here, the appeal for criticism can only indicate the desperate need for an "alliance" with science. In this context, however, it is worth noting the divergent opinion of another representative and fellow philosophical-practitioner, Shlomit C. Schuster. Unlike Cohen, Schuster does not contend that philosophical counseling exists as a hybrid, psychologized form: "Philosophical activity attempts to go beyond scientific established knowledge either by criticizing scientific 'truths' or through intellectual quest that in the future may lead to the establishment of new scientific knowledge" (Schuster 1999, p. 4). In post-Enlightenment era, the very task of demanding scientific evidence as the adherence of philosophical counseling to strictly defined professional standards, must be validated. At the least, such a demand should denude the potentially problematic nature of counseling. Yet the clients themselves, who may believe in the scientific "stylization" of psychotherapy, likewise share the need for scientific validation as to the efficacy of philosophical counseling services (necessitating a standardization of methods and procedures).

---

[6] The philosophical counseling program that I founded at the University of Silesia in Katowice therefore places a great emphasis on the study of psychology (general, social, emotional and motivational), interpersonal training, and coaching. Unlike the regular philosophy studies track, the program has a hands-on approach in teaching relationship-building, psychological assessment accuracy, communicating in a non-directive way concerning the different levels of logical expression.

In his definition of the profession,[7] Michael Davis draws attention to the fact that "Licensing, registration, and certification are all forms of consumer protection. Their purpose is (or, at least, should be) to protect the public from charlatans, mountebanks, imposters, incompetents, and others whom the public cannot sufficiently protect themselves from" (Davis 2013, p. 249). At the same time, Davis expresses doubts as to whether professionalism is synonymous with career licensing, arguing in favor of philosophical neutrality against standards derived from other fields (see: Davis 2013, pp. 237–250). Yet the apparent reality of the service market seems to support the role of the philosophical counselor as one who adheres to regulations in order to practice effectively. The problem with adopting heterogenic standards of professional practice means that philosophical counseling will play the part of *consolatio* for itself. In "disguising" itself as a similar field, the practice gains prestige and loses any sort of "inferiority complex." On the other hand, the adoption of any kind of professional limitation, brings with it, to a greater or lesser extent, the loss of normative dogmatism. Despite the anesthetizing effect that consolation might provide, the autonomy of philosophy lasts only as long as it retains an awakened, critical stance – particularly critical of itself.

Conclusions

Particularly in philosophy's applied form, that is to say, philosophical counseling, it might be tempting to say that criticism plays an essential role in protecting philosophical autonomy. How does this translate from a practical standpoint, in relation to a particular individual? The response concerns two issues: firstly, the attitude of the philosophical advisor who should remain autocritical, open to interpretations, humble in the face of professional challenges, ethically responsible, suspicious of the obvious, and acutely aware of the entanglements within the socio-cultural sphere. His education should thus be grounded on a historical-philosophical foundation, thereby allowing him to not only to appreciate the transformations in the history of ideas, but also to utilize a richer assortment of concepts and tools in the hopes of broadening the client's perspective. Secondly, this issue concerns a relational methodology in which the regulatory idea should remain as far as possible from a) a lack of set directives, b) a suspen-

---

[7] A profession is a number of individuals in the same occupation voluntarily organized to earn a living by openly serving a morally-permissible way beyond what law, market, morality, and public opinion would otherwise require (Davis 2013, p. 243).

sion of preconceived notions about the direction of the process, c) an avoidance of decision-making on behalf of the client in order to make room for a certain amount of independent study. It can be understood as following the client, his search, an understanding and appreciation of his point of view and relevant thought process vis-à-vis the whole experience. Furthermore, welcoming views from different philosophical positions and offering on-topic suggestions, will not disaffect the client's ability to decide the shape and purpose of the process. It is by far the most constructive critical attitude, in which interventions and procedural guidelines pave the way toward empathetic cooperation through an emotional and spiritual adjustment, thereby expressing an openness to the process occurring within the client himself. Recognizing the boundaries between "I" and "You" does not permit the "You" to become part of the thought form "I." Rather, such a recognition suspends judgment on what would be right for "You," (either critical methods or *consolatio*), possessing the transcendental correctness in form of being-for, which determines the rudimentary soundness of philosophical practice.

Bibliography

Achenbach, Gerd (1995): "Philosophy, Philosophical Practice, and Psychotherapy". In: R. Lahav, M.V. Tillmanns (eds.): *Essays on Philosophical Counselling*. Lanham. Maryland: University Press of America, pp. 61–74.

Allen, Richard (2002): "Philosophical Inquiry and Psychological Development", In: *International Journal of Philosophical Practice* 1, no. 3, pp. 1–16.

Amir, Lydia B. (2004): "Three Questionable Assumptions of Philosophical Counseling". In: *International Journal of Philosophical Practice* 2, no. 1, pp. 1–32.

Boethius (2005): "De Consolatione Philosophiae Opuscula Theologica". In: Claudio Moreschini (ed.): *Bibliotheca scriptorum graecorum et romanorum teubneriana*. München und Leipzig: De Gruyter.

Brown, Sam (2010): "The therapeutic status of philosophical counselling". In: *Practical Philosophy* 10:1, pp. 111–120.

Cohen, Elliot D. (2009): *Critical Thinking Unleashed*. Lanham – Boulder – New York – Toronto – Plymouth: Rowman & Littlefield Publishers.

Cohen, Elliot D. (2013): *Theory and Practice of Logic-Based Therapy: Integrating Critical Thinking and Philosophy into Psychotherapy*. Newcastle upon Tyne: Cambridge Scholars Publishing.

Cohen, Elliot D. (2015): "Counseling Hume: Using Logic-Based Therapy to Address Generalized Anxiety Disorder". In: *International Journal of Philosophical Practice* 3 (no. 4), pp. 1–8.

Dąbrowski, Kazimierz (2015): *Personality-Shaping Through Positive Disintegration*. Red Pill Press.

daVenza Tillmanns, Maria (2013): "Philosophical Counseling: Understanding the Unique Self and Other Through Dialogue". In: Elliot D. Cohen/Samuel Zinaich Jr (eds.): *Philosophy, Counseling and Psychotherapy*. Newcastle upon Tyne: Cambridge Scholars Publishing, pp. 132–138.

Davis, Michael (2013): "Licensing Philosophical Counselors". In: Elliot D. Cohen/Samuel Zinaich Jr (eds.): *Philosophy, Counseling and Psychotherapy*. Newcastle upon Tyne: Cambridge Scholars Publishing, pp. 237–250.

Falikowski, Anthony (2012): "Disciplinary Turf War: Philosophical Counseling in an Era of Psychological Hegemony, Philosophical Practice". In: *Journal of the American Philosophical Practitioners Association* 7, issue 1, pp. 889–902.

Fastvold, Morten (2015): "The Art of Questioning". In: Michael Noah Weiss (ed.): *The Socratic Handbook*. Wien – Zürich: Lit, pp. 11–18.

Foucault, Michel (2005): *The Hermeneutics of Subject. Lectures at the Collège de France 1981–82*. Transl. Graham Burchell. New York: Palgrave McMillan.

Fromm, Erich (2001): *The Sane Society*. London: Routledge.

Hansen, James T. (2014): *Philosophical Issues in Counseling and Psychotherapy. Encounters with Four Questions about Knowing, Effectiveness, and Truth*, Lanham – Boulder – New York – Toronto – Plymouth: Rowman & Littelfield.

Horkheimer, Max (2004): *Eclipse of reason*. London, New York: Continuum.

Knapp, S./Tjeltveit, A.C. (2005): "A Review and Critical Analysis of Philosophical Counseling". In: *Professional Psychology: Research and Practice* 36, no. 5, pp. 558–565.

Lahav, Ran (2013): "Philosophical Counseling and Self-Transformation". In: Elliot D. Cohen, Samuel Zinaich Jr. (eds.): *Philosophy, Counseling and Psychotherapy*. Newcastle upon Tyne: Cambridge Scholars Publishing, pp. 82–99.

Marinoff, Lou (1999): *Plato, Not Prozac!: Applying Eternal Wisdom to Everyday Problems*, New York: Quill.

Marinoff Lou (2002): *Philosophical Practice*. San Diego – New York – Boston – London – Sydney – Tokyo – Toronto: Academic Press.

McWilliams, Nancy (2011): *Psychoanalytic Diagnosis, Second Edition: Understanding Personality Structure in the Clinical Process*. New York: The Guilford Press.

Megone, Chris (2017): "Ancient Applied Philosophy". In: A Companion to Applied Philosophy". In: Kasper Lippert-Rasmussen/Kimberley Brownlee/David Coady (eds.): *Blackwell Companions to Philosophy*. Chichester – Hoboken: Wiley Blackwell, pp. 585–597.

Mills, Jon (2013): "Philosophical Counseling as Psychotherapy". In: Elliot D. Cohen/Samuel Zinaich Jr. (eds.): *Philosophy, Counseling and Psychotherapy*. Newcastle upon Tyne: Cambridge Scholars Publishing, pp. 100–111.

National Philosophical Counseling Association http://npcassoc.org/practice-areas-boundaries/, 12.05.2017.

Ostasz, Lech (2011): *Psychoterapia filozoficzna. O usprawnianiu rozumu i leczeniu psychiki*. Warszawa: Wydawnictwo ENETEIA.

Padin, Roger (2013): "Defining Philosophical Counseling". In: Elliot D. Cohen/Samuel Zinaich Jr. (eds.): *Philosophy, Counseling and Psychoterapy*. Newcastel upon Tyne: Cambridge Scholars Publishing, pp.16–33.

Raabe, Peter (2000): "Passionate Judgements in Philosophical Counselling". In: *Practical Philosophy* 3, no. 3, pp. 12–18.

Ricoeur, Paul (1970): *Freud and Philosophy: An Essay on Interpretation*. New Haven: Yale University Press.
Schuster, Shlomit C. (1991): "Philosophical Counseling". In: *Journal of Applied Philosophy* 8 (2), pp. 219–223.
Schuster, Shlomit C. (1999): *Philosophy Practice: An Alternative to Counseling and Psychotherapy*. Westport – Connecticut – London: Praeger.
Schuster, Shlomit C. (2004): "Marinoff's Therapy: A Critique of His Books on Philosophical Practice". In: *International Journal of Philosophical Practice* 2, no. 2, pp. 1–10.
Szasz, Thomas (1991): *Ideology and Insanity: Essays on the Psychiatric Dehumanization of Man*. Syracuse: Syracuse University Press.
Tillich, Paul (1980): *The Courage to Be*. London: Yale University Press, New-Haven.
Tukiainen, Arto (2010): "Philosophical Counselling as a Process of Fostering Wisdom in the Form of Virtues". In: *Practical Philosophy* 10, no. 1, pp. 47–56.
Van Deurzen, Emmy. (2010): *Everyday mysteries: A handbook of existential psychotherapy*. London – New York: Routledge.
Zinaich, Jr. Samuel. (2013): "Diagnosis, Philosophical Counseling and Culturally Recognizable Mental Illnesses". In: Elliot D. Cohen/Samuel Zinaich Jr (eds.): *Philosophy, Counseling and Psychotherapy*. Newcastle upon Tyne: Cambridge Scholars Publishing, pp. 204–226.

Dariusz Rymar
Plato's Dialectics as a Method of Critical Reflection on Art

Abstract: The article challenges the validity of stereotypical evaluations of Plato's reflection on art, which is often seen as a dogmatic attack on the artistic culture. However, the author argues that a more beneficial approach in our understanding of art is to interpret the artistic creation in context of Platonic dialectics. A study of the dialectical method manifested, among others, in the dialogues *Parmenides*, *Sophist* and *Philebus* shows that Plato in his attitude to art has presented only one of two complementary dialectic extremes. The founder of the Academy explicitly characterizes art negatively, but also calls for its defense (*Republic*, 607e-608b). Author of the article argues that the most important premises for the reconstruction of Plato's "theory of art" are included in the construction of the dialogues themselves, where aesthetic qualities are treated with as much care as the logical structure of the arguments. He illustrates this point with examples of Plato's myth–crafting (*Symposium*, *Phaedrus*, *Republic*, *Timaeus*) and contends that Plato's dialectics may also assist our reflections on contemporary issues related both to artistic culture and its theory.

In the further part of the article, the author refers to the most acclaimed philosophical concepts of the second half of the twentieth century, indicating that they have become a framework for contemporary thinking about art. He discusses the most important aporias of contemporary epistemological assumptions, then shows how shortcomings of these assumptions translate to simplifications in the understanding of art. He argues that art is substantially a hostage of mercantile thinking, pointing out that such concept of art is a reductionist understanding of the idea of freedom. Using these diagnoses, the author proposes a reconstruction of the "first philosophy", understood as a transcendental description of various forms of human experience.

Keywords: Plato's dialectics, critical methods, art, criticism

1 The open nature of Plato's dialectics

Plato's attitude to art happens to be a common object of attack for contemporary theory of art. The tradition of criticizing Platonism as a negative reference point for contemporary reflections on the artistic culture was initiated by Friedrich

Nietzsche, who saw him as. "[...] the greatest enemy of art Europe has yet produced" (Nietzsche 2011, p. 114).

Plato's remarks on art are as later a negative point of reference for Theodor Adorno, Gianni Vattimo, Richard Shustermann, Wolfgang Welsch, Arthur C. Danto, Matthew Kieran and others. The Founder of the Academy is blamed for initiating a tendency to limit the sphere of freedom. He is reproached for postulating the supervision of art and overseeing its education. The perception of Plato as "the enemy of art" is a symptom of a multidimensional misunderstanding. So is the extrapolation of these aspects of Plato's critique of art which are local and highly context-dependent, to modern disputes about art. The opponents often do not just miss the dialectical dimension of Plato's thought, but use aporetic reasoning that is close to internal contradiction.

A significant number of researchers (such as Martin Heidegger, Arthur C. Danto, George Dickie and Stanley Fish) treat art as having a highly contextual character. According to many hermeneuticians, works of art represent a state of local culture at a specific time, so understanding it in isolation from the context in which they occurred, is impossible. Plato's line of argument relates to a different context and to art different than that, which is being created in our times. Therefore, the dispute would be largely meaningless.

Plato is being criticized for his allegedly dogmatic attitude towards art and the introduction of strong metaphysics[1] which leads to contemptuous attitude towards weak manifestations of reality. In both cases, these assessments are a result of a stereotype repeated for centuries, which sees the founder of the Academy as a dogmatist.

A significant part of the opponents of Plato's conception of art ignores the essence of problematic nature of this philosophy. Plato postulated multidimensional analysis of problems in his dialectics. Meanwhile, many critics of Plato's concept use arguments in a fragmentary fashion, which distorts this concept.

Plato's approach to art seemed to be sufficient for understanding the role of art up to the mid-nineteenth century. This monolith of the *Great Theory* began to crack as early as the eighteenth century to break down in the second half of the nineteenth century.[2] Before it happened, inspired by Plato's teachings, a modern "theory" of genius was developed. The full basis for the formulation of this "theory" was made by Marcilio Ficino, who was inspired by sources that indicate the dichotomous nature of the artistic and philosophical talent. On one hand, he has to have a tendency for frenzy, on the other – an ability to penetrate the met-

---

[1] See: Vattimo 1999.
[2] See: Tatarkiewicz 1972.

aphysical and mystical realms. Ficino combined, among others, a description in *Phaedrus* with Aristotelian characteristic of human temperaments:

> Finally, not till then was the equation of the Aristotelian melancholy with Platonic "divine frenzy"—never clearly formulated by the ancients themselves—expressly made. Then—and not till then—did the modem age conceive the modem notion of genius, reviving ancient conceptions indeed, but filling them with a new meaning (Klibansky et al. 1979, p. 250).

In the twentieth century, along with the rejection of metaphysics, a departure from the category of beauty has occurred, despite the fact that it has been treated as the essence of art for more than two millennia. Soon, an attack on the idea of artistic genius followed. However, this one-sidedness of culture's choices may be problematic. It also seems dangerous that a significant part of philosophers support this unilateral turn, refusing to conduct any in-depth discussion.

Tendencies towards simplified understandings of Plato's teachings are rooted in the interpretation of Aristotle, who attributed the introduction of the "two worlds" aporia to Plato. This problem was noticed by Nicolai Hartmann, who indicated that superstitions associated with Platonic doctrine are already so deeply rooted in our understanding of the history of philosophy, that these errors seem almost impossible to remove: "This pseudoplatonic superstition remained, despite its early discovered weakness, surprisingly long-lasting" (Hartmann 1958, p. 283, transl. Dariusz Rymar).[3]

Hartmann notes that Plato himself vigorously opposed such interpretations of the theory of ideas. German philosopher indicates, that basing on the line of argument in *Parmenides*, Plato's concept can be interpreted in a significantly different way than it is in traditional approaches:

> One can also reverse the historical perspective and, looking back, enclose all dialectical studies of Platonic *Parmenides* as a kind of "a transcendental deduction" of the ideas – of course without a sign of subjectivity. Since, what has been finally overcome in it, is the separation (chorismos) of the ideas: combination (symploke) leads to "the opposite of the idea", concretum (Hartmann 1958, p. 283, transl. Dariusz Rymar).[4]

---

[3] "Dieses pseudoplatonische Vorurteil ist trotz seiner früh erkannten Schwäche ein merkwürdig langlebiges gewesen" (Hartmann 1958, p. 283).

[4] "Man kann geschichtlich die Perspektive auch umkehren und rückwärts schauend die großen dialektischen Untersuchungen der Platonischen "Parmenides" als eine Art ""transcendentaler Deduktion"" der Ideen – freilich ohne die Vorzeichen des Subjektivismus – auffassen. Denn was in ihnen schließlich überbrückt wird, ist eben der Chorismos der Ideen: die Symploke führt auf ""das Gegenstück der Idee"", das Conctretum, hinaus" (Hartmann 1958, p. 283, n. 1).

This treatment, however, only shows one of possible interpretations of *Parmenides*. Meanwhile, this work helps to develop a number of different approaches. Furthermore, one could risk a thesis, that in a philosophical line of argument, one cannot go beyond the general framework of a method outlined in this dialogue, since the dialogue indicates the limits, both in positive and nihilistic reasoning. Moreover, the dialogue uses some mechanisms of sophistic argumentation, that disguises the simplifications of reasoning and erroneous way of thinking due to aporetic nature of the dialogue, it was suspected that it is a boring, meaningless joke that brings the reader into the quibble of empty reasoning.[5] This problem can be captured clearly if one combines two evaluations of Wilamowitz-Moellendorff.

This famous researcher of Plato's works expresses a distinct disapproval of *Parmenides* dialogue in several places, although it is a work of exceptional logical discipline. For example, the authors of *Plato. Sein Leben und seine Werke* say: "This thought is a real philosophical mill, which stones grind themselves because there is no grain poured, it is as anti—platonic as only possible (Wilamowitz-Moellendorff and Snell 1959, p. 511, transl. Dariusz Rymar)."[6]

In history, the dialogue has been treated as: an exercise in eristics, a method of structurizing aporias, an exercise in logical division of concepts, ontology built from the bottom, teleological metaphysics. One can add here purely logical attempts, such as the interpretation of Rickless or mereological interpretation of Kutschera, which examines relationships between the part, the whole and the multitude.[7] Plato builds contradictory strategies of argumentation: each positive reasoning is contrasted by a negative approach. In both models of thinking, the reader should recognize the absurdities, paradoxes and gaps in reasoning.

Kenneth M. Sayre indicates that Plato, since sophist builds the dialectical method, develops it in *Statesman*, for it to reach full maturity in *Parmenides* (Sayre 2007, p. 193, p. 198, p. 211). This dialogue has no outer theme, it is somehow an *exercise* (γυμνασία) in itself, since its purpose is to develop a mature

---

5 See: Cornford 1939, p. vi.
6 *"Dies Denken ist die rechte philosophische Mühle, deren Steine sich zerreiben, weil kein Korn aufgeschüttet wird, so unplatonisch wie möglich"* (Wilamowitz-Moellendorff and Snell 1959, p. 511).
7 Potentially, the text can be approached from the perspective of dynamic logics, which attempt to deal with lack of continuity between the dierent levels of reasoning, like attitudes, partial negation, different strength of convictions, etc. See: Benthem 2011, p. 18, p. 131, pp. 274–275. J. van Benthem does not talk about the dialectic presented in the *Parmenides*, however, features such as running a line of argument on several levels of reasoning, suggestions on reasoning with incomplete data, a significant role of partial and total negation, allow to conclude that in this dialogue, among the Plato's works, dynamic nature of the dialectic is most visible.

method of philosophizing. Among other things, due to the lack of clear solutions it is the least dogmatic.

In the first part, Socrates presents a theory of forms, as we know it in the stereotypical approach to Plato's concepts. Parmenides, in a conversation with young Socrates refutes the assumption about participation of the sensuous in the Forms themselves, by pointing out that from the perspective of sensory experience one can never get a full set of information. In other words, in the bottom—up ontology, one will never come to grasp the Form itself. Parmenides, seeing the young Socrates' helplessness, reproaches his impatience, while encouraging him to deepen the reflection:

> For you are trying to mark off something beautiful, said he, and just, and good, and every single one of the forms, Socrates, too early, before you are trained. [...] Believe me, your urge toward arguments is indeed noble and divine; but while you are still young you should exercise and train yourself better in what the many call idle talk and think useless, else the truth will escape you (*Parmenides*, 135c8–136e4, transl. Samuel Scolnicov).[8]

In the first part of the dialogue *Parmenides* indicates that founding the thinking solely on sensual input may make conducting a substantive line of argument impossible. This is a consequence of a too indefinite character of sensual experiences. However, the static theory of an idea, proposed by young Socrates, is not a solution. Parmenides in turn proposes a dialectic of three fundamental reference points, that allow to capture the dynamic nature of reality, without losing the right order of reasoning. The assumptions of this method are made in an instruction closing the first part of the dialogue:

> Take, if you like, Parmenides said, Zeno's hypothesis, according to which 'if it is many,' what consequences ensue both for the many in relation to themselves, and in relation to the one, and for the one in relation to itself, and in relation to the many. And conversely, 'if it is not many,' you must again examine what consequences follow for both the one and the many, in relation to themselves and in relation to each other [...] (*Parmenides*, 136a-b, transl. Sylvana Chrysakopolou).

According to *Parmenides*, any substantial problems may be reduced to three main factors: what is a general (abstract) principle, its detailed exemplification, and what is opposed both to the rule and its specific manifestation. In the translation of Sylvana Chrysakopoulou, which is an exception to other translations, a

---

[8] Some fragments of *Parmenides* are quoted in translation of Scolnicov, and other of Sylvana Chrysakopolou, because in some places one of seems to be closer to the original text than the other.

distinction between the terms *polla* (πολλά) and *ta polla* (τὰ πολλά) is captured; they are respectably translated as many and the many.⁹

In a significant number of cases, whether *polus* occurs with an article or without it may not be relevant. In *Parmenides* a distinction appears in the plural in nominative case *polla* and *ta polla*, and in the plural genitive *tois pollois* (τοῖς πολλοῖς). As it results from the explanations in Liddell-Scott's dictionary, one of the meanings of the notation with an article is a "huge amount".¹⁰ The use of *polus* with an article may refer to the understanding of Socrates, who in his oration speaks on the form of plurality *tauta polla tô plêthous* (ταῦτα πολλὰ τῷ πλήθους) (*Parmenides*, 129b5–6). This has some importance, as in the second part of *Parmenides* an analogous distinction between *hen* (ἕν) and *to hen* (τὸ ἕν) is consistently applied. Hence, it appears that this distinction needs to be properly taken into account, both in translating the relevant passages and in the interpretation itself. The recommendation on the way of conducting exercises quoted above, can be adapted to the reflections on beauty. Sticking to the grammatical structure of the instruction, one should accept the distinction between the adjective "beautiful" and the noun "beauty". If there is beautiful, what consequences ensue both for the Beauty in relation to itself, and in relation to the others, and for the others in relation to themselves, and in relation to the Beauty. And conversely, if there is no beautiful, you must again examine what consequences follow for both the others and the Beauty, in relation to itself and in relation to themselves and in relation to each other.¹¹

This instruction generates eight hypotheses, but description of full implications for thinking about art is impossible to present in a short essay. Therefore, it is necessary to reduce the complexity of the analysis. One may remember that Plato bases on a much simpler dialectic structure in some of his dialogues. In the spirit of this simple dialectical structure, I shall limit my considerations to two hypotheses: one positive (opting for what is beautiful), and one negative (refuting the beauty in art) hypotheses, indicating hypothetically the implications that may have for our thinking about art.

The first hypothesis can be compared with the famous speech of Diotima from Plato's *Symposium*. Plato distinguishes between knowledge about the beauty and the beauty itself (*Symposium*, 211a5–7). Beauty itself is not only inde-

---

9 A distinction between *polus* (πολύς) and *to polu* (τὸ πολύ) —respectively, between Viele and das Viele, is also maintained in the German translation of Franz Susemihl from 1865.

10 The electronic version of an explanation of the different ways of understanding *polus*, can be found on the appropriate website of Perseus Project. On August 8, 2012 available at: http://www.perseus.tufts.edu/hopper/morph?l=polu\%2Fs&la=greek\#lexicon.

11 A paraphrase of *Parmenides*, 136a-b.

pendent of any specific sensations and things, but even of thinking about them (211b3–5). One can only contemplate this divine beauty. Our efforts to grasp the beauty are a never-ending road. Beauty itself is beyond our knowledge. Therefore, one can speak of Plato's agnosticism.[12]

A similar reasoning applies to the good itself in *Philebus* (59a-b), where Plato adds, that grasping the good is always partial and reveals itself somehow in between qualitative relationships of our thinking, as a result of the dialectics between beauty, truth and measure (62c). However, this compound cannot also be completely abstracted, it is a culmination of a road that begins with sensation. This raises a question of the final terms of possibility of an accurate judgment.

Although Plato's ontology is realistic, Plato avoids attempts to determine the status of the ideas themselves. The recognition of the highest objects of knowledge is covered in myth.

In *Parmenides* Plato shows, that any attempt to grasp the principle itself in its full purity ends in failure.

To sum up, one may say, that Beauty is the supreme object of spiritual eroticism [a passion for perfection]. One cannot fill the Beauty with any specific content. However, one can feel a tangible necessity of striving for perfection. However, this experience is not available to everyone.

For people dominated by external experience, such beauty does not mean anything. From this perspective, in relation to the beauty, one would use a formula enclosing the first hypothesis:

> So no name belongs to it, nor is there an account, nor any knowledge, nor perception, nor opinion of it. […] Therefore, it is not named nor spoken of, nor is it the object of opinion or knowledge, nor does anything among the 'things that are' perceive it (*Parmenides*, 142a, transl. Sylvana Chrysakopolou 2010).

2 Dialectics between shots empirical and intelligible

According to the second hypothesis, beauty in various exemplifications would be the subject of discussion. This approach includes both beauty itself and its incarnations. However, it focuses on the problem of equivocation. It reveals the para-

---

[12] See: Rowe 1998, pp. 198–200.

doxes that arise at the time, when the same concepts are used both in concrete and abstract senses. Still, it lacks positive conclusions.

Thus, relying on the second hypothesis one cannot obtain a method of distinguishing the ideal (abstract) beauty from the (concrete) incarnate beauty.

A similar problem can be indicated in discussions that are waged on beauty. Conceptual confusion is characteristic for those aesthetic reflections that treat the aesthetic ideal as a being itself. When it turns out that the ideals in the course of history have changed very significantly, and aesthetic sensitivity is context –dependent, the conclusion about the inconsistency of essential thinking with artistic practice seems to follow. Perhaps it would be difficult for us to become accustomed to the collection of ancient sculptures, if their polychromy was reconstructed. Painted marble of classic statues would appear to be lacking taste, proportionally to the intensity of their colors, for a significant part of the lovers of antiquity. Thus, this is not an evidence, as some aestheticians claim, of a misconception of Plato's concept on Forms, but of their naïve, stereotypical understanding.

The second hypothesis represents an aporetic state of horizontal reasoning that brings all differences to a single level, which is a model of naïvely understood pluralism. It seems that for solutions in the field of art, particularly interesting is the relationship between what is specified and what is not.

Aporetic relationship between the boundary and the indefiniteness[13] finds a development and application in *Philebus*, where qualitatively indefinite pleasure will be subjected to determination and qualitative division through mind's activity. Moreover, dynamics of quantitative relations in *Parmenides* gain an additional axiological dimension in *Philebus*. I can only indicate, due to lack of space, the affinity of reflections in the initial parts of *Philebus* (14e-23c), concerning relations "the one – many," with the argumentation of the second part of *Parmenides*.

Overall, it appears that Plato requires an advancement of reader's own way of thinking, which also applies to art. For example, in *Phaedrus*, speeches on divine madness (*mania* [μανία]), are ambiguous – aspects that can be taken seriously are interspersed with ironic descriptions, as Socrates informs at the end of *palinodia* (*Phaedrus*, 265b-c). It may be considered that equalization of the mania of poets and philosophers belongs to serious argumentation, especially as Socrates returns to this matter in the rational part of the argumentation.

Plato's opinions expressed in various places show that art has the potential for both good and evil, may betray the truth, but it can help a man to find it (see

---

[13] See: *Parmenides*, 145a and 158d.

e.g. *Phaedrus*, 277b5–279b8 and 278d6-c3). Due to this ambiguity, art does not reach the highest territory of human experience. Thus it is not art, as such, that has a privilege of judging the human world, but only art whose patron is truth—compliance with the requirements of a real being.[14]

So it is not art that evaluates philosophy, but it is philosophy that may make a judgment on art. This line of argument is also complemented by the fact that a philosopher cannot provide a specific recipe for the implementation of a successful work of art. One can, in the spirit of Hegel, say that philosophy has no sufficient insight into specific problems of implementation of the works. Exceeding the framework of legitimate interpretation is a risk to both parties. An artist is usually not a good philosopher, same as philosopher is not a good artist.

One can say that the empirical approaches have no meta-critical level and therefore are not competent to assess their own position in the entirety of human knowledge.

In turn, philosophy usually does not possess knowledge on a detailed level. Hence, dialectical "mediation" between different, fragmented views of reality is one of the tasks of philosophy. This approach may indeed counteract the tendencies for defragmentation of culture.

3 Negative Hypotheses

A significant part of contemporary art theorists refers to metaphysics in a negative way. Theodor Adorno, speaking about a possible spirituality in art, argues that it is to be achieved through negation of its references to transcendentals:

> The primacy of spirit in art and the inroads made by what was previously taboo are two sides of the same coin. It is concerned with what has not yet been socially approved and preformed and thereby becomes a social condition of determinate negation. Spiritualization takes place not through ideas announced by art but by the force with which it penetrates layers that are intention–less and hostile to the conceptual. This is not the least of the reasons why the proscribed and forbidden tempt artistic sensibilities [Ingenium[15] – D.R.]. Spiritualization in new art prohibits it from tarnishing itself any further with the topical preferences of philistine culture: the true, the beautiful, and the good. Into its innermost core what is usually called art's social critique or engagement, all that is critical or negative in art, has been fused with spirit, with art's law of form. That these elements are at present

---

14 See: *Sophist*, 234c2-e2, especially the argumentation from 265d5 until the end of the work.
15 In the original version, the term *Ingenium* is used, which indicates an inherent ability, the talent, but also a genius. In the English version used here sensibilities weakens the vividness of interpretation (see: Adorno 1970, p. 228).

stubbornly played off against each other is a symptom of the regression of consciousness (Adorno 2013, p. 128 [1970, p. 93]).

In another place, he states:

[...] art became the tumbling mat of the true, the beautiful, and the good, which in aesthetic reflection forced valuable art out of the way of what the broad, polluted mainstream of spirit drew in its current (Adorno 2013, p. 86 [1970, p. 62]).

According to Adorno, references to the beauty not only petrify the spirituality, but are an expression of violence:

Hitler's empire put this theorem to the test, as it put the whole of bourgeois ideology to the test: The more torture went on in the basement, the more insistently they made sure that the roof rested on columns (Adorno 2013, p. 68 [1970, p. 49]).

This German philosopher puts the task of ennobling what has been humiliated in front of the art:

Art must take up the cause of what is proscribed as ugly, though no longer in order to integrate or mitigate it or to reconcile it with its own existence through humor that is more offensive than anything repulsive. Rather, in the ugly, art must denounce the world that creates and reproduces the ugly in its own image, even if in this too the possibility persists that sympathy with the degraded will reverse into concurrence with degradation (Adorno 2013, p. 68 [1970, pp. 48–49]).

A little further, he adds:

Art need not defend itself against the rebuke that it is degenerate; art meets this rebuke by refusing to affirm the miserable course of the world as the iron law of nature (Adorno 2013, p. 68 [1970, p. 49]).

Adorno criticizes transcendentals, seeing them as a sign of spiritual poverty, since they are rules limiting the creative freedom of a genius. The conflation of transcendentals with philistine culture, done by him raises serious doubts. Philistine approach focuses on creating external appearances, while being completely false. Such an attitude is associated with inadequate understanding of the phenomena and strong convictions. However, exactly due to lack of understanding, it does not reach the truth, and therefore, under Plato's assumptions, philistine attitude is neither good nor beautiful.

Adorno did not notice that an analogous problem concerns also the experience of ugliness. A philistine may "contemplate" disgusting items as well. It seems that it is easier than recognising beautiful works of non-trivial character.

It is easier to recognize ugliness, scandal and abomination than to differentiate the Beauty from the kitsch. One only needs to accept that ugliness, scandal and shock are the greatest achievements of art in order to enjoy participation in the creative "genius." Some interpreters reinforce such tendencies, using a sophistic strategy, for example, by arguing that art has always tried to shock. For instance, one can point to the elaboration of Kerstin Mey's *Art and Obscenity*; according to the author, self-mutilation, defecation or sexual intercourse carried out under the banner of art are supposed to broaden our understanding of the world:

> [...] provocation and shock have been part and parcel of western art from the modern period onwards—testing, pushing and expanding the established aesthetic parameters closely linked to intellectual, religious, ethical and legal concerns of the time (Mey 2007, p. 1)

In another place, she states:

> In the early 1960s, a loose grouping of artists gained notoriety in Vienna and beyond through taboo-breaking performative actions. Hermann Nitsch, Otto Muehl, Writer Brus and Rudolf Schwarzkogler were responsible for those highly 'provocative, insurgent and challenging' interventions. Known as the Vienna Action Group or Vienna Actionists, they performed their own bodies or the bodies of friends in highly charged sexual ways on Vienna's streets and in the city's cellar spaces, that is to say, outside of the art establishment's reaim, collaboratively as well as individually.' In the increasingly politicized climate of the post–war period, the 'sons' sought to break with the social value continuum, and the authoritarianism of the pre–war 'father' generation. Muehl, with male and female collaborators, indulged in opulent material actions. Employing foodstuff, paint, blood and other organic materials, those scripted experiments centered on the manipulation of erogenous body zones and collective sexual 'interchanges'. Nitsch choreographed lengthy, spectacular and exhaustive 'abreact games' in his Orgy–Mystery (O: M.) theatre. These performances featured the slaughter of animals, scenes of crucifixion, blood pouring and washing in order to reawaken primordial instincts and desires in the service of purification and catharsis (Mey 2007, p. 20).

In the ending of a lecture on the Actionists Kerstin Mey says:

> At the time, their concerted onslaughts against the reigning reactionary ideology and authoritarian violence provoked severe crackdowns by Austria's legal apparatus and eventually forced the artists to 'leave': Schwarzkogler committed suicide in 1969, Brus and Nitsch went into exile, and Muehl withdrew into the Austrian countryside to continue his life–art project, shaping an 'egalitarian' and liberal community outside of bourgeois (sexual) economy (Mey 2007, p. 21).

In a series of studies devoted to Actionists, a significantly different image, than one shown by K. Mey, emerges. Actionists were promoted by a part of Austrian establishment.[16] Especially significant is the casus of Otto Muehl, who founded around 1972 *Commune freie Sexualität:* Otto Muehl's trial in Eisenstadt ended with a conviction and a seven-year sentence for "the sexual abuse of minors, rape and forced abortion" (Kuhner 2008, p. 4).

Against this background, slogans that Muehl popularized in his manifestos are not of neutral, merely aesthetic nature:

> Everything is worthy of presentation [...] That includes rape and murder. Coitus, torture and the annihilation of man and beast is the only drama worth viewing. Murder is an integral part of sex. House pets have to serve as surrogates I intend to commit the perfect murder on a goat that will serve as a substitute for a woman (Rumler 1968, p. 254).[17]

Kerstin Mey believes that art influencing our primal instincts also frees us from negative emotional tensions. It is difficult, however, to accept uncritically that by interacting with such experiences a catharsis is obtained. A significant part of interpreters willingly support their arguments by referring to Heraclitus. Meanwhile the philosopher of Ephesus, warning about the danger of Dionisia, says:

> They vainly purify themselves with blood when defiled with it, as if a man who had stepped into mud were to wash it off with mud. He would be thought mad if anyone noticed him acting thus (fr 105 (D-K, B 5), transl. Cohen et al. 2016, p. 25).

In another place we read:

> Eyes and ears are bad witnesses to people if they have barbarian souls (fr. 13 (D-K, B 107), transl. Cohen et al. 2016, p. 21).

Modern psychology seems to confirm the objections of Heraclitus. Elliot Aronson in his well-known monograph *The Social Animal* warns that stimulating strong emotions does not purify our feelings but on the contrary, leads to an escalation of tensions (Aronson 2003, pp. 263–265).

Intellectual effort of a large part of modern thinkers seems to aim to paralyze forms of positive reflection on the relationship between the world and man. They

---

[16] See: Herbert Kuhner, *Monsignor Otto Mauer. Austrian Patron of the Arts* (24.02.2013: http://viennanet.info/wp-content/uploads/2008/12/monsignor-otto-mauer_english.pdf); Andreas Schlothauer: *Die Diktatur der freien Sexualitdt – vom Ende einer 'Sekte'* (24. 02.2013: http://www.report.de/Die\%20Diktatur\%2@der\%2@freien\ %20Sexualitaet.html).

[17] See: Kuhner 2008, p. 4.

accuse the traditional philosophy of failing to reform the moral order. Some blame it for the social disasters of the last century. One might also ask why the attack on metaphysics is so one-sided. One might also ask lo a different question: why is philosophy so socially powerless? Why, during over twenty centuries, the evil resulting from the lack of control of lust has not been "exorcised"? What is the conviction that resignation of philosophy from the public debate could revive pacifist thinking among us and lead to the decrease in conflicts, built upon? Once philosophy is deserted, no attempt of reaching a positive response is available. Lyotard, as well as a number of other postmodern thinkers (and post-structuralists) oppose to metaphysics, seeing in it what the ancients called *hubris*: The threatiste, however, is a genre that incites arrogance, and the arrogance of philosophers is metaphysics (Lyotard 1993, p. 331).

In turn, Odo Marquard says goodbye to philosophy with cheerful irony:

> Philosophy was competent in everything; then it was competent in some things; today philosophy is competent for one thing only—namely, to ac-knowledge its own incompetence. And if that is the way things stand, then what is left for philosophy is: absolutely nothing— that is, pure, unadulterated, naked incompetence, as well as, to cite Socrates, only a single little trifling something, an admittedly very un–Socratic trifle that, rather than making philosophy somewhat less problematic, on the contrary makes it 100 percent problematic; and I should like to name this item, in view of the radical incompetence that philosophy lias arrived at: it is philosophy's competence in compensating for its incompetence (Marquard 1989, p. 28).

In one of the essays Alain Badiou evokes Lacanian theme of the hysteric:
"We know that the hysteric comes to the master and says: "Truth speaks through my mouth, I am here. You have knowledge, tell me who I am"" (Badiou 2005, p. 1). One could add a response of a master (post-philosopher): "Your hysteria is good, so give up the truth." However, less entertaining is the question: is the refusal of treatment more arrogant than attempting it, even if the effectiveness of treatment seems insignificant?

Promoters of anti-art use methods tested in the last century. The first step in the anatomy of success of a modern artist is to provoke a scandal that starts an avalanche of emotional reactions. Apologists of anti-art, when faced with harsh criticism, turn its blade around, accusing the opponents of an attack on freedom, reminding about the cases of reviewing art. If one manages to keep a discussion longer, this artifact gets strong enough to effectively replace the substantial works of art. One could say, that avant-garde artists have developed a strategy used by today's celebrities, which is essentially based on provoking a media uproar.[18]

Well-known art philosophies of the late twentieth century sanctioned this mechanism by giving the final word to World Art (Arthur C. Danto), or artistic institutions (George Dickie). Rosenstein rightfully notes, that these theories mask the absence of theory.[19] One could only add the conclusion that they mask the absence of art itself and its works for over a century, thanks to the power of beliefs of the philistines of negativity.

4 Closing Remarks

The dialectics undertook in Rosenstein's article notes that the role of philosophy is not an apology of dominant practices in certain spheres of society, but the testing of convictions. Only such a philosophy is critical and only the art having a base in such a philosophy could deserve its title.

One might recall that the word *critic* comes from the Greek *kritikos*, which in adjective form means a person capable of issuing a judgement, while the noun *kritikon* – an ability to judge. The mission of philosophy is coming closer to fair verdicts, which requires weighing the arguments.

Initially, one may notice that the promotion of the art of scandal, despite its libertarian declarations, drastically restricts more subtle artistic creations. Classical art is accused of conformism and lack of ideological orientation. As Danto noted:

> The injunction is to sneer at genius, mock the masterpiece, giggle at aesthetic values – and to try to begin a new history, nonexploitative, in which art is put to some end more immediately human and important (Danto 1997, p. 302).

Indirectly, it follows that as a result of World Ares massive attack, genius was incapacitated. There is no climate for maturation of artistic styles and subtle forms of creative expression in the art.

However, I do not see grounds to assume that this is a final verdict. The situation of contemporary art can be illustrated by a famous Albrecht Dürer's print – Melancholia I. It depicts three figures that are likely to enter in a dialectical relationship. This raises a triad: winged Melancholia, putto, sleeping dog

---

[18] See: Boorstin 1998, Marshall 1997 and Turner 2004.
[19] See: Rosenstein 2002.

(*canis dormitans*). This is an allegory of elementary human activity and a state of complete lack of awareness, as authors of *Saturn and Melancholy* explain.[20]

The dog symbolizes total ignorance, but it is also a symbol of fidelity. A dog can depict a philistine, but also an apologist of the art, who remains faithful to it, even if it changes into an anti—art. Putto represents mindless activity, a scribbling child creates some minimal aspect of substantial art of genius. Putto does not get tired with doubts, constantly produces, just as late Warhol "his" works at the art factory. Melancholia, symbolizing the artistic genius, has frozen in lethargy. Lack of inspiration is a reason of lack of metaphysical intuitions. However, one can hope for the "perverse" nature of philosophy, that after current metaphysical numbness will undertake a question of deepened forms of spirituality. Then Melancholia (genius) will finally wake up from her nap.

Bibliography

Adorno, Theodor W. (2013): *Aesthetic Theory*. Transl. Robert Hullot-Kentor. London, New Delhi, New York, Sydney: Blommsbury [Adorno Theodor W. (1970): *Ästhetische Theorie*. Frankfurt am Main: Surkhamp Verlag].
Aronson, Elliot (2007): *The Social Animal*. New York: Worth Publishers.
Badiou, Alain (2005): *Handbook of Inaesthtics*. Stanford: Stanford University Press.
Benthem, Johan van (2011): *Logical Dynamics of Information and Interaction*. Cambridge: Cambridge University Press.
Boorstin, Daniel J. (1998): *The Image: A Guide to Pseudo-Events in America*. New York: Vintage Books.
Clay, Diskin (2007): "Plato Philomythos". In: Roger D. Woodard (ed.): *The Cambridge Companion to Greek Mythology*. Cambridge: Cambridge University Press.
Cohen, Marc, Curd Patricia, and Reeve C.D.C. (2016): *Readings in Ancient Greek Philosophy from Thales to Aristotle*. Indianapolis/Cambridge: Hackett Publishing Company, Inc.
Cornford, Francis M. (1939): *Plato and Parmenides*. London: Routledge and Kegan Paul.
Corrigan, Kevin (2010): "The Placed of the Parmenides in Plato's Thought and in the Subsequent Tradition". In: John D. Turner and Kevin Corrigan (ed.): *Plato's* Parmenides *and its Heritage*. Vol. I: *History and Interpretation from the Old Academy to Later Platonism and Gnosticism*. Atlanta: Society of Biblical Literature, pp. 34–36.
Cürsgen, Dirk (2002): *Die Rationalität des Mythischen*. Berlin: Walter de Gruyter.
Danto, Arthur C. (1997): *Encounters & Reflections. Art in the Historical Present*. Berkeley, Los Angeles, London: University Of California Press.
Foucault, Michel (1983): "Preface". In: Gilles Deleuze, Félix Guattari: *Anti- Oedipus. Capitalism and Schizophrenia*. Minneapolis: University of Minnesota.
Hartmann, Nicolai (1958): "Vom Neukantianismus Zur Ontologie". In: *Kleinere Schriften*, Bd. III. Berlin: Walter de Gruyter.

---

[20] See: Klibansky et al. 1979, pp. 320–321.

Hyland, Drew A. (2008): *Plato and the Question of Beauty*. Bloomington & Indianapolis: Indiana University Press.
Kieran, Matthew (2005): *Revealing Art*. London and New York: Routledge.
Klibansky, Raymond, Panofsky Erwin, Saxl Fritz (1979): *Saturn and Melancholy. Studies in the History of Natural Philosophy Religion and Art*. Liechtenstein: Kraus-Thomson Organization Limited.
Kuhner, Herbert (2008): *Monsignor Otto Mauer, Austrian Patron of the Arts:* http://viennanet.info/wp-content/uploads/2008/12/monsignor-otto-mauer_english.pdf (visited: 24.02.2013).
Lyotard, Jean-François (1993): "Philosophy and Painting in the Age of Their Experimentation: Contribution to an Idea of Postmodernity". Transl. Mária Minich Brewer and Daniel Brewer. In: Galen A. Johnson and Michael B. Smith (eds.): *The Merleau-Ponty Aesthetics Reader: Philosophy and Painting*. Evanston: Northwestern University Press.
Marquard, Odo (1989): *Farewell to Matters of Principle. Philosophical Studies*. Transl. Robert M. Wallace, Susan Bernstein and James I. Porter. New York; Oxford: Oxford University Press.
Marshall, David P. (1997): *Celebrity and Power: Fame in Contemporary Culture*. Minneapolis: University of Minnesota Press.
Mey, Kerstin (2007): *Art and Obscenity*. London; New York: I.B.Tauris & Co Ltd.
Morgan, Kathryn A. (2000): *Myth and Philosophy from the pre-Socratics to Plato*. Cambridge: Cambridge University Press.
Nietzsche, Friedrich (2011): *On the Genealogy of Morality*. Transl. Carol Diethe. Cambridge: Cambridge University Press.
Plato (2010): "Parmenides". Transl. Sylvana Chrysakopolou. In: Arnold Herman (ed.): *Plato's Parmenides*. Las Vegas, Zurich, Athens: Parmenides Publishing.
Plato (2003): "Parmenides". In: Samuel Scolnicov: *Plato's Parmenides. Translated with Introduction and Commentary*. Berkeley, Los Angeles, London: University of California Press.
Rickless, Samuel C. (2007): *Plato's Forms in Transition: A Reading of the Parmenides*. Cambridge: Cambridge University Press.
Robb, Peter (2011): *M: The Caravaggio Enigma*, London: Bloomsbury Publishing Plc.
Rosenstein, Leon (2002): "The End of Art Theory". In: *Humanitas* XV, no. 1.
Rowe, Christopher J. (1998): *Plato: Symposium*. Warminster: Aris & Phillips.
Rumler, Fritz (1970): "Ein Problem der Umweltverschmutzung?". In: *Der Spiegel* 47.
Sayre, Kenneth M. (2007): "Dialectic by negation in Three Dialogues". In: Suzanne Stern-Gillet and Kevin Corrigan (ed.): *Reading Ancient Texts*. Vol. 1: *Presocratics and Plato*. Leiden: Brill, pp. 189–212.
Schlothauer, Andreas (1992): Die Diktatur der freien Sexualität – vom Ende einer 'Sekte' (24.02.2013):http://www.report.de/Die%20Diktatur%20der%20freien%20Sexualitaet.html
Sciberras, Keith (2002): "Frater Michael Angelus in Tumultu: The Cause of Caravaggio's Imprisonment in Malta". In: *The Burlington Magazine* 144, no. 1189, pp. 229–232.
Sextus Empiricus (1998): *Against the Grammarians*, I 63–72. Translate and commentary David L. Blank, Oxford: Clarendon Press.
Susemihl, Franz (2004): "Parmenides". In: Erich Loewenthal (Hrsg.): *Platon: Sämtliche Werke in drei Bänden*. Bd. 2. Darmstadt: Wissenschaftliche Buchgesellschaft.

Tatarkiewicz, Władysław (1972): "The Great Theory of Beauty and Its Decline". In: *The Journal of Aesthetics and Art Criticism* 31, No. 2, pp. 165–180.
Turner, Graeme (2004): *Understanding Celebrity*. London: Sage.
Vattimo, Gianni (1999): *Belief*. Transl. Luca D'Isanto and David Webb. Stanford: Stanford University Press.
Wilamowitz-Moellendorff, Ulrich von (1920): *Platon. Sein Leben und seine Werke*. Erster Band. Berlin: Weidmannsche Buchhandlung.

Register

Achenbach, Gerd 266 f.
Adamus, Jan 260
Adorno, Theodor W. 192, 213, 215–220, 223–229, 231 f., 282, 289–291
Aenesidemus 65, 86 f.
Ajdukiewicz, Kazimierz 161, 167–170, 179–183, 186, 188
Allen, Richard 266
Althusser, Louis 215, 226
Amir, Lydia B. 267
Anaximander 12, 16, 29 f.
Anaximenes 12, 30
Annas, Julia 6, 48
Anstey, Peter 95 f.
Antisthenes 31 f., 37
Arcesilaus 86 f.
Archilochus of Paros 13
Aristoteles→Aristotle
Aristotle 8, 11, 26–29, 37, 44, 65–71, 94 f., 135, 140, 166, 283
Arnobius 241
Aronson, Elliot 292
Ashworth, William B. Jr. 95
Attfield, Robin 89
Aubrey, John 95
Augustin St. 74, 274
Austin, Scott 90
Axtell, James L. 96

Bacon, Francis 95–97, 107, 197, 223
Bacon, Roger 198
Baczkowski, Krzysztof 260
Badiou, Alain 293
Bailey, D. T. J. 55
Baker, Gordon 200
Balibar, Étienne 214
Barnes, Jonathan 6, 17 f., 48
Barth, Hans 223
Bauer, Bruno 222
Bayle, Pierre 241, 243
Belfiore, Elizabeth S. 49
Bell, Martin 241, 243
Benjamin, Walter 218
Bentham, Jeremy 230

Benthem, Johan van 284
Berkeley, George 100, 198, 241
Bird, Colin 252
Bobrzyński, Michał 260
Boethius 265
Bohlender, Matthias 221
Boltanski, Luc 195, 213, 215
Boorstin, Daniel J. 294
Botwinick, Aryeh 75, 84
Bourdieu, Pierre 195
Boyle, Robert 96 f.
Brandt, Andreas 120 f.
Brecht, Bertolt 194
Breitenstein, Peggy H. 213
Brennan, Jason 252
Brentano, Franz 161 f., 166 f., 183
Brickhouse, Thomas C. 57
Brown, Sam 266, 273
Bruin, Boudewijn de 252
Brus, Writer 291
Bryan, Jenny 90
Burnet, John 16
Bury, Robert Gregg 31

Cackowski, Zdzisław 5
Callicles 32
Carnap, Rudolf 86
Carneades 86 f., 89
Cassirer, Ernst 136
Celikates, Robin 194 f., 203, 213, 215
Cherniss, Harold 16, 27
Chiapello, Ève 213, 215
Chrysakopolou, Sylvana 285, 287
Cicero 86
Classen, Carl Joachim 69
Cloeren, Hermann J. 197
Coats, Wendell John, Jr. 74
Cohen, Elliot D. 271, 274 f.
Cohen, Hermann 127–137, 139 f., 142–158
Cohen, Marc 292
Cohen, Martin 252
Comte, Auguste 3
Constant, Benjamin 74, 260
Cooper, John M. 50

Cornford, Francis Macdonald 26, 43, 284
Crary, Alice 200
Critias 238
Curd Kenig, Patricia 16, 20
Czeżowski, Tadeusz 179 f., 183–185, 187

Dąbrowski, Kazimierz 271
Dąmbska, Izydora 162, 166, 176, 184
Danto, Arthur C. 282, 294
daVenza Tillmanns, Maria 269
Davis, Michael 276
Demetrius of Phalerum 19, 21
Demmerling, Christoph 191 f.
Dennett, Daniel 244 f., 247
Descartes, René 58, 85 f., 93, 96 f., 101, 108
Desjardin, Rosemary 66
Detel, Wolfgang 216
d'Holbach, Paul-Henri Thiry, Baron 241
Diagoras of Melos 238
Dickie, George 282, 294
Diels, Hermann 11, 16, 27, 79, 89
Dierse, Ulrich 221
Diogenes Laertius 18, 26, 88
Dionysius II 42
Diotima 36, 49, 286
Dostoyevsky, Fyodor 274
Dreyfus, Hubert 201
Duhem, Pierre 180
Dupréel, Eugène 66, 69
Dürer, Albrecht 294
Dürr, Karl 26

Eagleton, Terry 214
Eamon, William 95
Echecrates 39
Eggeling, Heinrich 124
Ehrenberg, Alain 197, 233
Eisler, Rudolf 123
Ellis, Albert 271
Elsenhans, Theodor 123
Engels, Friedrich 204, 223, 227, 229
Erasmus of Rotterdam 241, 246
Euhemerus 238

Falikowski, Anthony 269
Fastvold, Morten 271
Ferber, Rafael 59

Feuerbach, Ludwig 227
Fichte, Johann Gottlieb 119, 122
Ficino, Marcilio 282 f.
Fiorato, Pierfrancesco 136
Fischer, Kuno 128
Fish, Stanley 282
Flach, Werner 118
Forster, Michael N. 87, 115 f.
Foucault, Michel 268
Franco, Paul 85
Fraser, Nancy 213, 215
Frege, Gottlob 198
Fretschel, Lisa 179–181, 183, 185–187
Fried, Gregory 53 f., 60
Fries, Jakob Friedrich 111, 120–124
Fritz von, Kurt 16, 20
Fromm, Erich 267
Frycz Modrzewski, Andrzej 260

Gadamer, Hans-Georg 54, 139, 143, 149 f., 155–157
Gaiser, Konrad 26, 29
Gajda, Janina→Gajda-Krynicka, Janina
Gajda-Krynicka, Janina 25, 28, 30, 39
Galen 239
Galilei, Galileo 95, 107
Gaukroger, Stephen 95 f.
Gebauer, Gunter 202
Gerencser, Steven Anthony 75
Geuss, Raymond 194, 216 f.
Gigon, Olof 16 f.
Glock, Hans Johann 202
Gombrowicz, Witold 251 f., 254–262
Gonzalez, Francisco J. 54, 58 f.
Gorgias 28, 253
Görland, Albert 136
Gramsci, Antonio 226
Granger, Herbert 18
Griswold, Charles L. 54
Grocholski, Zygmunt 260
Grzeliński, Adam 93, 96
Guthrie, William Keith Chambers 16, 66

Habermas, Jürgen 3 f., 194 f., 203
Hacker, Peter Michael Stephan 200
Hansen, James T. 272
Harman, Gilbert 252

Hartle, Ann 240 f.
Hartmann, Nicolai 283
Haslanger, Sally 213 f.
Haug, Wolfgang Fritz 226
Hecataeus of Miletus 13, 15 f., 19, 21
Hegel, Georg Wilhelm Friedrich 3, 74, 87, 206, 219, 224, 226 f., 289
Heidegger, Martin 282
Heidel, William Arthur 16 f.
Helnont, Jan Babtist von 97
Heraclitus 11–15, 17–22, 29 f., 34, 65, 70 f., 79, 292
Herder, Johann Gottfried 140, 198
Herrmann, Steffen Kitty 192
Hesiod 12 f., 15 f., 18 f., 21
Hobbes, Thomas 74, 86 f., 113
Hölscher, Uvo 20
Holzhey, Helmut 128, 139 f.
Homer 13
Honneth, Axel 206
Horkheimer, Max 194, 209, 217 f., 225, 267
Hosiasson-Lindenbaum, Janina 180
Huard, Roger L. 51
Huffman, Carl A. 18
Hume, David 74, 86, 94, 98, 164, 198, 237, 241–244, 248
Hyland, Drew A. 54, 59 f.

Jacobs, Struan 81 f.
Jadczak, Ryszard 167
Jaeger, Werner 16
Jaeggi, Rahel 194, 206, 213, 215, 226
Jakobson, Roman 30
Jakuszko, Honorata 103
Janik, Piotr 176
Jędrzejko, Paweł 209, 234
John of Salisbury 241
Jones, Henry Stuart 15
Jonkisz, Adam 173
Jowett, Benjamin 43

Kahn, Charles H. 11, 13–19, 26, 37, 55 f.
Kalaš, Andrej 31
Kant, Immanuel 1, 3, 6 f., 75, 93, 95, 108 f., 111–124, 127–134, 136 f., 139–158, 166, 193
Kaute, Wojciech 260

Kerferd, George 43
Kieran, Matthew 282
Kierkegaard, Søren 246, 274
Kirk, Geoffrey Stephen 14, 90
Kjell Kvalø 214
Kleszcz, Ryszard 161, 166, 169
Klibansky, Raymond 283, 295
Knapp, S. 269
Knowles, Dudley 252
Kojève, Alexandre 48
König, Helmut 219
Kotarbińska, Janina 7, 180, 186
Kotarbiński, Tadeusz 6 f., 184
Krämer, Hans J. 26, 29, 57, 59
Kranz Walther 11, 16, 27, 79, 89
Krijnen, Christian 111
Kubalica, Tomasz 111, 120
Kubok, Dariusz 1, 5, 7 f., 13, 73, 90, 252 f.
Kuch, Hannes 192
Kuhn, Thomas 180
Kuhne, Frank 219
Kuhner, Herbert 292
Kulas, Piotr 252
Kutschera, Franz von 284

Lactantius 241
Lahav, Ran 268 f.
Lakatos, Imre 173
Larmore, Charles 252
Larrain, Jorge 214, 219
Laursen, John Christian 75, 86 f.
Lecercle, Jean-Jacques 204
Leibniz, Gottfried Wilhelm 112, 123, 132 f.
Lelewel, Joachim 260
Lenk, Kurt 219
Lesher, James H. 90
Leśniewski, Stanisław 167 f.
Lessing, Gotthold Ephraim 140
Liddell, Henry George 8, 15, 286
Lloyd, A. C. 26
Lloyd, Geoffrey Ernest Richard 12, 90
Locke, John 93–109, 198
Lucian of Samosata 32
Lukács, Georg 206
Łukasiewicz, Jan 167 f., 179, 181, 183, 186, 188
Łuszczewska-Romahnowa, Seweryna 179

Luther, Martin 246
Lyotard, Jean-François 293

Mackenzie, Mary Margaret 20
Maia Neto, Jose Raimundo 87
Malebranche, Nicolas 102
Mannheim, Karl 220, 225
Marcovich, Miroslav 15, 21f.
Margański, Janusz 257
Marinoff, Lou 269f., 272
Marquard, Odo 4, 79, 83, 293
Marshall, David P. 294
Marx, Karl 191, 199, 203–208, 213, 215f., 218–224, 227–233
Marx, Wolfgang 137
Mauer, Otto 292
McKenzie, Roderick 15
McWilliams, Nancy 267
Megone, Chris 273
Melissus of Samos 28
Mendelssohn, Moses 140, 144
Merleau-Ponty, Maurice 6
Mey, Kerstin 291f.
Michelet, Ludwig 122
Miller, David 252
Mills, Jon 275
Mnesesarchus 19
Montaigne, Michel de. 74, 86, 89, 237, 239–241, 244–246, 248
Mrówka, Kazimierz 14
Muehl, Otto 291f.
Myron 153

Næss, Arne 214
Nehamas, Alexander 52
Nerczuk, Zbigniew 65
Newton, Isaac 96f., 107f., 131, 133f.
Ng, Karen 215
Nicholas of Cusa 241
Nietzsche, Friedrich 274, 282
Nitsch, Hermann 291
Noras, Andrzej Jan 111, 127f.

Oakeshott, Michael 73–88, 90
Olesiński, Dariusz 47, 57
Orsi, Davide 75

Orzechowski, Stanisław 260
Ostasz, Lech 270f.

Padin, Roger 266
Paganini, Gianni 87
Pareto, Vilfredo 224
Parmenides 27f., 32, 37, 40f.
Pascal, Blaise 49, 77, 86, 246
Pawiński, Adolf 260
Pelc, Jerzy 2
Perzanowski, Jerzy 176
Philip, James. A 26
Philo of Larissa 89
Pico della Mirandola, Giovanni 241
Plantinga, Alvin 6f., 161
Plato 11, 25–29, 31–44, 47–50, 52–60, 65–71, 83f., 87, 132, 135, 140, 268, 274, 281–284, 286–288, 290
Platon→Plato
Plotinus 140
Plutarch 14
Podoksik, Efraim 74
Polykleitos 153
Popkin, Richard H. 87, 240f.
Popper, Karl R. 4f., 73–86, 88–90, 173f., 176–178, 180–188
Press, Gerald A. 48f., 54
Prodicus of Ceos 238
Protagoras 32, 65–71
Proudhon, Pierre-Joseph 208, 227
Pyrrho 65, 86–88, 115f.
Pythagoras 13, 15–17, 19–21, 31

Quine, Willard Van Orman 180

Raabe, Peter 269
Rayner, Jeremy 74
Read, Rupert 200
Reale, Giovanni 26, 28f., 37, 57
Rehmann, Jan 215, 226
Reichenbach, Hans 176
Reinhold, Karl Leonhard 122
Reitz, Tilman 222
Rickless, Samuel C. 284
Ricoeur, Paul 273
Riehl, Alois 7
Robinson, Richard 52

Romberg, Reinhard 221
Roochnik, David 51f.
Rosa, Hartmut 207, 233
Rosenstein, Leon 294
Ross, William David 67f.
Rossi-Landi, Ferrucio 204
Rousseau, Jean-Jacques 74
Rowe, Christopher J. 287
Rumler, Fritz 292
Russell, Bertrand 161, 163
Russell, Paul 243
Rymar, Dariusz 281, 283f.

Sayre, Kenneth M. 26, 43, 284
Scheler, Max 6, 135, 225
Schellenberg, J.L. 237, 244–248
Schelling, Friedrich Wilhelm Joseph 151
Schiller, Johann Christoph Friedrich von 139, 151
Schindler, D. C. 51, 54, 60
Schlosser, Joel A. 51
Schlothauer, Andreas 292
Schulte, Joachim 202
Schuster, John 96
Schuster, Shlomit C. 266f., 269, 275
Schwarzkogler, Rudolf 291
Scolnicov, Samuel 56, 285
Scott, Dominic 26
Scott, Robert 8, 15, 286
Sennert, Daniel 97
Sextus Empiricus 6, 14, 28, 65, 69, 77, 86, 88, 237–240, 244, 248, 253
Shustermann, Richard 282
Siemek, Marek J. 219
Simmons, Peter 166f.
Simpson, Tim 51
Smith, Nicholas D. 57
Sneed, Joseph D. 184
Snell, Bruno 284
Sobieski, Wacław 260
Socrates 28, 31f., 36–41, 43, 48–54, 57, 59, 253, 285f., 288, 293
Śpiewak, Sebastian 11
Spinoza, Baruch 87, 246
Stahl, Titus 213, 215
Stefanini, Luigi 48
Stegmüller, Wolfgang 184

Stolzenberg, Jürgen 135
Strauss, Leo 48f., 77
Susemihl, Franz 286
Sutton John 96
Suvák, Vladislav 31
Świercz, Piotr 251, 260
Sydenham, Thomas 96f.
Symotiuk, Stefan 4
Szaniawski, Klemens 176
Szasz, Thomas 273
Szlezak, Thomas Alexander 26, 29
Szymankiewicz, Błażej 252

Talbot, Ann 95
Tarski, Alfred 182, 188
Tatarkiewicz, Władysław 282
Taylor, Charles 201
Tetens, Holm 193
Thales 12, 29f., 83f.
Theodorus of Cyrene 238
Tigerstedt, Eugène N. 48
Tillich, Paul 271
Tjeltveit, A.C. 269
Tolstoy, Leo 274
Tregenza, Ian 81f.
Trendelenburg, Friedrich Adolf 128
Trochimska-Kubacka, Beata 139
Tseng, Roy 75
Tukiainen, Arto 265
Tuominen, Miira 55, 57
Turner, Graeme 294
Twardowski, Kazimierz 161–170, 176, 179, 183f., 187f.

Unger, Peter 244

Vaihinger, Hans 128
Van Deurzen, Emmy 273
Vattimo, Gianni 282
Verdenius, Willem Jacob 18
Vlastos, Gregory 53
Vološinov, Valentin Nikolaevich 204

Walmsley, Jonathan C. 97, 101
Walmsley, Peter 95
Warhol, Andy 295
Warren, Mark E. 252

Weber, Max 224
Welsh, Wolfgang 282
Weydemeyer, Joseph 223, 227, 229
Wiggershaus, Rolf 192
Wilamowitz-Moellendorff, Ulrich von 284
Winckelmann, Johann Joachim 140, 154f.
Winter, Eggert 127
Wittgenstein, Ludwig 191f., 198–208
Witwicki, Władysław 168
Woleński, Jan 174, 176, 178–180, 182–184, 187f.
Wolff, Christian 112, 123
Wood, Neal 74
Woodruff, Paul 48

Woolhouse, Roger 96
Woszczyk, Agnieszka 265

Xenophanes 13, 15–17, 19, 21, 28, 89f.

Yolton, John 99

Zamecki, Stefan 174, 176, 178f., 182–187
Zawirski, Zygmunt 183, 186
Zeller, Eduard 16
Zeno of Elea 26f., 41
Ziemińska, Renata 237, 239
Zinaich, Samuel Jr 275
Žižek, Slavoj 213, 215
Zurn, Christopher F. 252

www.ingramcontent.com/pod-product-compliance
Lightning Source LLC
Chambersburg PA
CBHW030335240426
43661CB00052B/1640